Building for Belgium

BUILDING FOR BELGIUM

BELGIAN EMBASSIES IN A GLOBALISING WORLD
(1945-2020)

Bram De Maeyer

LEUVEN UNIVERSITY PRESS

The publication of this book was supported by Universitaire Stichting van België, KU Leuven Fund for Fair Open Access, KU Leuven Faculty of Architecture, and the Open Book Collective (see www.lup.be/obc).

Published in 2025 by Leuven University Press / Presses Universitaires de Louvain / Universitaire Pers Leuven. Minderbroedersstraat 4, B-3000 Leuven (Belgium).
© 2025, Bram De Maeyer

All TDM (Text and Data Mining) rights reserved.

This book is published under a Creative Commons Attribution Non-Commercial Non-Derivative 4.0 License. For more information, please visit https://creativecommons.org/share-your-work/cclicenses/

Attribution should include the following information:
Bram De Maeyer, *Building For Belgium: Belgian Embassies in a Globalising World (1945-2020)*. Leuven: Leuven University Press, 2025. (CC BY-NC-ND 4.0)

Unless otherwise indicated all images are reproduced with the permission of the rightsholders acknowledged in the illustration credits. All images are expressly excluded from the CC BY-NC-ND 4.0 license covering the rest of this publication. Permission for reuse should be sought from the rightsholders.

ISBN 978 94 6270 481 7 (Paperback, colour)
ISBN 978 94 6270 488 6 (Paperback, B/W)
ISBN 978 94 6166 677 2 (ePDF)
ISBN 978 94 6166 678 9 (ePub)
https://doi.org/10.11116/9789461666789
D/2025/1869/34
NUR: 648

Layout: Crius Group
Cover design: Daniel Benneworth-Gray
Cover illustration: Main entrance of the Belgian ambassadorial residence in New Delhi with its exposed brickwork and lingam-shaped structures, 1985 (© Massachusetts Institute of Technology, courtesy of Peter Serenyi).

This book is dedicated to my family for their unwavering love and support and especially to my mother Mieke Van Staeyen, who has endless faith in her last-born child. Having four older siblings, I have been blessed to stand on the shoulders of these giants.

To my beloved friends and hilarious colleagues at the Federal Public Service Finance, who somehow survived my lengthy monologues about Belgian embassies and never once rolled their eyes when I talked about my book project.

And to Phil Collins and Frank Boeijen whose timeless songs have faithfully accompanied me during the writing and revision processes of this book.

Table of Contents

Foreword by Mark Eyskens · 9
Acknowledgments · 11
Abbreviations · 13
Notes regarding the maps and the monetary values used in the book · 14

Introduction · 17

Chapter I. The Ambassador's Agency: The Head of Mission as Project Developer (1945-1957) · 37

Chapter II. Building Embassies on Demand: The Steering Role of the Receiving State (1958-1974) · 97
   A. Building an Embassy in the Land Down Under: Diplomatic Housing as Political Leverage · 98
   B. The Reconstruction of the Mniszech Palace: The Diplomatic Cornerstone of Belgian-Polish Relations · 122
   C. Building in Brasília, Brazil: Moving Out of One's Comfort Zone · 144

Chapter III. "It's the Economy, Stupid!": Constructing Embassies as Venues for Economic Diplomacy (1980-1985) · 167

Chapter IV. Plugging the Holes in the Federal Budget: Monetising the Belgian Embassy Patrimony (1999-2020) · 233
   A. Redeveloping the Belgian Embassy Grounds in Japan: A Public-Private Partnership · 235
   B. Diplomatic Co-housing: The Kinshasa Project · 275

Epilogue · 307

Notes · 313
Bibliography · 329
Illustration Credits · 339
Index · 343

Foreword

It is a privilege for me to write the foreword to this particularly original book by Dr. Bram De Maeyer. As a long-serving minister, and especially in my capacity as Prime Minister and Minister of Foreign Affairs, I have had the opportunity to visit many of the Belgian embassies that Dr. De Maeyer explores in terms of their architectural history and significance.

This book, written with great talent by Bram De Maeyer, Doctor of Architecture at KU Leuven, offers an impressive analysis of the mutual interaction between architecture, diplomacy, and national identity. His impressive publication is a particularly original and timely theme, especially in an era of growing internationalization and rising global tensions. The book's title, *Building for Belgium: Belgian Embassies in a Globalizing World*, is therefore a fitting reflection of its content.

In his research, the author has analyzed several Belgian embassies, encompassing both the ambassador's residence and the chancery which houses administrative services, in order to examine the complexity of their existence and functioning abroad. Embassies need to be built, purchased, or at times renovated and modernized. An architect and a construction company must be appointed, and numerous concrete administrative difficulties must be resolved. Financing such projects is always a heavy burden for the Kingdom of Belgium, which is continually plagued by budget deficits.

The multifaceted nature of these challenges means that the Belgian ambassador on-site, the diplomats at the Ministry in Brussels, and the competent Minister of Foreign Affairs, who is sometimes replaced by a newcomer when a new government is formed, often react strongly to the many and diverging issues. Decision-makers frequently engage in heated discussions and defend differing opinions about the construction of a Belgian embassy abroad.

One of the commendable conclusions drawn by author Bram De Maeyer is that Belgium lacks a coordinated and coherent policy regarding the acquisition, whether by construction or purchase, of embassies abroad. Through his thorough analysis of the challenges involved in constructing, furnishing, and utilizing Belgian embassies overseas, De Maeyer highlights the complex interplay between the physical appearance and architectural appeal of an embassy on the one hand, and the diplomatic and political interests it serves on the other. An architecturally remarkable embassy impresses visitors and undoubtedly enhances a country's prestige.

I have visited most Belgian embassies abroad and attended numerous receptions and dinners. The spontaneous political and diplomatic discussions among the guests often captivated me. These gatherings offer the ambassador an opportunity to spark interest among foreign guests in Belgium's artistic and cultural achievements.

Such occasions allow dynamic ambassadors to host cultural events at the embassy, sometimes with the goal of softening the sharp edges of political disagreements. They also provide an elegant setting in which ambassadors can invite important figures for discussions within the splendor of the embassy's salons. The presence of elegant ladies contributes to the creation of a warm and hospitable atmosphere.

The salons of the embassy foster a warm and welcoming atmosphere in which confidential and diplomatically useful exchanges become possible. In this context, Baudelaire's verse becomes fitting: *"Here reign calm, luxury, and pleasure."*

The fact that Belgium typically maintains attractive and impressive ambassadorial residences, along with well-functioning chancery buildings and offices in major foreign capitals, is not an unnecessary luxury, but rather a strategic investment. It serves to enhance our country's diplomatic influence in a world characterized by both international cooperation and competing interests.

Upholding peace in a world full of tensions by "preparing for war" is sometimes seen as necessary, but it remains a paradox—one that can have harmful consequences. In contrast, maintaining peace and resolving conflicts through negotiation—through diplomacy—is not only often more effective, but also a morally responsible approach.

The coziness, the intimate setting, and the informal hospitality of our embassies can contribute meaningfully to this diplomatic effort. Bram De Maeyer's thorough study offers many valuable lessons for Belgian political and diplomatic decision-makers.

Mark Eyskens
Former Belgian Prime Minister and Minister of Foreign Affairs

Acknowledgments

This book would have never seen the light of day if it were not for Fredie Floré and Anne-Françoise Morel. As my former supervisors, Fredie and Anne-Françoise granted me the opportunity to join KU Leuven's Department of Architecture and conduct the PhD research on which this book is based. I would like to express my deepest and most sincere gratitude to Fredie and Anne-Françoise for believing in me. Their guidance, advice and continuous moral support carried me through the PhD trajectory. Additionally, I owe a debt of gratitude to KU Leuven for generously funding my PhD project.

I would also like to thank the members of my doctoral commission for sharing their expertise with me. Their insightful comments, constructive critiques and valuable suggestions have tremendously contributed to enriching and expanding my research. My sincere appreciation also goes out to my fellow PhD candidates at the Sint-Niklaasstraat in Ghent. I have fond memories of amusing conversations during lunch breaks. It was especially wholesome for me to share the joys and disappointments intrinsically linked to the world of academia. A special note of thanks goes out to my dear colleague Charlotte Rottiers. Charlotte knows first-hand the challenges and hurdles one faces when studying Belgian diplomatic architecture. I will always treasure our in-depth discussions on diplomatic housing.

My utmost gratitude goes to the Federal Public Service (FPS) Foreign Affairs, Foreign Trade and Development Cooperation. Its generous support has been key to scrutinising the Belgian embassy-building programme. I would especially like to thank Markus Maes, head of the real estate department, for being my go-to person within the FPS Foreign Affairs. Markus granted me access to the archives, shed light on the Ministry's housing policy and brought me into contact with Belgian embassies in my search for primary sources. Moreover, I would like to thank Ambassadors François Delhaye, Patrick Herman, Luc Jacobs and Dirk Wouters for sharing relevant source material with me. Moreover, I would like to thank chief archivist Didier Amaury of the Diplomatic Archive of Belgium for his assistance in consulting archival records. I would also like to acknowledge Ilse Dauwe, the Ministry's art curator, for shedding light on the art policy and the importance of art in embassy interiors.

Moreover, I would like to express my heartfelt gratitude to my publisher, Leuven University Press, and especially Mirjam Truwant, for believing in my book proposal and guiding me throughout the journey of bringing this book project to life. My publisher made my dream of publishing my very own book come true. Furthermore, I would like to thank the University Foundation, KU Leuven's Fund for Fair Open Access and KU Leuven's Faculty of Architecture for financially supporting the publication of this book.

It is difficult to give adequate thanks to my long-time friends. They have not only offered me moral support but several friends also made significant contributions to this book. I would like to express my gratitude to my long-time friend Christophe De Coster for producing maps on embassy locations and the spatial layouts of embassy interiors. I would also like to praise my close companion and colleague Thomas Bresseleers, my personal proofreader, for sifting through the manuscript. Moreover, I would also like to thank my friends Christophe Bellens for introducing me to the world of diplomacy, Anton Rombaut for shedding light on an embassy's legal status, and Nick Ceyssens for translating Portuguese sources to Dutch.

Ekeren, 10 May 2025

Abbreviations

CD&V	Christen-Democratisch en Vlaams
CEKOP	Centrali Eksportu Kompletnych Obiektów Przemysłowych
CIAM	Congrès Internationaux d'Architecture Moderne
DAB	Diplomatic Archive of Belgium
FPS Foreign Affairs	Federal Public Service Foreign Affairs
MP	Member of Parliament
MR	Mouvement Réformateur
MTOB	Mitsubishi-Takenaka-Okabe-Bank of Tokyo
NATO	North Atlantic Treaty Organisation
N-VA	Nieuw-Vlaamse Alliantie
OPEC	Organisation of the Petroleum Exporting Countries
P&O	Personnel & Organisation
USSR	Union of Soviet Socialist Republics
VLD	Vlaamse Liberalen en Democraten

Notes regarding the maps and the monetary values used in the book

The maps used in this book are based on background layers of OpenStreetMap. OpenStreetMap is open data, licensed under the Open Data Commons Open Database License by the OpenStreetMap Foundation.

To ensure comparability over time, historical monetary values are often deflated. This can be done in different ways, such as through a GDP-deflator or a wage deflator. PhD student Matthias Van Laer (University of Antwerp), who was kind enough to help me, has therefore used a consumer price index (CPI) deflation method for the monetary values mentioned in this book. A CPI is an index, usually constructed using price data, that reflects the cost of living over time, expressed in nominal monetary values. This cost of living is then expressed as the price of a basket of goods, to be determined by whomever collects the price data or constructs the index. An index expresses this cost in relation to a base year, and is thus unit neutral. For example, if the value of the index equals 100 in 1950 and 200 in year 1970, then the price of that basket of goods has doubled in 1970 compared to 1950. *Static* CPIs are indices that measure the price evolution of an unchanging basket of goods (e.g. the price of 1 HL of grain in 1900 vs. 1950). While they are less data-heavy, they lack historical realism; consumption patterns change over time. *Dynamic* CPIs allow the basket of goods to change over time (e.g. 1 HL of grain in 1950 vs. 0.5 HL of grain and 0.5 kg of beef in 1970). What they lack in ease of data collection, they make up for in historical realism. CPIs are not value-neutral; their nature and composition reflects the presuppositions of its author regarding historical reality and change. Lastly, a CPI can be calculated in the following ways: (1) via (weighted) inflation data that describes the price evolution of (all) goods over time; and (2) via a price index of different goods. The latter is more data intensive, but has the advantage that weights can be attributed by the author of the eventual index. The former is less labour intensive, and therefore the most suitable for most purposes. Official institutions such as national banks or statistical bureaus often report their own, already weighted, inflation data or index.

In this case, Van Laer has opted for the CPI index of the National Bank of Belgium (NBB) (https://stat.nbb.be/Index.aspx; prices; consumer prices and inflation; historical CPI) and the inflation calculator of the Bureau of Labour statistics of the US. (https://www.bls.gov/data/inflation_calculator.htm). The NBB reports an annual inflation number as well as an off-the-shelf CPI. It is a dynamic index based on price data provided by the Federal Public Service Economy of Belgium that spans from the early 20th century until the present day. Due to the reliability of the institution, the range of the data and the fact that the CPI is already weighted, it was considered the best option among the many historical indices that are out there (e.g. Clio-infra, Statbel …). All data were converted using an annual index, since the monthly price data does not reach back far enough. The US Bureau of Labor Statistics, which is as reliable as the NBB, has an online inflation calculator with monthly inflation data. If no month was reported, values were deflated using the inflation rates from December of that year. In both cases, all non-euro values were converted to euros. BEF using the 2002 exchange rate, US dollars using the 31 December exchange rate. Correcting for inflation can happen to a historical base year, or to a year as close to the present day as possible. Deflating to the present day has the advantage of making the monetary values directly interpretable, with the necessary caveats in mind. In this case, all values were deflated to December 2024 using the following formula:

$$\text{Value}_t = \text{Value}_{t-n} * \text{CPI}_t / \text{CPI}_{t-n} * \text{ExchangeRate}$$

Where value = historical monetary value; CPI = NBB consumer price index; t = base year or month (2024 or December 2024); t – n = historical year or month (e.g. 1953 or February 1953); ExchangeRate = exchange rate from BEF or USD to EUR.

Introduction

"A Building That Represents a Country Abroad"

In the spring of 2016, the Belgian Ministry of Foreign Affairs decided to move its embassy offices in Washington, D.C. to a new location. The Ministry purchased two floors in an apartment block in the city centre, situated within a stone's throw of the White House. Before the embassy staff could move into the apartment, the Ministry instructed its real estate department, Personnel & Organisation (P&O) 5.1. Buildings Abroad, to renovate the interiors. P&O 5.1 launched a public tender in which candidates were briefed on the specifics of the renovation project. In the programme of requirements, P&O 5.1 officials stressed to candidates that the embassy project was by no means a mundane commission.

The programme of requirements stated that an embassy building is far more than just the accommodation of diplomats abroad. According to P&O 5.1, an embassy is the architectural calling card of the Belgian state on foreign soil, describing the building's function in the following terms:

> An embassy is a building that represents a country abroad; through this building a country shows itself to the outside world. Therefore it is important that embassy buildings show a certain style, class without exaggeration, as they are in fact a visit card of the country in question.[1]

Such a statement obviously raises a series of compelling questions. From an architectural perspective, P&O 5.1 officials underscore that embassies have to express a specific style, defined as class without exaggeration, in order to be national emblems abroad. Candidates wondering what exactly is understood by class without exaggeration were, however, kept in the dark. The programme of requirements did not elaborate on this rather vague description. Nonetheless, the statement indicates that P&O 5.1 upholds a certain architectural vision as to what an embassy building should ideally look like. This begs the question of what kind of architectural aesthetic the Ministry of Foreign Affairs deems worthy of representing Belgium abroad. What are Ministry's architectural preferences and to what extent has national specificity been expressed in relation to the style, form and materiality of Belgian embassy architecture?

From a historical perspective, the Ministry's statement gives rise to the question of whether establishing an architectural standard is a recent practice or rather a long-standing architectural policy. Moreover, if such an architectural policy has indeed been established for a long time, what changes and continuities can be noticed in the way the Ministry has represented Belgium through embassy architecture? After all, the Ministry is anything but an entity frozen in time. Founded in 1831, it is one of the oldest ministries making up the Belgian state apparatus. Successive foreign ministers and top officials with diverging political leanings and foreign policy goals have been at its helm. Did they develop an overarching architectural policy that was closely guided and redefined over the years? Given the fact that the Ministry frames its embassy patrimony as a national calling card, the obvious question is to what extent its leadership has invested in embassy architecture to express diplomatic and ideological stances on the international stage. When scrutinising such a question, the overarching geopolitical context cannot be overlooked. In the second half of the 20th century, when the number of Belgian embassies grew significantly, the international stage witnessed profound changes. Since 1945, Belgian diplomats have witnessed the decolonisation process, the emergence of newly independent African and Asian countries, the Cold War and the birth of the transatlantic alliance, the growth of multilateralism in international relations, Asia's economic rise, the surge of terrorist attacks on embassies, globalisation, and the establishment of an ever more interconnected world, among other events. To what extent did these profound geopolitical themes affect the architecture of the very buildings housing Belgian diplomats?

By intertwining the architectural and historical perspectives, the overarching question that arises is whether the Belgian Ministry of Foreign Affairs has actually practised what it preached in its programme of requirements for the new Washington embassy in 2018. It is one thing to solemnly state that embassy architecture plays a key role in forging a national identity abroad but quite another to actually put such ambitions into practice. The book *Building for Belgium: Belgian Embassies in a Globalising World (1945-2020)* gets to the bottom of the matter by retracing the historical trajectory of Belgian embassy projects and the Ministry's quest for an appropriate architectural expression across the world since 1945.

The premise of *Building for Belgium* is elementary. The book examines to what extent the Ministry has purposefully invested in the architectural design and representational role of embassy buildings to convey diplomatic and political messages abroad and, more significantly, what kind of architectural designs were considered appropriate to convey those messages. Therefore, this book focuses on the phenomenon of purpose-built embassies.

The Phenomenon of Purpose-built Embassies

Throughout history, the majority of Belgian embassies have been established in purchased and leased premises but this book focuses solely on purpose-built embassies. *Building for Belgium* makes the case that scrutinising this building activity offers a particular insight into the Ministry's architectural stances. There are two main reasons why scrutinising purpose-built embassies is especially worthwhile when considering the topic at hand.

Firstly, the Belgian Ministry of Foreign Affairs has traditionally commissioned purpose-built embassies. Whereas Belgian government buildings have been constructed by either the former Ministry of Public Works (1837-1992) or the Belgian Buildings Agency (1971-present), the construction of embassy buildings has fallen outside their mandate.[2] Commissioning purpose-built embassies has always been the Ministry's exclusive prerogative. In its capacity as awarding authority, the Ministry has guided purpose-built embassy projects from start to finish. A plausible explanation for this anomaly might be the special status of the Ministry of Foreign Affairs within the Belgian state apparatus. The Ministry has often been portrayed as the maverick of the state apparatus, a state within a state adhering to its own customs and traditions.[3] As its diplomats are the ones working and living in embassies, the Ministry of Foreign Affairs has most likely made the case that practicalities such as constructing an embassy fall within its area of responsibility. However, this practice is not solely a Belgian anomaly. For instance, the foreign ministries of the United States, the United Kingdom, and France have also been responsible for the construction of their respective embassies.[4]

The second reason to focus solely on purpose-built embassies has to do with the very nature of this building commission. Whereas the Ministry of Foreign Affairs finds itself in a pre-existing architectural context when it purchases or leases a property, a purpose-built embassy is by its very essence developed from scratch. What better way to uncover the Ministry's attitude towards architecture than by examining its role in the construction of its own embassy-building projects? After all, commissioning a purpose-built embassy requires far more commitment than purchasing or leasing properties. In the case of constructing an embassy, ministry officials have to roll up their sleeves and guide the project through multiple stages. These include selecting a building plot, drafting a programme of requirements, hiring an architect and building contractor, making adjustments to the preliminary design, securing a building permit, supervising construction works, and furnishing and decorating the embassy interiors. During such stages, ministry officials have to make fundamental choices affecting the embassy's architectural, scenic and spatial qualities.

These choices have representational, diplomatic and political ramifications as purpose-built embassies are, by their very essence, highly charged building commissions. For instance, does the Ministry perceive the new embassy as an urban landmark by purchasing a prominent building site in the city centre or does it instead acquire land in a secluded suburb so that diplomats can work and live far away from any prying eyes? Moreover, does the Ministry approach the building project as an opportunity to showcase national craftsmanship on foreign soil by hiring a Belgian architect and calling for a design in which national character and specificity are expressed through style and form? Or does the Ministry hire a local architect and call for an architectural design that pays tribute to local architectural traditions and practices? By paying tribute to the host country, the Ministry may aspire to build up goodwill among the local elite and population at large.

By analysing the choices made during the design and construction phases, Belgian purpose-built embassies offer us invaluable insights into the Ministry's architectural stances. As such, *Building for Belgium* argues that a discussion on the Belgian embassy-building programme makes for a convincing case to assess the level of importance the Ministry has historically attached to embassy architecture. Scrutinising the building programme is particularly insightful when assessing whether the Ministry has practised what it preached in the Washington programme of requirements and what kind of architecture was deemed worthy of representing the state abroad.

Quid Embassy?

By now, the word *embassy* has already popped up 30 times in the introduction. As embassies are the main subject of this book, it is imperative to define exactly what is meant by this term. Such a definition is especially necessary given the fact that *embassy* has an institutional and an architectural meaning.

Institutionally, an embassy refers to the highest diplomatic mission which permanently represents the sending state in the receiving state.[5] Generally, the sending state establishes an embassy in the capital of the receiving state. As the highest diplomatic mission, an embassy protects the national interests of the sending state, negotiates with the receiving state and reports on local developments. Additionally, an embassy protects the interests of its nationals residing in or visiting the receiving state, and offers them administrative assistance in their bureaucratic business with the government of the sending state. This diverse range of tasks is the responsibility of the diplomatic staff employed at the embassy. The diplomatic staff is headed by an ambassador who is also referred to as the head of mission. To ensure that they can execute their functions without foreign meddling, diplomats enjoy a special legal status. They have diplomatic immunity for the duration of their posting, shielding them from legal prosecution.

In order to carry out their duties, embassy staff members need proper accommodation. This brings us to the architectural meaning of an embassy. In architectural terms, an embassy refers to the building or constellation of buildings housing the diplomatic mission. In fact, an embassy is a collective infrastructural term made up of two parts. The first part consists of the ambassadorial residence. As the name suggests, the ambassadorial residence functions as the official residence where the ambassador and his/her family reside for the duration of the ambassadorship. Besides its primary housing function, the ambassadorial residence also serves as a high-end venue for social events. As the art of socialising and networking plays a pivotal role during an ambassadorship, ambassadors frequently open the doors of their residence. The head of mission uses the residence as a venue to host social events. The residence is an invaluable asset for any ambassador who is keen to further strengthen personal relations with the local elite. Already in 1522, Niccolò Machiavelli (1469-1527) advised a befriended ambassador to frequently invite local dignitaries over for dinner and gambling parties in his residence.[6]

Machiavelli claimed that wining and dining in style helps to loosen the tongues of those within the ruling power base. Given its function as a social venue and representational flagship, ambassadorial residences have often been housed in majestic buildings with lavishly furnished and decorated interiors. Sending states tend to provide such residences in order to ensure ambassadors live comfortably, boost national prestige and symbolise state power abroad.

The second part of an embassy consists of the chancery. Housing the embassy offices, the chancery functions as the bureaucratic heart of a diplomatic mission. From the chancery, the ambassador and embassy staff draft reports on developments occurring in the receiving state. As an administrative workspace that generates an abundance of paperwork, the chancery includes an archival section where sensitive documents are stored. Additionally, the chancery has meeting rooms where discussions with delegations take place. In some cases, the chancery can also include enquiry counters where nationals can conduct their bureaucratic business and foreigners can apply for a visa to visit the sending state. Whereas foreign ministries have invested considerably in housing ambassadorial residences in majestic premises, this is much less the case for chanceries. As will become apparent throughout this book, Belgian chanceries were often housed in far less splendid and spacious buildings. Belgian diplomats frequently had to work in mundane rowhouses and apartments, often in cramped conditions.

In general parlance, the strict distinction between the ambassadorial residence and chancery is rarely made. Whether the distinction is clearly articulated often depends on the spatial ratio between both parts. The ambassadorial residence and chancery can either be clustered together in the same building, located on the same site, or housed in separate buildings spread across the capital city.

More recently, there is a growing tendency to establish embassies in compounds for security reasons, especially in politically unstable countries. This leads us to consider the exclusive nature of embassy buildings. One does not simply walk into an embassy. With the rise of global terrorism in the second half of the 20th century, sending states have considerably beefed up security as embassies have become prized targets for terrorist groups. Nowadays, embassies and walls, fences, surveillance cameras, armed guards, bulletproof glass and panic rooms go hand-in-hand. This creates a certain tension between the embassy's status as a venue for social events and public service on the one hand, and its increasingly fortress-like appearance on the other hand. This tension is further emphasised by the special legal status of an embassy building. Like diplomatic staff, embassy premises enjoy legal protection as these buildings are inviolable. Reflecting the privileged position diplomatic missions occupy in society, the *United Nations Vienna Convention on Diplomatic Relations* of 1961 offers legal protection to diplomatic premises. Local authorities can only enter an embassy with the consent of the ambassador. Consequently, embassies have often been safe havens for political refugees and whistle-blowers who want to avoid prosecution, with the seven year stay of Julian Assange in the Ecuadorian embassy in London one of the most striking examples. Contrary to popular belief, however, embassy grounds are not exclaves of the sending state in the receiving state. The plot of land on which the embassy stands is still part of the receiving state's national territory but it is an area with special privileges and protection.

Taking all these elements into consideration, embassy buildings perform an abundance of functions, being the sending state's architectural calling card, an official residence, a venue for social gatherings, an administrative workspace, and an inquiry counter to conduct administrative business. This hybrid programme makes purpose-built embassies a special kind of building commission to examine, which is made evident by the growing body of literature devoted to the topic.

Embassy Architecture as Research Topic: A Novel Academic Field

In architectural history, the topic of government architecture has traditionally aroused wide interest. Scholars have devoted a great deal of attention to how nation states have historically invested in commissioning vast and majestic government buildings on their national territory. Government architecture is as a medium through which state authorities aim to express political beliefs, ideas and aspirations, and project power over their subjects and territory, making it a political force in its own right.[7] Architectural historian Lawrence Vale has convincingly demonstrated that the abiding role of government architecture has been to symbolise state power and make the regime visible as the ruling entity to the masses.[8] Moreover, authors have abundantly illustrated how regimes have wielded architecture to create a national identity, legitimise their political rule and showcase their character and effectiveness.[9]

Continuing along these lines, scholars have expanded the scope by examining how state authorities have invested in government architecture on foreign soil in order to express state sovereignty and mould their self-image abroad. This leads us to the body of literature on purpose-built embassies. In recent decades, architectural historians have increasingly scrutinised the embassy-building programme of Western states, especially the building activity of their respective country. Perceiving such a building programme as the most tangible evidence of a nation's diplomatic presence abroad, this body of literature frames purpose-built embassies as a country's foreign policy distilled to its most basic essence. The existing literature has mainly examined the building programme of (former) great powers and their efforts to showcase power, radiate nationhood and foster respect abroad through embassy architecture. The lion's share of these publications discusses the diplomatic building activity of the United States, the United Kingdom, France, Germany and the former Soviet Union throughout the 20th century.[10]

The most canonical work on embassy architecture is Jane Loeffler's *The Architecture of Diplomacy: Building America's Embassies* which was first published in 1998. Widely hailed as one of the most comprehensive and enlightening studies on the topic, Loeffler presents a detailed overview of the building activity of the US State Department since 1945. Her time frame coincides with fundamental shifts in American foreign policy as the United States took up the role of the world's policeman and entered into a power struggle with the Soviet Union during the Cold War era. In this geopolitical context, Loeffler demonstrates how the State Department invested considerably in embassy architecture to beef up its diplomatic presence in all the corners of the globe. In the 1950s and 1960s, modernist architecture was the dominant architectural aesthetic as the US State Department commissioned high-profile embassy buildings designed by renowned architects such as Marcel Breuer (1902-1981), Eero Saarinen (1910-1961) and Walter Gropius (1883-1969). These embassy designs were intended to project an open, forward-looking image of the United States. In doing so, the US State Department aimed to showcase itself as the progressive superpower *par excellence* in the context of the cultural Cold War. Moreover, Loeffler puts a great deal of emphasis on how embassy designs have met the hybrid programme of diplomatic housing and tackled profound changes affecting the diplomatic profession. In this regard, she published a second edition of *The Architecture of Diplomacy* in 2011 in which she discusses more recent developments affecting the

US embassy-building programme. With the devastating Al-Qaeda attacks on US embassies in Dar es Salaam and Nairobi in 1998, the diplomatic building programme changed radically as security became the guiding principle in designing embassies.

In addition to studies on great powers, architectural historians have extended the scope to purpose-built embassies of so-called middle powers such as the Netherlands, Sweden, and Australia.[11] Middle powers are defined as countries that are neither great nor small powers in terms of their military and economic strength.[12] In general, middle powers use their diplomatic leverage in the service of international stability and collaboration by means of pursuing multilateral solutions to global issues. Moreover, middle powers tend to engage actively in the safeguarding of democratic values and general wellbeing of civil society. Whereas the literature on purpose-built embassies of great powers predominantly traces efforts to express nationhood and power through embassy architecture, the narrative of publications on middle power states tends to be more nuanced. Of course, the expression of nationhood through embassy architecture continues to run like a thread through this body of literature but a great deal of emphasis is put on the bilateral exchange of ideas, information and practices. Its line of inquiry approaches purpose-built embassies as more of a collaborative effort where both the sending and receiving state leave their stamp on the design.

However, the Belgian embassy-building programme has remained a blind spot in the literature on diplomatic architecture. Academic research on purpose-built, let alone purchased or leased, Belgian embassies was non-existent before the start of my PhD research in 2017. At the time, literature on Belgian embassies was mostly made up of richly illustrated coffee table books and promotional booklets made in cooperation with the Ministry of Foreign Affairs.[13] As the proprietor of a largely unknown patrimony, the Ministry has shown a growing interest in showcasing its diplomatic premises through a series of publications. As can be expected, this genre is predominantly characterised by a promotional, almost hagiographical, approach with telling book titles such as *Belgium's Most Beautiful Embassies From Around The World*. The narrative is often marked by a solemn tone, proclaiming just how aesthetically pleasing Belgian embassies are and how these buildings offer the foreign public a window into Belgian society and culture. As befits the genre's promotional nature, the printed text is of a descriptive nature with little to no room for analysis. In fact, printed text is of secondary importance as images of majestic façades and lavish interiors take centre stage in these publications.

Making a Case for Belgium

Whatever the merits of this promotional literature, the Belgian embassy-building programme has remained uncharted territory. *Building for Belgium* sets out to fill this gap through an in-depth study of Belgian purpose-built embassies. So what is the relevance of a study entirely devoted to Belgium? After all, filling a gap for the sake of filling a gap does not cut it. This book argues that there are three solid reasons that make a national focus on Belgium worthwhile.

Firstly, the Belgian state authorities do not enjoy an upstanding reputation when it comes to commissioning public and government buildings. Belgian architects and architecture critics alike have generally been critical of the national government in its capacity as awarding authority since the second half of the 20th century. Architectural historian Geert Bekaert has been one of the most vocal critics. Bekaert has often critiqued the role of the Belgian state authorities and the Belgian political climate in general towards architecture. He hammers home the argument that the Belgian state has lacked the ambition to invest in architecture. In his canonical work, *Bouwen in België 1945-1970*, Bekaert discusses how architectural projects that were ambitious on paper were watered down because of bureaucratic meddling, political intrigue and budget cuts.[14] In 1999, he went so far as to argue that policymakers have failed to develop, let alone create the illusion, that there has ever been an architectural policy worthy of the name.[15] In his derogatory writing style, Bekaert lambasts the government for its tendency to greenlight hideous and empty-headed architectural designs, bankrupt of any imagination.[16] In fact, according to Bekaert, the architect's political affiliation and willingness to adhere to the budget were often more decisive factors for being awarded commissions than the architectural merits of the design entry. Moreover, Bekaert claimed that policymakers lacked interest in clearly articulating the representational function of government architecture.

Taking this domestic context into account, a close reading of Belgian purpose-built embassies is particularly interesting. It helps to shed light on whether the Ministry lived up to its reputation as a maverick ministry by consciously investing in architecture as a means to forge an identity for itself and thus also the country it represents abroad.

Secondly, Belgium is an interesting case because of its evolving statehood. At the time that its first embassies were established in 1920, Belgium was a unitary state with a centralised administration. However, in the second half of the 20th century, mounting political, economic and cultural tensions between the linguistic regions, together with a growing subnational awareness, resulted in profound changes in national governance.[17] Since 1970, Belgium has witnessed six state reforms that have transformed the unitary state into a federal one composed of communities, regions and language areas. Through their respective parliaments, the regional governments wield executive powers in areas such as education, healthcare and socioeconomic policies. The federal government, however, is still responsible for maintaining diplomatic ties with foreign countries. Nevertheless, in the 1990s, the regions each created their own foreign trade agencies to conduct economic diplomacy abroad.[18]

Against this backdrop of subnationalism and devolution, a study on Belgian embassies is especially interesting. After all, leading scholars in the field of embassy architecture have labelled embassy buildings the architectural expression of nationhood abroad. As Fabien Bellat puts it so eloquently, an embassy forms an island of national representation surrounded by foreign waters.[19] In the case of Belgium, the process of devolution and subnationalism significantly challenges the task of expressing nationhood abroad. This makes a study of Belgian purpose-built embassies especially compelling as it figures out whether and to what extent such designs have been influenced by the country's multilayered foreign representation and growing subnational awareness.

Thirdly and lastly, Belgium's foreign policy has witnessed profound changes in the second half of the 20th century. In the wake of the Second World War, Belgian foreign policymakers abandoned the traditional policy of strict neutrality that had been the cornerstone of Belgian foreign policy. From 1947 onwards, Belgium increasingly aligned itself with the United States by joining the Marshall Plan (1947) and being a founding member of NATO (1949). Additionally, Belgium joined international and supranational organisations in order to gain greater international influence. In its capacity as a middle power, Belgium has played a proactive role in organisations such as the International Monetary Fund (1944), the World Bank (1944), the United Nations (1945) and the European Coal and Steel Community (1951) which evolved into the present-day European Union. Moreover, the post-war period marked the end of Belgium's status as colonial power. In the 1960s, the Belgian Congo and Ruanda-Urundi attained self-rule as a wave of decolonisation swept across Africa and Asia. Nevertheless, for better or worse, Belgium continued to be closely involved in the affairs of its former colonies.

The profound redirection of Belgian foreign policy is an additional reason to study its embassy-building programme. Investments in embassy buildings have traditionally been perceived as the architectural embodiment of the sending state's political goodwill, commitment and allegiance, or a show of force to the receiving state.[20] The decision to build an embassy often constitutes an event of extraordinary importance in bilateral relations. These buildings are the architectural testament of the Ministry's foreign policy aspirations and diplomatic achievements over time, set against the backdrop of key geopolitical themes and bilateral ties. With regard to Belgium, this raises the question of to what extent the Ministry of Foreign Affairs aimed to define its role on the international stage through the construction of embassies. Moreover, it begs the question of whether Belgian foreign policymakers considered such building projects to be critical to their foreign agenda, given that the projects are the architectural expression of foreign policy stances to the outside world.

All things considered, Belgium makes for an enticing case study given its capacity as a middle power on the international stage, the alleged lack of an architectural policy, its evolving statehood at home, and the profound redirection of its foreign policy since 1945. As Loeffler has argued, embassies are by their very essence highly charged building projects defined by three factors: a country's architectural policy, domestic politics and foreign affairs.[21] As far as Belgium is concerned, there is no shortage of profound changes affecting these three factors.

A Guide to Studying Embassies

Building for Belgium sets out to reconstruct the historical trajectory of the Belgian embassy-building programme. This approach aims to thoroughly embed embassy projects in time and place, putting special emphasis on the historical context in which projects were designed and built. Aspiring to scrutinise the political and diplomatic significance of this building activity from the point of view of both the sending and receiving state, this book aims to understand the conditions, historical events and agency of key actors that have guided building projects from start to finish, and how such conditions triggered change and continuity over time. This monograph aspires to make sense of how things unravelled and, more importantly, why they played out the way they did.

As part of this historical research, the book's methodological framework features three levels. The first level consists of a case study driven approach. As a study on purpose-built embassies entails, by its very essence, a global scope and the period under investigation covers more than half a century, it is imperative to pursue such a research strategy. The ambition to cover the global building programme in a set number of pages meant that choices had to be made as to which building projects were to be examined. Of necessity, the chosen case studies are a selected sample of building projects. Therefore, a representative benchmark of projects has been put together on the basis of four main criteria.

The first criterion entails choosing embassy projects set against the backdrop of key geopolitical themes, such as the emergence of newly independent states, decolonisation, the Cold War and the development of the transatlantic alliance, the economic rise of Asia, and the complex relationship between a former colonial power and its old colony. Secondly, the selected cases are a sample featuring a variety of architectural projects set in varying urban contexts. This ranges from a free-standing chancery in a residential suburb, a neoclassical palace situated in the city centre, and a fortress-like embassy compound in a diplomatic district, to a towering edifice in a high-rise metropolis. Thirdly, this book has selected embassy buildings that have been designed by respectively Belgian architects, local architects and a collaboration between both. Fourthly and finally, cases have been selected on the basis of their geographical location. In total, this book explores eight case studies (Washington, D.C., Canberra, Warsaw, Brasília, New Delhi, Riyadh, Tokyo, and Kinshasa) spread across different continents (see table p. 30). In doing so, this study aims to illustrate how Belgium has showcased itself through embassy architecture in all the corners of the world and against the backdrop of different cultures, building practices and codes. It is imperative to stress that not each case study carries the same weight in this book. This has to do with the availability of primary sources, resulting in the fact that the Washington and New Delhi cases are discussed in far more detail than, for instance, the Riyadh and Kinshasa cases.

Location	Land Acquisition	Building project	Completion	Architect(s)
Washington, D.C.	1947	Chancery	1957	Hugo Van Kuyck Voorhees, Walker, Foley & Smith
Canberra	1951	Chancery & Residence	1962	Fowell, Mansfield & Maclurcan
Warsaw	1959	Chancery & Residence	1962	Mieczysław Kuzma
Brasília	1960	Chancery & Residence	1974	Nicolaï Fikoff (chancery) Paulo Antunes Ribeiro (residence)
New Delhi	1954	Chancery & Residence	1983	Satish Gujral
Riyadh	1981	Chancery & Residence	1985	BESIX Group
Tokyo	1928	Chancery & Residence	2010	Noriaki Okabe Architecture Network
Kinshasa	2012	Chancery	2017	A2M

Overview of the embassy case studies

The second level consists of an analytical framework or model to study the case studies. *Building for Belgium* has coined a model to examine purpose-built embassies. In conceiving this model, this book has built on the observation that policymakers often describe how their foreign policy agenda centres around three Ds: diplomacy, defence and development aid. Being a source of inspiration, the three Ds model has been remoulded to correspond with the scope of this book.

The first **D** stands for the Decision-making process to build an embassy. At first glance, the decision to build an embassy seems to be a mundane one but this was definitely not the case for Belgium. As the launch of building projects deviated from the Ministry's dominant housing strategy of purchasing and leasing premises, it is imperative to uncover the main rationale behind the decision to build and how the project got off the ground. Did the purpose-built embassy have to solve existing accommodation problems, boost national prestige through architecture, and/or emphasise the earnestness of Belgian intentions to further cement bilateral ties with the receiving state? Therefore, it is instrumental to study the building project in relation to the national, bilateral and economic contexts. By uncovering such incentives, the decision-making process aims to identify the ambitions projected on the embassy and why the Ministry of Foreign Affairs considered that investing in embassy architecture would satisfy such needs. It serves as an indication as to what role has been attributed to embassy architecture over time. Moreover, the decision-making process sets out to emphasise that building plans often became the focal point of internal power struggles, personality clashes, rivalries and intrigues between ministers, ministry officials, diplomats and MPs alike.

Building on this foundation, the second **D** stands for **Design**. This part goes to the very essence of a purpose-built embassy by retracing how the building came into being. Of primary importance, this part questions how the architects involved have approached such a hybrid type of building commission. After all, an embassy building performs an abundance of functions, being the representational flagship of the sending state, an official residence, a venue for social events and an administrative workspace. Simultaneously, this part retraces the role the Ministry has played in the architectural design of embassies. Did the Ministry clearly communicate its preferences to the architect by formulating what kind of character, style and materials it considered to be aesthetically and representationally pleasing? Or did the Ministry only formulate programmatic needs and did the architect enjoy creative freedom to design an embassy? Moreover, the design level examines what kind of statement the actors involved aimed to make through architecture. Continuing along the lines of Le Corbusier's famous line in *Vers une architecture* that a house should be considered as a machine for living, one can frame an embassy as *une machine-à-représenter*, as a means of showcasing the nation through architecture.[22] This metaphor leads to insightful observations as to what the Ministry has considered worthy of representing the nation abroad, paying tribute to the host country and/or building up goodwill with the local population. Architecturally speaking, a great deal of emphasis is put on how architects have tackled the programmatic needs intrinsically linked to the diplomatic profession. An embassy project is a hybrid commission, providing a diplomatic mission with housing, a workspace and a venue for social events. How did the architectural designs meet the standards of the Ministry of Foreign Affairs and to what extent have the designs facilitated the diplomatic profession? As part of this discussion, emphasis is also put on the contemporary building activity of other sending states in the capital city in question. After all, the Ministry did not commission its embassies in a vacuum and quite possibly drew inspiration from purpose-built embassies of other nations.

The third and final **D** stands for **Decor**. This part discusses the furnishing and decoration of the diplomatic interiors. By their very nature, such interiors are politically charged spaces where the ambassador interacts with fellow diplomats, the local political-economic elite, journalists, countrymen, and family members. The physical confines of an embassy serve as a decor or scenery where the ambassador performs various roles, ranging from representative, negotiator, boss, host, partner to parent. Any ambassador worthy of the name aims to come across as a charming host, an entertaining conversationalist and a (wo)man of culture. Therefore, a head of mission needs a fitting decor that positively influences public opinion of his/her ambassadorship and the sending state as a whole. The embassy interiors serve as a stage where the ambassador showcases to others a way of working and living through furniture items, artwork, household equipment, food and clothing. As the metaphorical home of the nation abroad, embassy interiors tend to be carefully orchestrated decors where material objects serve as instruments of identity-building and national representation. This book identifies efforts to brand the nation through furniture, artwork and other household effects. It reveals if and to what extent the Ministry opted to showcase national craftsmanship and design in its embassy interiors to promote a national way of living and working to foreign recipients and thus create a favourable image of Belgium abroad. In order to identify and examine such efforts, this book turns to the concept of cultural diplomacy. Cultural diplomacy refers to the sending state's efforts to promote its national culture abroad through the arts, science, and technology.[23] Cultural diplomacy is a celebration of national prestige, an idealised and romanticised endeavour to mould a country's self-image abroad through culture.

The third and final level of this methodological framework consists of a series of dominant dynamics shaping the Belgian embassy-building programme since 1945. Acting as a force field surrounding the building programme, the dominant dynamics have both been the main rationale behind the construction of an embassy and the guiding principle in its architectural design. In total, four dominant dynamics have been identified. These dynamics are the ambassador's agency (1), initiatives taken by the receiving state (2), foreign economic interests (3), and the embassy as an income-producing property (4). Each of these dynamics reached its zenith during a specific period in time, making it possible to arrange this book in both a thematic and chronological order.

In Search of Sources

As is the case for every piece of historical research, this book has gathered voices from the past to reconstruct the historical trajectory of the Belgian embassy-building programme. So where does one find the necessary sources to do so?

With regard to retracing the decision-making process (1D), this book has primarily relied on the Diplomatic Archive of Belgium (DAB) where the records of the Belgian Ministry of Foreign Affairs are stored. The DAB collects and preserves the main sources for the study of the Ministry's inner workings, containing an abundance of personnel and administrative collections. The personal papers of Belgian diplomats, diplomatic correspondence, minutes of high-level meetings at the Ministry and inspection reports of Belgian embassy premises were especially insightful to retrace the rationale behind a building project. Additionally, the private archives of influential figures within the Ministry's hierarchy have been consulted. Scanning such archives is especially revealing as these leading figures use a far less formal tone to discuss building projects in their private correspondence. The archives reveal their personal aspirations, incentives and objections towards investing in embassy architecture and help to flesh out the main protagonists. Finally, this book has also used the parliamentary records of the Belgian Chamber of Representatives to shed light on the political stances towards investing in purpose-built embassies. These include the proceedings of the plenary sessions and the Parliamentary Committee for Foreign Affairs.

As far as casting light on the design process (2D) has been concerned, the search for sources was especially complicated. Much to my astonishment, I was informed that the Ministry's real estate department has been exempted from depositing its records with the DAB. Fortunately, I was granted access to the archival records of P&O 5.1 Buildings Abroad, the Ministry's real estate department. The P&O archive, however, is by no means a historical one where documents related to building projects are meticulously stored. Instead, the main purpose of this archival room is to support the current real estate operations of P&O 5.1. I was appalled to hear that the real estate department had periodically destroyed and thrown out documents that would have undoubtably been valuable for this book as they were considered useless in the day-to-day management of P&O 5.1. In addition to having dire consequences on the availability of contemporary documents, this preservation policy – or lack thereof – is a testament to the lack of a historical mindset within the Ministry's walls concerning the heritage value of its embassy patrimony. Consequently, these archival gaps make it extremely difficult to compile a complete overview of all purpose-built embassies constructed by the Belgian Ministry of Foreign Affairs. Such an overview thus falls outside the scope of this book.

The Belgian case with its archival gaps, however, is far from unique. My experiences are reminiscent to what Jane Loeffler has previously experienced in the context of her research on American purpose-built embassies. Confronted with a lack of primary historical sources at the real estate department, Loeffler openly questioned whether the US State Department was actually interested in documenting these building projects for future generations.[24]

Finding records on older embassy projects at P&O 5.1 turned out to be a dead end but its archival records did contain valuable information on more recent embassy projects. With regard to documenting older cases, however, I had to explore other options to find original documents. Acting on the advice of Markus Maes, head of P&O 5.1, I got in touch with Belgian embassies, asking them whether their archives contained any paperwork related to the design and construction of their respective embassy. Fortunately, ambassadors often responded positively to my inquiries, indicating that stacks of relevant sketches, blueprints, letters, reports and meeting minutes were stored in their archives. It is telling that this paperwork has been collecting dust in embassy archives rather than being sent to Brussels for preservation. Several ambassadors were kind enough to digitise archival records and email copies to me. Additionally, several heads of mission sent archival records to Brussels by means of a diplomatic bag. In tandem with sifting through these documents, I consulted the private archives of the Belgian go-to architects of the Ministry of Foreign Affairs in the 1950s and 1960s. Additionally, contemporary architectural magazines have been used. Combining paperwork produced by both the Ministry of Foreign Affairs and the architects offered an intertwined perspective that reveals the aspirations, challenges and difficulties of both parties in designing and building an embassy abroad.

Fortunately, the search for primary sources to shed light on the embassy as diplomatic decor (3D) has been far more straightforward. In their correspondence with Brussels, ambassadors tend to give vivid descriptions as to how they have opened the doors of their embassy to host high-society events attended by esteemed guests. Going through their correspondence and personnel files, I frequently stumbled upon clippings of foreign newspapers. Ambassadors have had the tendency to carefully document their media appearance during their foreign posting. They tend to give interviews to local media outlets in the lavish interiors of the ambassadorial residence, aimed at showcasing a sophisticated lifestyle intrinsically linked to their diplomatic profession. Additionally, this book has extensively made use of Belgian newspapers thanks to the search engine BelgicaPress of the Royal Library of Belgium. In addition to popular media outlets, I consulted architectural magazines. Being richly illustrated, architectural magazines offer us insights into how the embassy interiors were originally furnished and decorated. Moreover, I have consulted memoirs of Belgian ambassadors and foreign ministers that give insights into what it was like to visit, live and work at an embassy.

Navigating this Book

Building for Belgium comprises four chapters arranged in chronological order. Each chapter centres around one of the abovementioned dominant dynamics shaping the embassy-building programme since 1945. Therefore, each dominant dynamic will be made evident by one or multiple cases that form the architectural expression of the dynamic in question.

Chapter I sets the stage and discusses the agency ambassadors used to enjoy in commissioning purpose-built embassies. Chapter I examines the construction of the Washington chancery (1957) against the backdrop of the emerging transatlantic alliance between Belgium and the United States. It aims to demonstrate how the chancery was a personal project of the serving ambassador at the time. The chapter highlights the importance of personal involvement by appointed diplomats in the construction and utilisation of embassy buildings. Diplomats have had a big say in choosing the embassy's location, the architect, the architectural aesthetic, the furniture elements and artwork.

Chapter II touches upon the efforts of foreign governments to incentivise Belgium to construct embassies in their respective capitals. Examining Belgian embassy projects in Canberra (1962), Warsaw (1962) and Brasília (1974), Chapter II approaches purpose-built embassies from a bilateral point of view. It elaborates as to how commissioning said projects entailed a complex and often complicated collaboration between the sending and receiving state.

The relationship between foreign economic interests and the construction of embassies form the subject of Chapter III. Chapter III discusses how the Ministry allocated considerable resources to the construction of striking embassy buildings in New Delhi (1983) and Riyadh (1985) in times of economic crisis. By investing in prolific embassy buildings, the Ministry aimed to both provide its diplomats with a high-end venue to conduct economic diplomacy and boost its presence in these emerging markets.

Chapter IV puts the emphasis on how embassy projects became entangled in complex real estate operations intended to generate funding for the Belgian state finances. Since the turn of the millennium, the Ministry of Foreign Affairs has been compelled to approach its diplomatic patrimony as an income producing real estate portfolio. Therefore, Chapter IV discusses the embassy-building projects in Tokyo (2010) and Kinshasa (2017).

Chapter 1
The Ambassador's Agency
The Head of Mission as Project Developer (1945-1957)

On 28 April 1952, Hervé de Gruben (1894-1967) undoubtedly heaved a deep sigh as he was going through a letter of complaint addressed to him. In his capacity as Secretary-General of the Belgian Ministry of Foreign Affairs, de Gruben served as the main point of contact for Belgian diplomats to express their grievances. In this context, he received a letter of complaint from Arthur Wauters (1890-1960), the newly appointed Belgian ambassador to the USSR. In his letter, Wauters expressed his dismay at the apparently poor living and working conditions in the embassy. He vividly pointed out the many shortcomings of the building and urged his superiors to greenlight the necessary alteration works at once.[25]

Whether Wauters' assessment of the embassy's material conditions was truthful or should be taken with a pinch of salt might be interesting *pour la petite histoire*, but the reaction of Secretary-General Hervé de Gruben to the letter is far more telling. In an internal report, de Gruben indicated that Wauters' letter was just the latest in a series of letters of complaints from Belgian heads of mission who had recently arrived at their new diplomatic posting:

> The letter from Mr. Wauters on the state of the building occupied by our Embassy in Moscow takes its place among the literary exercises that our heads of mission engage in on their arrival at their posting. Over several pages, and with a wealth of adjectives, they explain that the building occupied by their predecessor is in a state of complete disrepair and quite simply uninhabitable. Recently, the Department has received samples of this literature from Tehran, Rio, Rome Q., Athens, and so on.[26]

Indeed, following their arrival at a new diplomatic posting, Belgian ambassadors had the tendency to write such letters of complaint on the embassy's material conditions. Given that they have to work and live in an embassy for several years on end, ambassadors have felt entitled to call for thorough renovations, extensive refurbishments or the relocation of the embassy.

In order to initiate such investments, ambassadors sent letters of complaints to the Ministry's highest echelons. In fact, such letters were a common part of the day-to-day routine of the Ministry in the 1950s. However, Secretary-General Hervé de Gruben was worried by a new trend that he noticed in this kind of correspondence. De Gruben witnessed first-hand how Belgian ambassadors were increasingly calling in the help of local real estate agents, architects and project developers. Such professionals were consulted to make detailed reports on the possibility of making alterations to the existing embassy or relocating the embassy to a new building. De Gruben argued that, by using external expertise, the ambassadors were pushing their own agenda and showing to Brussels that their grievances were anything but unfounded. Such moves were the direct result of the Ministry's lack of in-house expertise to assess the diplomatic housing situation. As the Ministry lacked a well-organised real estate department and did not employ any in-house architects or engineers at the time, ambassadors resorted to the know-how of third parties to fill the void. Secretary-General de Gruben was alarmed by the tendency to call upon external expertise. He strongly believed that local experts tended to exaggerate the embassy's material conditions in order to be awarded contracts.[27]

This example goes to show that Belgian ambassadors showed considerable interest in beefing up diplomatic housing. If the embassy's material settings did not correspond to their preferences, heads of mission would not hesitate to take action. Building on this observation, chapter I aims to illustrate that this proactive attitude among ambassadors was not limited to carrying out alteration works to existing premises or purchasing new buildings. Such an attitude also had a profound impact on the Belgian embassy-building programme. The current chapter explores the agency of the ambassador – the first dominant dynamic – that has guided the Belgian embassy-building programme. In line with the ambassadors of other countries in the 1950s, Belgian ambassadors have played a pivotal role in commissioning purpose-built embassies and they had a big say in the design and building process.[28]

The construction of the Belgian chancery in Washington, D.C. (1956-1957) serves as a striking case in point of this dynamic. The Washington chancery was the first major building project of the post-war period. Instead of being the result of a top-down supervised building project, the Washington chancery was more of a personal endeavour of the serving

Belgian ambassador to the United States at the time. This chapter showcases how one of Belgium's most seasoned diplomats was determined to wield architecture and interior design as representational instruments to enhance his country's prestige across the Atlantic, against the backdrop of the ever-growing importance of the United States in the post-war world order. The ambassador faced strong opposition to his building plans from within the Ministry but he successfully pulled the necessary political strings and was able to micromanage the entire building project from start to finish. So who exactly was this ambassador who also took on the role of project developer as a side hustle?

A New Sheriff in Town

On 8 March 1945, Baron Robert Silvercruys (1893-1971) was appointed the new Belgian ambassador to the United States. His new ambassadorship was nothing short of a dream come true for him. Back in the 1920s, he had already served as junior diplomat at the Belgian embassy in the American capital. Silvercruys was an admirer of the United States and wished to strengthen the transatlantic alliance.[29] The immediate post-war period provided a significant opportunity for Silvercruys to do so. In 1947, for instance, Belgium accepted American aid through the Marshall Plan and, as a founding member of NATO, it became militarily affiliated to the United States. Ambassador Silvercruys served as the Belgian representative during these key negotiations and was determined to make the transatlantic alliance the bedrock of Belgian foreign policy in the immediate post-war period. Successive Belgian governments in the 1940s and 1950s expressed their appreciation for Silvercruys' track record. This is reflected in the fact that he would go on to serve as Belgian ambassador to the United States until his retirement in 1959. Whereas an ambassadorship usually spans four years, Silvercruys had the opportunity to represent Belgium for 14 years.

During his ambassadorship, Silvercruys invested considerably in developing a social network that reached the highest echelons of American politics. In 1953, Silvercruys married Rosemary Turner (1917-1986), widow of the Democratic Senator Brien McMahon (1903-1952). The marriage boosted the already esteemed status of Silvercruys in Washington's *beau monde* and gave him access to his wife's political connections. It speaks volumes that the wedding party was attended by none other than Mamie Eisenhower (1896-1979), first lady of the United States.

His ambassadorship was also marked by a burning desire to beef up the material conditions of the Belgian embassy. As this chapter will highlight, he leveraged diplomatic architecture and interior decoration to increase Belgian prestige in the United States. In the eyes of Silvercruys, the embassy's material conditions did not do justice to the growing importance of the United States to Belgian foreign policy. For him, it was paramount to invest in diplomatic housing.

Upon his arrival in Washington, D.C., Silvercruys set out to find a new ambassadorial residence. At the time, the ambassadorial residence was situated at 1780 Massachusetts Avenue. Massachusetts Avenue was the capital's main diplomatic hub where the majority of foreign embassies and legations were located, earning this street the nickname Embassy Row.[30] Massachusetts Avenue was strategically situated just north of political hotspots such as the US State Department, Capitol Hill and the White House.

The ambassadorial residence was located in a majestic Beaux-Arts mansion and was one of the architectural showpieces of Belgium's diplomatic real estate portfolio. Upon his arrival in 1945, Silvercruys assumed that he could simply take up residence in the urban mansion as his predecessors had done since 1920. However, things worked out differently to what he had anticipated. The urban mansion was requisitioned by Paul Kronacker (1897-1994), the liberal Minister of Provision. The requisitioning was intrinsically linked to Belgium's precarious socioeconomic situation following the harsh German occupation. In December 1944, Kronacker set up his headquarters in the ambassadorial residence from where he coordinated the shipping of essentials to war-ravaged Belgium.[31]

As such, Silvercruys was forced to find a new residence. As a seasoned diplomat, Silvercruys knew that he could largely steer this purchase in the direction that he wanted. After all, the Ministry of Foreign Affairs tended to call upon the know-how of its diplomatic corps to scan the local real estate market. Knowing the American capital and its real estate market like the back of his hand, Silvercruys had no difficulties in finding a new residence that was up to par with his lavish lifestyle.

A majestic mansion (Fig. 1) situated in the north-western suburbs of Washington, D.C. along Foxhall Road caught his eye. Originally, the mansion had been commissioned by Anna Dodge Dillman (1866-1970), widow to Horace Elgin Dodge Sr. (1868-1920) who amassed his wealth as an automobile manufacturer. As her daughter, Delphine Cromwell (1899-1943), was getting married in 1928, Anna Dodge Dillman financed the construction of the Foxhall Road residence as a wedding gift for her daughter, the cost of which amounted to 310,000 US dollars (5.5 million euros). Whereas several authors indicate that Horace Trumbauer (1868-1938) was the architect, the estate was actually designed by the African-American architect Julian Abele (1881-1950) who worked as chief designer for Trumbauer.[32] In the context of racial segregation in the United States during the 1930s, the Foxhall Road estate was attributed to Trumbauer who frequently designed lavish French-style mansions for the rich and famous in the United States. Completed in 1931, the estate is an architectural reproduction of the *Hôtel de Rothelin-Charolais*, a Parisian *hôtel particulier* that was constructed in 1703. Rumour has it that Delphine Cromwell saw this *hôtel particulier* during one of her visits to Paris in the 1920s and subsequently asked her mother to construct a copy of the estate as a wedding gift.[33] This demonstrates the predilection for French architecture, furniture and culture in America's high society at the time. Erected on a densely wooded domain in front of a paved roundabout, the French Neo-Renaissance estate features a limestone façade with a central portico consisting of Ionic columns and a pediment depicting mythical figures. The estate's interiors comprise 44 rooms and marble flooring on the ground floor.

Silvercruys' enthusiasm for purchasing the estate was enormous and made him go to great lengths to secure political support in Brussels. He reached out to befriended politicians in an effort to obtain political backing outside of the Ministry's walls. Well aware that the Belgian Ministry of Finance would ultimately decide whether the estate would be purchased, Silvercruys personally reached out to Finance Minister Camille Gutt (1884-1971). During the Second World War, both men had developed a

Figure 1. The Foxhall Road residence, 2025.

Figure 2: The interiors of the Foxhall Road residence, 2025

strong friendship and continued to correspond with one another on a regular basis. Gutt convinced his fellow ministers to allocate 325,000 US dollars (5.4 million euros) to the Ministry in order to purchase the French neo-Renaissance estate.

Before moving into the new ambassadorial residence, Silvercruys oversaw a thorough refurbishment of the interiors (Fig. 2) to restore the estate to its former glory. Showing a keen interest in the residence's interiors and material settings, he called upon the services of the renowned French decoration company Alavoine et Cie that had originally furnished the estate in 1931. All the public rooms on the ground floor, such as the dining room, grand salon and library, were extensively redecorated. Given his preference for the French decorative arts, Silvercruys decorated the interiors to his own liking. He personally selected the crystal chandeliers, Aubusson carpets, parquet floors and carved panelling all of which were imported from France.[34] In line with this aesthetic, Silvercruys hand-picked French period furniture, such as Regency armchairs covered with silk Beauvais tapestry and Louis XVI-style commodes in the grand salon.

The Belgian baron was keenly aware that the residence had the potential to boost national prestige significantly. He wielded the Foxhall Road residence as a diplomatic tool, using it as a stately scenery for media interviews. As such, the new Belgian ambassadorial residence did not go unnoticed in the American press. Seeing the residence's spatial and architectural qualities as an indication of Belgium's socioeconomic status, *The Washington Times Herald* commented "Belgium is in good shape; Silvercruys lives in one of the most magnificent estates in Washington."[35] Meanwhile, *The Washington Post* marvelled at the lavish interiors: "[...] decorated in the style of Louis XVI with beauty and line down to the smallest detail. Panelled walls are finely carved, and leaves of ice-thin crystal hang by slender stems from chandeliers."[36]

If the Ministry's highest echelons were hoping that Silvercruys would now be satisfied following his move into the Foxhall Road residence, they were in for a rude awakening. The baron had no intention of resting on his laurels. For him, the purchase of the Foxhall Road residence was just the beginning of his endeavours to invest in high-end diplomatic housing.

The Washington Chancery: Rebooting the Bureaucratic Machine

Building on his success, Silvercruys now turned his sights to improving the working conditions in the Belgian chancery. At the time, the chancery was housed in a detached townhouse at 1715 22nd Street, situated just a stone's throw from Embassy Row. The Ministry of Foreign Affairs had purchased the property for 25,000 US dollars (417,000 euros) in January 1945, just two months before the start of Silvercruys' ambassadorship.[37]

The Ministry may have purchased the townhouse only recently, but Silvercruys had no intention of working there. In his eyes, the property was ill-suited to house the embassy's bureaucratic nerve centre. In a letter to a befriended politician, he complained about the deplorable working conditions in the townhouse. He argued that the building's spatial layout and infrastructure severely hindered working conditions.[38] It was unfeasible to give each embassy staffer an individual workspace as there were not enough offices to go around. Furthermore, there was no separate room available to accommodate the encryption devices used for safely communicating with Brussels or to store archival documents in an orderly fashion. As a temporary solution, the archives were stored in the townhouse's cellar but the American authorities warned the Belgian ambassador that a separate archival room was necessary to prevent fires from breaking out.[39] Furthermore, there was no central telephone system installed in the building which, Silvercruys argued, only added to the difficult working conditions at 1715 22nd Street.

Given the ambassador's voluntarism to turn things around, Silvercruys asked and received permission to carry out alteration works in the chancery during the spring of 1945. Following the completion of the works in June, Ambassador Silvercruys confided to a befriended politician that the alteration works were nothing more than simply papering over the cracks:

> The refurbishments at the 22nd Street Chancery is now almost complete. We were really cramped, with poor working conditions, and our offices looked pretty shabby. We have reclaimed seven offices from the premises formerly occupied by the building's caretaker (!), who is now housed in the basement. We carried out further partitioning work. We've set up a telephone exchange, and rooms for filing, ciphers, etc. There's also a visitors' office. There's an office for visitors and one specially reserved for Ministers who are travelling. It's not all perfect, but it will keep the machine running.[40]

To complicate matters more, the number of embassy staffers was increasing significantly. This was intrinsically linked to the growing importance of the transatlantic alliance. Whereas the Belgian embassy staff consisted of just seven people in 1939, this number would increase to 15 by the late 1940s. The staff increase was not solely due to diplomats but also government officials working for other Belgian ministries. With the rise of multilateralism in the post-war period, ministry departments such as the agriculture, colonial affairs, defence and economic affairs departments were poised to tighten their grip on the international dimension of their specific policy domain. Believing that diplomats lacked the expertise to adequately protect their interests abroad, these ministries increasingly dispatched their own officials, more commonly known as attachés, to Belgian diplomatic missions in order to have a man on the inside.[41] In the case of the Washington embassy, the number of attachés increased from just two in 1945 to six by 1957. The staff increase put further strain on the already cramped working conditions in the chancery at 22nd Street.

As the head of mission, it was up to Ambassador Silvercruys to make room for the arriving diplomats and attachés in his already cramped chancery. He wanted to locate his entire staff on one site but it proved impossible to cluster all the offices under the same roof at 22nd Street. The townhouse may have undergone considerable alteration works in 1945, but it had once again become too cramped by 1947. As such, Silvercruys was back to square one as he found himself in exactly the same situation as at the start of his ambassadorship. Given his desire to improve the working conditions at his embassy and his interest in architecture, Silvercruys cooked up an out-of-the-box solution, namely the construction of a chancery in the new *caput mundi*.

Silvercruys: A Man with a Plan

Ambassador Silvercruys conjured up the plan to build a chancery that would be spacious enough to cluster all the offices under the same roof. His building plans stood in stark contrast to the Ministry's real estate policy in the late 1940s. At the time, the Ministry preferred to purchase or lease properties abroad to accommodate embassy offices and the launch of a diplomatic building project was a highly unusual move for Belgium. By 1947, the number of purpose-built embassies and legations could be counted on one hand.[42] Moreover, this limited building activity was mostly carried out on the African and Asian continents as the Ministry believed that the local housing market in these regions was not equipped to meet the so-called Western living standard. Silvercruys hoped that the construction of the Washington chancery would be the first embassy-building project in a western country.

Even in the streetscape of Washington, D.C., purpose-built embassies were a rare sight to come across in the late 1940s. Sending states had primarily opted to purchase or lease premises along Embassy Row to house their diplomatic missions.[43] A notable exception was the purpose-built British embassy (Fig. 3) situated along Massachusetts Avenue. Completed in 1930, the embassy was designed by the renowned British architect Sir Edwin Lutyens (1869-1944) who made a name for himself by designing imperial New Delhi as well as vernacular-style houses with classical motifs in the English countryside.[44] Continuing along these architectural lines, Lutyens opted for a neoclassical approach when designing the new British embassy.

The chancery building was oriented towards Massachusetts Avenue. The building volumes were arranged in a U-shape, creating an inner courtyard that gives an inviting appearance to the diplomatic premises from the streetscape. In a similar fashion to the ambassadorial residence which is situated just behind the embassy offices, the chancery's architecture features a neo-Georgian Palladian façade with a characteristic portico and consists of brickwork and Indiana limestone to pay tribute to local building traditions.[45] Lutyens emphasised the chancery's strong verticality by

Figure 3: The British chancery, undated

means of accentuated chimneys that were inspired by Christopher Wren's (1632-1723) design of the Royal Chelsea Hospital which was completed in 1692. The opening of the purpose-built British embassy contributed to cementing the status of Massachusetts Avenue as the capital's diplomatic hotspot. The British embassy served as a magnet that attracted other diplomatic missions to purchase or lease premises along Embassy Row.[46]

The British building activity incentivised the Apostolic Nunciature of the Holy See, the Vatican's equivalent of an embassy, to commission a new diplomatic building (Fig. 4) for its papal nuncio to the United States. In 1931, the Vatican purchased a plot of land at 3339 Massachusetts Avenue just a stone's throw away from the British purpose-built embassy. The Holy See reached out to the American architect Frank Vernon Murphy to design its new diplomatic premises. Murphy ticked all the boxes for the Vatican. He was the chairman of the architecture department at the Catholic University of Washington, D.C., had designed several churches in the United States, and was a man of faith.[47] Murphy opted for an architectural design that resonated well with the preferences of his religious client. As part of his scheme to evoke an image of Rome in Washington,

Figure 4: The Apostolic Nunciature of the Holy See, undated

D.C., he designed a three-story Renaissance palazzo for the papal nuncio situated on top of a granite base.

Completed in 1939, its austere façade features three distinctive horizontal layers made of Indiana limestone and evenly spaced windows. These windows were made of stained-glass, depicting scenes from Dante Alighieri's (1265-1321) *Divine Comedy*, several popes and saints, and historical figures such as Christopher Columbus (1451-1506) and the first American President George Washington (1732-1799).[48] Whereas governments use taxpayer money to finance diplomatic building projects, the Vatican raised the necessary funding among the different Catholic dioceses across America.[49] Ambassador Robert Silvercruys had a special connection with the diplomatic grounds of the Apostolic Nunciature of the Holy See. As part of the baron's wedding to his American wife Rosemary Turner on 21 September 1953, the Apostolic Delegate Amleto Cicognani (1883-1973) presided over a small wedding ceremony in the small chapel situated in the gardens of his diplomatic premises.[50]

One cannot help but think that Silvercruys wanted to join this select group of diplomatic missions with purpose-built diplomatic housing in

Figure 5: Spaak (left) and Ambassador Silvercruys (right), 1948

the contemporary *caput mundi*. The lack of office space was of course the main rationale for constructing new embassy offices, but Ambassador Silvercruys envisaged a purpose-built chancery to be more than just a work environment. As the purchase of the Foxhall Road residence demonstrated, Silvercruys framed this construction project as yet another opportunity to put Belgium on the map by means of brick and mortar. Architecturally speaking, Silvercruys wanted to put his chancery on a par with the Foxhall Road residence.

It is one thing to come up with such an idea, but quite another to put it into practice, especially as the Belgian Ministry of Foreign Affairs did not have a strong building tradition at the time. As such, it was imperative for Silvercruys to gain support among the highest political echelons. Whereas he had previously called upon the support of Finance Minister Camille Gutt in the context of purchasing the residence, this was no longer possible as his close friend had left national politics by 1947. Consequently, Silvercruys opted for another strategy to gain support for his building endeavour. He opted to immediately reach out to Foreign Minister Paul-Henri Spaak (1899-1972) (Fig. 5). In March 1947, an opportunity presented itself through the annual diplomatic conference organised by the Ministry. As part of this conference, all Belgian ambassadors were recalled to Brussels to attend lectures and seminars. Believing that it would be more fruitful to pitch his building proposal to Spaak in person, Silvercruys arranged a personal meeting with him on the margins of the conference.

During his pitch to Spaak, Silvercruys tried to convince his boss of the merits of the building project. Silvercruys hammered home the argument that a new chancery would tremendously improve the working conditions of all Belgian representatives in the American capital.[51] It would serve as a diplomatic hub where the offices of diplomats and attachés would be clustered together under the same roof. Demonstrating his diplomatic skills, Silvercruys succeeded in piquing Spaak's interest. The latter instructed Silvercruys to conduct a preparatory study that would involve scanning the Washington real estate market for a suitable building plot.

Wandering through Washington

Ambassador Silvercruys did not waste any time following his return to the United States. In March 1947, he scanned the local real estate market for a suitable building plot. As part of his preparatory study, Silvercruys was driven around Washington, D.C. by his German chauffeur. They made stops at over a dozen different building plots up for sale. The ambassador enjoyed a significant amount of freedom as he was not accompanied by an official of the Ministry of Finance. On 5 April 1947, he sent a detailed report on his findings to Spaak. The report clearly illustrates how Silvercruys had his own interpretation of the task Spaak had entrusted to him. Whereas Spaak had instructed him to compare the available building plots, Silvercruys only discussed the building plot he deemed most suitable to locate the future chancery.

He urged Spaak to purchase a plot of almost 5,000 m² situated in Washington's northern suburbs at the corner of 34th Street and Garfield Street. From a diplomatic point of view, the suggestion to move to the northern suburbs was remarkable. Silvercruys wanted to leave Embassy Row, an area that greatly facilitated diplomatic interaction as it is situated in the vicinity of the State Department, Capitol Hill and the White House. By building the new chancery on the north-western edge of Embassy Row, Silvercruys wanted to join a select group of diplomatic missions which had previously constructed purpose-built diplomatic properties in this neighbourhood, such as the aforementioned British embassy and Apostolic Nunciature.

Silvercruys' report to Spaak reads like a vigorous sales pitch. He made the case that the plot on Garfield Street was the most ideal site. The site, Silvercruys argued, met three important criteria. The first criterion concerned the financial aspect. The report started off by emphasising that the plot's price tag of 21,000 US dollars (272,000 euros) was a bargain. Whereas the average price of undeveloped land ranged between 1.5 (20 euros) and 5 US dollars (64 euros) per square foot, the ambassador highlighted that his preferred plot of land only cost 43 US cents (5 euros) per square foot.[52] The second criterion put forward by Silvercruys echoes the main catchphrase of real estate agents: location, location, location. He touched upon the scenic qualities of the site, indicating that the plot was situated in an upstanding residential neighbourhood on the wooded outskirts of Rock Creek Park. Although not explicitly mentioned in the report, personal grounds may have influenced the ambassador's choice for this building plot. The proposed site was located close to the Foxhall Road residence. This would significantly reduce the ambassador's commute between the chancery and the residence. Furthermore, he stressed that the site was situated opposite to Washington National Cathedral. Conceived as Washington's equivalent to Westminster Abbey, the neo-Gothic cathedral was and still is the religious landmark of the city. The cathedral has historically served as the venue for state funerals of American presidents. At the time Silvercruys drafted his report, the cathedral was the third tallest structure the American capital had to offer.

Additionally, the Silvercruys report highlighted that the site was situated on an elevated part of the American capital. As one drives up the hill coming from Massachusetts Avenue, the building plot has a prominent position that is visible from afar. Its prominent position did, however, come with a price. Being situated on a sloped area, the building plot was not a flat landscape. As will become apparent, these geographical conditions had a significant impact on the eventual design of the future chancery. In his report, Silvercruys also anticipated any objections to moving the chancery away from the city centre. The report indicated that the proposed site would be easy to reach for embassy staffers and visitors alike as two important bus lines were situated nearby. The report also stated that there was a growing tendency among diplomatic missions to leave the city centre and move to the north-western residential suburbs to escape the busy city centre with its traffic congestion and noise pollution.

As such, the ambassador argued that the future chancery would certainly not be isolated from other diplomatic missions.⁵³ Thirdly and most importantly, Silvercruys highlighted the size of the building plot. With a surface area of almost 5,000 m², the plot would be large enough to construct a spacious chancery with thirty offices for diplomats and attachés.

Given his commitment to the chancery project, Silvercruys stated in his report that he had taken the liberty to reach out to William Waverly Taylor Jr. (1896-1986) – an American architect that he had befriended – to make a preliminary design for the new chancery. Silvercruys had already introduced Waverly Taylor to the project back in November 1946.⁵⁴ This move makes two things crystal-clear. Firstly, Silvercruys was already toying with the idea of building a chancery even before the embassy staff significantly increased from 1947 onwards. While Silvercruys brought up practical issues, such as a shortage of office space, as leverage to build a new chancery, this was not the basis of his building plans. Judging from the aforementioned purchase of the Foxhall Road residence, Silvercruys envisaged his purpose-built chancery as a project to boost national prestige in the United States. Secondly, his talks with Waverly Taylor go to show that the personal network of Belgian diplomats played a significant role in bringing the Ministry of Foreign Affairs into contact with architects. In a letter to the Ministry, Waverly Taylor indicated that he normally did not design office buildings, but that his "[...] interest in the proposed Chancery for your government was motivated primarily by my desire to be helpful to its Ambassador here, and by my warm feeling toward your country."⁵⁵

Ambassador Silvercruys concluded his report by stating that the site formed the ideal location for the future Belgian chancery. In his eyes, such an opportunity should not be squandered. Worried that the building plot he so desired may already be sold before Spaak made up his mind, he put pressure on the foreign minister to act swiftly. He indicated to Spaak that he had already talked to the owner of the site and personally negotiated an option to purchase it for 21,000 US dollars (272,000 euros) that would transpire by the end of April 1947:

> In return for a deposit of 50 dollars [650 euros], I have obtained an option to purchase this plot of land and would be grateful if you could send me your instructions before the last day of this month. I can assure you that the choice I am proposing is the result of a meticulous investigation and that I do not think it will be possible to find, in the future, a plot of land as well located under such advantageous conditions.⁵⁶

His efforts were not in vain. By the end of April, Spaak wired the necessary funding to the embassy's bank account. On 12 May 1947, Silvercruys personally signed the deed of purchase. So what initially started out as a preparatory study in March 1947 resulted in the purchase of a building plot less than two months later. As will become apparent, this quick decision-making process was and still is highly unusual for the Belgian embassy-building programme.

Subsequent purchases of sites for embassy buildings moved at a snail's pace through the Ministry's bureaucratic apparatus. It goes to show that Silvercruys was a highly influential figure within the Ministry who could get things done quickly. Judging from the swift purchase of the site and the talks he had with an architect, there was seemingly nothing that stood in his way to develop the site. Little did Silvercruys know that his main rival within the Ministry was gearing up to thwart his building endeavours.

Opposition within the Ministry: Less is More

Judging by the swift action Spaak had taken in acquiring the building plot, one would assume that it would be a mere formality for Silvercruys to secure the necessary funding. In reality, however, nothing could be further from the truth. By June 1947, Spaak did not undertake any further initiatives related to the chancery project. It remains unclear why the foreign minister suddenly lost interest in the project, but there is reason to believe that his packed agenda had something to do with it. Spaak began to combine the position as foreign minister with that of prime minister. Combining both public functions turned out to be quite a challenge. Walter Loridan (1909-1997), Spaak's Chief of Cabinet, wrote a letter to Silvercruys in which he revealed that Spaak was biting off more than he could chew. Loridan complained that it was not easy to get hold of Spaak. He was often absent from the Ministry and if he did show his face it was only a lightning visit of just a few minutes.[57]

With Spaak out of the picture, the chancery project landed on the desk of Secretary-General Hervé de Gruben who managed the Ministry's day-to-day operations. De Gruben was known for his aversion towards launching building projects abroad. Back in 1935, he had talked the Ministry's leadership out of the idea of constructing a legation in Moscow.[58] According to de Gruben, the Ministry lacked the necessary in-house expertise and financial means to build abroad. In his eyes, the

Ministry should rather purchase and lease existing properties to house diplomatic missions.

To complicate matters even further for Silvercruys, he had a strained personal relationship with de Gruben. In an interview with Mark Eyskens, the former Belgian prime minister recalls how both men were rivals.[59] In late 1944, this rivalry reached its zenith as the two senior diplomats were competing for the prestigious function of Belgian ambassador to the United States. As Silvercruys was eventually awarded the diplomatic posting, the already strained relationship turned sour. With Spaak outsourcing the Ministry's management to de Gruben, Silvercruys now had to discuss the building project with his rival who was already not keen to launch building projects for budgetary reasons.

Given their history, Silvercruys was anticipating financial criticism from Secretary-General Hervé de Gruben. In his report to de Gruben, Silvercruys therefore made the case that one should not envisage the building project as a costly investment, but rather as a reallocation of funds and assets.[60] More specifically, Silvercruys argued that the project's price tag could largely be covered by selling and ending the lease of the four residential buildings accommodating the embassy offices at the time. The Belgian ambassador, however, did not back this statement with exact figures of the estimated value of these properties or the price tag of constructing a new chancery.

The lack of budgetary details did not go by unnoticed. Secretary-General de Gruben criticised Silvercruys for leaving out this information. Moreover, de Gruben was not convinced that the sale of the properties at Massachusetts Avenue and 22nd Street would largely cover the construction costs. Such concerns did not appear out of nowhere. Just as Ambassador Silvercruys, Hervé de Gruben knew the city of Washington, D.C. like the back of his hand as he had been posted as counsellor at the Belgian embassy between 1937 and 1945, leaving just before the arrival of Silvercruys. He had a clear understanding of the local real estate market and thus a good indication of the value of the Belgian embassy buildings. In a follow-up report, Silvercruys reluctantly admitted that he might have painted a picture that was too rosy. He indicated that selling the diplomatic premises would generate only 200,000 US dollars (2.5 million euros) whereas the construction costs for the new chancery would amount to 485,000 US dollars (6.2 million euros).[61] The real estate operation cooked up by Silvercruys would not even cover half of the chancery's price tag. In a similar fashion to real estate magnate Donald Trump, Ambassador

Silvercruys apparently had the tendency to overvalue real estate assets for personal gain. Consequently, Secretary-General de Gruben pulled the plug on the project.

Confronted with this rejection, Ambassador Silvercruys reconsidered his options. By the summer of 1948, he pursued a strategy similar to the one he had used in the case of purchasing the Foxhall Road residence in 1945. He once again reached out to his close friend Camille Gutt to help convince Spaak of the merits of the project. At the time, Gutt served as the first managing director of the International Monetary Fund, the headquarters of which were located in the American capital. This enabled Silvercruys to speak with Gutt in person and fill him in on the details of the project. On 18 August 1948, Gutt came to the aid of his friend by writing a letter to Spaak. He pleaded with Spaak to send more diplomats to the Belgian embassy in Washington, D.C. and went on to highlight the advantages of constructing a new chancery:

> I am more familiar with the second question, which is that of a building to be constructed on the land we own, to house our various departments. You will remember that, although I hold the purse strings, I was in favour of the purchase of our present embassy [residence at Foxhall Road], and I think that you feel, as I do, that it was a useful investment. I think the same would be true for the construction of the building which would house the chancery, the commercial and military attachés, and the procurement department, which are now spread over four different buildings. Silvercruys tells me that selling these buildings, plus the unused balance, would cover the building costs. This seems to me to be a valid assertion, although I have not been able to verify this of course. If this is the case, there is no doubt that the efficiency of the work and the good appearance of the Belgian departments would gain a lot from this transformation. This is a personal opinion which I thought would be useful to share with you.[62]

Echoing the arguments made by Silvercruys, Gutt made the case that commissioning a modern and spacious office building would tremendously increase the bureaucratic efficiency of one of the nation's most important embassies. As a technocrat, Gutt implicitly reasoned that investing in modern and comfortable offices would improve the working conditions of diplomats posted in the contemporary *caput mundi*. Interestingly, Gutt repeated Silvercruys' unfounded claim that the sale of the current diplomatic premises would largely cover the construction costs. As Hervé de Gruben had already debunked this claim, Silvercruys was walking on thin ice walking as he asked his friend Gutt to pass on this incorrect information to Spaak. The questionable working method illustrates that the senior diplomat would go to great lengths to greenlight the chancery's construction.

Unfortunately for Silvercruys, Gutt's letter did not have the effect he was hoping for. In contrast, his plan blew up in his face. Spaak did not show any signs of greenlighting the construction proposal. Moreover, Hervé de Gruben was not amused that Silvercruys was undermining his authority as secretary-general by talking behind his back with Spaak and calling on the help of his political friends to do his bidding. The tendency of Silvercruys to operate outside of official channels did not go down well with Secretary-General de Gruben. He was so fed up with the Silvercruys' concerted efforts that he reprimanded the Belgian ambassador.[63]

In early 1949, Silvercruys made a last-ditch attempt to change the mind of his superior, but his efforts were in vain. Secretary-General Hervé de Gruben once again argued that the building project was dead in the water. To justify his decision to Silvercruys, he indicated that erecting a new chancery with a price tag of some 13.6 million Belgian francs (3.7 million euros) would tremendously exceed the financial means of Ministry of Foreign Affairs.[64] To get his point across, he stressed that the Ministry was only allocated 12.6 million Belgian francs (3.4 million euros) to finance the purchase and construction of new diplomatic premises for 1949. As such, the Washington project alone would have already exceeded the total budget of 1949.

De Gruben twisted the knife further by revealing to Silvercruys that he would not consider greenlighting the project even if the necessary funds were available. He reasoned that the current working conditions in Washington, D.C. were not as bad as Silvercruys claimed. Secretary-General de Gruben labelled the entire building project as costly and unnecessarily expensive. He went so far as to argue that the entire plan was not driven by a desire to improve the working conditions in Washington, D.C., but by the ambassador's wish to have a nice and lavish office for himself.[65]

De Gruben's budgetary objections demonstrated his 'less is more' management style during his tenure as secretary-general. On 2 December 1947, for instance, he issued a directive in which he instructed all ministry staffers to limit their travel expenses.[66] The Secretary-General spoke out against staying in high-end hotels or having dinner in fancy restaurants. To justify his decision, Hervé de Gruben reasoned that a frugal policy would significantly strengthen the country's prestige abroad following the war.[67] It would show to the eyes of the world that Belgium had suffered greatly from the German occupation and had prompted the Belgian diplomatic apparatus to tighten its belt. As such, the construction of a chancery did not correspond with the frugal policy he wanted to uphold.

Building up Political Support

Facing strong opposition from the Ministry's highest echelons, Ambassador Silvercruys put his lobbying skills as a seasoned diplomat to good use. In the spring of 1949, he started an intensive lobbying campaign in the hope of convincing key figures in Brussels. His correspondence on this topic reads like a who's who of Belgian politics at the time. As part of his scheme to build up a coalition of the willing, Silvercruys reached out to Finance Minister Gaston Eyskens (1905-1988), who was one of the strongmen of the Christian Social Party. Silvercruys did not face any difficulties in convincing Eyskens of the merits of his building project. On 23 March 1949, for instance, Eyskens confided to Silvercruys that he was trying to convince Spaak to greenlight the chancery project:

> Knowing that this construction project is so close to your heart, I have done my utmost to persuade Mr. Spaak of the advantages of going ahead with it. Unfortunately, I have not been able to obtain his support, as he feels we must wait a little longer.[68]

Spaak's apathy towards the chancery project goes to show that he attached great importance to the judgment of Hervé de Gruben, whom he had personally appointed as secretary-general back in 1947.

Ambassador Silvercruys would, however, get help from an unexpected source: the Belgian electorate participating in the elections of 1949. The victorious Christian Social Party came out on top and formed a coalition government with the liberals, casting the Belgian Socialist Party into the opposition. As such, Spaak's dual mandate as prime minister and foreign minister came to an end. Following a decade of Spaak at the helm, Spaak was succeeded by the Christian-democrat Paul van Zeeland (1893-1973). Furthermore, Gaston Eyskens of the Christian Social Party succeeded Spaak as prime minister. As Eyskens had previously expressed his support for the Washington project, the stars were seemingly aligned for Silvercruys. On 17 November 1949, Prime Minister Eyskens attempted to set the Washington project back in motion during a budgetary meeting with high-level officials of the Ministry. Among those present were Foreign Minister Paul van Zeeland, Secretary-General Hervé de Gruben and Roger Ockrent who served as Secretary-General of the Department of Foreign Trade. Ockrent was a close friend of Silvercruys and always made sure that Silvercruys caught up on all the latest gossip in Brussels.[69] Being the faithful friend that he was, Ockrent sent a summary of the meeting to Silvercruys to keep his friend in the loop:

> I would like to tell you about a small incident. At the end of the meeting, Prime Minister Eyskens asked with a smile: Are you going to build the new Chancellery in Washington?
> De Gruben: Certainly not, it's a lavish, unnecessary and superfluous expense.
> Van Zeeland: Slow down, slow down... I'm looking into it. Mr. de Gruben has just given you his opinion, which will not necessarily be mine. Obviously, his opinion matters.[70]

Silvercruys may have got rid of Spaak but Secretary-General Hervé de Gruben stuck to his guns. He continued to make objections to the building project which he labelled as nothing more than an unnecessary and excessive expense. Ockrent half-jokingly suggested to Silvercruys that they should pray together that de Gruben would be quickly relieved of his duties as secretary-general and sent as ambassador to Timbuktu.[71] Fortunately for Silvercruys, de Gruben clashed not only with his subordinates but also with Foreign Minister van Zeeland. From 1951 onward, rumours began to spread in Brussels that van Zeeland was seriously thinking of replacing de Gruben.[72]

Unsurprisingly, it was only with the departure of Hervé de Gruben as secretary-general in March 1953 that the tide finally turned in favour of Ambassador Silvercruys. In March 1953, van Zeeland appointed Hervé de Gruben as Belgian ambassador to West Germany. Louis Scheyven (1904-1979), the Director-General of Political Affairs, was appointed secretary-general. As the brother of Raymond Scheyven (1911-1987), the treasurer of the Christian Social Party, Louis Scheyven was closely affiliated with the ruling Christian democrats which played to the advantage of Ambassador Silvercruys. As Louis Scheyven was closely affiliated to Paul van Zeeland's political party and supported the idea of constructing new embassy offices in Washington, D.C., the chancery project finally gathered pace in 1953.

Paul van Zeeland at the Wheel

With Hervé de Gruben out of the picture, Foreign Minister Paul van Zeeland finally showed his true colours. The building project had already piqued his interest from the start of his ministership in August 1949. As the chancery project would be the biggest and most expensive building project of the Ministry, van Zeeland wanted to be sure that he and his secretary-general were on the same page, which was definitely not the case with Hervé de Gruben. It does not come as much of a surprise that van Zeeland was a strong supporter of the project. Van Zeeland framed the United States as a key partner in military and economic affairs. In return, American support would enable the European powers to build up a unified Europe.[73] In his eyes, the new Washington chancery would not only provide Belgian diplomats with a state-of-the-art work environment but would also serve as an architectural testament to the importance of the transatlantic alliance. On a personal level, van Zeeland framed the Washington project as a unique opportunity to leave behind an architectural mark on his ministership for decades to come.

Such aspirations became apparent in his efforts to handpick the architect for the project. Notwithstanding that Silvercruys had already reached out to William Waverly Taylor Jr., van Zeeland pushed the American architect aside. Instead, he wanted to call upon the services of an architect with whom he was friends. Such a move helps to explain why van Zeeland first wanted to get rid of Hervé de Gruben before proceeding with the building project. During his tenure as secretary-general, Hervé de Gruben put forward the proposal to professionalise the procedure by which public contracts were awarded. In January 1948, de Gruben called for the creation of an independent commission that would guide the Ministry in awarding architectural contracts.[74] Such a commission would review bids independently, without the meddling of diplomats, ministry officials and the foreign minister. However, given the Ministry's status as a state within a state that adhered to its own rules and procedures, de Gruben's proposed reform never saw the light of day.

As such, Foreign Minister Paul van Zeeland could reach out to his friend and architect Max Winders (1882-1982) to make a preliminary design of the future Washington chancery. Born and raised in Antwerp, Winders was the son of the renowned architect Jean-Jacques Winders (1849-1936), whose designs included the neoclassical Royal Museum of Fine Arts in Antwerp and several neo-Renaissance town halls and post offices at the end of the nineteenth century. Following in his father's footsteps, Max Winders studied architecture, painting and sculpture at the *Académie Royal des Beaux-Arts* in Antwerp.[75] Thanks to his marriage to the daughter of the director of the National Bank of Belgium, Max Winders was given the opportunity to design several Beaux-Arts bank buildings in Antwerp, Huy and Leuven. Winders' architectural oeuvre was marked by a classical and neo-Gothic approach. His classical designs showcase a certain French allure and radiate a sense of monumentality and stateliness.[76] During both world wars, Winders cemented his ties with the political elite of Belgium. Given his association with high finance, Winders helped to evacuate the national gold reserve to Britain during the early stages of the First World War. During the Second World War, the government entrusted him with the task of keeping valuable Belgian artwork and church bells out of the hands of German occupiers.[77]

Believing that the chancery project had been delayed long enough, Paul van Zeeland sent Max Winders to Washington, D.C. to acquaint himself with the local conditions and especially the features of the building plot. During Winders' stay, Ambassador Silvercruys spared no expense to pamper the Belgian architect. Winders stayed at the luxurious Mayflower Hotel and was also invited to the Foxhall Road residence for an intimate dinner party with Silvercruys. During his stay in Washington, D.C., Winders gained as much relevant information as possible to make a design for the new chancery.

Firstly, he visited the building plot and examined its spatial qualities. As mentioned previously, the plot is situated on a slope. It drops off into a declivity beginning at approximately 40 meters from the curb line on 34th Street. Winders believed that this height difference should not be seen as an obstacle, but rather as an opportunity. He conceived the idea to position the building volume on the slope, so the basement could be accessed from the rear façade and could not be seen from the street side. Furthermore, he examined the building regulations and the zoning laws that were applied to this area. The Washington authorities had zoned the area around Garfield Street as Residential A, which was the highest type of residential zoning. This implies that only the construction of single-family and detached dwellings was permitted.[78] As diplomatic missions began to move away from the city centre, however, the Washington Board of Zoning Adjustment adopted a more lenient attitude and gave permission to diplomatic missions to construct residences and chanceries in the area. To remain in touch with the neighbourhood's surroundings, however, the diplomatic buildings had to be low-rise constructions no more than two-storeys high.

Secondly, Winders held several talks with Ambassador Silvercruys and the embassy staff on the programmatic needs of the future chancery.[79] As Silvercruys had already conceived his plan for this chancery back in 1946, he knew exactly what he wanted. He informed Winders that the new chancery should have at least 59 offices. He made it crystal clear that the offices had to have different dimensions in order to accentuate the pecking-order within the embassy staff. Ambassador Silvercruys wanted to give himself and his senior diplomats the most spacious offices, whereas the offices of lower-ranked diplomats and attachés ought to be considerably smaller. Furthermore, his wish list also featured a large conference room, an exhibition room and a library. The inclusion of an exhibition room and library illustrates how Ambassador Silvercruys envisaged the chancery to be not only an office building, but also a cultural centre where American visitors could be introduced to Belgian artwork and literature. Investing in cultural diplomacy was the ambassador's favourite *modus operandi* to strengthen bilateral ties. As an art connoisseur and literature lover, the ambassador frequently offered Belgian artwork and books as gifts to foreign leaders and fellow diplomats.[80]

Additionally, the chancery's basement had to include an apartment for the caretaker. The basement would also be used to store the embassy's archives. As the chancery would house the offices of Belgian military attachés, the archival room would contain sensitive military documents. As a result of Belgium joining NATO in 1949, this had a profound effect on the design of the archival room. Silvercruys made it clear to Winders that each diplomatic mission of a NATO member state was required to store its military documents in a well-secured archival room. NATO even issued security guidelines to its member states. The archival room had to be closed off by a steel door, the walls had to be made of reinforced concrete that was 30 cm thick, and the ceiling had to be 20 cm thick.[81]

Thirdly, Winders contemplated how he would tackle this building commission in terms of aesthetics. Together with Silvercruys, Winders believed that the Belgian embassy building should pay tribute to Washington's government architecture. Therefore, he toured the city to draw inspiration. His archival records of the trip contain several city guides and brochures on government buildings. One of these brochures was devoted to the headquarters of the United States Department of Defence, more commonly known as the Pentagon (Fig. 6). Judging from the various circles he drew with his pencil in the brochure, this landmark caught his eye. Completed in 1943, the Pentagon was – and still is – one of the largest office buildings in the world. The building, with its Indiana limestone façade, was designed by the American architect George Bergstrom (1876-1955) and constructed by the building contractor John McShain (1898-1989). The massive office building, with a floor area of more than 600,000 m², was nicknamed the Pentagon because of its five-sided structure and equal amount of concentric rings making up the building volume.[82]

In his design of the Pentagon, Bergstrom paid tribute to a long-standing American tradition to draw inspiration from antiquity for government buildings. From Washington's grid plan, conceived by the French-American engineer Pierre L'Enfant (1754-1825), to the monumental architecture of several public buildings, American policymakers and architects have frequently modelled the American capital after the classical principles of Greco-Roman architecture, seeing these 'democracies' of antiquity as a source of inspiration for the United States.[83] Throughout the 20th century, neoclassical architecture witnessed several revivals in the context of commissioning government buildings in the United States. During the Roosevelt presidency (1933-1945), the federal government favoured stripped classicism when commissioning public buildings. This stripped classical style was a modern derivation of Greco-Roman architecture that featured its main architectural principles but left out any ornamentation. This aesthetic shaped several government projects in Washington, D.C., such as the Folger Shakespeare Library (1933), the Federal Reserve Building (1937) and the Pentagon building which drew Winders' attention.

Winders' aesthetic approach matched the personal preferences of Ambassador Silvercruys. Silvercruys had also expressed his desire to construct a stripped classical office building. In a letter to van Zeeland, Silvercruys suggested constructing the chancery with "[...] top notch

Figure 6: The Pentagon, 1940s

building materials and sandstone exteriors in the tradition of US government buildings."[84]

Following his return to Brussels, Winders held talks with the Ministry's highest echelons on the design. His main conversational partner was Baron Etienne Ruzette who served as Director-General of the Personnel Department. Director-General Ruzette approved the suggestion to blend into the surroundings of Washington's government architecture. However, he stressed that the building project would also be the perfect opportunity to incorporate Belgian elements into the design to express nationhood on American soil. In his discussions with Winders, Ruzette brought up a memo from a previous meeting he had held with Foreign Minister van Zeeland. During this meeting, van Zeeland had put forward the idea of using building materials endemic to Belgium and the Belgian Congo:

> In the event of the construction of an office building, it would be preferable to arrange for natural or manufactured products (stone, bricks, wood from the Congo, beams for metal framing, frames, partitions, etc.) to be shipped from Belgium to the USA.[85]

Perceiving the future embassy as *une machine-à-représenter*, he wanted to give the building a clear Belgian touch and to ensure that the building served as an architectural expression of Belgian craftsmanship and culture. Van Zeeland even explicitly expressed his desire that the chancery's interior prominently feature Belgian black marble – the so-called *noir belge* – and Congolese woodwork. His suggestion to use Congolese woodwork underscores that materials from the colony were generally perceived to be assets of the Belgian metropole and thus also paid tribute to the country's status as a colonial power.

On 16 March 1953, Winders sent his preliminary design to his friend Paul van Zeeland. Unfortunately, the drawings and blueprints have not withstood the test of time. This makes it difficult to discuss the main features of the design, but some paragraphs in the accompanying letter give us some clues. Winders designed a U-shaped two-storey building with a concrete structure, the exterior of which would be covered with Indiana limestone.[86] The U-shaped building would be oriented towards the intersection of Garfield Street and 34th Street to give the building an inviting appearance from the street side. The sixty offices for diplomats and attachés would be spread over two floors, while the technical installations, archival room and caretaker's apartment would be situated in the basement. As the building was positioned on the slope, the basement would only be situated below ground level at the northern and western sides of the building.

Winders urged van Zeeland to construct the new chancery as it would not only boost national prestige but also significantly improve working conditions for embassy staffers.[87] He estimated that the price tag would not exceed 650,000 US dollars (7.4 million euros) and prominently highlighted, as though Silvercruys were telling him what to write, that selling the current chancery buildings would generate some 180,000 US dollars (2 million euros).[88] Winders concluded his letter by expressing his hope to van Zeeland that the Ministry of Foreign Affairs would proceed with his preliminary design and eventually award the commission to him. As luck would have it, however, Winders' involvement caused political upheaval in Brussels.

Paul van Zeeland versus Camille Huysmans: Allegations of a *quid pro quo*

Van Zeeland's decision to handpick Max Winders would come back to haunt him. The socialist opposition in parliament got wind of it and began to scrutinise the conduct of van Zeeland in hiring Winders. Camille Huysmans (1871-1968), who was a heavyweight of the Belgian Socialist Party, interpellated van Zeeland to shed light on the matter during Question Time in the Chamber of Representatives. Huysmans had built up an impressive political career, serving as the first socialist mayor of Antwerp (1933-1940; 1944-1946), president of the Chamber of Representatives (1936-1939; 1954-1958) and prime minister (1946-1947). By 1953, the 82-year-old Huysmans was the oldest MP in the Chamber of Representatives. Notwithstanding his age, Huysmans stood his ground in parliamentary debates, as Paul van Zeeland would find out during Question Time on 16 June 1953.

That day, Huysmans took the stage and blasted van Zeeland for his apparent lack of transparency concerning the hiring of an architect. If it were not for the rumours circulating in Brussels, Huysmans stated, he and his fellow MPs would not have known that the Ministry had selected an architect for the Washington project. Moreover, Huysmans blasted van Zeeland for withholding the identity of the architect and openly questioned why the Ministry had not organised a public tendering procedure as was common practice for any other ministry department:

> I asked you who the architect was who was given the job. In the Dutch text you say 'a famous architect' and in the French text 'a renowned architect'.

If this architect is so famous, I'd like to know his name, to see if he really is a renowned architect, even in America. I see [...] that an architect has been designated, but nothing more. I don't think that's a recommendable way of working. I don't even think that ministers should make any distinction between foreign countries and their own where, fortunately, other rules apply.[89]

Huysmans vented his frustration regarding how the Ministry of Foreign Affairs used its foreign sphere of action as a pretext to bend the rules and ignore the regular tendering procedure for public buildings erected on Belgian soil.

Responding to the fierce criticism, van Zeeland revealed that Max Winders was the architect in question and went on to defend his decision to hire him. Van Zeeland indicated that his decision was solely based on Winders' merits as an architect and not the result of any personal ties. Subsequently, he enumerated the benefits of working together with a highly reputed architect such as Winders by highlighting his architectural oeuvre, his various positions in the world of academia, and his various awards and decorations.

As both Paul van Zeeland and Camille Huysmans were big names in national politics, their heated argument was widely covered in the press. Most newspapers only gave a summary of the parliamentary discussion but the francophone newspaper *La Libre Belgique* seized the debate as an opportunity to take a critical look at how the Ministry was hiring architects. *La Libre Belgique* concurred with Huysmans and criticised the lack of a tendering procedure worthy of the name. The foreign minister could simply choose an architect of his own liking and was exempt from organising an architectural competition.[90]

Meanwhile, the Flemish Christian-democratic newspaper *De Standaard* presented very different views in its coverage of the parliamentary debate. *De Standaard* made the case that Camille Huysmans was only criticising the Washington project because he had ulterior political motives.[91] *De Standaard* did not elaborate further on the alleged political motives but it was most likely referring to Huysmans' political views on Belgium's foreign policy at the time. As a devoted Marxist, Huysmans fiercely opposed the transatlantic alliance between Belgium and the United States and strongly condemned the harsh anti-communist rhetoric in national politics and media outlets.[92] Huysmans propagated the idea of deepening bilateral ties with Moscow and the communist countries in Eastern Europe. *De Standaard* reasoned that Huysmans was only criticising the building project because the future chancery would serve as the architectural symbol of the flourishing transatlantic ties.

Interestingly, the wide media coverage provided Huysmans with inside information on van Zeeland's alleged motives for awarding this commission to Winders. At the end of June 1953, Huysmans received a letter from a certain Mr. Smet. The self-proclaimed whistle-blower claimed that van Zeeland had a hidden agenda in hiring Max Winders:

> Why did Mr. van Zeeland award the commission to build the new embassy to architect Winders? Only because Winders, a corresponding member of the Institute de France, beaux-arts, architecture, painting and sculpture, had recommended him as a member of that institute. This was something van Zeeland had wanted for a long time, and many dinners were held for the academicians at the Ministry of Foreign Affairs and the Avenue de Belgique to achieve this result. [...] What are van Zeeland's talents as a painter, sculptor and architect? Once again we are paying for van Zeeland's follies of grandeur.[93]

Whether Mr. Smet spoke the truth or fabricated the story remains unclear. Paul van Zeeland did indeed become a member of the Institute de France in 1953, but there is no solid evidence in writing that there was a so-called *quid pro quo* arrangement between both men.

Mr. Smet's letter and the parliamentary debate do, however, demonstrate how the absence of a transparent awarding procedure for architectural commissions came at a price for the Ministry. In its capacity as awarding authority, the foreign minister and the Ministry's highest echelons could handpick an architect without organising a competition. In doing so, they manoeuvred themselves into a tricky position as the outside world could easily get the impression that such public contracts were awarded through shady backroom deals that could not stand the light of day. The lack of parliamentary scrutiny, let alone any internal procedures to award commissions at the time, made the Ministry especially vulnerable to such allegations.

The Elections of 1954: A Calculated Political Gamble

The parliamentary debate had a profound impact on the Washington project. Van Zeeland took on a more prudent and cautious approach until the criticism died down. He first wanted to secure the necessary funding for the project from his fellow ministers in the Christian-democratic government. Knowing the ins and outs of national politics, van Zeeland knew that the Ministerial Council tended to greenlight proposals more easily at the end of a parliamentary legislature when national elections were right around the corner. In doing so, governments could announce popular measures on the eve of elections. Whether such measures were financially feasible usually remained unaddressed. As such, any financial issues were simply passed on to the new government. Van Zeeland put the Washington project temporarily on hold and would only introduce his building proposal at the last Ministerial Council before the national elections of 11 April 1954.

However, architect Max Winders was not thrilled by such stalling tactics. He had hoped to submit his final design in 1953 but was forced to wait. Moreover, there was no guarantee that he would eventually be awarded the commission. Given the unpredictability of elections, van Zeeland could be replaced as foreign minister by another politician who could handpick another architect or abandon the building project all together.

Winders' uncertain future eventually caused his professional relationship with the Ministry to turn sour. This becomes apparent in a financial dispute between him and the Ministry. Following the completion of his preliminary studies, Winders sent an invoice to the Ministry. The architect charged 100,000 Belgian francs (24,915 euros) to cover his architectural fees, preparatory studies and the drafting of several blueprints.[94] Somewhat taken aback by the amount, Foreign Minister van Zeeland asked Winders to clarify how he had come up with the figure. Far from happy with van Zeeland's response, Winders sent a detailed overview of the various steps he had taken for the preparatory study of the Washington project. He highlighted that he had attended several meetings in Brussels, predefined the building's requirements in a rulebook, and written a detailed report estimating the construction price.[95]

However, this explanatory note did not resolve the financial dispute. On the contrary, tensions between architect and client reached unprecedented heights. The Ministry refused to pay the architectural fees, reasoning that it did not have to because the building was not yet constructed. Confronted with the Ministry's refusal to pay, Winders argued that he could easily win a civil court case. In one of his letters to the Ministry, he attached a court ruling from 1926 that dealt with a similar dispute between an architect in Liège and his client.[96] The attached verdict stated that the client was in the wrong and had to pay the architectural fees and an indemnity to the architect. Alarmed that Winders would take the matter to court and prevail, the Ministry reluctantly paid the full amount of 100,000 Belgian francs (24,915 euros).

Meanwhile, Paul van Zeeland introduced his building plans to the Ministerial Council. During the meeting held on 9 April 1954, just two days before the elections, van Zeeland urged his fellow Christian-democratic ministers to allocate the necessary funding. He did not face any difficulties in persuading the Ministerial Council. The Christian-democratic government allocated 50 million Belgian francs (12.3 million euros) to the project.[97] To put this amount into more concrete terms, the Ministry had only spent 32.5 million Belgian francs (8 million euros) to cover the rent, refurbishment and maintenance of its entire diplomatic patrimony in 1956.[98] It may have taken Ambassador Silvercruys seven years of lobbying in Brussels, but he had finally secured the necessary funding. His excellent ties with prominent figures within, or aligned to, the Christian Social Party had paid off. One can only wonder whether another Belgian ambassador who lacked the necessary contacts among the upper political echelons would have been able to pull this off.

Just two days after the decision, however, the elections profoundly shifted the balance of power in Belgian politics. The ruling Christian Social Party lost its majority and was succeeded by an unprecedented coalition government consisting of socialists and liberals. Consequently, Paul van Zeeland was succeeded as foreign minister by none other than Paul-Henri Spaak who made his triumphant return. Given that Spaak had not previously been a big supporter of the building project, it seems that the fate of the Washington chancery once again hung in the balance. Fortunately for Silvercruys, the return of Spaak was a blessing in disguise. Spaak had no intention of rolling back the decision of the previous Christian-democratic government to fund the Washington project. In fact, Spaak's return ensured that Silvercruys once again played the leading role in commissioning the chancery. Whereas van Zeeland had practically taken over the project and hired his friend Max Winders, Spaak was not particularly interested in managing the project and once again outsourced it to Silvercruys.

The Search for an Architect (bis): Old Atlantic Acquaintances

With the necessary funding secured, the Ministry was in need of an architect to design the Washington chancery. The most straightforward decision would have been to award the commission to Max Winders who knew the ins and outs of the project. The Ministry, however, cut ties with Winders all together. The decision was both incentivised by Winders' personal ties with Paul van Zeeland, whose party was now in opposition, and the aforementioned financial dispute. As such, the Ministry needed another architect to take over Winders' role. Ambassador Silvercruys played a pivotal role in finding another architect, showcasing that he was back at the helm of the project.

The architect who appeared on the ambassador's radar was Hugo Van Kuyck (1902-1975) whose biography reads like an adventure novel. Born and raised in Antwerp, Hugo Van Kuyck followed in his father's footsteps as he studied architecture at the *Académie Royale des Beaux-Arts* in Antwerp. In 1926, he completed an internship at the design studio of the renowned Belgian architect Victor Horta (1861-1947) during which he studied the acoustics for the Henry Le Boeuf concert hall in the recently completed *Palais des Beaux-Arts* in Brussels.[99] His main interests, however, lay in modernist architecture and urbanism which incentivised him to study civil engineering at the State University of Ghent.

Following his graduation in 1932, the architect and civil engineer gave a series of well-attended lectures in Scandinavia on his urban plans for Antwerp. He made a name for himself and was offered a lectureship in urbanism at Yale University where he taught from 1936 until 1940. Gradually swapping his Beaux-Arts training for a more functionalist and rationalist approach towards architecture, Van Kuyck was drawn to the modernist building principles of the *Congrès Internationaux d'Architecture Moderne* (CIAM), especially its take on social housing. His reorientation was crystalised in the design of the so-called Canada blocks (1937-39), a large-scale social housing project in the Luchtbal neighbourhood just north of Antwerp.[100] Tasked with constructing 350 apartment units, Van Kuyck designed a series of five-storey blocks around two inner courtyards. From a bird's eye view, the housing complex was shaped in a figure of eight. In accordance with CIAM-doctrine, collective facilities such as a school, laundry room and shops were situated on the ground level.

Following the German invasion of Belgium on 10 May 1940, Van Kuyck fled the country and made his way to the United States. Arriving in July 1940, Van Kuyck resumed his teaching assignment at Yale University and carried out urban studies for the Massachusetts Institute of Technology. Around this time, he also began to work at the New York-based architectural firm Voorhees, Walker, Foley & Smith. Under the leadership of the American architect Ralph Walker (1889-1973), the firm had become a well-established

Figure 7: Major Hugo Van Kuyck, 1944

name in America's architectural scene by the mid-1940s.[101] Its most notable commissions were a series of skyscrapers with Art Deco detailing in New York such as the Western Union Building (1930) and the Irving Trust Building (1932). As Hugo Van Kuyck did not yet have a degree in architecture from an American university, he initially worked as an advisor at the firm. Meanwhile, he studied architecture at the University of Richmond where he obtained his degree in architecture on 9 July 1941. Henceforth, he was officially licensed to take on work as an architect on American soil.

His employment at the firm was, however, short-lived. Following America's entry into the Second World War in December 1941, Van Kuyck enlisted in the United States Army (Fig. 7) and joined the Development Section of the Engineer Amphibian Command on 25 July 1942. As an experienced sailor who was familiar with the tides in the English Channel, Van Kuyck played a pivotal role in planning the amphibious landings on the Normandy beaches on 6 June 1944.[102] For his efforts, he was awarded with the American Bronze Star Medal and the Order of the British Empire.

Hugo Van Kuyck may have built up quite the career in the United States but this still does not explain how he appeared on Silvercruys' radar. Once again, the Kronacker missions, running like a red thread through the ambassador's real estate endeavours, brought both men into contact with each other. As part of the Kronacker missions, the Belgian government was poised to study new building techniques in the United States in an effort to speed up Belgium's reconstruction and modernise the building industry.[103]

Baron Kronacker added his friend Hugo Van Kuyck to the Washington staff. Van Kuyck was instructed to study prefabricated building techniques in the United States. Having his office in the former ambassadorial residence at 1780 Massachusetts Avenue and working closely with Belgian embassy staffers, Hugo Van Kuyck came into contact with Ambassador Silvercruys.

As such, Hugo Van Kuyck crossed the ambassador's mind when he was searching for an architect in 1954. Van Kuyck had the ideal profile to work for the Belgian state and design a chancery on American soil. At the political level, Hugo Van Kuyck was closely affiliated to the ruling socialist and liberal parties. He had designed social housing projects for the socialist mayor Camille Huysmans, and his grandfather Frans Van Kuyck (1852-1915) had been a prominent liberal politician in Antwerp. On a professional level, Hugo Van Kuyck knew the right people in America to navigate the design and construction processes successfully. He was not only licensed to work as an architect in the United States, but was also affiliated to the firm Voorhees, Walker, Foley & Smith. Van Kuyck thus brought in partners who were familiar with local building codes and had the necessary contacts among American building contractors. Acting upon the suggestion made by Silvercruys, the Ministry of Foreign Affairs officially awarded the commission to Voorhees, Walker, Foley & Smith where Hugo Van Kuyck and his American colleagues were assigned to the chancery project. As such, the Ministry's decision to hire a Belgian architect resulted from practical considerations rather than a desire to showcase national craftsmanship.

By the time the commission was awarded, Hugo Van Kuyck had made a name for himself as an architect back in Belgium as he significantly contributed to the introduction of prefabricated building techniques.[104] While working and living in the United States during the 1930s and 1940s, Hugo Van Kuyck became imbued with the idea that a rationalised industrial basis should become the future of the Belgian building industry. This becomes apparent in a 1946 publication that he wrote during his time working for the Kronacker missions:

> Maybe the time is approaching when our men, proud of the traditions of their Flemish and Walloon forefathers, like the great builders of cathedrals and palaces, will plan on a scale which is beyond the vision of the good bourgeois of today. Maybe our towns of tomorrow integrated with parks and roads, built with the tremendous technical means now at our disposal, will take an outstanding place in the history of architecture.[105]

In subsequent projects, Van Kuyck increasingly opted for a functionalist approach by relying on industrialised building techniques such as prefabrication methods. This was reflected in the second social housing project he designed in the Luchtbal neighbourhood, among other projects.

In 1948, the Antwerp social housing company hired Van Kuyck to design social housing estates for the employees of General Motors. In accordance with CIAM-doctrine, he opted for an orthogonal grid in which the social housing estates were immersed in greenery and had access to collective and recreational facilities.[106] The housing estates comprised six high-rise towers and four high-rise slabs, positioned parallel to each other and all constructed by means of modulated, prefabricated and monolithically cast concrete.

It would, however, be too short-sighted to portray Hugo Van Kuyck as a dogmatic modernist architect. He did opt for the modern type of high-rise blocks and towers made of concrete, but he regularly opted to cover exteriors with traditional materials such as bricks.[107] As architectural historian Michael Ryckewaert illustrates, the Luchtbal estate serves as a prime example of moderate modernism. Moderate modernism intertwines modernist building principles with traditional materials such as limestone and brickwork which adds a certain degree of monumentality.[108] Van Kuyck adopted a similar approach in designing the headquarters of the International Bell Telephone Company in Antwerp in 1953. The office complex comprised a 14-storey tower flanked by two medium-rise wings. In a similar fashion to the Luchtbal estate, this office complex forms an example of moderate modernism as the concrete structure was covered with bluestone to give the building a statelier appearance.

One year later, in 1954, construction works began on another noteworthy office building designed by Hugo Van Kuyck. The insurance company *Prévoyance Sociale* hired the Belgian architect to design its new head office (1954-1957) in Brussels. Hugo Van Kuyck designed a 17-story skyscraper which was a novelty in the skyline of the Belgian capital at the time.[109] The head office of the *Prévoyance Sociale* formed a locally embedded approach to American corporate modernism and was characterised by repetitive modular forms and the use of modern building materials, such as steel and concrete, and a glazed façade to express transparency. Hugo Van Kuyck's versatile take on designing office buildings raises the following questions: what kind of design would the Belgian architect submit to the Ministry of Foreign Affairs for the new Washington chancery? Would he and his American colleagues opt for a modernist office building that would resonate with American corporate modernism or did they have something else in store, something that would correspond with Ambassador Silvercruys' soft spot for revival styles?

Designing the Chancery: "Reminiscent of the Country it Represents"

Together with his American colleagues, Van Kuyck set about designing the new embassy offices. At the end of 1954, the architects submitted their design to the Ministry through the publication of a presentation booklet. The American-Belgian proposal called for the construction of a two-storey office building, with a basement, with a total floor area of 2,700 m². Drawing inspiration from Max Winders who had proposed to construct a U-shaped building, Van Kuyck and his American associates opted to mould the structure into a crescent form. The building was strategically positioned on the slope so that the basement could be accessed from the back. This crescent-shaped structure would be oriented towards the intersection of 34th Street and Garfield Street to give the building an inviting appearance from the street side.

In front of the chancery, a roundabout was to be paved to facilitate the coming and going of visa applicants, foreign diplomats and American state officials. The roundabout served as both a car park for visitors and a driveway where chauffeurs could drop off guests. The architects also included a car park just south of the chancery for embassy staff. As the embassy building would only take up 800 m² of the building plot, the design called for planting greenery on the embassy grounds. As the chancery would be constructed in a high-end residential neighbourhood with well-tended gardens, the architects deemed it appropriate to bring the embassy grounds up to par with the green surroundings. They proposed to landscape the terrain by laying lawns and planting trees. Continuing along these lines, the architects wanted to include greenery on the street side by surrounding the chancery building with trees and hedges. At the north-western edge of the plot, the architects included a spot immersed in hedges to install a flagpole where the national colours could be hoisted.

Architecturally speaking, the design of Van Kuyck and Voorhees, Walker, Foley & Smith largely corresponded with the preliminary design of Winders and the suggestions made by van Zeeland in 1953. In their presentation booklet, the architects highlighted that the design would both pay tribute to Washington's government architecture and radiate nationhood by using building materials endemic to Belgium and the Belgian Congo:

> Having in mind the classical aspects of Washington, we have attempted to give the building a fresh approach through the design of its architectural features

and yet be happily reminiscent of the country its represents. [...] The building has been designed with a great deal of thought to the materials which might be used from both Belgium and the Belgian Congo.[110]

With regard to Washington's classical design features, the crescent-shaped chancery (Fig. 8) would comprise a concrete structure. The exteriors would be covered with Indiana limestone. Indiana limestone was extensively used to clad Washington's government buildings, such as the Pentagon. The Belgian chancery would feature limestone tiles arranged in a square pattern to accentuate the building's strong horizontality. This was further reinforced by the symmetrical composition of the front façade with a centrally positioned main entrance flanked by evenly spaced windows to add a sense of rhythm. To conform with the residential surroundings, the architects opted for a pitched roof. This roof structure would be covered with dark brownish-yellow tiles produced in Belgium to accentuate national craftsmanship. The most overt element of national representation was the large national coat of arms with the distinctive lion figures strategically positioned above the main entrance. The large copper coat of arms was to be sculpted into a large circular window and flanked by the seals of the nine provinces making up Belgium at the time.

Figure 8: The Washington chancery, 1954

The design of the main entrance serves as a prime example of how Van Kuyck and his American colleagues intertwined stripped classical exteriors with modern building elements. The stately entrance featured two concrete columns covered with red marble, more commonly known as the *rouge belge*, obtained from Walloon quarries. The steps were to be covered with bluestone, and the walls with white marble. This classical vocabulary of pillars and marble elements was intertwined with a fully glazed revolving door, a design feature often used to project an image of progress and technological refinement.[111] Stripped classicism not only corresponded with the aesthetic of Washington's public buildings but also with that of grand public buildings constructed in Brussels in the postwar period such as the National Bank of Belgium and the Belgian Royal Library.[112] This goes to show that the Belgian Ministry of Foreign Affairs considered stripped classicism also appropriate for nationally inspired building projects erected on foreign soil.

The chosen aesthetic was also expressed in the chancery's interiors. Upon accessing the chancery through the revolving doors, visitors entered the grand lobby area (Fig. 9). The lobby had a high ceiling, giving an additional effect of space and light to the room. At the end of the lobby, the architects included a spiral staircase – the focal point of the room – leading to the mezzanine level and the diplomats' offices. The architects suggested including a large tapestry behind the spiral staircase. The mezzanine level is supported by two concrete pillars covered with Belgian black marble or *noir belge*. This material was also used to cover the steps of the stairs leading to the elevated platform on which the spiral staircase is situated. Even though Paul van Zeeland was no longer foreign minister, the architects heeded his call to include materials endemic to Belgium in their design.

Additionally, the architects envisaged the lobby as a venue to accentuate Belgium's status as a colonial power. They suggested including Congolese woodwork in the lobby area. The lobby's concrete walls would be covered with plywood panels made of limba, a tree known for its light yellowish to golden brown colour. Limba is endemic to the tropical regions of Central Africa, growing in the western parts of the Democratic Republic of the Congo. The limba plywood panels were to be arranged in a chequered pattern to give a sense of warmth to the lobby. By including Congolese woodwork, the architects followed another suggestion originally put forward by Paul van Zeeland. It is not beyond the realm of possibility that Ambassador Silvercruys may also have had a hand in this choice. As

RECEPTION LOBBY
BELGIAN CHANCELLERY

Figure 9: The chancery's lobby, 1954

historian Thomas Vanwing indicates, the Belgian ambassador served as a committee member of the *Institut des Parcs Nationaux du Congo belge* at the time.[113] Founded in 1934, this institute was tasked with the protection and conservation of the national parks established by the colonial authorities. In 1948, the Belgian ambassador travelled to the Belgian Congo to participate in a study tour organised by the wildlife institute. Given his interest in the fauna and flora of the colony, one can assume that he was keen to include Congolese woodwork in his new embassy.

From a bilateral point of view, however, the use of Congolese woodwork was controversial. Against the backdrop of the Cold War rivalry between East and West, the Soviet Union criticised Western European countries for holding on to their colonial empires in Africa and Asia. In doing so, the USSR both aimed to win over the hearts and minds of the colonised peoples and simultaneously destabilise the transatlantic partnership between the United States and Western Europe.[114] Confronted with the unsettling prospect that the Soviet Union held the moral high ground through its strong condemnation of European colonialism, the United States gradually began to propagate the idea of self-government for colonies across Africa and Asia. In the case of the Belgian Congo, the State Department argued that Congolese self-government could be best achieved through close collaboration with Brussels to ensure an orderly transition of power.¹¹⁵ While the State Department gradually put pressure on Brussels to prepare the Belgian Congo for self-rule from the mid-1950s onward, the Ministry saw no harm in including Congolese woodwork in the Washington chancery. Its presence was clearly not seen as politically problematic at the time as no objections were raised to using this kind of woodwork in the interiors. To a certain extent, the presence of Congolese woodwork can be read as a statement of the Ministry to Washington, D.C. that Belgium had no intention of leaving the Congo any time soon.

Designing a Hierarchical and Hybrid Work Environment

The chancery's main function was of course to offer the growing diplomatic staff a modern and spacious work environment. Washington, D.C. was one of the most important diplomatic postings for Belgium in the 1950s. Its political significance becomes tangible by the sheer amount of paperwork produced by the embassy staffers. In 1955, for instance, the embassy sent 4,924 reports, 294 telegrams and 8,918 letters to Brussels.¹¹⁶

The workforce responsible for this large amount of paperwork was a hybrid one comprising diplomats, attachés and government delegations attending high-level meetings in the American capital. Corresponding with the aspiration of Silvercruys to house this workforce under the same roof, Van Kuyck and Voorhees, Walker, Foley & Smith invested considerably in designing a state-of-the-art work environment with sufficient office space.

The basement served as the chancery's engine room, ensuring that the bureaucratic machine ran smoothly. Covering a floor area of 800 m², the basement comprised an apartment for the janitor, rooms for shipping and receiving mail, and a spacious archival room that could be locked. The ground floor comprised the aforementioned lobby area. Upon entering the centrally positioned lobby, visitors could either turn right to the visa section or make their way to the left towards the offices of the military attachés and the large conference room. The walls of the conference room were panelled with Congolese woodwork and a large, sculpted coat of arms served as the room's focal point. In front of the conference room, the architects proposed to include a small and intimate landscaped garden.

The architects reserved the entire first floor as office space for Ambassador Silvercruys, the diplomatic staff and attachés. The offices' importance was expressed in the building's exteriors by accentuating the window frames "[…] in height to lend more dignity to the more important rooms of the chancery."[117] Van Kuyck and his American colleagues opted for a cellular office layout running through the length of the building in which each embassy staffer was given an individual office. The use of a cellular or so-called compartmented office layout stands in stark contrast to the growing preference within corporate America at the time for an open-plan work environment where employees work in the same room. In his 1960 publication *Office Building and Office Layout Planning*, the American architect Kenneth H. Ripnen indicated that cellular offices had become a thing of the past and promoted the use of an open office layout:

> Basically, the theory of integrated space calls for open general office areas with a minimum of partitioning, of either the fixed or movable type. This type of plan is gaining many adherents today, since it generally offers more flexibility, economy of space, easier work supervision, and equality of facilities for all parts of the office in comparison with the older, more conventional compartmented layout of office space in which partitions are used to create custom-built departmental units.[118]

As the diplomatic profession was and still is known for its highly hierarchical work culture, it is understandable why the architects opted for cellular offices. This spatial layout not only ensured that each staff member could work and meet people undisturbed but also increased the sense of ownership of the workspace.[119]

The cellular office layout was ideal for accentuating the hierarchy within the embassy staff. As can be expected, Ambassador Silvercruys was given the largest individual office (Fig. 10) situated at the northern end of the hallway. The office's importance was further accentuated by its walnut wood flooring and high ceiling, giving it an additional effect of space and light. In his capacity as head of mission, Silvercruys also enjoyed the benefits of having a private dressing room and toilet. From the outside, the ambassador's workspace further distinguished itself from the other offices by having two balconies. In architecture, the balcony is traditionally perceived as a theatrical stage from which political actors tower above the masses.[120] As the chancery was first and foremost an office building, the two balconies served as a platform from which Ambassador Silvercruys could peer over Garfield Street and its green surroundings while benefitting from fresh air and sunshine. The balconies increased his visibility as passers-by could see the senior Belgian diplomat during his breaks.

AMBASSADOR'S OFFICE
BELGIAN CHANCELLERY

Figure 10: The ambassador's office, 1954

To further emphasise the pecking order on the first floor, the offices of the senior diplomats were clustered together in the northern end of the crescent shaped hallway in close proximity to Silvercruys' office (Fig. 11). A small staff of typists and clerks was accommodated adjacently in order to keep the bureaucratic wheels turning. As one leaves the spacious office of Silvercruys and walks down the hallway, one would come across seven empty offices near the spiral staircase. The vacant offices were emblematic of the changing dynamics affecting Belgian diplomacy. At the time, there was a growing tendency among Belgian ministers to manifest themselves on the international stage as they opted to attend international summits personally.[121] The American capital had become a popular travel destination for Belgian members of government since the late 1940s. As such, seven offices remained unassigned in the new Washington chancery, providing office space to Belgian ministers and their staffers. Most of these unassigned offices were oriented towards the intersection of Garfield Street and 34th Street, offering Belgian ministers an excellent view on Washington National Cathedral.

The new chancery also had to accommodate officials, the so-called attachés, who worked for ministry departments such as the agriculture, defence, colonial affairs and economic affairs departments. As can be

THE AMBASSADOR'S AGENCY 79

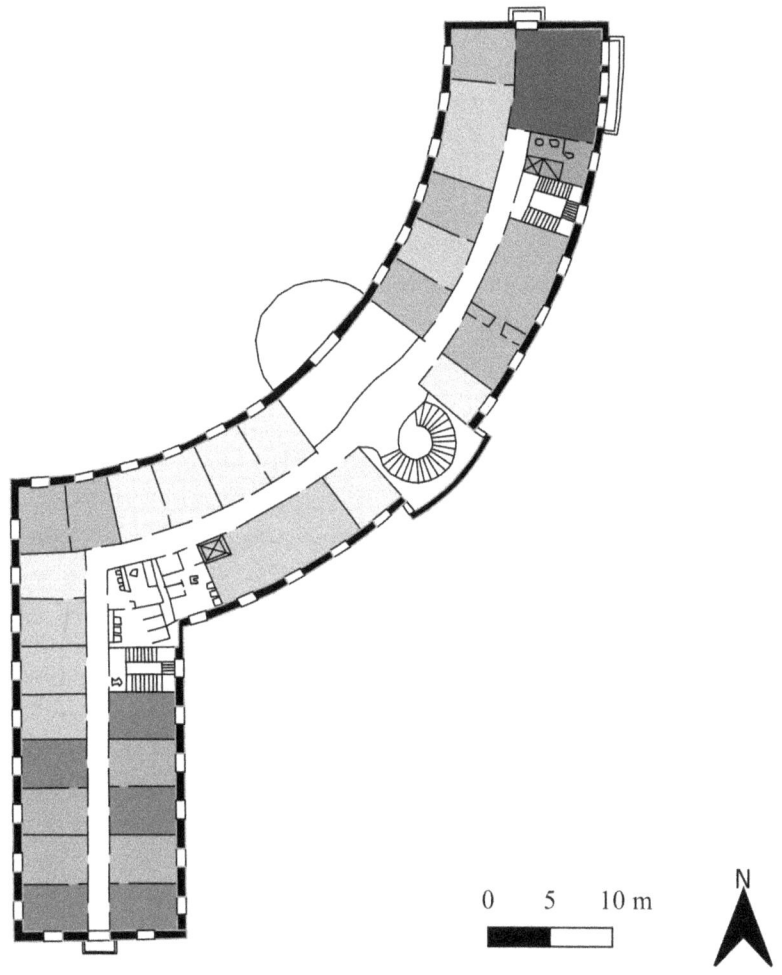

Legenda

- Office of Ambassador Silvercruys
- Ambassador's Dressing Room
- Offices of Attachés
- Offices of the Diplomatic Staff
- Supporting Staff
- Unassigned

Based on: FelixArchief, Architect Hugo Van Kuyck, 28#9562, Presentation Booklet 'The Belgian Chancery'.

Map created by Christophe De Coster

Figure 11: The chancery's political section

expected, the arrival of attachés in several embassies caused tensions with Belgian diplomats who felt that the handling of foreign matters was their prerogative.[122] This strained inter-ministerial relationship and the perception of attachés as 'strangers in our midst' was clearly accentuated in the chancery's office layout. The five offices assigned to attachés were clustered together in the southern end of the hallway, situated as far away as possible from the offices of Silvercruys and his senior diplomats. Moreover, these offices were significantly smaller and were situated adjacent to those assigned to lower-ranked diplomats, typists and clerks. Separate stairwells were included at both the northern and southern end of the hallway. While such stairwells were first and foremost included because of security concerns, the separate stairwells made sure that the movements of senior diplomats and attachés across the chancery were separated from one another, adding to the hierarchical character.

The attachés who eventually moved into the new chancery were, however, far from intimidated by the hierarchical workspace. This becomes apparent in the memoirs of the Christian-democratic Foreign Minister Pierre Wigny (1905-1986) who visited the chancery in 1959. During his stay, he witnessed first-hand how the attachés made fun of Silvercruys' meticulous eye for detail. Wigny recalls how "[...] the attachés liked to repeat an innocent joke. They would surreptitiously move a magazine or knick-knack and calculate the number of minutes it would take the ambassador to see the mess and put the object back in its place."[123] This goes to show that the new chancery not only served as a workplace for diplomats and attachés, but also as a playground where colleagues ridiculed each other's character traits.

Public-Private Diplomacy: The Need for External Funding

By late 1954, Ambassador Silvercruys had seemingly overcome all major obstacles standing in his way. The support of Paul van Zeeland was the game changer Silvercruys so desperately needed. In April of that year, the Christian-democratic foreign minister vowed to allocate 50 million Belgian francs (12.3 million euros) to the building project. Unfortunately for Silvercruys, the Court of Audit spoke out against the deal. As the financial watchdog monitoring the government's financial dealings, the Court of Audit notified the Belgian government that the chancery's price tag would exceed the budget reserved for extraordinary expenditures.[124]

According to the Court of Audit, it would be far more feasible to call upon a financial intermediary. A private partner could be reimbursed in instalments to stretch the total cost of the building project over a long period of time which would be more manageable for the state finances.

By the time the Court of Audit vetoed van Zeeland's financial scheme, the Christian Social Party were in opposition and there was a coalition government of socialists and liberals. Paul-Henri Spaak once again made his return as foreign minister and it was up to him to find private funding. Reflecting his disinterest in the building project, Spaak did not put much effort in coming up with private funding. As such, the purpose-built chancery once again became a distant dream for Ambassador Silvercruys. Finding a private investor appeared to be a near impossible task. To put it bluntly, who among his friends was financially capable, let alone willing, to lend money to the Belgian government?

Fortunately for Silvercruys, his old friend Camille Gutt occupied a new function in the world of high finance which enabled him to come to his friend's aid yet again. By 1954, Gutt served as an influential board member at Banque Lambert.[125] At the time, Banque Lambert was one of Belgium's leading financial institutions. Immobilière Lambert, one of the bank's subsidiaries, was specialised in financing real estate deals and projects.[126]

In a letter to Silvercruys, Gutt confided that he would do his utmost to convince chairman Léon Lambert (1928-1987) and his fellow board members to finance the chancery project.[127] Given his esteemed position in the world of high finance, Gutt did not face any noteworthy difficulties in garnering support within the walls of Banque Lambert.

The financial support of Banque Lambert was another major success for Silvercruys but he was by no means out of the woods yet. The Belgian Ministry of Finance expressed concerns about the feasibility of such a public-private partnership. For budgetary reasons, the Ministry of Finance vetoed the plan to refund the Banque Lambert in instalments.

Tensions ran high in Brussels. The Ministry of Foreign Affairs and the Ministry of Finance were diametrically opposed to each other. Louis Scheyven, Secretary-General of the Ministry of Foreign Affairs, personally mediated on behalf of Silvercruys to break the inter-ministerial stalemate. These negotiations were nothing short of a war of attrition. Scheyven spent over sixteen months working towards a breakthrough. On 29 March 1956, Secretary-General Scheyven could finally deliver some good news to Silvercruys. He had just struck a deal with the Ministry of Finance on the payment procedure to reimburse Banque Lambert. In his letter to Silvercruys, Scheyven revealed that the inter-ministerial discussions were not without difficulties:

> I've been dealing with this issue personally, and the reason it's taken so long to resolve is because of some minor internal dramas and unfortunate personal issues, the details of which I'll spare you. The important thing is that yesterday we finally obtained the agreement of the Ministry of Finance on the payments to be made.[128]

In April of that year, Banque Lambert wired the necessary funding to the bank account of the Washington embassy. The construction of the chancery could finally commence.

Contracting The Man Who Built Washington, D.C.

The loan arrived not a moment too soon for Ambassador Silvercruys. Given his enthusiasm for the project, he had already instructed the architects to pick a building contractor, even before the financial issues were resolved. The New York architecture firm was awarded the commission on turnkey basis, making them also responsible for the chancery's construction. This hands-off Belgian approach was a far cry from the American and British way of working. Both the British Foreign Office and the US State Department had well-staffed real estate departments that closely monitored building projects from the drawing board to their completion.[129]

In November 1955, Voorhees, Walker, Foley & Smith launched a tender process to select a building contractor. This guided approach stands in stark contrast to the tendering procedure, or rather lack thereof, at the Ministry. Whereas personal ties between architect Hugo Van Kuyck and Ambassador Silvercruys were the deciding factor in being awarded the commission, the architects instead opted for a structured bidding process with competing bids from various building contractors. Ironically, the architects who were selected on the grounds of personal contacts assessed in return several bids on the basis of objective criteria.

The architects emphasised to candidates that speed was of the essence, highlighting that the time estimated by bidders to construct the chancery would be a crucial factor in reviewing the bids.[130] Apparently, the patience of Ambassador Silvercruys to finally move into his new chancery was wearing thin as it had already been eight years since he first introduced his building plans.

Arguing that his firm could construct the new chancery in just ten months, the American building contractor John McShain was selected to build the chancery. Taking over the Philadelphia-based family business in 1919, John McShain was a well-established contractor by the 1950s, running one of the ten largest building firms in the United States. McShain had excellent ties with both Republican and Democratic lawmakers which played to his advantage in winning government contracts. His company, John McShain Inc., carried out several landmark projects in the American capital such as the construction of the Jefferson Memorial (1939-1943), Washington National Airport (1940-1941), the aforementioned Pentagon (1941-1943) and the extensive renovation of the White House (1949-1951).[131] Such prestigious commissions earned John McShain the nickname of the man who built Washington, D.C. In addition to McShain's esteemed reputation, practical considerations may have also influenced the architects' decision to call upon his services. Firstly, the engineers employed at McShain Inc. were accustomed to the building techniques put forward by the architects such as cast-in-place concrete which significantly reduced construction time and was far more economical than the use of steel or brick. Secondly, Indiana limestone, the main building material used in the chancery's façade, was intrinsically linked to the business dealings of John McShain. As part of his strategy to supply his firm with a continuous flow of building materials and tighten his grip on the American building industry, McShain bought the Indiana Limestone Company in 1950. It made him the premier supplier of this high-end building material. As such, it was in the best interest of the architects to hire McShain.

On 26 January 1956, McShain Inc. started cutting down the trees on the building plot as a preliminary step to the chancery's construction.[132] In retrospect, this was an extremely risky move from the architects and Silvercruys as the budgetary issues with the Belgian Ministry of Finance were only resolved by late March of that year. Had the Ministry of Finance continued to veto the financial scheme with Banque Lambert, the project would have had to be halted even before the building process was well and truly underway. One can only wonder what the reputational damage for Belgium in Washington, D.C. would have been and whether McShain would have taken legal action taken against the Belgian state if the building project had to be abandoned. Fortunately for Ambassador Silvercruys, such a scenario did not occur and the chancery's construction began in the spring of 1956.

When comparing the original design of 1954 with the chancery under construction in 1956, it becomes apparent that several alterations were made to the architectural features of the chancery. Unfortunately, the archival records do not provide us with the reason for these changes. Judging from the budgetary issues, however, there is reason to believe that the Ministry had a hand in making alterations to the original design. This assumption is backed up by an article in *The Washington Daily News*. The article stated that the purpose-built chancery came with a price tag of 1.1 million US dollars (12.5 million euros), some ten percent higher than originally estimated by the architects in 1954.[133]

The alterations made to the chancery's exteriors were not so much fundamental changes to the original design, but rather small adjustments that did not significantly alter the architectural features of the chancery. For instance, above the main entrance, the architects had originally suggested including a large copper-made national coat of arms flanked by the seals of the nine Belgian provinces. Eventually, this political symbol was downsized as only the national coat of arms was sculpted into the building's limestone façade. Additionally, the use of Indiana limestone was reduced to cut corners. As the rear façade (Fig. 12) was hidden from the street side, parts of the concrete exterior were covered with grey bricks instead of the more expensive limestone façade.

The suggestion to include a small, landscaped garden in front of the conference room was also left out because of budgetary reasons. Regarding the chancery's interior, the architects made only one change, but it was significant. Originally, the lobby area would feature a spiral staircase leading to the political section on the first floor. The spiral staircase was, however, modified into a double staircase. As such, the hierarchical layout of the office section was further accentuated as the staircase on the left-hand side led to the offices of Silvercruys and his senior diplomats, whereas the staircase on the right-hand side led to those of the attachés and lower-ranked diplomats. Furthermore, the idea to include a mezzanine level in the lobby was abandoned all together. The double staircase would now lead to a regular storey situated above the lobby. As such, the lobby lost the effect of space and light generated by the mezzanine level.

McShain Inc. was also tasked with completing the chancery's interior. It was up to the company to cover the lobby's walls with limba plywood panels. With regard to the production of these panels, the architects brought McShain Inc. into contact with the Belgian wood and furniture producer Kortrijkse Kunstwerkstede Gebroeders De Coene. De Coene had access to tropical wood species from the Belgian Congo. De Coene was an important shareholder and client of a French wood supplier that

Figure 12: The chancery under construction, 4 September 1956

imported African wood species to Europe.[134] Since the interwar period, Congolese wood species were increasingly used by Belgian architects to design floors, wall panelling, movable and built-in-furniture, and stairs in suburban bourgeois townhouses.[135] De Coene was generally perceived as the leading wood producer that was accustomed to working with tropical wood species originating from the Belgian Congo.[136]

Furnishing the Chancery: *Tene Quod Bene*

Ambassador Silvercruys now turned his attention to furnishing the chancery. He convinced the Ministry to purchase new office furniture to accentuate the chancery's novel appearance. At the time, the branch *A/Matériel* was tasked with furnishing diplomatic interiors. *A/Matériel* had a commission procedure in place for awarding contracts to furniture producers.[137] Silvercruys, however, wanted to play first fiddle in furnishing his chancery. As the lavish Louis XVI style furniture of his ambassadorial residence has made abundantly clear, he had expensive taste.

In order to continue with such an aesthetic in the chancery's interiors, the senior Belgian diplomat wanted to handpick the furniture company, which entailed bypassing the commission procedure of *A/Matériel*. From the outset, he was determined to call upon the services of a Belgian furniture brand. This was part of his economic agenda to promote national craftsmanship and entrepreneurship in the United States. During his ambassadorship, he frequently sponsored Belgian commercial exhibitions and arranged meetings between Belgian entrepreneurs and chambers of commerce in different American cities.[138] Buying Belgian was also promoted within the Ministry's walls. In a memo, *A/Matériel* made the case that diplomatic interiors served as an ideal display window where Belgian-made furniture and artwork could be showcased to foreign audiences.[139]

Ambassador Silvercruys reached out to the aforementioned Belgian furniture firm Kortrijkse Kunstwerkstede Gebroeders De Coene to furnish his new embassy offices in 1956. It was thanks to the efforts of Pol Provost (1907-1990), De Coene's general director, that the firm appeared on the radar of Ambassador Silvercruys. Back in January 1953, when architect Max Winders was visiting Washington, D.C., Provost was also in the United States conducting a study tour. Provost got wind of the plans to construct a new chancery. Poised to be awarded the prestigious commission of furnishing the new chancery, Provost personally reached out to Winders to offer his services.[140] The lobbying activities yielded results as Winders suggested Ambassador Silvercruys award the contract to De Coene.

At the time, De Coene was one of the leading Belgian brands in the furniture and wood industry.[141] Founded in 1887, the Courtrai-based family business initially made its mark on the domestic market for its top-notch Art Deco furniture during the interwar period. One of its most notable commissions was the production of a rosewood desk for the Belgian monarch Leopold III (1901-1983) in 1935, designed by the well-reputed architect Henry Van de Velde (1863-1957). The business' esteemed reputation was, however, shattered during the Second World War for its dubious relationship with the German occupying authorities. De Coene collaborated with the German military administration on an economic level by constructing dummy wooden aircraft for the Luftwaffe. Following the liberation of Belgium in September 1944, De Coene was sequestered for its wartime activities and became a state-controlled enterprise.

With the restrictions lifted in 1952, De Coene's new management reoriented the commercial activities in an effort to turn the page on its wartime past. The firm redeemed itself by working for the victors of the Second

World War. De Coene produced 1,800 trailers for the United States Army Air Force in 1955.[142] At the same time, the new management made considerable efforts to reorient its furniture production. Director-General Pol Provost obtained a license to produce and sell furniture from the high end American furniture brand Knoll in the Benelux and the Belgian Congo in 1954. At the time, Knoll was one of the leading furniture brands producing modern domestic and office furniture designed by big names such as Eero Saarinen (1910-1961), Isamu Noguchi (1904-1988) and Ludwig Mies van der Rohe (1886-1969).[143] As such, Van der Rohe's iconic Barcelona chair, originally designed for the German pavilion at the world's fair of 1929, was manufactured in the workshops of De Coene. This refined design object comprising a chromed steel framework and two leather cushions was widely used by De Coene to furnish the lobbies of several high-profile companies in the Benelux.

It is telling that Silvercruys once again contracted a Belgian partner with an outspoken American connection, as was the case with architect Hugo Van Kuyck. Ambassador Silvercruys had, however, no intention of purchasing the modern Knoll designs. Instead, he opted for the period furniture that De Coene continued to produce alongside the innovative Knoll pieces. Just as the chancery's stripped classical design did not quite reflect Hugo Van Kuyck's architectural oeuvre at the time, the baron's decision to purchase period furniture did not reflect De Coene's state-of-the-art designs produced at the time.

Echoing his preference for French decorative arts and interior design, the ambassador opted for a conservative approach to furnish the new chancery. De Coene's line of Neo-Empire furniture (Fig. 13) caught his eye. Taking its name from the First French Empire (1804-1814), Neo-Empire furniture forms a revival of the Napoleonic era and is characterised by its classical ornamentation, carvings and dark finish. Such period furniture reflected not only Silvercruys' personal taste, but also the general preference of his fellow heads of mission. Period furniture was perceived to be a symbol of wealth and status in the diplomatic realm at the time.

The Ministry's archives do not contain any contemporary records or images of the interior design of the Washington embassy offices. Fortunately, a personal letter from Silvercruys to De Coene and two sketches of his personal office have been preserved in the private collection of Noël Hostens, a De Coene enthusiast. Both sketches first and foremost show how the importance of the ambassador's office was emphasised by the office furniture made by De Coene. Labelling the room's interior design as an *interprétation classique*, the Courtrai-based manufacturer produced

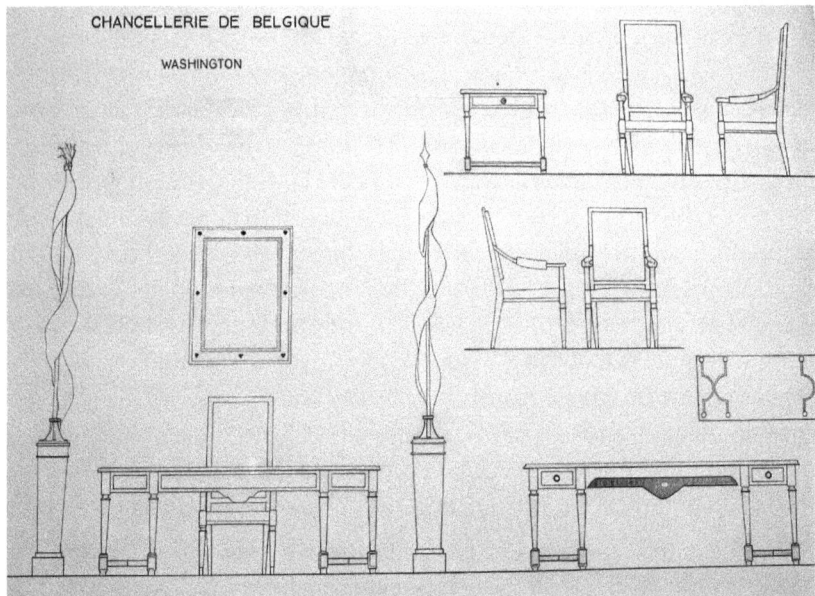

Figure 13: Furniture for the ambassador's office, undated

a wooden office desk with a carved tabletop. Accentuating the esteemed status of the head of mission, the backrest of his office chair was slightly higher than those of the chairs facing him which were used by visitors. This status was also underlined by two wooden pedestals strategically positioned behind the ambassador's desk. Being clear markers of nationhood, these pedestals served as flagpoles of the Belgian tricolour. The top of the flagpole on the left-hand side featured a carved lion, a traditional emblem of the Belgian state. Above the personal desk of Silvercruys, the state portrait of the Belgian monarch Baudouin (1930-1993) was placed, suggesting that the King of the Belgians was constantly looking over the shoulder of his diplomatic representative in the American capital.

When the furniture was delivered to Washington, D.C. in the spring of 1957, Ambassador Silvercruys was most satisfied. On 3 May 1957, he personally wrote a thank-you letter to Pierre De Coene (1916-2001). In his letter, the baron spoke words of praise for the pieces of furniture, stating that they resonated Belgian craftsmanship and were most fitting to furnish the diplomatic interiors:

> This furniture, which has found its place in our new building, reflects sobriety in the elegance of the design, the best taste in the choice of colours, and perfection

in the execution. It is a testament to your company and all its staff, as well as to this Embassy. I would like to thank you for the care you have taken with this delivery and I am grateful for your kind gesture of offering the Embassy a charming tea table, listed in the inventory of the residence's furniture, for the Ambassador's use. I hope that I will have the opportunity to welcome you on a future trip to the United States, and I am sure that you will be pleased to see for yourself, as all VIPs who come here do, the positive impression made by your furnishings.[144]

The excellent ties with Pierre De Coene were also expressed by the tea table the latter had offered free of charge to the Belgian ambassador. This was most likely as a token of gratitude from De Coene for being awarded this prestigious commission. As Silvercruys had simply bypassed *A/ Matériel*'s tendering process, the personal gift also illustrates once more that having close relationships with Belgian diplomats was of the utmost importance to winning contracts for the Ministry in the 1950s.

3330 Garfield Street: A Venue for Cultural Diplomacy

Determined to showcase Belgian craftsmanship, Silvercruys envisaged the chancery's interiors as a venue to exhibit artwork. In his search for artwork, the baron came across two large tapestries preserved in the storage rooms of the old ambassadorial residence at 1780 Massachusetts Avenue. Originally, these tapestries were manufactured to decorate the interiors of the Belgian pavilion at the New York World's Fair of 1939. Based on drawings made by the Belgian expressionist painter Floris Jespers (1889-1965), the large tapestries – each measuring 30 square metres – were woven by the Belgian manufactures Chaudoir and Braquenié.[145]

Both tapestries were textbook examples of cultural diplomacy as the works of art not only demonstrated national craftsmanship but sent strong political messages through art. The first tapestry depicts America's military and industrial might coming to Belgium's aid during the First World War and includes images of American soldiers and weapons of war en route to liberate Europe. Floris Jespers especially accentuated the efforts of the Commission for Relief of Belgium, an American organisation which had raised money to set up a steady supply of food to German-occupied Belgium from 1914 onward. The American businessman and future president Herbert Hoover (1874-1964) served as the Commission's chairman and is strategically depicted next to the burning library of the Catholic University of Leuven which was set ablaze by the German army in August 1914. Following the liberation of Belgium, Hoover's Commission for Relief in Belgium generated the necessary funds to build a new library in Leuven.

During his ambassadorship, Silvercruys entertained the idea of donating the tapestry to the Hoover Institution. Founded by Herbert Hoover in 1919, this research centre collects archival material and publications related to global conflicts and is closely affiliated to Stanford University, Hoover's alma mater. The donation demonstrates Silvercruys' efforts to wield artwork as an instrument to cement bilateral ties with the United States. During his ambassadorship, the baron inaugurated and financially supported Belgian art expositions in America. On 10 March 1953, Silvercruys handed over the tapestry during a solemn ceremony at the Hoover Institution. As part of this ceremony, Silvercruys gave a high-flown speech in which he accentuated that the tapestry not only reflected his country's age-old craftsmanship, but also its undying gratitude to the American war effort:

> This tapestry, designed by one of our best artists, was woven in Brussels, a city which for ages has produced excellent craftsmen in that field. It is this tapestry I have the honour to present today to the Hoover Library on War, Revolution and Peace, on behalf of the government of Belgium. [...] When future generations of this Alma Mater look up from their books and stand before this tapestry, may they be reminded always that Belgium finds happiness and pride in the practice of the simplest virtues of all: gratefulness and loyalty in friendship.[146]

The second tapestry (Fig. 14) that decorated the Belgian pavilion at the New York World's Fair also depicts a transatlantic encounter, but one in the more distant past long before Belgium or the United States were founded. The tapestry pictures the priest Louis Hennepin (1626-1704), born in Hainaut which is part of modern-day Belgium, who explored the Mississippi River in 1680 at the request of the French monarchy.[147] Depicting a romanticised past connecting modern-day Belgium and the United States with one another, Silvercruys was especially fond of this tapestry. In his eyes, the tapestry illustrated how Christianity has been the bedrock of both the 'old' and the 'new' world.[148] Acting on the architects' suggestion to hang a tapestry in the chancery's lobby, the baron picked the Hennepin tapestry. The presence of this religiously inspired artwork

Figure 14: The Belgian community in the United States assembling in front of the Hennepin tapestry as they await the arrival of King Baudouin, May 1959

fitted neatly in the Catholic surroundings of the new chancery with the Washington National Cathedral and the Apostolic Nunciature of the Holy See situated just a stone's throw away.

The Chancery as Flagship Project

The Hennepin tapestry found its place in the lobby just in time for the chancery's inauguration ceremony on 9 February 1957. The inauguration coincided with the visit of Foreign Minister Spaak to the American capital. It is somewhat ironic that Spaak, who had not shown much interest in the chancery, was presiding over the inauguration. Moreover, it is telling how Spaak seized the ceremony as an opportunity to ingratiate himself with the American government. As he hoisted the national colours over the new embassy premises, Spaak gave a speech to the Republican Under Secretary of State Christian Herter (1895-1966) and several foreign diplomats. In his pompous speech, he framed the new chancery as an architectural testament to America's leading role in the world and somewhat stretched the truth regarding his involvement towards its commissioning:

> The new building is the fulfilment of a dream which I have had, and which Ambassador Silvercruys has had, for some years. It is a token of the high regard we Belgians have for the position of the United States in the world. We have tried to adapt to a beautiful city a building whose walls will, I hope, house activities of interest and benefit to all.[149]

One can only wonder what went through the mind of Silvercruys as Spaak was taking credit for the chancery's construction. In fact, Spaak's pro-American speech needs to be seen in light of a political career shift coming his way. Within a matter of weeks, Spaak would be appointed as the new Secretary General of NATO. Well aware that it was of the utmost importance to be in the good books of Washington, D.C. to turn his mandate into a success, Spaak thus capitalised on the chancery's opening by framing the project as a symbol of America's prominent position in the world.

During the ceremony, Spaak awarded the Order of the Crown, one of Belgium's highest honorary orders of knighthood, to Ralph Walker and John McShain to accentuate the input of the American partners in the design and construction of the chancery. As the ceremonial ribbon was cut, Spaak and Silvercruys guided American officials and foreign diplomats through the new embassy offices. During the tour, Silvercruys and Spaak were constantly accentuating how the chancery's architecture and interiors incorporated Belgian and American elements which, they argued, showcased the strong bilateral ties between both countries.[150]

The esteemed guests wandering through the corridors included the Apostolic Delegate Amleto Giovanni Cicognani (Fig. 15), who had officiated the baron's marriage in 1953, the Dutch Ambassador Herman van Roijen (1905-1991) and the Luxembourgish Ambassador Hugues Le Gallais (1896-1965). According to a Belgian journalist, foreign diplomats envied Silvercruys for his modern and above all spacious chancery.[151] The journalist gave no indication of their identity, but he likely referred to the Dutch ambassador van Roijen. At the time, van Roijen was unsuccessfully lobbying in The Hague to construct a chancery.[152]

Judging from the press coverage, Spaak and Silvercruys succeeded in their goal to showcase the new chancery as the symbol of the transatlantic

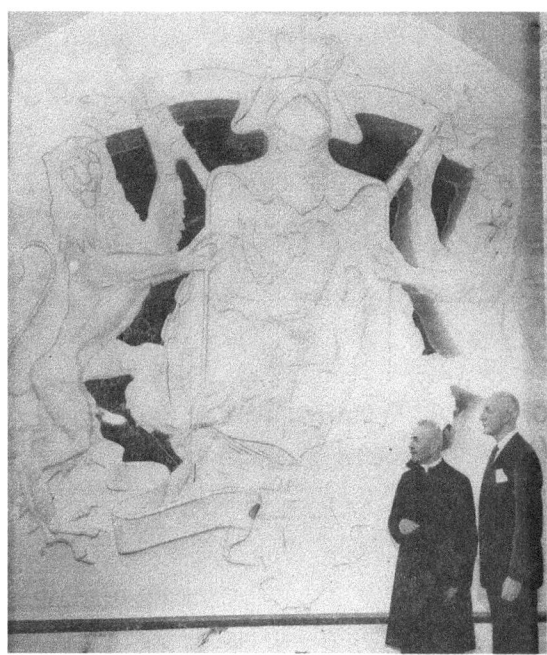

Figure 15: Apostolic Delegate Amleto Giovanni Cicognani (left) and Ambassador Silvercruys (right), 10 February 1957

alliance. Several journalists mentioned the Indiana limestone façade, the Congolese woodwork, and the furniture manufactured by De Coene. Both Belgian and American reporters spoke words of praise for the new chancery, but it is striking that they accentuated different design qualities. The American press primarily addressed the building's functionality as a spacious and modern work environment.[153] Belgian journalists, however, highlighted the aesthetic qualities. In a moment of chauvinism, a journalist from *Le Soir* called the new chancery one of the most beautiful buildings Washington had to offer.[154] In contrast to the jubilant mood prevailing in the bourgeois media, a Belgian journalist from *Le Drapeau Rouge*, the official newspaper of the Communist Party of Belgium, only mentioned factual information on the new chancery such as its location, dimensions and price tag.[155] Against the backdrop of the Cold War, it was apparently a bridge too far for the Belgian equivalent of *Pravda* to praise the building's design, let alone its political significance for the transatlantic alliance.

The new chancery also received much acclaim from the highest echelons of Belgian politics and diplomacy. During a parliamentary debate on diplomatic housing on 19 May 1959, the liberal MP Adolphe Van Glabbeke (1904-1959) called for additional funding to construct and renovate embassy offices. Van Glabbeke stressed to Foreign Minister Pierre

Wigny that new and modern chanceries not only reflected positively on Belgium, but also on the professionalism of its diplomatic agents posted in foreign capitals far and wide. To get his point across, the liberal MP stated that the newly built Belgian chancery in Washington, D.C. was a flagship project which should set the standard for future projects.[156] In his unpublished memoirs, Wigny joined Van Glabbeke in praising the design of the Washington chancery. Wigny drew particular attention to the pivotal role played by Silvercruys in commissioning the new embassy offices, stating how the ambassador set an example to be proud of.[157]

The Washington chancery did indeed set the standard for the future building activity of the Ministry of Foreign Affairs. This so-called Washington model did not involve the Ministry commissioning stripped classical embassies; rather, it refers to the Ministry's strategy of awarding future commissions to key actors involved in the Washington chancery project for future commissions. Hugo Van Kuyck became the Ministry's go-to architect, designing the new embassy compound in Tokyo (see Chapter IV) and renovating embassy buildings in Bangkok, Lebanon and Caracas at the end of the 1950s. Additionally, De Coene was hired to furnish Belgian embassies in Bonn, Budapest, Canberra, Copenhagen, Lisbon and The Hague.[158]

The chancery's inauguration did not go unnoticed in the American capital. According to the Belgian diplomat Freddy Cogels (1910-2000), the Washington chancery not only served as the political landmark of the Belgian state but also as a tourist attraction. In his memoirs, Cogels recalls how sightseeing tours included the embassy in their itineraries.[159]

Several local residents along Garfield Street, however, did not share the rosy picture Freddy Cogels painted of the Belgian chancery. As part of the Dutch plans to erect a new chancery in the early 1960s, the Dutch diplomat Emile Schiff (1918-2007) carried out a survey on different purpose-built chanceries which included the Belgian one. In his report, Schiff indicated how local residents told him that the Belgian chancery was out of tune with its surroundings.[160] Apparently, its stripped classical appearance was disliked by the owners of the predominately Neo-Georgian style homes along Garfield Street.

Notwithstanding such dissonant voices, the Belgian chancery was generally perceived as a tremendous success by the different actors involved. As the process of greenlighting the project was nothing short of a Herculean task, Baron Silvercruys personally thanked his political friends who had enabled him to launch this building project. In a letter to

Camille Gutt, Silvercruys reassured his friend that "un bureau Gutt" would always be at his disposal in his "belle ambassade" whenever he happened to be in the American capital.[161] Silvercruys also used the chancery as a stately location for pompous events. On the occasion of the royal visit of King Baudouin to Washington, D.C. in May 1959, the chancery was used as a venue where the Belgian community in the United States, the embassy staff and their families could meet the young monarch.

By hosting such a solemn moment in the new embassy offices instead of the majestic Foxhall Road estate, Silvercruys illustrated how the chancery was finally up to par with his ambassadorial residence. It may have taken him over 12 years, but the baron now deemed both sections of his embassy worthy of representing Belgium in the contemporary *caput mundi*. However, Ambassador Silvercruys could not enjoy the fruits of his labour for that long. Just two years following the chancery's inauguration, his diplomatic career came to an end as he retired in 1959. Together with his wife, Silvercruys moved to a property at 3201 Woodland Drive, less than 300 metres from the purpose-built chancery at Garfield Street. As such, the Belgian baron kept a watchful eye over the architectural legacy of his ambassadorship until he passed away in 1975.

Chapter II
Building Embassies on Demand
The Steering Role of the Receiving State (1958-1974)

On 17 June 1988, the Ministry's highest echelons discussed the planned renovation of the Belgian chancery in Moscow. The Ministry had recently started to lease an office building from the Soviet authorities. As there was no such thing as a private real estate market in the USSR, all buildings were communally owned by the Soviet regime. Unsatisfied with the working conditions in the chancery, the Ministry requested its Soviet landlord to carry out a renovation. However, the Belgian request was not a priority for the Soviet bureaucracy and the renovation plans were at a deadlock. On top of that, the Soviet authorities had suddenly increased the rent by 50 per cent without prior notice. In its capacity as landlord, the USSR was notorious among Western countries for such capricious actions. In times of geopolitical animosity, the Soviet Union had a tendency to increase the rent of diplomatic premises occupied by NATO member states.

Being fed up with how the USSR politicised diplomatic housing, the Belgian Ministry of Foreign Affairs was poised to give the communist superpower a taste of its own medicine. Therefore, the Ministry used a Soviet building project in Brussels as leverage to put an end to the deadlock. At the time, the Soviet authorities were about to construct a new office building for its commercial representation. To this end, 30 Soviet construction workers would be sent to Brussels. Determined to settle the score with the USSR, the Ministry refused the labourers' visa applications.[162] Belgium would only grant the necessary visa if the USSR would fully support the renovation of the Belgian chancery in Moscow. As luck would have it, the gamble paid off immediately. The Soviet authorities had a sudden change of heart and the chancery's renovation got underway.

This compelling case emphasises how both the USSR and Belgium politicised each other's investments in diplomatic housing. In their capacity as receiving states, both countries were in a privileged position to influence the projects of sending states. After all, such investments take place abroad, on foreign territory where sending states wield no legal authority. Consequently, the receiving state plays an instrumental role in turning investments in diplomatic housing into a success or failure. This is especially true in the context of commissioning purpose-built embassies. Local authorities enforce building regulations and issue building permits to sending states. If the construction plans of the latter do not meet the standards, the receiving state can veto building plans and send sending states back to the drawing board.

The receiving state can, however, also make considerable efforts to boost the construction of purpose-built embassies on its territory. Several receiving states have taken up the role of facilitator by creating favourable conditions to construct embassies. Such conditions range from allocating building plots to foreign governments, to inviting foreign governments to restore historical premises in exchange for using them as their embassies. Receiving states have done this to help the diplomatic corps sort out living arrangements, legitimise the ruling power base and support their own urban projects.

The premise of chapter II is to demonstrate how several receiving states have kickstarted Belgian embassy projects and tremendously influenced their architectural design. Their efforts form the second important dominant dynamic shaping the Belgian embassy-building programme since 1945. Chapter II turns to embassy projects in Australia, Poland and Brazil, illustrating how these receiving states incentivised Belgium to build on their demand. Throughout the chapter, emphasis will be put on the fact that commissioning purpose-built embassies is essentially a two-way street in which both the receiving and sending states have to give and take. Consequently, the Belgian embassies erected in Canberra, Warsaw and Brasília are by their very essence the architectural expression of a bilateral compromise.

A. BUILDING AN EMBASSY IN THE LAND DOWN UNDER: DIPLOMATIC HOUSING AS POLITICAL LEVERAGE

Establishing Diplomatic Ties With Australia: A Dilemma Between Sydney and Canberra

In the immediate post-war period, Foreign Minister Spaak set about expanding the network of diplomatic and consular postings. In 1947, he set his sights on establishing diplomatic ties with Australia. The absence of a Belgian diplomatic mission had to do with Australia's status as a British dominion. Australia's foreign policy was largely defined by London. By the 1940s, however, the Australian government veered away from London and set up its own diplomatic missions across the globe. In return, foreign countries began to open a diplomatic mission in Australia during the 1940s, a trend that had not escaped Spaak's notice. He deemed the time right to establish diplomatic ties with Australia formally by opening a legation.

High-ranking ministry officials such as Hervé de Gruben, however, spoke out against the idea. His opposition had everything to do with the location of the future legation. The Australian government expected that diplomatic missions would be located in the federal capital of Canberra. According to de Gruben, however, locating the legation in Canberra would go against Belgium's economic interests in Australia. He called Canberra a purely administrative city that stood in the shadow of Sydney, the nation's economic heartland.[163] Posting Belgian diplomats in Canberra would be ludicrous as they would have to travel up and down to Sydney constantly. Moreover, he warned Spaak that it would be difficult to find suitable and affordable housing as Canberra was still in full development.

Founded in 1913, Canberra is situated some 150 kilometres from Australia's east coast in between Sydney and Melbourne. The city's foundation is intrinsically linked to the rivalry between Sydney and Melbourne. As both cities were at odds with one another as to which city would become the nation's capital, the Australian parliament developed a purpose-built capital.[164] The American architect couple Walter Burley Griffin (1876-1937) and Marion Mahony Griffin (1871-1961) was commissioned to design Canberra. Adhering to the principles of the City Beautiful movement that called for a more harmonious social order through the embellishment of cities, the Griffins conceived an urban plan (Fig. 16) in which the built environment interacted with the natural environment. Nestled into the mountainous terrain surrounding the Canberra area, the horizontal city that the Griffins designed was characterised by a low building density and a low-rise aesthetic. The city's design diagram was to be made up of interlocking circles and hexagons set on an equilateral triangle of three main boulevards. The three boulevards form the crux of the design diagram, connecting the Capitol, the Civic Centre and the Market Centre. On the city's southern edge, radial residential suburbs were to be developed with distinctive curved, English-style streets to give a more organic appearance to the urban fabric and to contrast with Sydney's and Melbourne's grid plan. To evoke a sense of harmony with the hilled grasslands, a series of landscaped parks and a large artificial lake

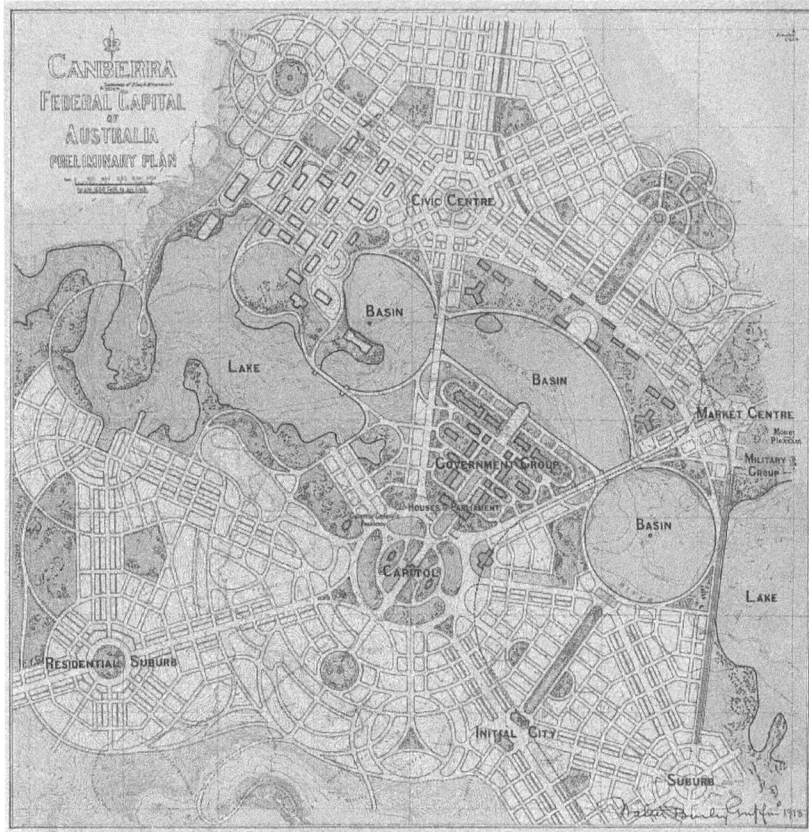

Figure 16: Canberra, 1914

were to be included. The development of Canberra, however, faced several hiccups along the way, such as a lack of funding, creative differences and two world wars.

On top of that, Canberra had a serious image problem. Critics framed Canberra as a soulless city that was far away from the buzzing coastal cities and inhabited by politicians and bureaucrats who were out of touch with the average Australian.[165] Such notions were further reinforced by Canberra's small population. By 1947, the city had just 25,000 residents and was regarded as a ghost town.

Secretary-General De Gruben did his best to talk Spaak out of the idea of opening a legation in Canberra. Demonstrating the great deal of sway that de Gruben had, Spaak altered his plans. Instead of moving to Canberra, the consulate in Sydney was elevated to a legation in November 1947. The

Australian Department of External Affairs had little choice but to accept the Belgian plans. Firstly, several sending states had already opened their diplomatic mission in Sydney because of Canberra's housing shortage. Secondly, the Australian government did not have the moral authority to force such a move to Canberra as it did not lead by example. By 1947, half of the Australian ministry departments were still located in Sydney. Thirdly and lastly, the Australian Department of External Affairs had its own shortcomings. At the time, the Department did not have an Australian legation in Brussels. This imbalance did not adhere to the principal of reciprocity, one of the main building blocks of bilateral diplomacy.

The More the Merrier: The Development of Diplomatic Hill

The Australian government may have been pleased with the establishment of diplomatic missions on its territory but the fact that Sydney was the preferred location was a thorn in its side. The absence of diplomatic missions undermined Canberra's prestige. Determined to turn things around, the Australian authorities developed a diplomatic district in Canberra to facilitate the opening of diplomatic missions. More commonly known as Diplomatic Hill, the diplomatic district is situated in the hilly suburb of Yarralumla. On the basis of long-term leaseholds, undeveloped land was allocated to sending states that were interested in constructing diplomatic premises.

The United States was the first country to accept the offer and was allocated a prime building plot on the district's most elevated part, giving the American embassy a commanding view over Yarralumla. In early 1941, the State Department tasked in-house architect Paul Franz Jaquet (1889-1951) to design the new embassy. Approaching the commission as an opportunity to express nationhood abroad, Jaquet designed a majestic ambassadorial residence (Fig. 17) in colonial Georgian style. The residence was modelled after the grand edifices of Williamsburg, the capital city of the former American colony of Virginia.[166] Jaquet designed a stately residence with a symmetrical façade. It included a centrally positioned portico with columns and it was topped off by a steeply pitched roof with chimneys to accentuate the height. On 7 December 1941, the very day the lease for the land was signed, Japan started its war of aggression against the United States and Australia. The signing thus turned from a mundane administrative procedure into an oath of allegiance between

Figure 17: The American embassy in Canberra, 1957

the two allies. Due to the war, local building materials had to be used, such as bricks and marble from New South Wales. Completed in 1943, the purpose-built American embassy was and still is one of the landmarks in Canberra and has served as a magnet that attracted sending states to launch their very own building projects.

Following in America's footsteps, the South African Department of Foreign Affairs constructed a diplomatic residence on Diplomatic Hill. Malcolm Moir (1903-1971) was hired to design a residence. Moir was a well-reputed architect in Canberra, being one of Canberra's earliest privately practising architects. Moreover, he had supervised the construction of the US embassy. Cementing his status as the go-to architect for diplomats, Moir was instructed by the South African state to evoke a sense of home on Australian soil. Complying with the client's wishes, Moir designed a diplomatic residence in Cape Dutch style. This architectural style is intrinsically linked to South Africa's history, mimicking the vernacular architecture of farmhouses constructed around the Cape of Good Hope during the Dutch colonial rule in the 17th and 18th centuries. Completed in 1957, the South African residence showcased distinctive architectural features of the Cape Dutch style. The exteriors featured ornately rounded gables and whitewashed walls topped off by a pitched roof covered with red terracotta tile. The timber-framed windows were flanked by teak louvered shutters, giving the residence a rural character and offering protection from natural light. The residence was immersed in a well-tended garden, made up of plants endemic to South Africa.

The foreign building activity may have strengthened Canberra's status as the national capital but not everyone welcomed the design choices made by foreign governments. In his 1960 book with the telling title *The Australian Ugliness*, the Australian architect and critic Robin Boyd (1919-1971) argued that the country's built landscape was a hotchpotch of foreign architectural styles with excessive decorative elements that were ignorant of local conditions, such as the countryside and climate, and he coined this phenomenon Featurism. The epitome of Featurism, Boyd reasoned, could be found on Diplomatic Hill. Sending states and their obsession with radiating nationhood turned Diplomatic Hill into an architectural travesty:

> But the best Featurism and the main tourist attraction of Canberra is the number of official buildings designed and erected by foreign or other Commonwealth countries. Most of the diplomatic visitors have felt obliged to feature themselves for reasons of public relations or propaganda, to display as much as possible of their own national architectural character. [...] They embarked on projects apparently calculated to make Canberra the architectural equivalent of a full-dress diplomatic levee. Unfortunately the falsity of the costumes becomes so apparent in the bright light that the effect is more like a fancy-dress party. [...] Thus bureaucratic architecture from all nations finally reduces Canberra's architectural mood to a farce.[167]

Signing the Crown Lease: Diffusing a Difficult Situation for the Time Being

The Belgian diplomatic corps, however, begged to differ. Minister Plenipotentiary Paul Verstraeten was dazzled by the Neo-Georgian American embassy. Verstraeten wrote that the American embassy was a magnificent sight to behold that set the standard for future diplomatic building projects in Canberra.[168] Such statements underscore how Belgian diplomats had a soft spot for historical and monumental designs for diplomatic buildings.

Supporting the relocation of diplomatic missions to Canberra, the Australian Department of External Affairs expressed its desire to Verstraeten that Belgium construct a new legation. In talks with Verstraeten, Australian officials stressed that Belgium should select a building plot on Diplomatic Hill as soon as possible or run the risk that the best sites would be already taken. In doing so, Australian officials put pressure on Belgium to build and thus speed up the transfer to Canberra.

Verstraeten was, however, anything but excited about the prospect of moving to Canberra. In his correspondence with Brussels, he did not speak highly of the Australian capital. Canberra was only a city in name. Compared to the vibrant city of Sydney, he argued, Canberra was nothing more than a little, sleepy ghost town.[169] Moreover, Verstraeten reasoned that moving the Belgian legation to Canberra would complicate his diplomatic work. As bilateral ties mainly revolved around trade, it would be ludicrous to leave the financial and economic hub of Sydney. As such, Verstraeten made the case to his superiors to stay in Sydney and turn down the Australian offer. Even if Verstraeten had suggested that his superiors launch a building project in the late 1940s, the Ministry's highest echelons would have undoubtedly curbed his enthusiasm. As demonstrated in the previous chapter, Secretary-General de Gruben was notorious for vetoing building plans. Moreover, Australia's insignificance to Belgian foreign policy did not justify the construction of a legation.

By 1951, however, the Ministry was forced to reconsider its options. As more diplomatic missions were moving to Canberra, the Belgian diplomatic corps was worried that its legation in Sydney would become isolated. Running the risk of becoming a diplomatic outcast, the Belgian state explored the possibility of entering into a lease agreement. A desire for prestige also incentivised this change of heart. If Belgium continued to sit on the fence, it would miss out on the best plots of land that Diplomatic Hill had to offer. Consequently, the Belgian legation commenced negotiations with the Australian Capital Territory Government to acquire a site.

The Australian Capital Territory Government rewarded the Belgian state for its change of heart by allocating a prominent parcel of land to Belgium. Situated along Arkana Street, the site (Fig. 18) has a surface area of almost 30,000 m^2, standing in stark contrast to the smaller plots leased by the Netherlands, West Germany and Sweden. The sizeable parcel of land would enable Belgium to construct both a residence and chancery. Moreover, the plot had scenic qualities. Immersed in a green setting, the site is situated on the southern slope of Diplomatic Hill. The future legation premises would thus be visible from afar and had the potential to become a landmark. Additionally, the plot was situated adjacent to the majestic American embassy. Being a small country, it was a nice bonus for Belgium to have its parcel of land situated next to the embassy of the most powerful country at the time.

On 28 May 1951, the Belgian diplomat Felix Jansen signed the so-called Crown Lease by which Belgium acquired the land. As was the case for each Crown Lease, the site was allocated to Belgium for a period of 99 years. Moreover, foreign governments only had to pay 60 Australian pounds a year to lease the parcel of land, a fraction of the actual market value.

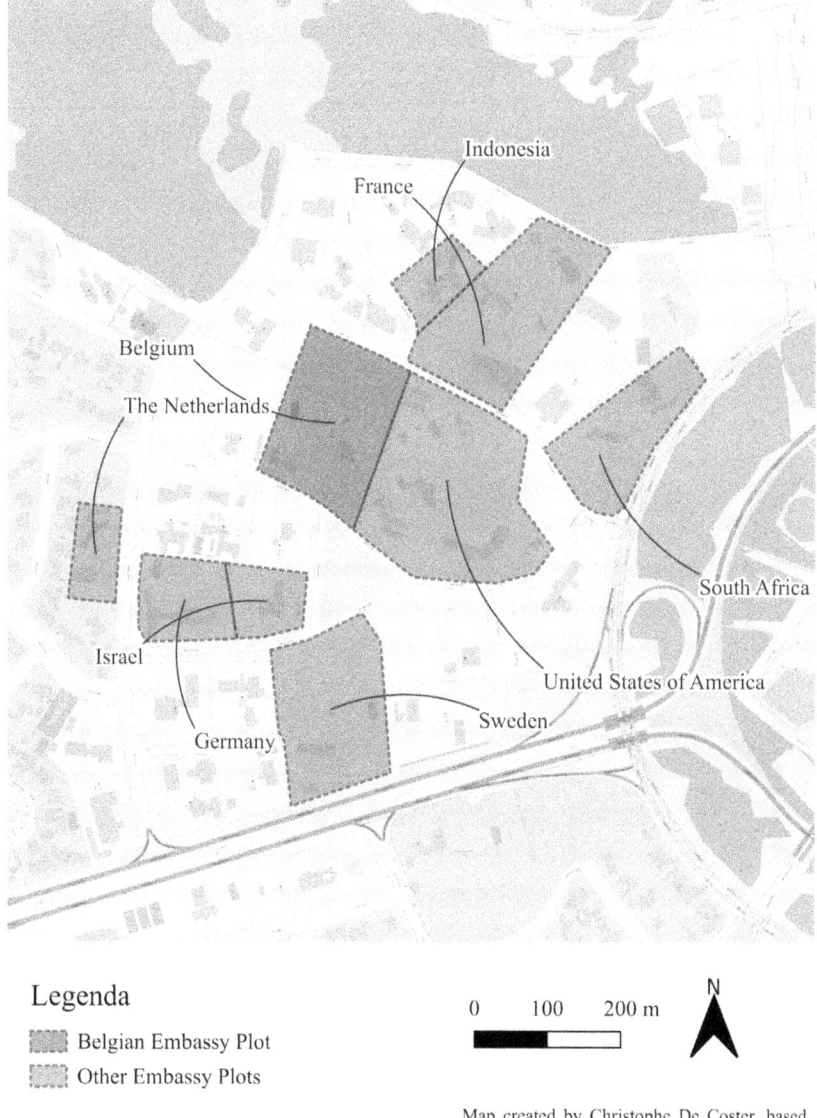

Legenda
▨ Belgian Embassy Plot
▨ Other Embassy Plots

0　　100　　200 m

N

Map created by Christophe De Coster, based on an earlier version by Elke Van den Broecke

Figure 18: Diplomatic Hill, 1951

In return, the Crown Lease stipulated the terms and conditions that sending states had to obey. Firstly, the Crown Lease stressed that sending states could only construct diplomatic buildings on the site. Secondly, sending states had to submit their building plans to the National Capital

Development Commission for review. It was in the best interest of sending states to submit blueprints quickly. After all, the third condition put forward a strict deadline. Construction works had to be completed within three years following the signing of the Crown Lease. In the case of Belgium, its purpose-built legation thus had to be completed by the summer of 1954 at the latest. Fourthly, the Crown Lease stipulated a noteworthy condition related to the construction phase. If construction workers were to stumble upon minerals during excavation works, the sending state would have to hand these raw materials over to the Australian authorities at once. Echoing a protectionist line of economic thinking, the Australian government clearly wanted to avoid a scenario in which the nation's raw materials would end up in foreign hands. Finally, the Crown Lease stipulated that sending states had to take care of their parcel of land once construction works were completed. Sending states were notified that their site had to be landscaped, planted and thereafter maintained in an adequate manner, stressing that "[...] the lessee will at all times keep the said land clean, tidy, and free from debris, dry herbage, rubbish, and other unsightly or offensive matter."[170]

It was in the best interest of Belgium to adhere to the terms and conditions. In its capacity as landlord, the Australian Capital Territory Government could terminate the lease unilaterally if the sending state failed to meet the above-mentioned requirements. Being expelled from Diplomatic Hill would have had severe consequences. It would undoubtedly sour the bilateral relationship with Australia and be a tremendous blow to national prestige. As such, one would assume that the Belgian state would roll up its sleeves and construct its legation at once. Things, however, unfolded very differently. By the time that the deadline to complete the legation by 1954 had passed, the Ministry had not even bothered to contact an architect. Fortunately, the Australian authorities did not reprimand the Belgian legation for policymakers' procrastination. Apparently, the Australian state took on a more lenient attitude in real life.

In retrospect, the Belgian lack of enthusiasm is understandable. The Australian government made little effort to improve bilateral ties with Belgium. By the mid-1950s, the Australian Department of External Affairs still had not opened a legation in Brussels. Moreover, in 1955, Australia turned down the invitation to participate in the 1958 Brussels World's Fair, much to the frustration of the Belgian state.[171] Consequently, the Ministry of Foreign Affairs was reluctant to invest in its diplomatic housing in Canberra, investments which would cement the city's status as undisputed capital.

On top of the bilateral context, constructing diplomatic buildings was still a rarity in the Ministry's housing policy at the time. By the time Belgium signed the Crown Lease, Ambassador Robert Silvercruys had been fruitlessly trying to greenlight the Washington project for four years. As this building project already progressed at a snail's pace in one of the most important diplomatic postings for Belgium, it is easy to understand why the Ministry was not willing to allocate its limited resources to the construction of a legation in Canberra.

As such, the Belgian state bought time for itself by signing the Crown Lease. Entering into a lease agreement already in 1951 was more of a preliminary step to anticipate better times. By signing the Crown Lease early on, Belgium was able to lay its hands on a prominent parcel of land. Moreover, the Belgian diplomatic corps got the Australian authorities off its back and bought time until there was enough political appetite and funding available for the project.

Kickstarting the Building Project on Diplomatic Hill

It was only in late 1955, more than a year after the Crown Lease deadline had expired, that the Ministry committed itself to developing the parcel of land. This move was triggered by growing Australian pressure and complaints from the Belgian Minister Plenipotentiary Jean Querton. Querton complained about having to commute from Sydney to Canberra to discuss political matters. Moreover, the absence of a diplomatic residence in Canberra thwarted his efforts to get to know Australian policymakers.[172]

Being sensitive to the Australian pressure and Querton's grievances, the Ministry reasoned that the time had finally come to launch a building project in Canberra. In a similar fashion to the Washington project, the Ministry instructed Minister Plenipotentiary Querton to find a local architect. This underscores yet again that it was common practice to outsource such a search to the diplomatic boots on the ground.

At first glance, the search for an architect seemed to be straightforward as Malcolm Moir was the go-to architect in Canberra for diplomats. Querton, however, reached out to the Sydney-based architecture firm Fowell, Mansfield & Maclurcan. Founded by Charles Fowell (1891-1970) and John Leslie Mansfield (1906-1965) in 1946, the architecture firm was one of the leading offices in New South Wales by the mid-1950s.[173] Trained in the United Kingdom, Charles Fowell worked as an assistant to the renowned Australian architect Leslie Wilkinson (1882-1973) during the interwar period. Fowell made a name for himself by designing over 40 churches in New South Wales and Victoria during the 1930s and 1940s. His associate John Leslie Mansfield had previously set up his own practice in Sydney in the 1930s and was the founder and chairman of the Town and Country Planning Institute of New South Wales. His oeuvre mainly consisted of the construction and renovation of houses, schools and public buildings. In the late 1940s, the Australian architect Donald Maclurcan (1918-1999) joined forces with Fowell and Mansfield, giving the firm its name of Fowell, Mansfield & Maclurcan. Serving as a captain in the Royal Australian Engineers during the war, Maclurcan was the firm's engineering-minded associate. Given his interest in large infrastructural works, he designed several prestressed concrete arch bridges across Australia.

There is no evidence in writing as to why Querton contacted Fowell, Mansfield & Maclurcan but circumstantial evidence may shed some light on the matter. In the mid-1950s, the architecture firm was commissioned to renovate and extend Kirribilli House, the Sydney residence of the Australian prime minister. One can assume that Querton deemed it only fitting that an architecture firm with such a prestigious commission would go on to design the Belgian legation. Moreover, one cannot help but think that his choice was influenced by practical considerations. As the Belgian legation was still located in Sydney, it would be far more convenient to work with a local architecture firm. The Ministry followed his recommendation and awarded the commission to Fowell, Mansfield & Maclurcan in 1956.

Fowell, Mansfield & Maclurcan had their work cut out for them as the commission entailed a comprehensive design brief. Both the residence and chancery had to be constructed on the sizeable parcel of land to facilitate the legation's day-to-day business. The residence and the chancery were to be housed in separate buildings to accentuate their different purposes in the diplomatic realm.

Fowell, Mansfield & Maclurcan's site plan clearly expresses the chancery's and residence's purpose, together with their respective hierarchy in relation to each other. In line with its public function as an administrative point of contact, the chancery was to be situated on the street side in the south-eastern corner of the plot. The chancery had a separate driveway leading to a parking lot for staffers and visitors. Just west of the chancery, a second driveway was to be paved. This driveway would lead to a large roundabout situated in front of the residence. The residence was to be strategically positioned further inland. Accentuating its status as the legation's representational flagship, the residence was to be constructed on the most elevated part of the parcel. Its elevated location ensured that the residence would be visible from afar and tower over the chancery, highlighting the pecking order between both diplomatic buildings. Moreover, its elevated position created a certain sense of ceremony for visitors making their way to the residence. One can already conjure images of guests driving up the sloped driveway and being greeted by the Belgian minister plenipotentiary and his family wearing their Sunday best.

Adhering to the conditions of the Crown Lease, the grounds had to be landscaped in an aesthetically pleasing manner. The preliminary design proposed to lay turf over the legation grounds and surround the edges with trees, bushes and hedges to create a harmonious ensemble resonating with Diplomatic Hill's green aesthetic. The architects were also instructed to include recreational facilities, specifically a tennis court. The tennis court would not only offer recreational facilities to Belgian diplomats but would also be an invaluable asset to conduct diplomacy in a more informal setting. The Belgian head of mission could invite fellow diplomats and Australian officials over for a game and discuss bilateral matters in between sets. Moreover, the tennis court would enable the Belgian legation to showcase its athletes to the local population. Its next-door neighbour on Diplomatic Hill had already set the example. In January 1954, the US embassy organised exhibition games between the American and Australian Davis Cup teams on its tennis court. The games drew over 400 spectators to the embassy grounds and the US embassy received positive media coverage for hosting the event.[174]

Designing the Belgian Legation: An Architectural Discrepancy on Diplomatic Hill

Sending states such as the United States and South Africa had constructed diplomatic buildings reflecting the vernacular architecture of their respective countries. These historical and pompous designs were conceived to be the architectural expression of a romanticised history that both nations wanted to re-evoke on Diplomatic Hill. As this approach received much acclaim from Belgian diplomats, one would assume that the Ministry wanted to follow in their footsteps.

It is, however, telling that there was no interest within the Ministry's walls to call for a traditional and historical design for the Canberra legation. Radiating nationhood on Australian soil through diplomatic

Figure 19: The legation residence, 1959

architecture did not cross the mind of the Ministry. In fact, Fowell, Mansfield & Maclurcan were given a free hand to design a legation as long as it ticked all the boxes in terms of programmatic needs.

The residence (Fig. 19) was to be the architectural centrepiece of the Belgian legation grounds. The architects designed a stately residence with the appearance of a high-end country retreat that would not have looked out of place in southern France or Italy. Situated on an elevated plaza, the residence was to be a three-storey building entirely made of bricks. The brick building shell was to be plastered in a striking apricot colour to give the residence a more elegant appearance while simultaneously creating a colour contrast with the green surroundings. The front façade featured several elements that gave the residence its characteristic homely appearance. These included a pitched roof with a series of dormers and chimneys, and the extensive use of shutters. These shutters were merely included for the sake of decoration as the southern façade is not exposed to natural sunlight given the fact that Australia is part of the southern hemisphere. Regarding the front façade, the architects did not lose sight of the representational character intrinsically linked to diplomatic architecture. In a similar fashion to the Washington embassy offices, a large Belgian coat of arms was to be included in the front façade. The coat of arms was strategically positioned at the main entrance, just above the canopy where guests were to be dropped off by car.

The residence's interior layout was adjusted to meet the dual function of living quarters for the Belgian minister and venue for social gatherings.

Figure 20: The residence's main staircase, 1961

Upon entering the residence, visitors passed the cloakroom where they could leave their coats and other outerwear behind. Subsequently, they entered the centrally positioned main stair hall (Fig. 20) where Fowell, Mansfield & Maclurcan had invested considerably in the use of high-end applied materials. The flooring and steps were covered with Carrara marble to give the stair hall a majestic appearance.

From the main hall, one could enter the semi-private areas of the residence such as the drawing room, sunroom and study. These spaces were designed for use in the diplomat's everyday life and for the hosting of guests. As social gatherings tend to vary in terms of attendees and atmosphere, the diversity of semi-private spaces came in handy. Guests could be seated in the drawing room or, in fine weather, in the sunroom with a splendid view on the garden. If the Belgian minister wanted to have a one-on-one conversation with a guest, he could move the conversation to his private study for a confidential talk. The three rooms were each fitted with parquet flooring that gave an Australian touch to the interiors. The wooden flooring was made of tallow-wood, a tree endemic to Australia's eastern

Figure 21: The Belgian legation offices, 1959

shores. The brownish-yellow tallow-wood parquet brought a feeling of warmth and radiated Australian craftsmanship in the residence's interiors.

Upon taking the marble staircase to the first floor, guests reached the dining room. The dining room has traditionally been perceived as the residence's most important room where well-attended dinner parties are thrown. Wining and dining in style with guests is paramount for every diplomat who craves to deepen personal relations with local dignitaries. The dining room also had a parquet floor made of tallow-wood. The dining room was conveniently situated next to the kitchen. Adjacent to the kitchen were the servant's quarters where the men and women who kept the household running resided. Separate servant staircases were also included, enabling the domestic staff to circulate throughout the building without being seen. The presence of servants' staircases, which are reminiscent of old bourgeois mansions, reinforces the conservative image of the diplomatic world. The minister's private living quarters were situated on the top floor. These living quarters featured a private drawing room, five bedrooms, three bathrooms, a dressing room and two balconies oriented to the north to enjoy the sun.

In designing the chancery, Fowell, Mansfield & Maclurcan opted for a very different approach. Whereas a country retreat-like building was deemed appropriate for the residence, the chancery's design (Fig. 21) was characterised by a far more functionalist approach. As it was situated on sloped terrain, the legation offices were to be constructed on an elevated plaza. On the plaza, a somewhat unobtrusive single-storey office building was to be erected. The office building was characterised by a sleek, box-like structure topped off by a slightly curved roof made of anodised steel. In a half-hearted effort to create at least some resemblance to the diplomatic residence, the chancery's brick exteriors were also plastered in the same striking apricot colour. A fully glazed entrance was included to evoke a sense of openness and lightness from the street.

The exterior featured a series of narrow but tall window frames reinforcing the chancery's sleek appearance. Another profound difference

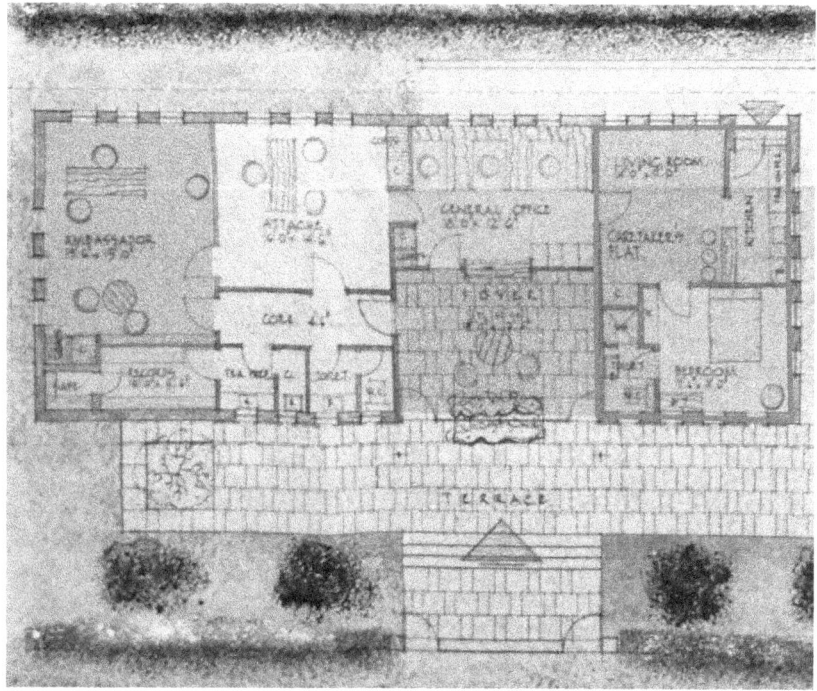

Legenda

- Caretaker's Apartment
- Archival Room and Safe
- Bedroom
- General Office with Enquiry Counters
- Kitchen
- Living Room
- Lobby
- Office of the First Secretary
- Office of the Minister Plenipotentiary
- Toilet
- Toilets

Based on: Belgian Embassy Archives Canberra, Architects Fowell, Mansfield & Maclurcan, 1958.

Map created by Christophe De Coster

Figure 22: The Belgian embassy offices, Canberra, 1958

with the residence was the absence of national symbols in the chancery's architecture. In contrast to the residence, there was no coat of arms on the front façade. It was up to the Belgian diplomatic corps to make their presence known by hoisting the national colours and hanging the coat of arms on the front façade.

The hierarchy between the residence and chancery was also made obvious by their respective surface area. With a surface area of 533 m², the chancery (Fig. 22) was significantly smaller than the 850 m² of the residence. This also had to do with the fact that the Belgian diplomatic staff was basically a skeleton crew. There were just two Belgian diplomats posted to Australia at the time. Given the limited staff, there was no apparent need to stress the pecking order in the office layout as was the case in the Washington chancery. Both offices were roughly the same size and were situated next to each other, reflecting a certain sense of collegiality. The chancery was also conceived as the place where citizens could conduct their bureaucratic business with the Belgian administration. Next to the lobby, enquiry counters were included where three clerks could process visa applications and other paperwork.

As the legation's workforce did not need an abundance of office space, the caretaker's apartment was also included in the chancery. The apartment took up approximately one third of the available space which was indicative of the size of the skeleton crew staffing the chancery. In designing the apartment, the architects paid attention to the fact that the housing unit was to be included in a public building. They purposefully installed the kitchen as far away from the lobby area as possible to safeguard the reputation of the Belgian diplomatic corps in Canberra. They reasoned that cooking odours and noise would raise eyebrows among the people waiting in the lobby area.

In September 1958, the Ministry greenlit the plans submitted by Fowell, Mansfield & Maclurcan. It therefore seemed as though nothing stood in the way of kickstarting construction works. However, things played out very differently. The Belgian parcel of land remained untouched throughout 1958 and the first half of 1959. Judging from the Washington case, one would easily assume that the postponement was caused by budgetary issues. There was, however, something far more intriguing going on, something that goes to the very core of how bilateral relations affect diplomatic building projects.

The Building Project as Diplomatic Bargaining Chip

The Belgian decision to stall the project was influenced by Australia's unwillingness to open a diplomatic mission in Brussels. Whereas Belgium had already opened a legation in Australia in 1947, the latter still had not returned the favour by the late 1950s. Australian procrastination was especially damaging to Belgian prestige given the fact that Australia did establish embassies in neighbouring capitals such as Paris, Bonn and The Hague. This was a thorn in the side of Willy Stevens who was appointed the new Belgian minister plenipotentiary to Australia in November 1957.

Determined to turn things around, Stevens frequently addressed the elephant in the room during talks with Australian officials. Much to Stevens' dismay, they continued to bring up practical issues that apparently stood in the way of establishing a legation in Brussels. Stevens grew increasingly frustrated and strongly advocated to his superiors in Brussels that the time for half measures and talk was well and truly over. He suggested that the Belgian state should flex its muscles as he cooked up a scheme to use the legation building project as a bargaining chip to put pressure on Australia. Stevens proposed to terminate the Crown Lease, pull the plug on the building project, and thus keep the legation in Sydney if Australia did not open a legation in Brussels at once.[175] In doing so, Stevens wanted to capitalise on the fact that the location of diplomatic missions was a sensitive issue for the Australian government. After all, the Australian authorities did not offer prime building plots in Canberra to sending states out of generosity but more to consolidate Canberra's position as the nation's true capital.

The Ministry's highest echelons were also fed up with Australia's procrastination and wholeheartedly supported the scheme of Stevens. Secretary-General Louis Scheyven even opted to raise the stakes by presenting the Australian authorities with an ultimatum in the hope of breaking the stalemate. Scheyven threatened to close the Belgian legation in Sydney if the latter failed to open a legation in Brussels.[176] Belgium may have been a small state actor but it was not afraid to show its teeth.

The Belgian ultimatum did not fall on deaf ears. In February 1959, the Australian Department for External Affairs caved to the pressure and greenlit the opening of an Australian diplomatic mission in Brussels. Moreover, in an effort to smooth things over, the Australian authorities suggested to open an embassy in Brussels instead of a lower-ranked legation. This move was very much appreciated by Willy Stevens as the Belgian legation in Sydney was elevated to an embassy in May 1959 on the basis of reciprocity.

The diplomatic upgrade did not go by unnoticed in the Belgian parliament. Upon hearing that the legation had been elevated to an embassy, the liberal MP Adolphe Van Glabbeke made the case that the Ministry should construct a new embassy building to do justice to the elevated diplomatic status.¹⁷⁷ Little did he know that the Ministry of Foreign Affairs had already been preoccupied with commissioning a building project in Canberra for quite some years and that the blueprints were already greenlit. This serves as a telling reminder that the embassy-building programme was a blind spot for Belgian lawmakers.

Succeeding in breaking the stalemate, the Ministry of Foreign Affairs revived its building plans on Diplomatic Hill at once. Following eight years of political indecisiveness and tug-of-war, the time had finally come to put the first shovel in the ground and construct the Canberra embassy. Therefore, the Ministry of Foreign Affairs put its faith in Ambassador Willy Stevens to be its eyes and ears on the building site.

Monitoring the Embassy's Construction: A Frustrated Ambassador Out of His Depth

Fowell, Mansfield & Maclurcan were awarded the project on a turnkey basis, making the firm responsible for selecting a building contractor and supervising construction works. Nevertheless, it was paramount that a Belgian official monitored the progress and examined whether construction works were carried out according to plan. Therefore, Brussels put its faith in Ambassador Stevens. This underscores yet again just how the Ministry lacked in-house experts to deal with such assignments.

In retrospect, one can raise serious doubts about whether an ambassador was the right person for such a task. Ambassadors often lacked the necessary qualifications and their ambassadorial duties were already demanding. Juggling the functions of an ambassador and a quality inspector was far from ideal, with the case of Ambassador Stevens serving as a textbook example.

The Canberra project turned out to be anything but smooth sailing for Willy Stevens. As stipulated in the Crown Lease, the Ministry first had to submit the building plans to the National Capital Development Commission to secure a building permit. Much to Stevens' frustration, the Commission vetoed the plans because of the proposed location of the chancery in the parcel's south-eastern corner. The Commission spoke out against the location because the Belgian chancery would be situated too close to the American embassy grounds. The Commission instructed the architects to alter the location and sent them back to the drawing board.

In response to the veto, the architects submitted a new plan in which the chancery was moved to the plot's south-western corner. Once again, the

Commission vetoed the scheme. This time, the Commission reasoned that the chancery was situated too close to Arkana Street and thus had to move some three metres further inland. Ambassador Stevens was not happy at all with the alterations proposed by the Commission. He reckoned that the chancery's new site would block the view on his ambassadorial residence from Arkana Street. He urged the architects to make his concerns known to the Commission:

> I think it is unfortunate that the Commission wants to move the building a further 11 ft. back. This will shorten the distance between the Chancellery and the Residence with great damage to the harmonious outlook of the whole. Perhaps the Commission will not be indifferent to this aesthetic aspect of the problem.[178]

The Commission, however, stuck to its guns. Much to the frustration of Stevens, the chancery thus had to be moved closer to the ambassadorial residence (Fig. 23). His frustration illustrates that ambassadors framed the residence and chancery as two completely different parts. A certain amount of distance between both parts was paramount in order to accentuate their diverging functions and increase the level of privacy at the ambassadorial residence.

Having secured a building permit, Fowell, Mansfield & Maclurcan organised a bidding process to select a building contractor. The Canberra-based construction firm Clements Langford submitted the lowest bid. The architects, however, urged Ambassador Stevens to dismiss the bid. Rumours were circulating that Clements Langford was drowning in debt and often worked below market prices in order to repay its creditors. Worried that the firm would soon go bankrupt, the architects recommended that Stevens exclude the firm from the bidding process. Back in Brussels, however, Clements Langford's low price offer attracted quite some interest.

Figure 23: The Belgian embassy grounds, 1962

Worried by the prospect of having to work with Clements Langford, the architects pressured Ambassador Willy Stevens to talk his superiors out of the idea. Stevens thus found himself caught between two sides with competing interests. Eventually, he had to concur with the architects and the commission was awarded to the Sydney-based construction firm C.H. Webb Bros. In total, the embassy's construction came with a price tag of 12 million Belgian francs (2.7 million euros). To put this figure into perspective, the construction budget took up almost 20 per cent of the Ministry's annual budget for diplomatic housing at the time. Working on a tight budget, it is therefore understandable why the Ministry was so keen to hire Clements Langford.

By the summer of 1959, C.H. Webb Bros kickstarted construction works. Due to budgetary constraints, the building project was split into two phases. In doing so, the building costs could be spread over several fiscal years to ease the financial burden for the Ministry. The first phase entailed the construction of the ambassadorial residence to ensure that Ambassador Stevens could move to Canberra as soon as possible. Monitoring the residence's construction phase took a toll on Stevens. He had to attend several meetings with the architects and make on-site visits. In reports to Brussels, Stevens complained that such commitments regularly prevented him from doing his job as ambassador and drained much of his energy.[179] Ambassador Stevens pleaded to his superiors for assistance in supervising the building project but his call for help went unanswered.

Nonetheless, Ambassador Stevens took his job as supervisor very seriously and set high standards for the residence. Upon inspecting the residence's interior finishing, he judged that the works had been carried out in a sloppy manner. On three different occasions, he instructed C.H. Webb Bros to replaster and repaint the main entrance hall. He also deemed the Carrara marble slabs to be of unacceptably poor quality and demanded their replacement at once. Ambassador Stevens was in a position of power to call out faulty works. After all, he was responsible for making payments to the architects and building contractor once a phase in the building works had been completed. If the quality of the works did not live up to his expectations, Stevens could simply stall payments until the works had been carried out accordingly.

As part of the second phase, the architects and C.H. Webb Bros turned their attention to the chancery's construction. The construction took more time than originally expected. This had to do with the National Capital Development Commission's demand to move the chancery to the south-western corner of the parcel of land. The soggy nature of the subsoil on the new site required concrete pier and beam footings to support the structure, forcing the architects to adjust the design.

The delay did not go down well with Ambassador Willy Stevens. Already fed up with the fact that he had to guide the building project, Stevens wanted to get it over and done with as soon as possible. He grew increasingly impatient with the delay, which caused tensions between him and Fowell, Mansfield & Maclurcan. In a letter to the architects, he vented his frustration regarding the slow work pace:

> Dear Sirs, I am not at all happy about the considerable delay for completing the working drawings and specifications regarding the construction of the Chancellery. You will remember that I asked you to proceed with those documents. On the 15th of February I wrote you a letter to express my surprise in the delay. It appears that from a telephone call of this Embassy that the working drawings will be completed early next week but that I will have to wait for the specifications. This is not at all satisfactory. I cannot understand how, after more than three months, those documents are not yet ready.[180]

The Stevens Residence, Lady of the House Speaking

Eventually, construction works were completed by the spring of 1961. In the eyes of Stevens, the embassy's completion presented itself as an excellent opportunity to put Belgium in a favourable light. Therefore, he counted on the support of his other half. He entrusted the task of furnishing and decorating the residence's interiors to his wife, Lucy Stevens.

Adhering to the normative idea that the diplomatic residence is the extension of the feminine household, Ambassador Stevens called upon her touch to turn the residence into a charming home with tastefully furnished and decorated interiors. The ambassadorial residence has traditionally been perceived as a feminine space where an ambassador's wife organises luncheons and dinner parties, oversees household chores, and creates a sense of domesticity. The Swedish Foreign Affairs Spouses Association, for instance, organised household management courses for ambassadors' wives in the 1960s, teaching them the ins and outs of arranging seating charts, furnishing a room and creating flower arrangements.[181]

Lacking in-house expertise, the Ministry gave Ambassador Willy Stevens – or rather his wife – a free hand in furnishing and decorating

Figure 24: The residence's drawing room, 1962

the residence's interiors. Her *pièce de résistance* was the drawing room (Fig. 24). Framing the drawing room as the space where visitors would get their first impression of the embassy and thus Belgium, Lucy Stevens deemed it important to include Belgian craftsmanship. Madame Stevens opted for a classic approach with De Coene furniture, the firm that had previously furnished the Washington chancery. Reminiscent of a bourgeois household, the drawing room featured upholstered seating, traditional rugs and crystal chandeliers that expressed both dignity and comfort. Moreover, she personally selected the wallpaper with a striking ice crystal motif. In order to showcase Belgian art in the residence, the Romantic painting *View of Ostend* by the Belgian painter François Musin (1820-1888) was displayed in the drawing room.

Whereas this classic approach was also applied to furnishing and decorating the dining room and study, the aesthetic approach in the sunroom (Fig. 25) clearly deviated from it. The sunroom's connection between the garden was expressed in the furniture. In line with the tallow-wood parquet, Lucy Stevens purchased bamboo furniture on the domestic market,

Figure 25: The residence's sunroom, 1962

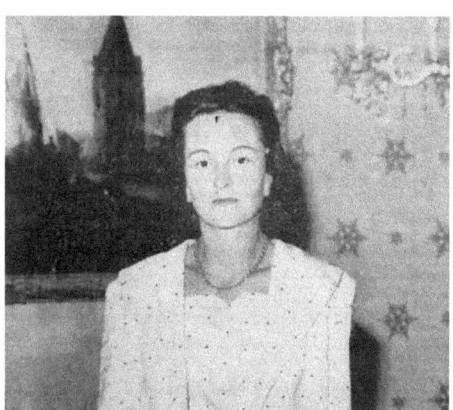

Figure 26: Lucy Stevens, 1963

yet another material found in abundance in Australia. To top it all off, curtains with a floral pattern were hung in the sunroom.

The residence was officially inaugurated on 21 July 1961. Ambassador Stevens had intentionally picked this date, which is also the Belgian national day, to further accentuate the solemn character of the occasion. To mark the occasion, a large reception was thrown in the embassy gardens. The reception was a true society event in Canberra and was attended by over 300 high-profile guests, including the Australian Prime Minister Sir Robert Gordon Menzies (1894-1978), several ministers of his cabinet, Canberra's *corps diplomatique*, and the Belgian community living in Australia. From then on, Ambassador Stevens put the residence to good use as he and his wife frequently hosted dinner parties, luncheons and cocktail parties. During these events, guests frequently spoke words of praise for the interior design.[182]

Seeing the residence's PR-value, the Stevens family made sure that it caught the public's eye. Lucy Stevens used the residence as a stately venue to give interviews to Australian media outlets such as the *Catholic*

Weekly and *The Sun* on what life is like as an ambassador's wife. In both interviews, Lucy Stevens (Fig. 26) posed in the residence's drawing room and proudly stated that she had personally furnished and decorated the interiors. Both media outlets spoke words of praise for her work, calling the residence a tastefully decorated and well-equipped venue.[183]

With the embassy completed, Ambassador Willy Stevens breathed a sigh of relief. The construction project may have been a demanding and time-consuming task but he now had an embassy at his disposal that boosted the nation's prestige and visibility on Australian soil. In a moment of true chauvinism, he boasted to Spaak that he was residing in the most beautiful embassy Canberra had to offer.[184]

B. THE RECONSTRUCTION OF THE MNISZECH PALACE: THE DIPLOMATIC CORNERSTONE OF BELGIAN-POLISH RELATIONS

The Mniszech Palace and the Belgian legation: Destruction as the Seed of Post-War Reconstruction

The Australian efforts were not an isolated case in the 1950s. Coinciding with the Canberra project, the Ministry received a similar invitation from behind the Iron Curtain that divided post-war Europe into a capitalist and communist bloc. The Polish People's Republic invited Belgium to reconstruct the war-ravaged Mniszech Palace and in return use it as the seat of the Belgian legation in Warsaw. To fully grasp the dynamics surrounding this project, it is paramount to first shed light on the devastating effects of the Second World War on the palace and the Belgian legation.

Situated along Senatorska Street in the heart of Warsaw, the Mniszech Palace was a majestic palace constructed at the beginning of the 17th century. The palace was originally commissioned by the Mniszech family, part of the Polish aristocracy, and witnessed several modifications throughout the centuries. By the early 19th century, the palace had its distinctive neoclassical touch. Its palatial architecture featured a central portico, a repetitive fenestration pattern and a pitched roof.

On the eve of the Second World War, the palace was the property of the Society of Merchants that used the spacious halls for lectures and concerts. Following the German invasion of Poland on 1 September 1939, the Mniszech Palace was converted into a hospital. The Mniszech Palace would continue to serve as a hospital for the remainder of the German

Figure 27: The war-ravaged Mniszech Palace, late 1940s

occupation. During the summer of 1944, when the victorious Red Army reached the gates of Warsaw, the Polish resistance took up arms against the German garrison in an effort to liberate the city. During the urban warfare, the Mniszech Palace served as one of the main frontline hospitals for Polish resistance fighters, while treating casualties from the German army side as well. Notwithstanding some initial success, the Warsaw Uprising was eventually crushed by the German army. On 14 August 1944, the *Wehrmacht* reoccupied the Mniszech Palace and ousted the sick and wounded from the hospital.

In retaliation to the insurrection, Adolf Hitler (1889-1945) ordered the levelling of Warsaw. As part of the city's systematic destruction, German troops targeted historically significant buildings such as palaces, castles and libraries. The Mniszech Palace did not escape their wrath. On 20 September 1944, German units set the palace ablaze which caused the building to collapse. Only the ruins of the exterior walls and the burned columns of the front portico were left standing (Fig. 27), serving as a silent reminder that the majestic Mniszech Palace once stood there. By January 1945, approximately 80 per cent of Warsaw's urban fabric had been reduced to rubble.[185]

The flames of war not only consumed the Mniszech Palace but also the Belgian legation. On the eve of the Second World War, the legation was housed in an apartment block along Ujazdów Avenue, one of the main north-south avenues of Warsaw. As war broke out in September 1939, the Luftwaffe bombed the legation. Completing its conquest of Poland, the Third Reich instructed all sending states to close their diplomatic missions and leave Poland at once. Eventually, during the final years of the war, the apartment building was completely destroyed like the Mniszech Palace. As both the Mniszech Palace and Belgian legation suffered the same fate, it was only fitting that their paths would cross each other in the post-war period.

Building Up Goodwill At Home and Abroad

Following the end of the Second World War, Poland became part of the Soviet sphere of influence as a Moscow-supported communist government took control from 1947 onwards. Ruling over a country in ruins, the Polish People's Republic launched a massive reconstruction scheme. The crown jewel of the scheme was the meticulous rebuilding of Warsaw's historic centre, more commonly known as the Old Town. The Old Town's reconstruction was not only launched to embellish the bombed-out capital but also to legitimise the new communist regime. Lacking broad support among the people, the communist leadership envisaged the urban project as the rebirth of Poland's cultural and historical identity. The government both aimed to ingratiate itself with the Varsovians and build up support for the new regime by establishing continuity with a glorified historic past.[186]

Once the reconstruction scheme was well underway by the mid-1950s, the Polish authorities expanded the scope to war-ravaged palaces situated just outside of the Old Town. Therefore, the Polish authorities invited foreign governments to fund such reconstruction projects. In return, the Polish government would offer sending states a long-term lease of 99 years on the property, enabling the latter to use it as the seat of its diplomatic mission. By cooking up such a scheme, the Polish authorities aimed to kill two birds with one stone. Firstly, foreign funding would tremendously speed up the reconstruction of historic palaces by which the government aimed to win over the hearts and minds of Varsovians. Secondly, these building projects would support the Polish Ministry of Foreign Affairs in providing housing to foreign diplomats. As private property was abolished following the communist takeover in 1947, there was no such thing as a private real estate market in Warsaw. It was therefore impossible for sending states to purchase properties to house their diplomatic mission. Instead, it was up to the Polish Ministry of Foreign Affairs to provide the *corps diplomatique* with rented premises. This was no small feat as housing was in short supply because of the wartime destruction of Warsaw. To ease the burden, the Polish Ministry of Foreign Affairs therefore invited foreign diplomatic missions to reconstruct majestic palaces. This type of building was and still is one the preferred types for diplomatic missions. By accepting the Polish offer, foreign governments could therefore move into more spacious and stately buildings that have traditionally housed diplomatic missions. Additionally, sending states could further ingratiate themselves among Varsovians by funding the reconstruction of the capital's architectural heritage.

In order to strike while the iron was still hot, the Polish Ministry of Foreign Affairs introduced reconstruction schemes to several diplomatic missions. In the 1950s, for instance, talks were held with France on reconstructing a historic palace at Piłsudski Square situated just south of the Old Town.[187] In the end, however, the French Ministry of Foreign Affairs declined the offer. The Polish Ministry of Foreign Affairs also tried its luck elsewhere. In 1950, the Polish state invited Belgium to rebuild the Mniszech Palace.[188] The Ministry's highest echelons neither accepted nor turned down the invitation and instead were considering how to respond to the invitation. The lack of enthusiasm to commit itself immediately to reconstructing the Mniszech Palace alongside the Polish People's Republic made sense, given the diplomatic context at the time. Bilateral ties with Poland were not particularly great. The Polish ideological climate was a far cry from that back home as Belgian diplomats reported how discussions often took place in a tense atmosphere. The Belgian diplomatic corps also did not think very highly of the Polish political leaders. They regarded them with much disdain, describing the Polish political elite as puppets who danced to the tune of the Kremlin.[189]

The Soviet Union did not make any particular efforts to nuance such perceptions as the USSR commissioned its purpose-built embassy (Fig. 28) in Warsaw in the mid-1950s. Designed by Soviet architects Igor Rozhin and Alexander Velikanov, the embassy was – in terms of architecture and volume – a true show of force in the streetscape of Warsaw. Rozhin and Velikanov designed a massive palatial building in a Stalinist Neoclassical style, intertwining innovative construction techniques with explicit references to classical architecture.[190] The front façade is made up of a careful

Figure 28: The former Soviet embassy in Warsaw, that now houses the embassy of the Russian Federation, 2022

composition of classical architectural elements, featuring a centrally positioned portico with the obligatory hammer and sickle sculpted into the pediment.[191] Across the entire length of the front façade, a repetitive arrangement of columns was incorporated to evoke a sense of rhythm to the building. Made up of Transcaucasian white marble, Ukrainian granite and Polish limestone, the monumental embassy structure was a prestige project for the USSR. Its design can be read as the architectural expression that Poland was a satellite state in orbit around the Kremlin.

The lack of Belgian enthusiasm can also be explained by the price tag of the building project. According to estimates, the reconstruction of the Mniszech Palace would cost approximately 45 million Belgian francs (12.3 million euros). The Ministry's highest echelons reasoned that it would be absurd to spend this considerable amount of money in Warsaw, the capital city of neither a close political ally nor an important trading partner. Moreover, if the Belgian state were to reconstruct the Mniszech Palace, it would indirectly support the Polish People's Republic in its efforts to wield architecture as an instrument to legitimise itself among the people. Taking all these things into consideration, the Ministry reasoned that it was not opportune to accept the Polish offer.

With Belgium sitting on the fence, the Polish authorities put additional pressure by bringing up the topic in conversations with Belgian diplomats.

One such occasion took place on 22 May 1954, the day Count Hadelin de Meeûs d'Argenteuil (1904-1993) presented his letters of credence as new Belgian minister plenipotentiary to Poland. As part of the ceremony, de Meeûs d'Argenteuil had an audience with Aleksander Zawadzki (1899-1964) who served as the Chairman of the Polish Council of State. During the audience, Zawadzki brought up the building proposal and once again invited Belgium to accept the offer.[192] His efforts yielded results in the following months. The Belgian Ministry of Foreign Affairs reached an agreement in principle and was open to the idea of financing the palace's construction and using it as the seat of the legation. De Meeûs d'Argenteuil stressed to Zawadzki that such a gesture should be interpreted as a sign of goodwill by Belgium to further cement bilateral ties with Poland. De Meeûs d'Argenteuil argued that, since Belgium and Poland were going to join forces in commissioning the new Mniszech Palace, the rebuilt palace would become the cornerstone of Belgian-Polish relations.

Such statements underscore how investments in diplomatic housing, next to its functional use, have often been framed as a means to improve bilateral ties. Minister Plenipotentiary Count Hadelin de Meeûs d'Argenteuil, however, got somewhat ahead of himself during his audience with President Zawadzki. The term 'agreement in principle' was and still is a flexible concept in Belgian politics. The Belgian Ministry of Foreign Affairs may have decided that the rebuilt Mniszech Palace would indeed make for a splendid location for its legation but it had not yet secured funding from the Belgian Ministry of Finance. In a similar fashion to the Washington project, the Ministry of Finance once again drove a hard bargain in allocating funding. Consequently, the ruins along Senatorska Street remained untouched in the mid-1950s, serving as a silent witness to both the wartime destruction of Warsaw and the lack of Belgian appetite to finance the reconstruction. It is telling that the Polish authorities had no intention of throwing in the towel just yet. Polish government officials sought support in Belgium through channels outside of the diplomatic realm. As luck would have it, such an opportunity presented itself in 1955.

Reaching Out to the Belgian Royalty

That year, Queen Elisabeth (1876-1965), a classical music enthusiast, was the honorary guest at the Fifth Chopin Piano Competition in Warsaw. The Belgian queen had gratefully accepted the Polish invitation despite pleas from Foreign Minister Spaak to turn it down, warning her that such a visit could damage her reputation. Elisabeth, however, begged to differ as she believed that Belgium should build up peaceful relations with communist countries. She wished to lead by example and firmly believed that the arts, which were universal, could transcend ideological differences.[193]

During her stay in Warsaw, it is claimed that Polish state officials introduced her to the idea of reconstructing the Mniszech Palace. This can be backed by circumstantial evidence. Firstly, Queen Elisabeth was the ideal person to pitch the idea to as she had an emotional connection with the Mniszech Palace through her late husband King Albert I (1875-1934). Back in 1919, the palace had hosted the state banquet in honour of the King of the Belgians to celebrate the establishment of diplomatic ties between Belgium and Poland. Moreover, a street in the vicinity of the Mniszech Palace was named after King Albert I following his death in 1934. Secondly, State Secretary Wilczek of the Polish Ministry of Culture and Art offered Her Royal Highness a sightseeing tour around Warsaw to show her the building frenzy that had taken hold of the city. Elisabeth was especially in awe of the efforts to meticulously restore the war-torn Old Town to its former glory.[194] One cannot help but think that State Secretary Wilczek also made a stop at the ruins of the Mniszech Palace to unveil the reconstruction scheme personally to her. Wilczek would have undoubtedly pointed out the symbolic value of Belgium reconstructing the Mniszech Palace, framing it as an architectural expression of the cordial relations between her husband King Albert I and Poland during the interwar period.

Her Royal Highness was an ardent supporter of the reconstruction scheme and did her utmost to build up support in Belgian diplomatic and political circles. Being sold on the idea, she sought support from Minister Plenipotentiary Count Hadelin de Meeûs d'Argenteuil. The Belgian head of mission had a personal connection with her as his uncle André de Meeûs d'Argenteuil (1879-1972) was the Grandmaster of the House of Queen Elisabeth. As the cousin of the queen's main confidant, Count de Meeûs d'Argenteuil had a tendency to go the extra mile for Her Royal Highness. In the context of her visit to Warsaw, for instance, he threw a marvellous reception for the queen and over 180 esteemed guests at the legation residence on 19 March 1955. In total, he paid 216,000 Belgian francs (53,000 euros) out of his own pocket on new furniture, artwork and food and beverages such as lobster, salmon, champagne, patisserie and ice cream. Given his cordial relations with Queen Elisabeth, de Meeûs d'Argenteuil notified his superiors that these expenditures were an expression of his personal devotion to the Belgian monarchy and did not have to be reimbursed.[195]

Queen Elisabeth called upon de Meeûs d'Argenteuil to gain political support for the reconstruction scheme. In the eyes of the head of mission, it was a nice prospect to move the Belgian legation into a majestic and spacious palace. As a seasoned diplomat, de Meeûs d'Argenteuil introduced the building scheme to Belgian politicians to forge a coalition of the willing. It is no coincidence that the liberal MP Ernest Demuyter (1893-1963) brought up the topic in parliament. In his capacity as chairman of the Belgian-Polish Friendship Association, Ernest Demuyter frequently visited the Warsaw legation and had an excellent relationship with de Meeûs d'Argenteuil. Coming to his friend's aid, Demuyter put the topic on the political agenda in Brussels. During a parliamentary debate on 24 November 1955, Demuyter urged Foreign Minister Spaak to accept the offer to rebuild the Mniszech Palace at once.[196] However, Spaak could do little as the Ministry of Finance refused to allocate funding. Moreover, Spaak's track record with regard to the Washington chancery had demonstrated his lack of appetite to commission purpose-built embassies.

Spaak may have been disinterested in the project altogether but he did elevate the Belgian legation to an embassy in April 1957 following several formal requests from the Polish People's Republic to do so. From a geopolitical point of view, such a decision was a significant diplomatic gesture. At the time, Belgium was only represented by means of a legation in the other communist states of Czechoslovakia, Hungary, Bulgaria and Romania making up the Eastern Bloc. The Polish authorities greatly appreciated the establishment of an embassy but its offer to reconstruct the Mniszech Palace continued to fall on deaf ears.

As such, the Mniszech project failed to materialise in the mid-1950s, much to the frustration of de Meeûs d'Argenteuil, Queen Elisabeth and the Polish government. However, in a similar fashion to Ambassador Silvercruys, they would get indirect support in greenlighting the project from an unexpected source: the Belgian electorate participating in the 1958 elections.

Wigny for the Win: Constructing Embassies, a Matter of National Prestige

The 1958 elections reshuffled the balance of power. The socialist-liberal coalition government lost its majority and was replaced by a homogenous Christian-democratic majority. With Spaak and the Socialists cast into the opposition, the Christian-democratic strongman Pierre Wigny became the new foreign minister. He had a keen interest in architecture and urban planning. Moreover, he was an ardent supporter of commissioning purpose-built embassies to boost national prestige abroad. Wigny confided in his diary that it was his personal ambition to house embassies in marvellous and stately buildings.[197] As such, the Polish proposal piqued his interest as he was determined to secure funding for the project.

This was, however, easier said than done. Finance Minister Jean Van Houtte (1907-1991), one of Wigny's fellow party members, drastically cut back on funding because of budgetary setbacks in the state finances. Whereas 90 million Belgian francs (20.7 million euros) had been allocated to diplomatic and consular housing in 1958, Van Houtte reduced the budget to 70 million Belgian francs (15.9 million euros) for 1959.[198] Such budget cuts did not go down well with Wigny. He was not afraid to openly criticise Van Houtte and his budget cuts. During a parliamentary debate in 1959, the liberal MP Adolphe Van Glabbeke criticised the government for reducing the diplomatic housing budget. At a time when Belgium was establishing embassies in newly independent countries, Van Glabbeke argued, it was absurd to reduce the real estate budget. Wigny's response to the criticism illustrates his strained relationship with the Ministry of Finance:

> If I may, Mr. Van Glabbeke, I would like to answer one of your questions before this House. You asked why we skimp on embassies and the purchase of buildings and land, which are necessary to maintain our prestige abroad, when this is not even an expense but an investment. My answer is the same. I think these budget cuts are bad.[199]

By complaining out loud in parliament, he called out Van Houtte and his budgetary policies. To a certain extent, his criticism vividly underscores the feeling of powerlessness Wigny experienced. Wigny could make up all the building plans he wanted but his efforts would be rebuffed without the support of the Ministry of Finance.

Nonetheless, Foreign Minister Wigny went above and beyond to revive the Mniszech palace project. He instructed Ambassador de Meeûs d'Argenteuil to start negotiations with the Polish Ministry of Foreign Affairs and personally wielded his influence in Brussels to receive funding. Ambassador de Meeûs d'Argenteuil put his skills as a negotiator to good use as he struck a favourable deal. The Polish Ministry of Foreign Affairs had re-estimated the building costs and believed that 15 million Belgian francs (3.4 million euros) would be sufficient to reconstruct the Mniszech Palace. If Belgium would put this amount of money on the table, the rebuilt palace would be offered to Belgium through a 99-year lease. From Belgium's point of view, the deal was far more beneficial than the original cost estimates of 45 million Belgian francs (12.3 million euros).

In his correspondence with Brussels, Ambassador de Meeûs d'Argenteuil praised himself for cutting the deal.[200] Meanwhile, the Polish government sang a very different tune as it argued that the Polish Ministry of Foreign Affairs had been far too generous. In all their enthusiasm to get the Belgians on board, Polish officials had grotesquely underestimated the construction costs. As the project would eventually cost more than expected, it was the Polish state that had to make up the difference out of its own pocket. As one can expect, the Polish Ministry of Foreign Affairs received backlash from the highest political echelons for this financial miscalculation. It was argued that they had practically given Belgium an embassy tied up in a little pink ribbon.[201] In retrospect, the tendency of Brussels to call upon its ambassadors in commissioning a purpose-built embassy was thus a double-edged sword. On the one hand, ambassadors were ideal for striking favourable deals but on the other hand they were often not cut out for supervising building project, as the case of the Canberra embassy made abundantly clear.

As part of the negotiations, de Meeûs d'Argenteuil discussed the embassy's overall design with the Polish authorities. It was agreed that the exteriors would be an exact copy of the pre-war Mniszech Palace, underscoring that the reconstruction project was intrinsically linked to restoring historically significant buildings to their former glory. By emphasising the restoration of the building's exteriors, the Polish state adhered to the tendency in architectural thought to consider the façade as the frontispiece where political and cultural meaning are expressed.[202] The restoration of the palace's façade was framed as an architectural expression of the government's aspiration to retain the historic character of Warsaw when reconstructing the war-torn capital. In reality, however, the careful restoration of the façade was actually an architectural *trompe-l'œil* as the interiors of the rebuilt Mniszech Palace would be fundamentally different to the pre-war design. As part of the deal, the Polish authorities gave the Belgian Ministry of Foreign Affairs *carte blanche* to rearrange the interior layout as it liked. Whereas the pre-war layout mainly featured spacious halls, the interior of the reconstructed Mniszech Palace was to be modified to accommodate an embassy with offices, living quarters and guestrooms.

Both parties also agreed on who would be responsible for reconstructing the palace. As befits a communist country where goods and services are provided by the state, the People's Republic of Poland would take overall control of the project. To this end, the state-run agency *Centrali Eksportu Kompletnych Obiektów Przemysłowych* (CEKOP) or Complete Industrial Facilities Export Centre would manage the entire project. CEKOP's core business entailed the construction of industrial facilities abroad and its officials were accustomed to working together with foreign clients.

CEKOP hired the renowned Polish architect Mieczysław Kuzma (1907-1983) for the project at hand. A graduate of the Warsaw University of Technology, Kuzma was appointed as professor in architecture and art history at his alma mater in the late 1930s. In the post-war period, Kuzma would go on to play a leading role in the restoration of historical buildings in Warsaw.[203] As the Polish authorities unveiled plans to reconstruct Warsaw's Old Town, they made Kuzma chief designer of the project. He was appointed director of the state-owned Monuments Conservation Workshop. Its workforce of engineers, decorators, painters and sculptors was specialised in rebuilding historical premises. In the case of rebuilding the Mniszech Palace, CEKOP both called upon the expertise of architect Kuzma and the Monuments Conservation Workshop. Ambassador de Meeûs d'Argenteuil gave his blessing to CEKOP to work together with the Polish architect. From the Belgian point of view, CEKOP's hands-on approach was a welcome change from what was simultaneously transpiring in Canberra on Diplomatic Hill. Whereas Ambassador Willy Stevens had to attend meetings with the Australian architects and make visits to the construction site, Ambassador de Meeûs d'Argenteuil could consider himself lucky that the entire building project was outsourced to CEKOP. Being a head of mission in a communist state had its perks, especially in the context of building a new embassy.

Meanwhile, on the home front, the lobbying efforts of Foreign Minister Wigny bore fruit. As the renegotiated deal with the Polish authorities would significantly reduce the price tag, Finance Minister Van Houtte eventually allocated funding to the project. In September 1959, Wigny dispatched the young ministry official Étienne Davignon to Warsaw to seal the deal. Davignon handed over a cheque of 15 million Belgian francs (3.4 million euros) to the Polish Ministry of Foreign Affairs. In the grand scheme of things, this was a considerable amount of money with regard to Belgian diplomatic housing, underscoring how Pierre Wigny spared no expense to boost national prestige abroad through diplomatic architecture. Queen Elisabeth and Ambassador de Meeûs d'Argenteuil could count themselves lucky that there was someone at the wheel of the Ministry of Foreign Affairs who saw the added value of investing in diplomatic housing.

Kuzma's Design: Converting the Mniszech Palace Into an Embassy

Having secured the necessary funding, architect Kuzma set about designing the Mniszech Palace. In a similar fashion to his other restoration projects in the Old Town, Kuzma's work was tremendously facilitated by the existence of a pre-war inventory of the Mniszech Palace. Moreover, the palace's ground floor was virtually intact which gave him a clear indication of the palace's dimensions.

Already on 15 December 1959, just three months after handing over the cheque, Professor Kuzma completed his plans. The new Mniszech Palace (Fig. 29) would be made up of a brick structure with a built area of just under 900 m². The brick structure was to be covered by lime mortar mixed with sandstone and marble that would give the building its distinctive white exteriors. The front façade was meticulously modelled after the pre-war Mniszech Palace, featuring the front portico made up of Corinthian columns, a repetitive fenestration pattern with window frames accentuated in height, and a pitched roof covered with red tiles. However, when comparing both designs, it becomes apparent that Kuzma made some slight adjustments to the front façade. The three windows situated just under the triangular pediment, for instance, were each fitted with a Baroque-style balcony with balustrades of wrought iron. These balconies were strategically positioned under the pediment that served as roofed point of entry where guests could be dropped off by car. From the balconies, the ambassador could greet guests upon their arrival at the embassy. Another noteworthy change to the original design was the addition of a series of small dormers that gave the majestic palace a more domestic appearance.

Whereas the alterations to the exterior were quite limited, Kuzma profoundly rearranged the spatial layout. At the request of the Belgian Ministry of Foreign Affairs, the interior layout (Fig. 30) had to be adjusted to the building's new function as the seat of an embassy. In contrast to the pre-war interior layout that featured a large hall and dining room, the ground floor of the new Mniszech Palace would house the chancery

Figure 29: The Mniszech Palace, 1959

where the offices of Ambassador Hadelin de Meeûs d'Argenteuil and his diplomatic staff were to be situated. In a similar fashion to the embassy offices in Washington, D.C. and Canberra, the usual cellular office layout also made its appearance in the Warsaw chancery. The most spacious office was to be allocated to Ambassador de Meeûs d'Argenteuil to accentuate his status as head of the embassy. His office was to be covered with a light-coloured parquet flooring with a striking star-shaped pattern.

From his office, the ambassador had an excellent view of the embassy gardens. Immersed in greenery, the garden's focal point was the small fountain on a paved, sandstone terrace. CEKOP labelled the garden a true asset, adding an atmosphere of privacy to the embassy where Belgian diplomats could have one-on-one talks with their guests in a tranquil setting.[204] To ensure that the wheels of the bureaucratic machine ran smoothly, the diplomats' offices were flanked by workspaces for personal assistants and typists to efficiently process the paperwork produced on a daily basis. The Warsaw chancery would also be the place where people could conduct their bureaucratic business. To this end, a visa section with front offices and an adjacent waiting room were strategically positioned near the main entrance. In a similar fashion to the Canberra embassy offices, the Warsaw chancery also included an apartment for the caretaker couple who would keep the Mniszech Palace neat and tidy. Interestingly, Ambassador de Meeûs d'Argenteuil had his preferences with regard to the background of the caretaker couple. The ambassador stressed that

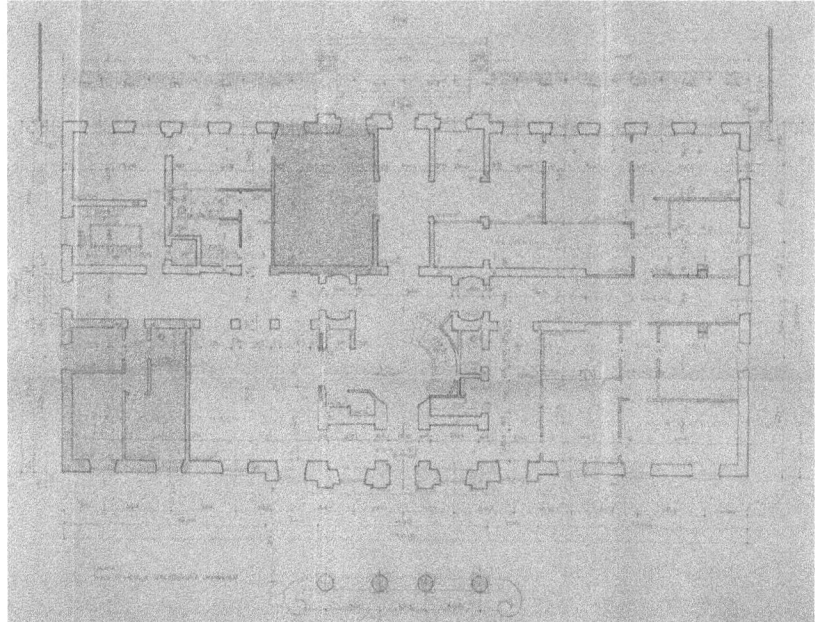

Legenda

Ambassador's Office
Living Quarters of the Caretaker
Visa Section

Based on: Belgian Embassy Archives Warsaw, Architect Mieczysław Kuzma, 1959.

Figure 30: The Mniszech Palace's ground floor, 1959

the couple had to have Belgian nationality and should not have any young children.[205] Apparently, the thought of toddlers running around the stately embassy sent shivers down his spine.

The ambassadorial residence was to be situated on the upper floors of the palace and could be reached by an *escalier d'honneur* (Fig. 31) or honorary staircase. In addition to connecting adjoining spaces, the honorary staircase was the high-end gateway to the residence, indicating to visitors that they were approaching the most prestigious floor of the embassy building. Therefore, Kuzma turned the honorary staircase into the architectural focal point of the embassy's interior by means of both

Figure 31: The residence's honorary staircase, 1962

composition and choice of material. The Polish architect designed a spiral staircase made of reinforced concrete, the dynamic shape of which was further accentuated by the sophisticated circular marble flooring near the staircase. To ensure that the spiral stairway lived up to its designation as honorary stairway, Kuzma opted to cover the steps with white marble.

Figure 32: The *salon jaune*, 1962

The marble used for the stairway had been mined in the quarries of Silesia to give it a clear Polish touch, echoing the metaphor of *une machine-à-représenter*. Its balustrade was made of wrought iron that was decorated with copper ornamentation. To top it all off, a large crystal chandelier was included as the main decorative light fixture.

Upon climbing the spiral staircase, visitors would make their way to the ambassadorial residence situated on the first floor and to the mansard roof which were considered the beating heart of the embassy. Kuzma accentuated their importance in the exteriors by making the windows of the first floor slightly higher than those on the ground floor. In line with the residence's dual function as living quarters and venue for social gatherings, the first floor included a gallery, two large reception lounges, a large dining room with an adjoining kitchen, and residential apartments for Ambassador de Meeûs d'Argenteuil and his wife, and guests staying at the embassy. Each apartment comprised a spacious drawing room, a bedroom with a walk-in wardrobe, and a bathroom. The mansard was also made up of residential apartments for the ambassador's children and the domestic staff who kept the embassy up and running. When designing the interiors, Kuzma paid particular attention to the large reception room on the first floor that would bear the nickname *salon jaune* (Fig. 32) because of the various yellow elements in the interior. Conceived to be the high-end venue for receptions, lectures and music concerts, Kuzma made sure that it would be a fitting scenery to receive guests in style by turning it into the most prestigious space. The *salon jaune* would be covered with the same light-coloured parquet flooring with the distinctive star-shaped pattern used in the ambassador's office. The room's focal point was a fireplace lavishly adorned with white marble. Traditionally perceived as the epitome of domesticity, the fireplace was included to provide an extra boost of heat to the spacious room while simultaneously evoking a sense of cosiness. The most striking elements of the reception room were the yellow columns. These columns were not structural elements; rather, they had been added for the sake of decoration, giving a more stately character to the room. The columns' richly decorated crowns were handcrafted by artisans employed at the Monuments Conservation Workshop. The room's ceiling was to be detailed by fine lines of Czech gold leaf. Crystal chandeliers were added to tie the room together.

Constructing in the Cold (War)

The Belgian Ministry of Foreign Affairs approved Kuzma's plans, seeing the new Mniszech Palace as the perfect setting to house its embassy. The fact that the building project was supervised by a state enterprise meant that securing a building permit was merely a formality. Already on 21 January 1960, Warsaw's municipal authorities granted a building permit to CEKOP. This stood in stark contrast to the course of action of Canberra's local authorities in commissioning the Belgian embassy. Whereas the local authorities and their objections gave Ambassador Willy Stevens headaches, Ambassador de Meeûs d'Argenteuil could count on the full cooperation of all levels of government in Poland. Commissioning a purpose-built embassy in concert with a communist regime had its advantages for Belgium. In January 1960, construction works along Senatorska Street began. Given his personal interest in the building project, de Meeûs d'Argenteuil frequently visited the building site and sent updates to Brussels. In the first months, construction works were hampered by the harsh winter of 1959-1960. By the beginning of March 1960, however, the building project picked up steam as Ambassador de Meeûs d'Argenteuil proudly reported that local construction workers were about to pour the concrete foundation. From then on, the building phase proceeded without noteworthy hiccups along the way.

Even on 15 February 1961, construction works on the new Belgian embassy continued unabated. That very day, news spread across Warsaw that Patrice Lumumba (1925-1961), the first democratically elected prime minister of the Democratic Republic of the Congo, had been executed by the secessionist regime of Katanga. As the Belgian government supported the Katangese secession and was involved in Lumumba's execution, mass demonstrations were held in front of over 60 Belgian embassies and consulates across the globe.[206] These demonstrations underscored the ambiguous relationship between diplomatic architecture and the popular masses. Traditionally conceived by sending states as architectural expressions to legitimate themselves and radiate nationhood on foreign soil, diplomatic buildings can overnight turn into arenas of contestation and conflict in times of political turmoil, adding a sinister side to their representational function. Demonstrators stormed the Belgian embassies in Belgrade and New Delhi, wreaking havoc on the interiors and looting valuable items such as furniture and artwork. Meanwhile, in Cairo, the Belgian embassy was set ablaze by rioters.

The Mniszech Palace, however, remained an oasis of tranquillity. This stood in stark contrast to events transpiring elsewhere in Warsaw. Less than four kilometres south of the Mniszech Palace, hundreds of Polish rioters stormed the Belgian embassy offices at Starościńska Street. They turned the Warsaw chancery into a scene of iconoclasm to avenge the death of Lumumba. The Polish rioters damaged furniture and typewriters, smashed the windows, set fire to archival records, and smeared red paint on the walls to symbolise that the Belgian government had blood on its hands.[207] The Warsaw police did arrive on the scene prior to the attack, but stood by idly as the rioters trespassed on the embassy. The attack on the Belgian embassy needs to be seen in the light of the Cold War. Against the backdrop of the Cold War rivalry, the communist world strongly criticised Western European countries such as Belgium for politically intervening in their former colonies.[208]

If the Polish rioters truly wanted to strike a serious blow against Belgium, one would assume that they would also target the Mniszech Palace that was being rebuilt. The palace was, however, left untouched. Two reasons come to mind. On the one hand, the Mniszech Palace could have been, in the eyes of the Polish rioters, far more than just the new seat of the Belgian embassy. It was first and foremost a historic landmark in the streetscape, a part of the city's architectural heritage that should be treasured. On the other hand, it is plausible that Polish government officials warned the rioters that the building site was off limits because the Polish People's Republic was co-financing the project.

Cold War tensions also manifested themselves on the construction site along Senatorska Street. The Belgian Ministry of Foreign Affairs wanted to install a state-of-the-art electronic system. Therefore, the Ministry reached out to the American technology company Honeywell. However, CEKOP did not take kindly to the fact that Belgium reached out to a foreign company and it felt somewhat offended that Polish technological knowhow was apparently deemed to be inferior. From a political point of view, the fact that the foreign company was American was especially delicate given the fact that Cold War tensions between East and West had culminated with the Berlin Crisis of 1961. Amidst these growing tensions between the capitalist and communist power blocs, one cannot help but think that Brussels had ulterior motives in entrusting the installation of the palace's electrical system to an American firm instead of CEKOP. It may well have been that the Ministry feared that Polish secret agents would infiltrate the construction site and install bugging devices during the installation of the electrical system. In doing so, they could tap confidential conversations in an embassy of a NATO country.

Such reasoning is not that far-fetched. In the summer of 1962, American security personnel inspected the construction site of the new American embassy in Warsaw. During their sweep of the site, they uncovered a hidden battery to power listening devices.[209] Two years later, when the chancery was nearing its completion, security agents discovered that the offices were bugged with dozens of listening devices. Whether this incident truly influenced the Belgian diplomatic corps remains unclear but it is telling that ministry officials went above and beyond to collaborate with Honeywell. It was no small feat for Freddy Cogels, the inspector of diplomatic and consular missions, to convince CEKOP to work with an American firm. Putting his diplomatic skills as bridgebuilder to good use, Cogels eventually succeeded in bringing CEKOP officials and Honeywell engineers around the table and letting them work together on the Warsaw project. In his memoirs, Cogels proudly calls this capitalist-communist collaboration at the height of the Cold War one of his greatest accomplishments as inspector of diplomatic and consular missions.[210]

If Freddy Cogels had had his way, he would have also played a leading role in furnishing and decorating the palace's interiors. Inspector Cogels had taken steps to professionalise the real estate department by calling upon the expertise of the Brussels-based antique shop Michiels. Upon hearing that

Lydia Michiels would visit the Mniszech Palace to discuss the furnishings and interior decoration, Ambassador de Meeûs d'Argenteuil vividly spoke out against such a move. Seeing Lydia Michiels as an intruder who had to disappear from the stage as soon as possible, the count informed Cogels that she was unqualified for the project at hand. In a derogatory remark, he referred to Lydia Michiels as nothing more than the wife of some upholsterer whose line of work would put the majestic interiors of the Mniszech Palace to shame.[211] Describing Michiels' approach as too contemporary and eclectic, de Meeûs d'Argenteuil advocated to Cogels for the purchase of period furniture in order to be in sync with the palatial architecture of the Mniszech Palace. The diverging views underscore the tensions that frequently manifested themselves between ambassadors and ministry officials working in Brussels. As the person who would work and live in the new embassy, de Meeûs d'Argenteuil reasoned that he was entitled to choose the furniture even though the Ministry of Foreign Affairs was paying for it.

In a true diplomatic spirit, a compromise was eventually reached to smooth things over between Cogels and de Meeûs d'Argenteuil. Lydia Michiels would still visit the embassy and share her advice while Ambassador de Meeûs d'Argenteuil was awarded 200,000 Belgian francs (44,000 euros) to purchase furniture to his own liking. As befits his aristocratic background, the count used the money to buy Louis XVI armchairs, sofas and chests of drawers on the local market.[212] Moreover, the obligatory mahogany dining table and library bookcase also found their place in the new embassy. In accordance with this traditional furnishing style, a series of tapestries was selected by de Meeûs d'Argenteuil and Cogels. Near the spiral staircase, they hung a large tapestry depicting a country landscape. It was an 18th century copy of a tapestry originally made by a manufacturer in Brussels following a commission from Sigismund II Augustus (1520-1572), the King of Poland and Grand Duke of Lithuania. By including this artwork, de Meeûs d'Argenteuil and Cogels aimed to showcase national craftsmanship that was intrinsically linked to Poland.

Showcasing the Mniszech Palace: A PR offensive

On 10 November 1962, CEKOP officially handed over the keys to Ambassador Count Hadelin de Meeûs d'Argenteuil. Five days later, on 15 November 1962, the count opened the doors for the palace's grand inauguration. The count had purposely picked this date to coincide with King's

Figure 33: The Mniszech Palace, 1962

Day, a holiday in honour of the King of the Belgians, underscoring the royal connection to the commission of the embassy. The inauguration ceremony was a true society event. The Belgian ambassador threw a well-attended reception in the lavish interiors, welcoming over 700 high-profile guests. Among those present were the members of the Polish Council of State, MPs, representatives of the Warsaw Chamber of Commerce, scholars of the Polish Academy of Sciences, Warsaw's *corps diplomatique*, the Belgian community living in Poland, and journalists.

The inaugural ceremony was an excellent networking event to further cement bilateral ties with the political elite of Poland. As the ceremony was the diplomatic equivalent of a house-warming party, Ambassador de Meeûs d'Argenteuil guided attendees through the new seat of the Belgian embassy. The attendees were in awe of the reconstructed Mniszech Palace (Fig. 33). A journalist from the Belgian magazine *L'Éventail*, for instance, was dazzled by the neoclassical palace with its lavishly furnished and decorated interiors, describing to his readers how the building was an architectural monument of outstanding class.[213] He deemed it the perfect type of diplomatic building, underscoring how contemporary voices in Belgium continued to uphold the idea that embassies should be housed in stately buildings with historic value in order to ensure prestige.

In line with the pompous character of the occasion, the ambassador made a solemn speech in which he expressed his hope that the reconstructed Mniszech Palace would open a new chapter in its centuries-old history and would become, for many years to come, the home of a cordial Belgian-Polish friendship in Warsaw. On the ambassador's suggestion, the Polish architect Kuzma was awarded an honorary Belgian medal for his efforts. Meanwhile, de Meeûs d'Argenteuil scathingly remarked to his superiors that he was still waiting on the medal Spaak had promised him, portraying himself as the unsung hero of the building project.[214]

Building on the success of the event, Ambassador de Meeûs d'Argenteuil pulled out all the stops to put his new embassy in the popular spotlight. To this end, he opened the palace's doors to the cameras of the *Polska Kronika Filmowa* or Polish Film Chronicle whose newsreels were shown in cinemas across Poland. Polish cinemagoers were shown footage of the newly built Mniszech Palace, while a voice-over narrator praised both the Belgian government and CEKOP for their efforts to restore one of Warsaw's architectural landmarks to its former glory. Additionally, de Meeûs d'Argenteuil once again joined forces with CEKOP to publish a richly illustrated booklet on the history of the Mniszech Palace and its recent reconstruction. The booklet served as a gift for guests visiting the Belgian embassy and was an instant success. Already in June 1963, 500 additional copies were printed as demand exceeded supply.

The ambassador sent a copy to Queen Elisabeth who had been present at the very beginning of the building project. She was very touched by the gesture and instructed André de Meeûs d'Argenteuil to pass on her words of praise to his nephew posted in Warsaw. In his letter, André de Meeûs d'Argenteuil highlighted how Elisabeth was in awe of the photos of the reconstructed Mniszech Palace, calling the interior a magnificent setting for hosting sensational receptions.[215] Booklets were also sent to fellow Belgian ambassadors. Although sending the booklet was a friendly gesture, one cannot help but think that Ambassador de Meeûs d'Argenteuil also wanted to brag about his stunning new embassy to his peers. After all, in terms of diplomatic housing, he was now in a different league to many of his fellow ambassadors.

Interestingly, Ambassador de Meeûs d'Argenteuil wanted to capitalise on his involvement in the building project in order to advance his diplomatic career. By 1962, rumours began to circulate that the position of Belgian ambassador to the USSR would become vacant. As an ambassadorship to the Soviet Union was his dream posting, de Meeûs d'Argenteuil announced his candidacy in a letter to Brussels, in which he called himself the perfect candidate for the job. In an effort to convince his superiors that he was well suited to represent Belgium in the heartland of the communist world, the count tooted his own horn by bringing up his prominent role in reconstructing the Mniszech Palace:

> It took a certain amount of ingenuity and a great deal of persistence to bring a project of this nature to fruition in a communist environment, where nothing, especially at that time, could compare with our ideas. It is well known that I devised the financial, administrative and practical solutions that were to serve as precedents for other Western missions, at the same time as I gave my country diplomatic headquarters that are both highly representative and functional.[216]

Reading between the lines, Count de Meeûs Argenteuil made the case to his superiors that if a Western ambassador, such as himself, were capable of bringing something as complex and demanding as reconstructing a palace to a good end alongside a communist regime, then he would undoubtedly be a fine ambassador to Moscow. Unfortunately for him, Spaak begged to differ. Instead, the socialist strongman offered him a diplomatic posting in South America. Far from thrilled at the prospect of packing his bags for South America, Count de Meeûs d'Argenteuil declined the offer and was instead recalled to Brussels where he was reassigned to office duty. However, as far as Chapter II is concerned, Spaak's suggested change of scenery reflects a shift in the geographical focus of this book towards South America where yet another receiving state incentivised Belgium to construct a new embassy in the late 1950s.

C. BUILDING IN BRASÍLIA, BRAZIL: MOVING OUT OF ONE'S COMFORT ZONE

Developing a Capital From Scratch: The Brasília Project

In 1956, the newly elected Brazilian President, Juscelino Kubitschek de Oliveira (1902-1976), revived the plans to build a new capital city in the heartland of Brazil. This massive urban project was to be the architectural expression of his '50 Years in Five' scheme. As the name suggests, President Kubitschek wanted to advance Brazil economically by 50 years in just five. The ambitious programme called for the nation's rapid industrialisation and modernisation through large infrastructural works. Moreover, the plan focused on the economic development of mainland Brazil, as most economic activity was still centred around the Atlantic port cities. In an effort to speed up the development of mainland Brazil, a new inland capital city with a new road network was to be constructed from scratch. By relocating the capital to a central position, Kubitschek wanted to give a serious impetus to his massive development initiative.[217] Interestingly enough, there was a Belgian link as to where the new capital city was to be located. The Belgian army engineer Louis Ferdinand Cruls (1848-1908) supervised the commission tasked with selecting the site for the future capital.[218] Cruls selected a site on the Brazilian Highlands situated some 1,000 kilometres north of Rio de Janeiro.

Cruls' decision would, however, have no real world effects until Kubitschek revived the massive urban project. In 1957, the design entry submitted by the Brazilian architect and urban planner Lúcio Costa (1902-1998) was selected as the blueprint for the new capital that was given the name Brasília. Costa's urban scheme, often compared to the shape of a bird in flight, comprised two intersecting axes that were to be the capital's main thoroughfares. Conceived as a monumental city, the majestic avenues stretched further than the naked eye can see. Inspired by Le Corbusier's Radiant City, Costa clearly defined the city's administrative and residential zones. The municipal centre, for instance, was to be located on the east end of the east-west axis, while housing for state officials was to be constructed along the north-south axis with its distinctive curved shape.

Meanwhile, the commission to design Brasília's grand public buildings was assigned to the Brazilian architect Oscar Niemeyer (1907-2012) in 1956. At the start of his career, Niemeyer was influenced by Le Corbusier. In 1936, he had the opportunity to work with his idol to design the office building of the Ministry of Education and Health in Rio de Janeiro. While working with Le Corbusier, it began to dawn on Niemeyer that the universalistic claims of modernist architecture were out of touch with the particularities of Brazil's culture and climate. He convinced Le Corbusier to include blinds in front of the building's windows and a popular Portuguese piece of tile-work to pay tribute to local building traditions. From then on, Niemeyer denounced the hard-edged universalist ideas of modernist architecture and instead opted for a regionally inspired kind of modernism. In contrast to the straighter lines traditionally associated with modernist architecture, Niemeyer's designs were characterised by curving geometric shapes in an effort to break away from the sterile aesthetic traditionally associated with modernism. He saw free and sensual curves as particularly Brazilian, claiming that curves are intrinsically linked to the country's mountains, rivers and, being the womaniser that he was, the bodies of Brazilian women.[219]

His line of work was praised around the world. The Belgian architectural community, for instance, was in awe of the Niemeyer's work. The architecture magazine *Bouwen en Wonen* praised Niemeyer for his innovative designs, stating that it was a prerequisite to build in such an imaginative way because of Brazil's wonderful landscape.[220] Moreover, the magazine framed Niemeyer as a guiding light for architects who wanted to free themselves from the shackles of tradition and convention. Architecturally, Brasília was to be the epitome of his innovative and imaginative take on architecture. Intended to be a monumental modernist city that marked a new dawn for Brazil, Brasília and its architectural landmarks were characterised by all-white buildings with curving geometric shapes immersed in grasslands. The most visually striking structures are the National Congress, with its distinctive bowl housing the Chamber of Representatives and dome housing the Senate, and the Cathedral of Brasília with its futuristic hyperboloid structure.

As is so often the case with planned capital cities, the Brasília project drew flak from public opinion. Belgian diplomats in Rio de Janeiro sent detailed reports to Brussels on the controversy surrounding the project. Political opponents of Kubitschek argued that nobody in their right mind would develop a new capital city from scratch. Framing it as a megalomanic project through which Kubitschek wanted to boost his ego, they reasoned that the money would be better spent on improving the living conditions in the existing cities.[221] In their reports, the Belgian diplomats also gave their own reading of Brasília. Following a visit to the building site of Brasília in October 1957, Ambassador René Van Meerbeke (1896-1971) raised serious doubts about whether the Brazilian people would ever embrace the new capital:

> The site of the future capital is on a plateau in the state of Goiás, which is fairly arid and desolate. It's an austere natural setting, very different from that of Rio de Janeiro and the eternal beauty of the Bay of Guanabara 'the Superb'. [...] Looking at the current site of this future city, one wonders whether the Brazilians, who are rather resistant to austerity, will have the tenacity and courage to settle in the new capital, where we can expect a particularly high cost of living, since everything will have to be brought in from elsewhere.[222]

Moving the Corps Diplomatique to Brasília: Making an Offer One Cannot Refuse

The Brazilian government could construct all the shiny public buildings it wanted but Brasília could only claim its place as the nation's true capital if sending states would leave Rio de Janeiro and move their embassies to the new capital. Incentivising sending states to do so was easier said than done in the late 1950s. Firstly, the initial building frenzy focused on the construction of government buildings and housing for officials. The private real estate market was still in its infancy. This would make it very difficult for sending states to purchase or lease premises to house their embassies. Secondly, Brasília had, and to a large extent still has, a serious image problem. In a similar fashion to Canberra, the capital is principally known as the city of government and bureaucracy.[223] Whereas Rio de Janeiro is widely considered to be the nation's cultural, recreational, and culinary capital, Brasília has a far less vibrant city life. To put it bluntly, the Kubitschek government was asking diplomats to leave Rio's white sandy beaches and entertainment industry behind and move to a ghost town in the middle of the rain forest. Thirdly, and most importantly, the Brazilian Ministry of Foreign Affairs was still located in Rio de Janeiro in the late 1950s. As the headquarters of its main speaking partner were still situated in Rio de Janeiro, it would be very impractical for the *corps diplomatique* to take up residence in a city situated almost 1,000 kilometres further inland.

The Kubitschek government was keenly aware that it had to create favourable conditions for sending states to move to Brasília. Therefore, it spared no expense. In a similar fashion to the development of Canberra's Diplomatic Hill, it was decided that a diplomatic district would be created where sending states could construct embassies. This district was given the rather unimaginative name of *Setor de Embaixadas Sul* or South Embassy Sector. The Embassy Sector was conveniently located on the southern edge of the municipal centre in close proximity to where political hotspots such as the Brazilian Ministry of Foreign Affairs and the National Congress would be erected. Adhering to the capital's neat and orderly urban fabric, the Embassy Sector was to be made up of large blocks consisting of rectangular sites. Interestingly, the main street of the Embassy Sector was named *Avenida das Nações* or Avenue of Nations. In so doing, the Brazilian authorities resorted to the nomenclature of world exhibitions that traditionally had an Avenue of Nations on the fairgrounds where national pavilions were clustered together. In terms of allocating building sites, Brasília's planning authority, NOVACAP, directed sending states to a particular site. NOVACAP approached each sending state with an invitation to acquire land. The terms and conditions to acquire land were far more generous than the Australian Crown Lease. The building plots were donated to sending states instead of being leased. Moreover, the building plots were very sizeable, having an average surface area of 25,000 m². In return for these favourable circumstances, NOVACAP imposed terms and conditions to sending states. Sending states could never sell the donated land or their diplomatic premises to other embassies or private individuals. As such, acquiring land was a clear commitment of the sending state that they would stay in the Embassy Sector for the long haul. Additionally, diplomatic missions had to submit their building plans to NOVACAP for review. Finally, foreign countries were obliged to develop their plot of land within two years following the move of the Brazilian Ministry of Foreign Affairs to Brasília.

NOVACAP called upon the aid of Brazil's diplomatic corps to pique foreign governments' interest in acquiring land in the Embassy Sector. Hugo Gouthier de Oliveira Gondim (1909-1992), the Brazilian ambassador to Belgium, personally introduced the plans to Foreign Minister Pierre Wigny. Wigny was immediately open to the idea and entered into negotiations with the Brazilian ambassador. Wigny's enthusiasm stands in stark contrast to the wait-and-see attitude of his predecessor Spaak. Wigny's eagerness is a testament to his keen interest in architecture and urban planning. This interest had already showed itself during his tenure as minister of the colonies in the late 1940s. During his time in office, Wigny laid the groundwork for the construction of 40,000 prefabricated houses to tackle the housing crisis affecting everyday life in the Belgian Congo.[224] In honour of Wigny, who had been present at the very beginning of the massive building programme, a new residential district near Léopoldville was called Cité Pierre Wigny. The commission to construct the Cité Pierre Wigny was awarded to the Belgian wood and furniture producer De Coene in 1952, the very brand that would go on to furnish the Washington embassy offices in 1956.[225] This underscores the excellent ties between the Belgian state and De Coene at the time and helps to explain why the Flemish wood company was the go-to furniture brand for the Ministry. Even though the Cité Pierre Wigny was only constructed after his ministership, Pierre Wigny closely followed its development. Framing the residential district as the architectural legacy of his ministership, the Christian-democratic strongman collected aerial photographs and blueprints of the site.[226]

BUILDING EMBASSIES ON DEMAND 149

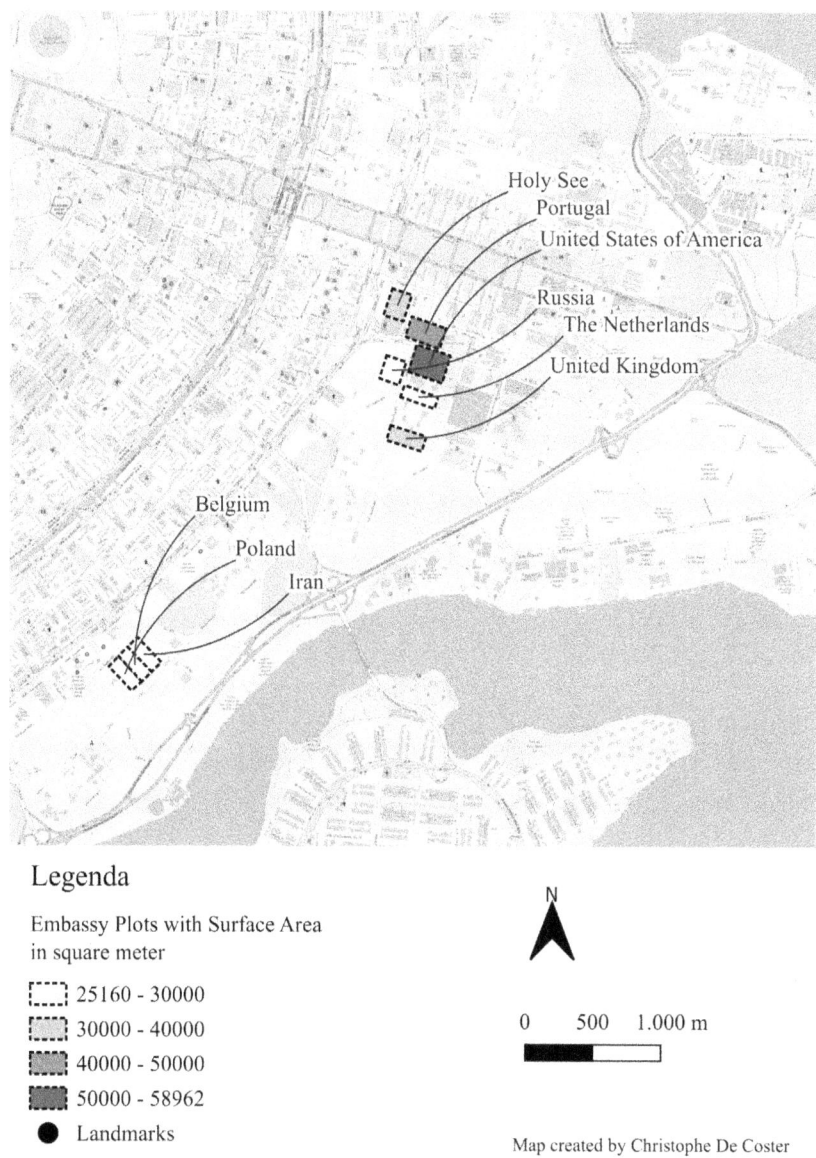

Legenda

Embassy Plots with Surface Area
in square meter

- 25160 - 30000
- 30000 - 40000
- 40000 - 50000
- 50000 - 58962
- Landmarks

N

0   500   1.000 m

Map created by Christophe De Coster

Figure 34: The *Setor de Embaixadas Sul*

Upon becoming foreign minister in 1958, Pierre Wigny also wanted to leave behind an architectural legacy by commissioning purpose-built embassies during his time in office. As a political career tends to be unpredictable, Wigny wanted to keep the momentum going by quickly acquiring land in Brasília. On 5 February 1960, a deal was struck by which plot 32 was officially donated to Belgium.[227] Plot 32 is a rectangular site of 25,000 m² situated in between the parcels of land allocated to Poland and Iran. In the grand scheme of things, the Belgian plot of land (Fig. 34) was certainly not the most prominent site NOVACAP had allocated to a small state. Looking at the parcel of land that was allocated to the Netherlands – the country that the Belgian diplomatic corps often used as a point of reference – the Belgian plot was in a far less prominent location. Whereas the Dutch plot is located between those of great powers and near Brasília's political hotspots, the Belgian plot is situated on the periphery of the Embassy Sector, immersed between less big names in world politics. The Brazilian authorities most likely allocated this well-located plot to the Dutch embassy to pay tribute to the colonial past of the Netherlands in Brazil, as was undoubtedly also the case for the Portuguese embassy.

Nonetheless, Foreign Minister Pierre Wigny was very pleased with the parcel of land. In his diary, he called plot 32 a magnificent site and went on to praise Ambassador Hugo Gouthier de Oliveira Gondim for his role in negotiating the deal.[228] In its capacity as receiving state, the Brazilian government had thus achieved its main objective of committing the Belgian embassy to eventually build an embassy in the new capital. As a token of appreciation towards Belgium, the Brazilian Ministry of Foreign Affairs presented Wigny with the opportunity to see Brasília with his own eyes.

The Belgians in Brasília: Laying the Foundation Stone Under Cover of Night

The Brazilian Ministry of Foreign Affairs kept the momentum going and invited Wigny to Brazil in January 1960. The visit's main goal was to sign a cultural treaty and attend the ceremony to lay the foundation stone of the future Belgian embassy. Given the fact that Belgium had not yet reached out to an architect, the ceremony was envisaged as merely a symbolic gesture. From the Brazilian point of view, such a ceremony was seen as a clear commitment from yet another sending state to move to Brasília. The Brazilian authorities aimed to further legitimise the new capital as its inauguration date of 21 April 1960 drew ever closer.

Arriving in Rio de Janeiro, Wigny had a busy schedule. He would visit over five Brazilian cities in ten days and attend various receptions and meetings. In his eyes, however, the highlight of the trip was the visit to Brasília. Given his enthusiasm for architecture and urban planning, Wigny was thrilled to visit this showcase of modernist urbanism. Upon seeing Brasília with his own eyes, he was mesmerised by the capital's scale and design. In his diary, he claimed that the Brasília project marked a new dawn for Brazil:

> The beauty of the city, which I won't dwell on describing: use of modern materials. Revolutionary urban planning. [...] Right in the heart of the country, one wants to create a new, more energetic humanity of pioneers who have escaped the soothing temptations of the beach.[229]

However, the modernist design of Brasília was not to everyone's taste. Several ministry officials of the Belgian delegation were shocked by the modernist aesthetic of the new capital.[230] As a conservative stronghold at the time, the Belgian diplomatic corps felt out of step with the purist approach in Brasília that disassociated itself from history and tradition. As part of the whirlwind visit, Wigny made his way to the Belgian plot of land along the *Avenida das Nações*. In the presence of the Brazilian President Kubitschek, a ceremony to lay the foundation stone was held during which Wigny gave a high-flown speech. Just as his predecessor Spaak had previously done in Washington, D.C., Wigny seized this ceremony to further deepen bilateral ties. The Christian-democratic strongman talked about his deep admiration for Brazil, expressing his respect for a country that could build a new capital city from scratch in just three years.[231] Moreover, he called the grand urban project a testament to the vigour and ingenuity of the Brazilian people and its leaders.

Amidst this jubilant atmosphere that prevailed during the ceremony, the Brazilian and Belgian delegations apparently did not pay close attention as to where this foundation stone was actually laid down. In a clumsy turn of events, the foundation stone was accidentally laid on the adjacent plot of land that had been allocated to Iran.[232] It was not until the spring of 1960 that the Iranian ambassador stumbled upon the foundation stone and notified his Belgian colleagues of the awkward mistake. The Belgian diplomatic corps feared that the embarrassing story would spread like wildfire and turn the Belgians into a laughing stock within diplomatic circles. Under the cover of night, the Belgian diplomat Serge de Robiano (1922-2012) moved the foundation stone to the Belgian plot of land.

Building to the Rhythm of the Receiving State

Having secured a building plot, the Ministry and especially architecture enthusiast Pierre Wigny were all set to launch their very own embassy project in the shiny new capital. Using the sizeable plot of land to its full potential, it was decided to construct an embassy compound made up of an ambassadorial residence, chancery and additional housing units for diplomats. The initial plan to erect all building units at once was, however, cut short. Instead, a decision was made to construct the embassy offices in the first phase and postpone work on the other buildings until further notice. Interestingly, this phased building activity had nothing to do with budgetary constraints, as had previously been the case for the Canberra project. Instead, the receiving state was the reason behind the phased building activity. More specifically, the construction of the new head office for the Brazilian Ministry of Foreign Affairs in Brasília did not run as smoothly as planned. As the ministry was forced to stay longer in Rio de Janeiro, it was not in the interest of diplomatic missions to move already to Brasília.

Nevertheless, Wigny decided to kickstart the project by constructing the chancery along the *Avenida das Nações*. Judging that the Brazilian Ministry of Foreign Affairs would move to Brasília sooner or later, Wigny wanted to commence the compound's construction during his ministership. In retrospect, one cannot help but think that personal pride had something to do with his decision as he would be remembered as the foreign minister who had overseen the embassy's construction.

As such, the Belgian diplomatic corps was in need of an architect. Both Niemeyer and Costa had expressed their desire that sending states would call upon leading architects in their respective countries. They argued that such well-reputed architects would design innovative embassy buildings that would pay tribute to the modernist urbanism of Brasília.[233] In the eyes of Niemeyer and Costa, Wigny would have undoubtedly done well to hire renowned Belgian architects such as Hugo Van Kuyck or Léon Stynen (1899-1990). However, the Christian-democratic strongman did no such thing. The commission was awarded to the Belgian-Bulgarian architect Nicolaï Fikoff. Fikoff is one of those unfortunate architects who has fallen through the cracks of history, as little to no information can be found on him. What we do know is that Fikoff worked and lived in Rio de Janeiro at the time and was closely affiliated to the local architectural community.[234] He had previously contributed to the design and construction of the Brazilian pavilion at the 1958 Brussels World Exhibition.[235]

Figure 35: The Brasília embassy offices, undated

Having been awarded the commission in 1960, Fikoff set about designing the Belgian embassy offices. The chancery would be situated on the northern edge of the parcel of land to separate the workspace from the ambassadorial residence that would be located on the southern edge. Architecturally, the design (Fig. 35) responded quite well to the symbolically charged modern context of the young capital city. Fikoff designed a single-storey building situated on a heightened concrete base plate. The building itself was rectangular, dominated by strong horizontal lines, and almost squeezed in between the whitish base plate and roof structure.

As the structure was made up of a grid of concrete beams and columns, the chancery's grey-blue limestone exteriors were non-load-bearing walls. This enabled Fikoff to extensively use ribbon windows for the external walls to bring in as much natural light as possible in the offices. Taking the tropical conditions into account, Fikoff paid particular attention to ensure that the windows would block incoming solar heat during the summer and keep indoor heat from escaping during the winter. Fikoff therefore called upon the Belgian glass manufacturer Glaverbel. Founded in 1961, Glaverbel made a name for itself with its so-called stop-ray insulating glass. This goes to show that Fikoff stayed up to date with developments in the Belgian building industry and wanted to showcase national technological knowhow in designing the embassy offices. Notwithstanding the modernist appearance of the chancery, its interior layout was to be far more conservative. In line with previous Belgian embassy projects, Fikoff opted for a cellular office layout instead of the more contemporary open office layout that was becoming more accepted in bureaucratic and corporate circles across the globe.[236] The Ministry most likely instructed Fikoff to include cellular offices as this type of layout suited the hierarchical work culture traditionally associated with the diplomatic realm.

Fikoff's plans were very much appreciated by Foreign Minister Wigny. In his diary, he praised the functional yet aesthetically pleasing design.[237] It is, however, striking that Belgian diplomats posted to Brasília did not share the minister's appraisal. One diplomat, for instance, described the chancery as nothing more than a hastily constructed pavilion that lacked the qualities to represent Belgium adequately abroad.[238] A more contemporary aesthetic in embassy design was not particularly welcome within the conservative Belgian diplomatic corps.

In the search of a building contractor, the Ministry took full advantage of the abundance of building companies operating in Brasília at the time. After comparing various quotes, the commission was awarded to the building firm Christiani & Nielsen which would construct the chancery for approximately two million Belgian francs (440,000 euros). Originally founded in Denmark at the beginning of the 1900s, Christiani & Nielsen had become a global player by the early 1960s with subsidiaries all over the world. The building phase continued without any hiccups as the chancery was completed by December 1962. However, by the time of the chancery's completion, Pierre Wigny was no longer serving as foreign minister. With the electoral defeat of the Christian Social Party on 26 March 1961, Wigny was succeeded by the socialist strongman Paul-Henri Spaak who started his fourth and final term as Belgian foreign minister. Nonetheless, the Ministry's leadership made sure that Wigny's pivotal contribution to commissioning the chancery was set in stone. Near the main entrance of the chancery, a bronze commemorative plaque was installed that referred to the foundation stone laying ceremony attended by Kubitschek and Wigny. This plaque was to be the most overt political marker in the building's façade as there was no coat of arms or other national references included on the exteriors.

In its capacity as sending state, Belgium had kept its end of the deal by already building a section of its embassy compound before the construction of the new seat of the Brazilian Ministry of Foreign Affairs in Brasília had even commenced. The Ministry's construction suffered several hiccups along the way, such as a lack of funding and a procrastinatory attitude among the Brazilian diplomatic corps that was far from keen to leave Rio de Janeiro behind. The postponement was a source of irritation among the Belgian diplomatic corps. It did not hesitate to complain about the course of events. During a visit to Brasília on 12 August 1963, Belgian Ambassador Count Paul Bihin shared his grievances with Manuel Mendes who worked as a press officer at the Brazilian Ministry of Foreign Affairs. Bihin confided to Mendes that he was very upset about the lack of progress in constructing the ministerial building in Brasília. He reasoned that Belgium had already done its part by constructing a modern and well-equipped chancery building but he could not put it to good use as the Brazilian Ministry of Foreign Affairs was still located in Rio de Janeiro. In a snide comment, Ambassador Bihin remarked that, if it were up to him, he would already have taken up residence in Brasília a long time ago.[239]

Three years later, in 1966, yet another Belgian public figure paid a visit to the new capital during which he called for efforts to speed up the construction of the ministry building. This figure was none other than the legendary and notorious Christian-democratic Prime Minister Paul Vanden Boeynants (1919-2001) whose witty one-liners dominated national politics in the 1960s and 1970s. At the end of his visit to Brasília, Prime Minister Vanden Boeynants joked to Belgian journalists that he would have liked to stay in the capital to help speed up the construction of this milestone of progress for humanity.[240] Reading between the lines, he was making the case that he would have done things differently and at a faster pace with regard to constructing the Brazilian Ministry of Foreign Affairs. Judging from his track record in Brussels, Vanden Boeynants was by no means exaggerating. In a similar fashion to his party member Pierre Wigny, his political career was marked by a burning desire to leave behind an architectural legacy.[241] In the mid-1960s, as president of the Christian Social Party, he launched the construction of new party headquarters in the heart of Brussels. However, his *pièce de resistance* was the redevelopment of the Northern Quarter in Brussels during his prime ministership.[242] The historically working-class neighbourhood was redeveloped into a central business district made up of high-rise office buildings. Reflecting his no-nonsense approach, Vanden Boeynants had little to no regard for the grievances of local residents whose houses were levelled to make way for skyscrapers. One can assume that Prime Minister Vanden Boeynants, being the builder-politician that he was, wanted to get on with the construction of the Brasília embassy compound to add it to his list of accomplishments. However, as luck would have it, the Brazilian Ministry of Foreign Affairs would put his patience and that of the entire *corps diplomatique* to the test.

Awarding the Commission: Money Trumps Prestige

Meanwhile, back in Belgium, the Ministry of Foreign Affairs took an important step in professionalising the embassy-building programme. For the first time in its long history, the Ministry hired an in-house architect. The appointment was intrinsically linked to the independence of the Democratic Republic of the Congo and Rwanda-Burundi in the early 1960s. As the Belgian Ministry of the Colonies had lost its *raison d'être*, its officials had to look for new career opportunities. One of these officials was Jean Loppe, an architect who oversaw the construction, renovation and maintenance of buildings housing the colonial administration in the Belgian Congo. As his ministry department was being dismantled in 1962, Loppe wanted to be reassigned to the Ministry of Foreign Affairs and sent an application letter to Spaak in February of that year. The Ministry went on to hire Loppe and tasked him with managing the vast diplomatic real estate portfolio and supervising building projects. Loppe did not design embassies himself but instead played an important role behind the scenes. He was responsible for drawing up specifications, discussing practicalities with the architect commissioned to design the embassy, and monitoring the building phase by making onsite visits. In his capacity as the Ministry's chief architect, Jean Loppe had his work cut out for him with regard to the Brasília project.

The first hurdle that Jean Loppe had to overcome was determining what would actually be constructed on the Belgian embassy parcel of land. From the outset, the Ministry had planned to use the plot of land to its full potential. The idea was to construct an embassy compound consisting of the already constructed chancery, an ambassadorial residence, a counsellor's residence and bungalows for lower-ranking diplomats. These plans were, however, called into question by the diplomatic boots on the ground. Ambassador Paul Bihin supported plans to construct the ambassadorial residence but spoke out against building additional housing units on the plot. Bihin noted that the site was not spacious enough:

> The relatively narrow plot of land, laid out lengthways, does not seem to me to lend itself to new constructions, which would inevitably encroach on the space intended for the residence or the chancery and would dangerously threaten the order of the existing plans, without providing the Ambassador and his family with the privacy to which he seems to me to be entitled.[243]

In his capacity as ambassador, Bihin was concerned about his privacy. The thought that he and his family would have to live on the same plot of land as the diplomatic staff worried him. This goes to show that the Belgian diplomatic corps still considered itself to be a strong hierarchical organisation in the mid-1960s. Architect Jean Loppe had to reassure Bihin. A belt of hedges and trees was to be strategically positioned between the ambassadorial residence and the other housing units to shield the ambassador and his family from next-door neighbours.

The second hurdle Jean Loppe had to overcome was figuring out when construction works could be launched. This was easier said than done. Belgian building activity was intrinsically linked to the construction of the Itamaraty Palace that would house the Brazilian Ministry of Foreign Affairs. Notwithstanding the fact that the palace was completed by 1967, the Brazilian Ministry of Foreign Affairs did not move to Brasília. Apartment buildings for its officials still had to be constructed and the Itamaraty Palace had to be fitted with international telephone lines to communicate with Brazilian embassies all over the world.[244] A regime change in Brazil made it especially difficult for the Brazilian Ministry of Foreign Affairs to receive the necessary funding. The military elite had seized power and were not particularly keen to move to Brasília, a futuristic city conceived as the architectural expression of progressivism and democracy.[245] At the time, high-ranking Brazilian officials were running a smear campaign against Brasília by spreading rumours among the government bureaucracy that Brasília was a rat-infested city.[246]

The Belgian embassy in Rio de Janeiro informed Brussels that it would be unwise to already launch construction works along the *Avenida das Nações* when the fate of Brasília hung in the balance. The Belgian embassy would run the risk of cutting itself off from the real locus of power in Rio de Janeiro. Nevertheless, the Brazilian Ministry of Foreign Affairs continued to make a strong case for Brasília in talks with Ambassador Bihin. It boasted that the inauguration of the Itamaraty Palace was just around the corner and pressured Belgium, just like other sending states, to launch construction works. However, their claims were not taken seriously by the Belgian diplomatic corps as several deadlines for the palace's inauguration had passed by silently without any noteworthy real-life changes. Eventually, it was not until 21 April 1970 – ten years after the official inauguration of Brasília – that the Itamaraty Place was officially inaugurated as the seat of the Brazilian Ministry of Foreign Affairs. It was only from this moment on that it was politically worthwhile for diplomatic missions to move to Brasília. The Brazilian receiving state imposed a deadline on sending states to make the move. By 7 September 1972, exactly 150 years after Brazil proclaimed its political independence from Portugal, all embassies had to be moved to Brasília.

The third and final hurdle Jean Loppe had to overcome was awarding the contract to design and build the embassy compound. As Nicolaï Fikoff had previously designed the chancery, Loppe first reached out to the Belgian-Bulgarian architect. Fikoff, however, made himself impossible from the outset. Upon hearing that he had to design an embassy compound, Fikoff complained that erecting more than two structures – the chancery and ambassadorial residence – would be out of tune with Brasília's urban landscape and would jeopardise the embassy's social cohesion:

> The original layout, with just two buildings on the site, would be retained. This would allow for larger green spaces and gardens, exactly as envisaged in the original plan drawn up by Brasília's official planning authorities, who have already agreed in principle on this point. This ensures that people working all day on the same site do not have to share the same space after working hours. This could lead to human conflicts (boss–subordinates; children–enjoyment and conservation of the garden, etc. etc....).[247]

Contributing to a project in which a boss and subordinates would have to work and live on the same domain did not quite correspond with Fikoff's beliefs. Eventually, the Ministry abandoned plans to work with Fikoff. Interestingly, none other than Oscar Niemeyer reached out to the Belgian diplomatic corps to design its embassy compound in 1968.[248] It goes without saying that a collaboration with such an internationally acclaimed architect would have been a tremendous PR stunt for a small country such as Belgium. From a prestige point of view, it is therefore almost incomprehensible that the Ministry did not bother to start exploratory talks with Niemeyer on the project.

There is no evidence in writing as to why Niemeyer's offer was turned down but judging from who was eventually awarded the contract, and for what reasons, one cannot help but think that money had something to do with it. After all, the contract was awarded to the Brazilian real estate tycoon José Pellegrino, one of the executives of the property developer Kosmos Engenharia. The Brazilian businessman had personally reached out to the Belgian embassy with a proposal that was especially appealing to the Belgian state finances. Pellegrino proposed to purchase the Belgian embassy in Rio de Janeiro and redevelop the site into a residential apartment building. He was prepared to pay top dollar for the property as he put 36 million Belgian francs (6.7 million euros) on the table. In return, the Ministry could reinvest the money into the construction of the Brasília compound. To make the deal even more straightforward, Pellegrino's business Kosmos Engenharia would design and construct an embassy compound with this amount of money. Basically, Pellegrino was proposing that the Ministry trade its Rio de Janeiro embassy for a new embassy compound in Brasília. Additionally, he boasted that his firm could complete the embassy by the summer of 1972, just in time to meet the deadline set by the Brazilian government. Ambassador August Lonnoy was an ardent supporter of teaming up with Kosmos Engenharia. In correspondence with Brussels, he described José Pellegrino to be a no-nonsense entrepreneur with deep pockets and an extensive social network.[249] Lonnoy claimed that Pellegrino was a man who gets things done.

Lonnoy's recommendation had its effect in Brussels. The Christian-democratic Foreign Minister Pierre Harmel (1911-2009) greenlit the real estate operation in the summer of 1970, seeing the trade-off with Pellegrino as the perfect fit for his tight real estate budget. As such, the prospect of getting an embassy for free was apparently more appealing than working with Oscar Niemeyer. In the end, money trumped prestige in the Brasília project. Nevertheless, the collaboration with Pellegrino drew flak within the Ministry's walls. Ministry officials argued that the Ministry of Foreign Affairs had succumbed to the lucrative temptation of acquiring an embassy for free. The Inspection of Diplomatic and Consular Missions even had to issue an internal statement, indicating that it had not intentionally searched for a real estate tycoon such as Pellegrino. The Inspection defended the collaboration with Pellegrino, arguing that "if property developers come to us spontaneously, before the Minister has made his final decision, why refuse to listen to them?"[250]

Lost in Translation: Building the Belgian Embassy Compound

José Pellegrino called upon his friend Paulo Antunes Ribeiro (1905-1973) to design the compound. A graduate of the National School of Fine Arts in Rio de Janeiro, Ribeiro went on to study urbanism in Paris at the end of the 1930s. During his time in France, he was introduced to the architectural ideas propagated by Le Corbusier. Upon returning to Brazil, Ribeiro became part of the modernist vanguard that called for a clear and honest expression of contemporary building methods and techniques. He made a name for himself by designing high-end houses and hotels.[251] Ribeiro's architectural oeuvre clearly drew inspiration from Le Corbusier but he made sure that his designs were well and truly rooted in the tropical Brazilian soil and sun. His line of work was characterised by the extensive use of *brise-soleils* and locally produced ceramic tiles. In the 1950s, Ribeiro's architectural career reached its zenith as he served as president of the *Instituto dos Arquitetos do Brasil* (Brazilian Architects Institute) and member of the selection board for Brasília.

The final embassy programme called for an ambassadorial residence, counsellor's residence, three secretary bungalows and a swimming pool. Whereas the chancery was situated on the plot's northern edge, Ribeiro situated the ambassadorial residence on the southern edge. By physically distancing both embassy buildings from one other, he accentuated the diverging functions of both buildings and, more importantly, complied with the ambassador's wish for privacy at the ambassadorial residence. Moreover, the ambassadorial residence and chancery would be shielded from each other by the counsellor's residence and the secretaries' bungalows that were to be constructed on the central area of the plot. In front of the ambassadorial residence, a paved roundabout was to be included. The roundabout, a trademark of any ambassadorial residence worthy of the name, facilitated the coming and going of guests visiting the residence.

In his design of the ambassadorial residence, Ribeiro stayed true to his modernist beliefs. He designed a two-storey residence (Fig. 36) in an exceedingly straightforward, functional manner. The building consists of a reinforced concrete structure with plain white exteriors. The ground floor was to be covered with white marble slabs while the first floor was to feature exposed concrete exteriors. The sobriety of its design was also made evident in the residence's front façade. The strong horizontal lines were accentuated by ribboned windows running along the façade's length. In a similar fashion to the embassy offices, the insulating window glass was produced by the Belgian manufacturer Glaverbel. Notwithstanding the sleek appearance of the building, Ribeiro wanted to reconcile the modernist aesthetic with more traditional elements intrinsically linked to Brazil. As part of a fusion between traditional and modern elements, he added a regional touch by including ceramic tiles from the north-eastern Brazilian province of Bahia in the front façade.

Figure 36: The ambassadorial residence, 1974

The clean-cut façade corresponded well with the clarity of the building's concise spatial layout. The diverging elements of the residence's hybrid programme – living quarters and social venue – were to be integrated into the building. The ground floor was to house the rooms where guests were traditionally received such as the drawing room, dining room and study. The drawing room and dining room were to be positioned at the rear of the building, behind a glazed façade. This ensured that residents and their guests had an excellent view on the embassy garden. Next to the residence, a paved terrace was to be included. The outdoor area was to be partially roofed by a series of concrete beams serving as sun-shading structure. This created spatial continuity between the interior and exterior, as though the terrace was an integral part of the structure. The first floor housed the living quarters of the ambassador and the guest rooms. The first floor was significantly smaller than the ground floor. Ribeiro envisaged it as a luxury penthouse towering above the embassy compound. It was made up of four bedrooms, five bathrooms, a drawing room and a dressing room. To top it all off, the building was to be surrounded by a capacious roof terrace. The terrace's concrete balustrade with clear lines was an additional feature accentuating both the simplicity of the building and the strong horizontality of Ribeiro's design. The strong emphasis on functionality and the expression of contemporary building methods and techniques corresponded with the symbolically charged modern context of Brasília.

There was, however, strong opposition against Ribeiro's plan. During the design phase, Baron Alexandre Paternotte de la Vaillée (1923-2014) was appointed the new Belgian ambassador to Brazil. As the first ambassador who would reside in the ambassadorial residence, Ambassador Paternotte de la Vaillée felt entitled to speak his mind on the design and did not hold back. The new ambassador was not at all pleased with the blueprints. In a letter to Brussels, he confided that the design of the residence was bad and without grace.[252] He pressured his superiors to send Ribeiro back to the drawing board. Architecturally, a more contemporary approach in which the design was simplified down to the essentials was considered a bridge too far for the Belgian diplomatic corps even if the embassy was situated in Brasília. Moreover, Ambassador Paternotte de la Vaillée was dissatisfied with the dimensions of the dining room on the ground floor. He argued that the dining room was far too cramped and had to be widened by at least two metres. He made the case that such an alteration was paramount to turn his ambassadorship into a success.[253]

Realising the importance of the room in the ambassador's everyday life, architect Jean Loppe instructed Ribeiro to increase the dimensions of the dining room. However, Brussels did not act on the ambassador's suggestion to send Ribeiro back to the drawing board and start from scratch. This was most likely due to the fact that Ribeiro was a protégé of José Pellegrino and any criticism of his friend could potentially sabotage the deal with the real estate tycoon. The general outline of Ribeiro's design remained the same, much to the frustration of Baron Ambassador Paternotte de la Vaillée. It did not help that the Bahia ceramic tiles, one of the few design features that he genuinely liked, were left out of the final design because architect Jean Loppe was worried that sunlight exposure could discolour or otherwise harmfully affect the finish of the earthwork.

As part of the deal with Pellegrino, the construction job was awarded to his construction firm Kosmos Engenharia. In preparation for the construction works, the engineers from Kosmos put together the building specifications outlining the scope of the works. The document was, however, written in Portuguese and it was up to the Belgian embassy staff to translate the lengthy document into French and forward it to Brussels. Given that the embassy staff was not familiar with the lexicon of the building industry, several important aspects were lost in translation. The Inspection of Diplomatic and Consular Missions frequently sent letters to the embassy asking them to clarify matters.

There was also miscommunication between individuals who spoke the same mother tongue. Upon seeing the blueprints of the ambassadorial residence, embassy staffer Ernest Vanderlinden was stunned that there was no air conditioning included. Vanderlinden expressed his concerns, making the case that it would be especially uncomfortable to live in Brazil in such conditions.[254] The Ministry's reaction speaks volumes on the questionable manner in which building projects were supervised at the time. Ministry officials shifted the blame to the embassy staff, arguing that they had never brought up the necessity to include air conditioning. Apparently, it was not common knowledge that Brazil had a profoundly different climate to Belgium as the embassy staff had to spell out the obvious to its superiors. Eventually, Kosmos Engenharia was instructed to install an air conditioning system but this caused some delay. Holes had to be drilled in the concrete walls to install the necessary ducts.

Another case of miscommunication involved the residence's sanitary installations. The ministry wanted to call upon a Belgian manufacturer for these installations, as it had done with Glaverbel for the embassy's insulating glass. The Brussels-based manufacturer Robinetterie AVH was commissioned to supply the Brasília residence with sanitary facilities.[255] For the sake of convenience, Robinetterie AVH contacted Ambassador Alexandre Paternotte de la Vaillée directly so that he could personally select the bathroom and kitchen taps. For unknown reasons, Robinetterie was under the impression that the ambassador was posted to Mexico City and sent its first quote to the wrong capital city. Several months passed by before the mistake was noticed.

These examples go to show that commissioning a purpose-built embassy, especially one far away from home, is by no means a simple and straightforward task. Different groups of people with different professional backgrounds, different mother tongues and working from different countries have to work together to construct a building, which is by its very essence already a complex undertaking.

Furnishing and Landscaping the Brasília Embassy: In with the Old and Out with the New

Baron Alexandre Paternotte de la Vaillée may not have got his way in reshaping the design but he was determined to leave his mark on the residence interiors. He made it crystal clear to the Ministry that furnishing and decorating the residence would be a personal project of his.[256] Together with his Italian wife, Eliane Orsolini-Cencelli (1923-1991), Paternotte de la Vaillée called upon Marquis Lottieri Lotteringhi Della Stufa (1919-1982), an Italian interior architect of noble descent who had moved to Brazil and worked for the rich and famous. To convince his superiors, Paternotte de la Vaillée stressed that Lotteringhi Della Stufa was willing to work for free, an indication that he was most likely a personal friend of the Paternotte de la Vaillée couple. The proposal was greenlit by Brussels, giving Lotteringhi Della Stufa and especially Eliane Orsolini-Cencelli free reign to furnish and decorate the interiors.

Their furnishings and decorations diametrically opposed the architectural design of Ribeiro. Following the example of many other Belgian diplomatic residences, they opted for a very traditional, somewhat old-fashioned, approach with an abundance of period furniture and antique art. To a certain extent, this choice can be read as a strong statement of Ambassador Paternotte de la Vaillée. The Ministry may have dictated that he take up residence in a building that was out of sync with his architectural preferences but he could still turn things around by overseeing the interior finishing. There was a certain mismatch between the modern aesthetic of the residence and its interiors that resembled something like an art museum. The drawing room (Fig. 37), for instance, was furnished in a very eclectic manner. It featured Persian rugs, Louis XVI armchairs, marble coffee tables, silver chandeliers and a massive tapestry.

The Italian roots of both Lotteringhi Della Stufa and Eliane Orsolini-Cencelli also showed themselves. Near the main entrance, a sculpted horsehead made entirely of high-end Carrara marble featured prominently next to a marble sculpture of a Roman goddess. The most museum-like atmosphere could be found in the ambassador's study (Fig. 38). The room was something of a personal hall of fame for Ambassador Paternotte de la Vaillée. Behind the main desk, a modern modular shelving system was installed where the ambassador showed off the various gifts and souvenirs he had accumulated throughout his diplomatic career alongside portraits of his ancestors. Ambassador Paternotte de la Vaillée was so proud of his interior decoration that he invited the Brazilian lifestyle magazine *Manchete* for a photoshoot. The journalist wrote a glowing review, describing the newly completed residence as a royal resort with tastefully furnished interiors.[257]

Whereas the interiors featured an abundance of old-fashioned elements, the embassy grounds were landscaped in a far more contemporary manner. As part of the deal with Pellegrino, Kosmos Engenharia would landscape the embassy grounds. Therefore, Pellegrino hired Roberto Burle

Figure 37: The residence's drawing room, 1974

Figure 38: The ambassador's study, 1974

Marx (1909-1994), the world-renowned Brazilian landscape architect. His line of work was characterised by a bold use of form and colour, giving his gardens an almost painterly aesthetic. He believed that gardens should not try to copy the natural landscape but rather create abstract spaces or snapshots capturing the lyrics of the landscape.[258] His career was marked by a profound ecological awareness. Throughout his life, Burle Marx spoke out against the deforestation of the Amazon rainforest and undertook plant-hunting trips, collecting unknown plants for conservation. In terms of commissions, Roberto Burle Marx had risen to fame for designing, among others, the Copacabana Promenade where he created a transition area between the city and the beach that was made of Portuguese stone mosaic and coconut palms. He was also the landscape architect of Brasília and designed the gardens of the Itamaraty Palace. Before accepting the embassy commission, he already had a professional connection with Belgium. During the 1958 Brussels World Exhibition, he had designed the tropical gardens of the Brazilian pavilion. In line with the general theme to showcase Brazil as a tropical civilisation, he had included species endemic to Brazil. For his contribution to the world's fair, the Belgian government had awarded him the Order of the Crown in 1959.[259]

Baron Paternotte de la Vaillée was thrilled that an internationally acclaimed landscape architect would design his embassy gardens. In a letter to the Ministry, he reasoned that the Belgian diplomatic corps should count itself lucky that someone such as Roberto Burle Marx would be involved in the embassy project.[260] At the roundabout near the ambassadorial residence, Burle Marx planted palm trees and curved, almost kidney-shaped, flowerbeds with colourful species. This colour scheme contrasted pleasantly with the residence's white exteriors. Particular attention was also paid to the area where the swimming pool was situated. Strategically positioned between the two residences and the bungalows, the swimming pool was envisaged to be far more than just a recreational facility. During the design phase, the Belgian diplomatic corps stressed that adding a swimming pool was a necessity as it would strengthen the bonds between embassy staffers. It ought to be an informal meeting place for staffers to unwind after a long day of meetings and deskwork together with their families. To create an intimate and tranquil environment around the swimming pool, Burle Marx included hedges, eucalyptus trees and plants endemic to the flora of Brazil. By August 1974, the new embassy compound was officially inaugurated. Ever since, it has been the seat of the Belgian embassy.

Chapter III
"It's the Economy, Stupid!"
Constructing Embassies as Venues for Economic Diplomacy (1980-1985)

On 14 June 1926, high-ranking ministry officials gathered for their monthly meeting. Among the various items listed on the agenda, was a request made by three Belgian companies with business dealings in Greece. Representatives of the three companies frequently made business trips to Athens in order to keep a watchful eye on their investments and build up a business network to capitalise on future investment opportunities. During their visits to Athens, however, the representatives were shocked by the appalling housing situation of Minister Plenipotentiary Baron Jules Guillaume.[261] At the time, Baron Guillaume was residing in a cramped hotel room because the Ministry lacked the funding to purchase, let alone lease, a property for the head of mission. So much for the stereotypical image of diplomats always residing in majestic estates with lavishly furnished and decorated interiors.

During his diplomatic posting in Athens, Guillaume frequently advocated for the improvement of diplomatic housing. Guillaume made it crystal clear to Brussels that his credibility as a diplomat was severely undermined by the absence of a diplomatic residence worthy of that name. He stressed that he could not host any grand events which was nothing short of a national embarrassment in a country such as Greece: "In a country where decorum is so highly prized, a head of mission must be able to represent himself with dignity and entertain guests at his table often enough."[262] The senior diplomat laid down plans to either lease, purchase or construct a new residence in the Greek capital but such proposals fell on deaf ears because of budgetary constraints.

Moreover, the lack of a diplomatic residence was a thorn in the side of the three Belgian businesses. It was common practice that serving Belgian heads of mission opened the doors of their diplomatic residence and invited their entrepreneurial countrymen, together with local politicians, officials, investors and businessmen, to attend receptions and dinner parties. In so doing, the Belgian diplomatic corps offered their country's entrepreneurs the opportunity to talk business with the local elite. In the case of Athens, however, Baron Guillaume could not render the same support to Belgian businesses as his diplomatic residence was nothing more than a mundane and cramped hotel room. Reasoning that the stay at the hotel reflected poorly on the image of both Belgium and its businesses, the Belgian companies called on the Ministry of Foreign Affairs to act swiftly to improve the country's diplomatic housing in the Greek capital.

Interestingly, the Belgian companies suggested taking matters into their own hands in the hope of turning things around quickly. The companies made a very unusual proposal to the highest ministerial echelons. They proposed to pool some three million Belgian francs (3.6 million euros) together and use this money to purchase a luxurious residence in Athens.[263] In return, this company-owned property would be leased to the Belgian Ministry of Foreign Affairs which could use it as a diplomatic residence. As such, Baron Guillaume would have a high-end venue at his disposal to throw receptions and dinner parties in a fitting scenery. The highest echelons of the Ministry were, however, split on this proposal. Whereas some framed it as an offer that they could not refuse, others believed that it was too risky to put their faith in corporations. In the end, the Ministry declined the offer and instead opted to purchase a property on its own terms in Athens in 1929. The proposal of the Belgian companies may have been turned down, but their course of action reveals that the Belgian business community considered the nation's diplomatic patrimony as important venues for economic diplomacy.

The efforts of the Belgian businesses do not come as much of a surprise. As Belgium has historically been an export-oriented economy, it was and still is of the utmost importance for Belgian companies to cement ties abroad if they have any hope of tapping into new markets. Consequently, the importance of trade relations has trickled down to the inner workings of the Ministry, making economic diplomacy the main cornerstone of Belgium's foreign policy from the outset.[264] Throughout this book, plenty of examples have illustrated how economic interests have been a pivotal factor in the Belgian embassy-building programme. Belgian investments in diplomatic housing have been intrinsically linked to economic interests. As discussed in the previous chapter, the Ministry was far from keen to build embassies in Canberra and Brasília and therefore leave economic hubs such as Sydney and Rio de Janeiro.

Figure 39: The New Delhi ambassadorial residence, 1985

The current chapter further elaborates on the symbiosis between economic interests and the Belgian embassy-building programme. The chapter highlights how economic incentives have been the third steering mechanism shaping the building policy and practice of the Belgian Ministry of Foreign Affairs. This influence reached its zenith in the first half of the 1980s. At the time, the Belgian economy was going through a rough patch in the wake of the 1970s energy crisis. Confronted with the nation's adverse financial-economic climate, the Ministry of Foreign Affairs supported Belgian businesses in their efforts to tap into new export markets. Ministry officials in particular set their sights on Asia, believing that this continent was a sleeping economic giant. The Ministry organised several economic missions to Asia during which Belgian captains of industry came into direct contact with clients and investors during networking events. To provide these economic missions with a high-end venue for such events, Brussels invested in the construction of purpose-built embassies in emerging Asian markets.

A telling example was the construction of the Belgian embassy in New Delhi. As part of its aspirations to put Belgium on the map in India, the Ministry of Foreign Affairs brought out the big guns as it constructed one of, if not the most, conspicuous Belgian embassies in terms of architecture. The entire embassy compound was designed by the Indian artist-architect Satish Gujral (1925-2020) in the late 1970s. Completed in 1983, the purpose-built embassy comprises a compound made up of the ambassadorial residence (Fig. 39), chancery, and additional housing for diplomats and servants' quarters. The embassy's sculptural design, with its irregular shape, exposed brickwork and moulded geometric forms such as arches and domes, is mind-boggling to say the least, especially for a Western country such as Belgium.

The current chapter goes to the very heart of this noteworthy embassy project by shedding light on the story how this compound came into being. It will argue that the Ministry's decision to build was incentivised by economic ambitions. This had a profound impact on the programmatic needs as Gujral was instructed to design a dazzling and spacious embassy where Belgian economic missions could network with the Indian elite. The programme may have been very clear, but the Ministry did not have an explicit view on what the new embassy should look like in terms of architecture. Instead, Satish Gujral was given *carte blanche* in terms of design.

The peculiar New Delhi design was therefore not the product of a well-considered building policy introduced by Brussels as it played no significant role in designing the new embassy. However, the decision to give Gujral free reign had a positive effect on Belgium's prestige in India. The metaphorical, historical and symbolic associations found throughout the design were very much appreciated by the Indian visitors. They perceived Belgium as a country that paid tribute to the receiving state in designing its embassy. In conclusion, the chapter will argue that the New Delhi embassy was not an isolated case in the 1980s. The Ministry of Foreign Affairs followed a similar architectural approach when constructing a new embassy in Saudi Arabia in the mid-1980s, yet another foreign market that caught the eye of Belgian foreign policymakers. But let us first shed light on the historical trajectory behind the design and building process of the New Delhi embassy set against the backdrop of Belgo-Indian relations.

Opening an Embassy in New Delhi: The Political Awakening of the Indian Giant

On 18 September 1947, a Douglas DC-6 of the Belgian airline Sabena touched down on an airstrip on the outskirts of New Delhi. The aircraft was chartered by the Ministry and flew the Belgian diplomat Prince Eugène de Ligne (1893-1960) to New Delhi to become the first Belgian ambassador to India. A descendent of the noble house of de Ligne, Prince Eugène de Ligne was a seasoned diplomat. Passing the diplomatic exam with distinction in 1920, Prince de Ligne worked at esteemed diplomatic postings such as Paris, Madrid, London and Washington, D.C. during the interwar period.[265] In 1926, he was sent to British India to draft a study on how to improve trade relations with the crown colony. As a well-reputed diplomat who had previously visited India, it was most likely in this context that the name of Prince Eugène de Ligne crossed the mind of Foreign Minister Spaak as he was looking for a diplomat to become the first Belgian ambassador to India. Upon informing the Royal Palace that de Ligne would become the first Belgian ambassador to India, Spaak called him the right man for the right place.[266]

The establishment of diplomatic ties with India was intrinsically linked to the rapidly changing political context on the Indian subcontinent. Following the Second World War, British hegemony disintegrated in the region as the call for Indian self-rule grew ever louder.[267] Lacking the resources and political will to once again tighten its grip on the Indian subcontinent, Great Britain decided to decolonise British India. In 1946, a provisional government led by the charismatic Jawaharlal Nehru (1889-1964), the face of the Indian independence movement and the Congress Party, was set up to prepare the forthcoming independence of India. Believing that the establishment of durable diplomatic ties with the rest of the world would cement India's position as a sovereign state on the international stage, Nehru sent his diplomatic adviser Krishna Menon (1896-1974) to Europe. Menon also paid a visit to Brussels where he met Paul-Henri Spaak. Both men agreed to establish diplomatic ties between Belgium and India. As India was the second most populous country in the world and the largest democracy, Spaak opted to immediately open an embassy instead of a lower-ranked legation.

Establishing diplomatic ties with a foreign country is one thing, but such a move raises forth practical issues such as finding diplomatic housing. To this end, Spaak instructed Albert Hupperts (1911-1974), the Belgian consul in Calcutta, to travel to New Delhi and find suitable diplomatic housing. Consul Hupperts had his work cut out for him. In the late 1940s, the local real estate market faced a housing shortage as New Delhi had become a magnet for both the growing bureaucratic apparatus of the nascent Indian state and refugees affected by the partition of British India in 1947.[268] As part of its decolonisation, British India was divided into the newly independent countries of India and Pakistan. This ill-prepared division separated families and religious communities from one another overnight. It led to ethnic cleansing between Sikhs, Muslims and Hindus, resulting in the death of approximately one million people.[269] Moreover, the arriving *corps diplomatique* was in need of diplomatic housing which led to competition among diplomats to get their hands on prime real estate. These circumstances made it extremely difficult for Consul Hupperts to purchase, let alone lease, a property. As demand surpassed supply, Indian landlords capitalised on this housing shortage by overcharging for rent.

Forced to pay extra, sending states filed complaints with the Indian Ministry of External Affairs and asked for assistance to overcome the hurdle of finding housing in New Delhi. In a letter to Spaak, Hupperts revealed that the Indian authorities were cooking up a scheme to come to the aid of foreign diplomats. More specifically, the authorities were toying with the idea of developing a purpose-built diplomatic neighbourhood in New Delhi. In a similar fashion to Canberra and Brasília, sending states would be invited to acquire a sizeable building plot on which they could construct diplomatic housing.[270] Hupperts, however, told Spaak that these plans were only preliminary and it was therefore necessary to continue scanning the real estate market for a property to purchase or lease. In retrospect, it remains doubtful whether Spaak would have been interested in acquiring a building plot in the diplomatic district, even if the Indian plans had been more concrete. As previously demonstrated, the socialist bigwig did not show much enthusiasm for constructing Belgian embassies in Washington, D.C. and Warsaw in the 1950s.

In August 1947, just one month prior to the arrival of Prince Eugène de Ligne, Consul Hupperts still did not have any luck in his house-hunting efforts. Worried that Ambassador de Ligne and his family would have to take up residence in a hotel room, Hupperts stepped up his efforts to find a property. He asked and got a one-on-one meeting with Prime Minister Jawaharlal Nehru to discuss the matter. In a letter to Spaak, he gave a summary of the meeting:

> The meeting lasted about twenty minutes, and after a message that I addressed to Nehru, I took the opportunity to insist very energetically that a house be allocated to us for the needs of the Embassy. Reminding my interlocutor that the Prince and Princess de Ligne would be arriving in Delhi on 15 September, I stressed how difficult it was to work and establish the services of an Embassy with only a hotel room at one's disposal. [...] Nehru seemed sensitive to my request, took note of my request and promised to intervene personally with the

Public Works Department, on which the allocation of buildings depends. The housing crisis has reached an extraordinary level and the diplomatic missions are not particularly helped by the Government of India.[271]

However, Nehru's reassurance that he would intervene personally on Hupperts' behalf did not yield any results. By the time Ambassador Eugène de Ligne and his family arrived in New Delhi on 18 September 1947, Hupperts still had not found an ambassadorial residence let alone offices for the chancery.

De Ligne and his family were forced to take up residence in a hotel room for the time being. De Ligne aimed to make his temporary stay in a hotel as comfortable as possible. Therefore, he moved into a room in a high-end hotel as befitted his noble background. The luxurious Maidens Hotel caught his eye. Established by the British Maidens family in 1903, the majestical Maidens Hotel was one of the most popular hotels for Westerners because of its air-conditioned rooms and European cuisine.[272] The Ministry, however, wanted to reduce his stay to a bare minimum as it had to cover these hotel expenses. Consequently, the Personnel Department instructed Ambassador de Ligne to take over Consul Albert Hupperts' fruitless house-hunting efforts and find an ambassadorial residence at once.

As New Delhi's *corps diplomatique* and the Indian government apparatus faced difficulties in acquiring premises in the overheated housing market, Prime Minister Nehru eventually took matters into his own hands to turn things around. He reintroduced the Requisition and Acquisition of Immovable Property Act that was first implemented by the British colonial administration at the outbreak of the Second World War. This act enabled the Indian government to temporarily acquire the second and third homes of the well-to-do and use these properties to house civil services and diplomatic missions.[273] Moreover, the Indian government requisitioned the properties of nationals who had fled to Pakistan following the tumultuous partition of British India in August 1947. Among the various properties that were seized by the Indian government was a colonial bungalow situated on 2.5 acres of land at 24 Hardinge Avenue, located just north-east of the city centre. At the end of 1947, the Indian authorities struck a deal with the Belgian state. Belgium would lease the property and use it as the seat of the ambassadorial residence.[274] The property was rented to Belgium on favourable terms, as the Ministry paid just 6,300 Belgian francs (1570 euros) a month.

Given the archival gaps in Belgian diplomatic housing, no images of this ambassadorial residence could be retrieved in the archives. Fortunately, the memoirs of the Belgian diplomat Serge de Robiano offer us a glimpse of its architectural design.[275] He recalls that the ambassadorial residence was a typical English bungalow. The single-storey building featured several high-end architectural elements such as white stone exteriors, a series of columns flanking the main entrance and exotic wood flooring. Behind the bungalow was a columned terrace where Belgian ambassadors threw well-attended cocktail parties. At the edge of the plot were two small housing units where the Indian household staff resided with their families.

By the time Ambassador de Ligne took up residence in the bungalow, the Ministry's Personnel Department was in the process of supplying each diplomatic mission with state-owned furniture. The Personnel Department prioritised the furnishing and decorating of diplomatic postings that were politically and economically significant for Belgium. As India ticked neither box at the time, it was up to Ambassador de Ligne to furnish and decorate his new residence. As an old-timer at the Ministry, Prince Eugène de Ligne was used to the old practice of bringing furniture and artwork with him. Throughout his diplomatic career, he had built up his own furniture collection that moved with him from one diplomatic posting to another. His furniture collection was the perfect fit for the bungalow residence. In line with the predilection of his colleagues for period furniture, de Ligne's collection mainly comprised Louis XV style items such couches and cabriolet armchairs upholstered with expensive damask silk.[276] He also brought a mahogany dining table and crystal chandeliers with him to New Delhi.

Moreover, Ambassador de Ligne used his influence within the Ministry to receive funding to refurbish the bungalow's interiors to his own taste. De Ligne was able to purchase top-notch table crystals produced by the high-end Belgian crystal glassware manufacturer Val Saint Lambert. Since 1826, Val Saint Lambert has made a name for itself as one of the world's leading crystal glassware manufacturers.[277] By 1947, Val Saint Lambert had built up an international clientele for its crystal artwork, glasswork and table sets. Approximately 90 per cent of the items produced in the workshops in the Walloon city of Seraing were exported to foreign clients.[278] Ambassador de Ligne saw the table crystals of the Belgian luxury brand as the perfect fit for his residence. As the name suggests, the table crystals were strategically positioned on the large mahogany dining table to reflect the light of the crystal chandeliers, adding a touch of glamour to the dining room. By showcasing Belgian design and craftsmanship to foreign guests in the dining room, Ambassador de Ligne used the residence's interiors as the perfect setting for national product placement.

Finding Common Ground in Chanakyapuri

Belgium was of course not the only country that was invited to open an embassy in New Delhi. As part of his scheme to further cement India's position at the international level, Nehru invested considerably in forging diplomatic relations with foreign governments. By 1949, 32 countries had accepted his invitation to open a diplomatic mission.[279] The arrival of foreign diplomats was a triumph for the nascent country and Nehru in particular, but this put further strain on New Delhi's overheated real estate market. Sending states faced many difficulties in finding prime real estate in the overcrowded Indian capital. In the late 1940s, foreign diplomats increasingly complained to the Indian Ministry of External Affairs that finding housing was no easy feat.

Confronted with such grievances, Prime Minister Nehru sped up the plans to build a diplomatic district. In a similar fashion to Canberra and Brasília, the Indian authorities would allocate large plots of land to sending states on which they could construct diplomatic premises. As one of the first urban expansions of Edwin Lutyens' New Delhi in the post-war period, the diplomatic district was to be situated just south-west of New Delhi in close proximity to the Presidential Palace and the seat of the Indian Ministry of External Affairs.

The diplomatic district was part of Nehru's agenda to shake off the shackles of India's colonial past. Whereas the grand urban project of New Delhi (1912-1931), with its distinctive street grid of hexagonal nodes and majestic colonial architecture, was the urban expression of British hegemony, the future diplomatic district was envisaged as a demonstration that India was now a sovereign state claiming its place on the international stage. The new diplomatic neighbourhood was part of Nehru's investments in both urban planning and architecture to brand India as an independent and modern state.[280] Coinciding with the development of New Delhi's diplomatic district in 1950, Nehru greenlit the construction of Chandigarh which forms the best-known example of his aspirations to give India a modern image. Nehru commissioned Le Corbusier to design a new capital city for Punjab with a team of European and Indian architects and engineers. Completed in 1960, the urban design of Chandigarh was based on Le Corbusier's functionalist zoning principles and included the introduction of vast open spaces scattered with isolated architectural structures.[281]

New Delhi's diplomatic district (Fig. 40) was given the name Chanakyapuri which means 'City of Chanakya' in Hindi. This was a nod to Chanakya (375 B.C.-283 B.C.), one of the founding fathers of the ancient Maurya Empire which politically unified the Indian subcontinent. Chanakya made a name for himself with his political writings and was a source of inspiration for Nehru. The Indian statesman idolised Chanakya and used the name as an alias while working as a journalist in the 1930s.[282] In terms of urban planning, Chanakyapuri's grid plan is characterised by a central avenue running along a north-south axis. The main avenue bears the name of *Shanti Path*, Hindi for 'the Path of Peace', and is flanked by lawns and a series of side streets dividing the district into large rectangular parcels. On the southern edge of the diplomatic neighbourhood, two semi-circular streets were paved which gives Chanakyapuri's its distinct U-shaped street pattern. With the development of Chanakyapuri in full swing, the Indian Ministry of External Affairs set up a meeting with the diplomatic corps in January 1950 where the plans were unveiled. Among those present was the Belgian Ambassador Eugène de Ligne. Upon receiving the blueprint for Chanakyapuri, de Ligne could see how the Indian authorities were considering allocating a prominent building plot of almost 32,000 m² to Belgium. Moreover, the site was situated near the Presidential Palace and just north of the British and American parcels of land.

The intention to allocate such a large and well-located parcel of land to Belgium was striking. After all, Belgium was neither a significant political ally nor an important trading partner to India. So what was the rationale behind this decision? It seems as though the excellent personal ties between Prime Minister Nehru and Ambassador Eugène de Ligne may have had a positive effect on the procedure for allocating building sites. During his ambassadorship, de Ligne bonded with Nehru. On 20 September 1947, for instance, de Ligne invited Nehru to take a pleasure flight over the Himalayas on board the Douglas DC-6 of Sabena. In a letter to Spaak, de Ligne tooted his own horn by highlighting how the flight had brought him closer to Nehru on a personal level.[283] Moreover, de Ligne and his wife accompanied Nehru to the play *Discovery of India* which was based on a book Nehru had written. On a professional level, Ambassador de Ligne earned Nehru's respect for trying to find a diplomatic solution to end the Indo-Pakistani War of 1947-48.[284]

Eugène de Ligne was inclined to accept the Indian offer. After all, de Ligne was not entirely happy with his diplomatic housing. The colonial bungalow at Hardinge Avenue did live up to his expectations but the embassy offices were quite a different story. The Belgian chancery was housed in an apartment at Connaught Place. Made up of a ring of

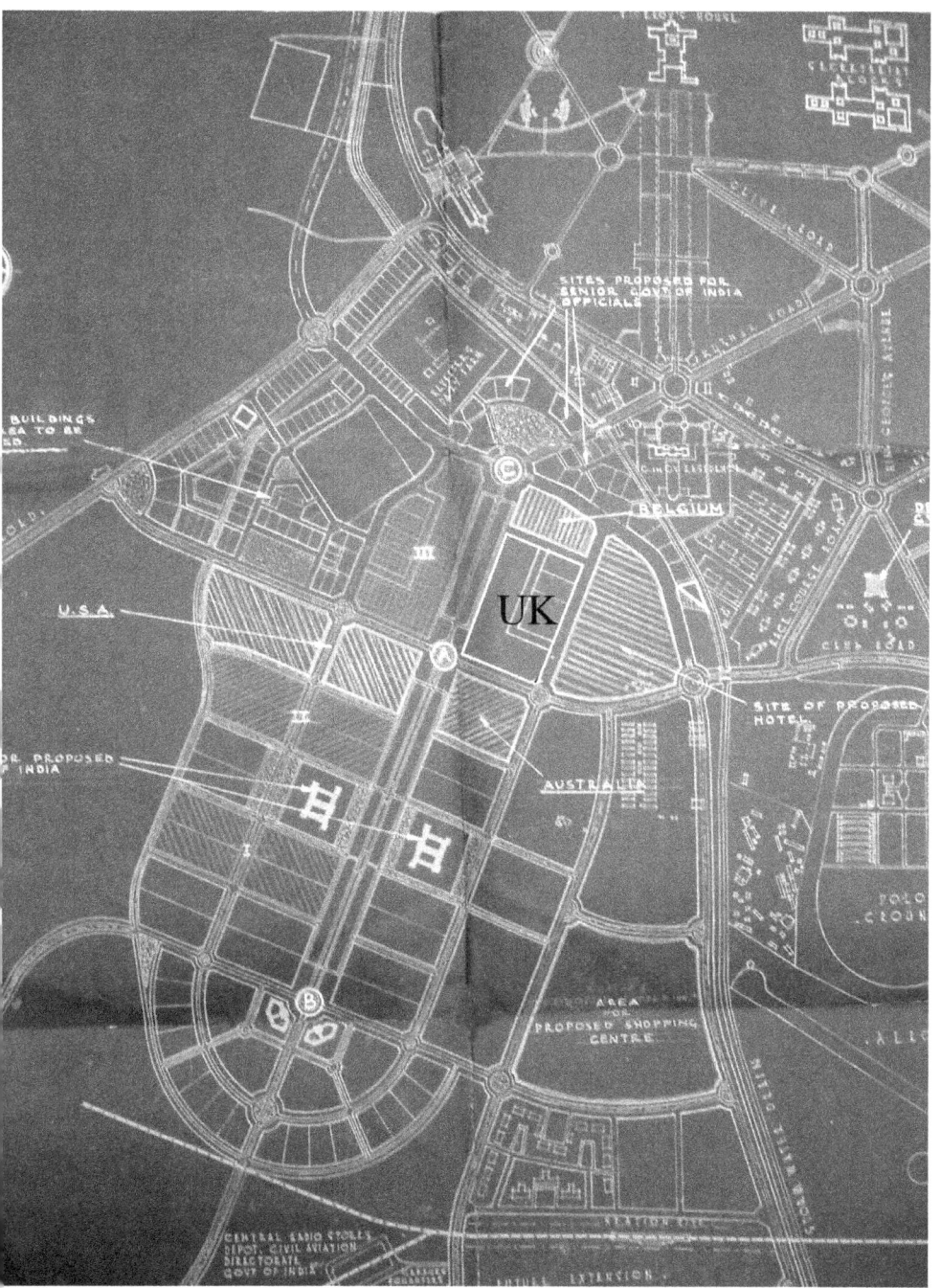

Figure 40: Chanakyapuri, 1952

colonnaded Georgian-style buildings, Connaught Place was conceived by the British architect Robert T. Russel (1888-1972) in 1933 to be the financial-economic hub of New Delhi.[285] The leased apartment was not the ideal work environment for de Ligne because of its small dimensions and the busy traffic affecting the central business district.

De Ligne was therefore keen to construct a chancery in Chanakyapuri. On the large plot of land in Chanakyapuri, de Ligne wanted to construct a spacious and comfortable chancery in a more tranquil area of the Indian metropolis. He briefed his superiors on the Indian proposal to acquire the large building plot and hoped for a quick response. As the Washington and Canberra cases have illustrated, a rapid decision-making process was not the Ministry's strong suit. The case of New Delhi would be no exception.

Before Brussels had even made up its mind, the ambassadorship of Eugène de Ligne in New Delhi came to an end as he was appointed the new Belgian ambassador to Spain in 1951. With de Ligne out of the picture, the Indian authorities now reached out to Stéphane Halot (1897-1958), the new Belgian ambassador, to convince his superiors to acquire land in Chanakyapuri.

In an effort to put the Indian proposal into more concrete terms, Ambassador Halot calculated the projected costs for his superiors. He indicated that the plot of land could be acquired for four million Belgian francs (993,000 euros) and the chancery's construction would cost 12 million Belgian francs (2.9 million euros).[286] Well aware that this total figure of 16 million Belgian francs (3,893,000 euros) would be a considerable expense for the Ministry, Halot accentuated the diplomatic significance of acquiring land in Chanakyapuri. He highlighted how 22 sending states, such as the United States and the United Kingdom, had already accepted the Indian offer. He reasoned that, if Belgium wanted to keep up with Western diplomatic missions, it was necessary to acquire a site in the diplomatic district. Halot's efforts were, however, in vain as key officials were far from keen to build a new chancery. The Inspector of Diplomatic and Consular Missions vetoed the proposal to acquire land in Chanakyapuri because of budgetary reasons.[287]

However, Ambassador Halot was not taken aback by the veto and tried his luck elsewhere. He personally reached out to Secretary-General Hervé de Gruben himself. Halot had therefore unwittingly presented his plans to the nemesis of the Belgian embassy-building programme. Fate, it seems, is not without a sense of irony. Unsurprisingly, de Gruben spoke out against the project. In a memo to Foreign Minister Paul van Zeeland, de

Gruben argued that moving to Chanakyapuri would entail excessive costs. Interestingly, Hervé de Gruben indicated that the budgetary limitations were not the main reason why he opposed the project:

> This budgetary aspect may be part of the problem, but it is not the main one. The major consideration that is holding us back is the amount of the planned investment: 16 million francs [3,893,000 euros]. Given the sums we are investing in other capitals for our embassy buildings, we feel that this amount is exaggerated in the case of India. For example, Athens 6.5 million [1.6 million euros], Lisbon 7 million [1.7 million euros], Strasbourg 2.5 million [620,000 euros].[288]

De Gruben argued that it would be ludicrous to allocate such funding to diplomatic housing in New Delhi. Such investments would be disproportionate to the economic importance of India to Belgium. Belgian exports to India had plummeted to an all-time low by 1950.[289] This was a direct result of the economic policies of the Nehruvian state. As part of his aspirations to reduce India's dependency on foreign nations and become a self-sufficient nation, Nehru largely closed off the Indian domestic market from foreign investments through import restrictions and high trade tariffs. In doing so, Nehru and his economic advisors adhered to the concept of 'the drain of wealth' which formed the core belief of their economic agenda. Originally coined during the British colonisation in the late 19th century, this economic theory argued that the Indian people were not reimbursed in terms of economic growth for all the wealth that flowed from India to Great Britain.[290] As such, the Indian subcontinent was gradually drained of its natural wealth which significantly contributed to the abject poverty and inequality.

Additionally, there was another reason why Hervé de Gruben vetoed the building plans. He was not a big fan of the diplomatic district of Chanakyapuri and the mechanism of acquiring building plots from the Indian authorities. In a memo to van Zeeland, he reasoned that the Nehruvian state could draw the Ministry into a tricky situation if the latter did decide to acquire a site:

> Indeed, if we exercise the option on the land and become its owners, we make a moral commitment to build and we can never sell it again. In a few years' time, 25 or more countries will have built their diplomatic missions' residences in this district, and the head of mission at the time will invoke reasons of prestige to consider it impossible not to do the same.[291]

In his eyes, the prospect of acquisitioning the plot would be nothing short of a poisoned chalice. As Belgian ambassadors have a tendency to compare their diplomatic housing with that of others, de Gruben was certain that they would use the building activity of other sending states in Chanakyapuri as leverage to construct an ambassadorial residence as well. According to the Secretary-General, this would be a pointless expenditure as the bungalow at Hardinge Avenue was an ideal ambassadorial residence.

Instead, de Gruben suggested purchasing the bungalow at Hardinge Avenue when the opportunity presented itself. If Belgium became the proprietor of the site, the Ministry could one day look into the possibility of constructing embassy offices in the spacious garden.[292] Given de Gruben's tight grip over the Ministry's day-to-day management, van Zeeland followed his advice. Consequently, Ambassador Halot notified the Indian government that Belgium kindly declined the offer to acquire the prominent plot of land in Chanakyapuri.

Interestingly, Ambassador Halot did not put up a fight. Whereas Ambassador Silvercruys drew strength from the opposition towards his building project, Ambassador Halot could not be bothered to go the extra mile. It was likely that his sense of resignation had to do with the fact that he wanted to leave his diplomatic posting in New Delhi. He had heard rumours that there was a vacant position for the post of ambassador to Austria and announced his candidacy to van Zeeland. To generate sympathy for a move to a European posting, the 56-year-old Halot complained that India's tropical climate was taking a toll on his health. Moreover, the ambassador indicated that his family had not joined him to New Delhi as they had opted to stay behind in Belgium. Halot's request, however, fell on deaf ears in Brussels. He was instructed to stay on as Belgian ambassador to India. His eagerness to leave New Delhi as soon as possible reveals that one cannot overstate the ambassador's role in launching a diplomatic building project. As Halot lost interest in his ambassadorship to India and therefore also in commissioning a purpose-built chancery in Chanakyapuri, the building plans seemed to be dead in the water.

De Gruben out and Scheyven in: New Bosses Mean New Rules

Stéphane Halot's transfer request may not have been granted but his boss Hervé de Gruben had more success in advancing his diplomatic career. As his mandate as Secretary-General came to an end in 1953, de Gruben got his dream job as ambassador to West Germany. As discussed in Chapter I, the departure of Hervé de Gruben and the appointment of Louis Scheyven as Secretary-General had a positive effect on the Washington project. The same can be said for the New Delhi project. Whereas Hervé de Gruben vetoed the scheme to acquire land in Chanakyapuri, the newly appointed Secretary-General Louis Scheyven was open to the idea. He firmly believed that moving to the diplomatic district could boost Belgian prestige in India. Under the leadership of Scheyven, Ambassador Halot was instructed to reopen negotiations with the Indian authorities.

By the time the negotiations between the Indian government and Ambassador Halot entered their final stages in May 1954, eight sending states had already acquired building plots in Chanakyapuri. Between January 1953 and May 1954, the Indian state had allocated plots of land to Western countries which included the United States, the United Kingdom, Australia and the Vatican together with recently decolonised Asian countries such as Burma, Pakistan, Indonesia and Sri Lanka.[293] It is true that Belgium could have acquisitioned a building plot even sooner than May 1954 but in its capacity as a small Western European country its presence clearly stands out from those of great (religious) powers and the Asian allies of the nascent Indian state.

Belgium was still among the first group of countries to accept India's offer but the Ministry's initial rejection did have repercussions on the size and location of the plot. As a token of recognition for both their diplomatic importance and willingness to move to Chanakyapuri, these sending states were rewarded with the most prominently situated sites. These countries were awarded large parcels of land with an average size of 45,000 m² which were all situated on the enclave's northern edge in close proximity to the Presidential Palace and the Indian Ministry of External Affairs. As Belgium had initially turned down the offer to acquire the prime site of 32,000 m², the Indian authorities had split the plot into two and allocated the eastern parcel of land to the Holy See and the western parcel of land to Norway instead in 1954. The pontificate of Pope Pius XII (1876-1958) wasted no time in constructing the new seat of its Apostolic Nunciature. Just one year later, in 1955, the new embassy (Fig. 41) was completed. Conceived by the Austrian architect Karl Malte von Heinz (1904-1971), the architectural design of the purpose-built seat of the Apostolic Nunciature evoked the image of Rome.[294] Meticulously following the preferences of his religious client, von Heinz designed a majestic palatial building on Indian soil. Its symmetrical classical façade with a centrally positioned portico, Ionic

Figure 41: The Apostolic Nunciature of the Holy See in Chanakyapuri, undated

columns, arches and balconies would not have looked out of place in the Eternal City. Its interiors were decorated with artwork depicting saints and popes that belonged to the rich collection of the Vatican Museums.

Whereas the palatial building was the kind of architectural self-expression one could expect from the Holy See, the same could also be said for the design of the Norwegian embassy compound (Fig. 42). A graduate of the Norwegian Institute of Technology in Trondheim, the Norwegian architect Rolf Ramm Østgaard (1923-2014) was hired to design his country's embassy. The compound included the ambassadorial residence, chancery, additional housing units for diplomats and servants' quarters. As a disciple of the renowned modernist Finnish architect Alvar Aalto (1898-1976), Østgaard's embassy design was characterised by a functionalist approach showcasing a keen sense of place and purpose. Completed in 1960, the compound was made up of a homogenous architectural ensemble of sober single-storied structures with white exteriors. Linked seamlessly with the low-rise embassy offices, the ambassadorial residence is the only building with an additional floor. Taking the intensity of the Indian sun into account, Østgaard included a shade-giving arcade in the southern and western façades of the chancery and residence. A similar approach was also used in the design of the Swedish embassy in Chanakyapuri that was

Figure 42: The Norwegian embassy compound in New Delhi, 1950s

completed in 1959.[295] Both the Norwegian and Swedish embassies were prime architectural expressions of the sophisticated simplicity and functional efficiency that hallmarked Scandinavian architecture at the time.

With the original site already divided between the Holy See and Norway, Belgium was offered a new site in Chanakyapuri. The plot (Fig. 43) was situated on the southern periphery of Chanakyapuri, far away from the plots of the contemporary world powers. At the time, Belgium was the first country to be allocated land on the southern edge of the diplomatic district. It was only from the late 1950s onward that the Indian authorities began to allocate the adjacent plots of land to countries such as the Philippines (allocated in 1958), Malaysia (1961), Bhutan (1962), New Zealand (1962), Poland (1973), Turkey (2005) and Ghana (2006). Moreover, the plot had a distinctive pentagonal shape and was significantly smaller, with a surface area of almost 22,000 m² whereas the initially offered site had a total surface area of 32,000 m². Nevertheless, Belgium was still offered a prominent parcel of land within the horseshoe-shaped diplomatic enclave. For instance, the site is still located along the central avenue of *Shanti Path* where the embassy compounds of the world powers are located. Additionally, the site is located just south of the rose garden. Together with the large Nehru Park situated on Chanakyapuri's eastern edge, the rosarium forms one of the more intimate green areas of the diplomatic neighbourhood giving the neighbourhood its quiet, verdant setting.

Framing the building plot as the ideal location for the future chancery, Secretary-General Scheyven instructed Ambassador Halot to seal the deal. On 24 May 1954, just days before the end of his ambassadorship, Halot

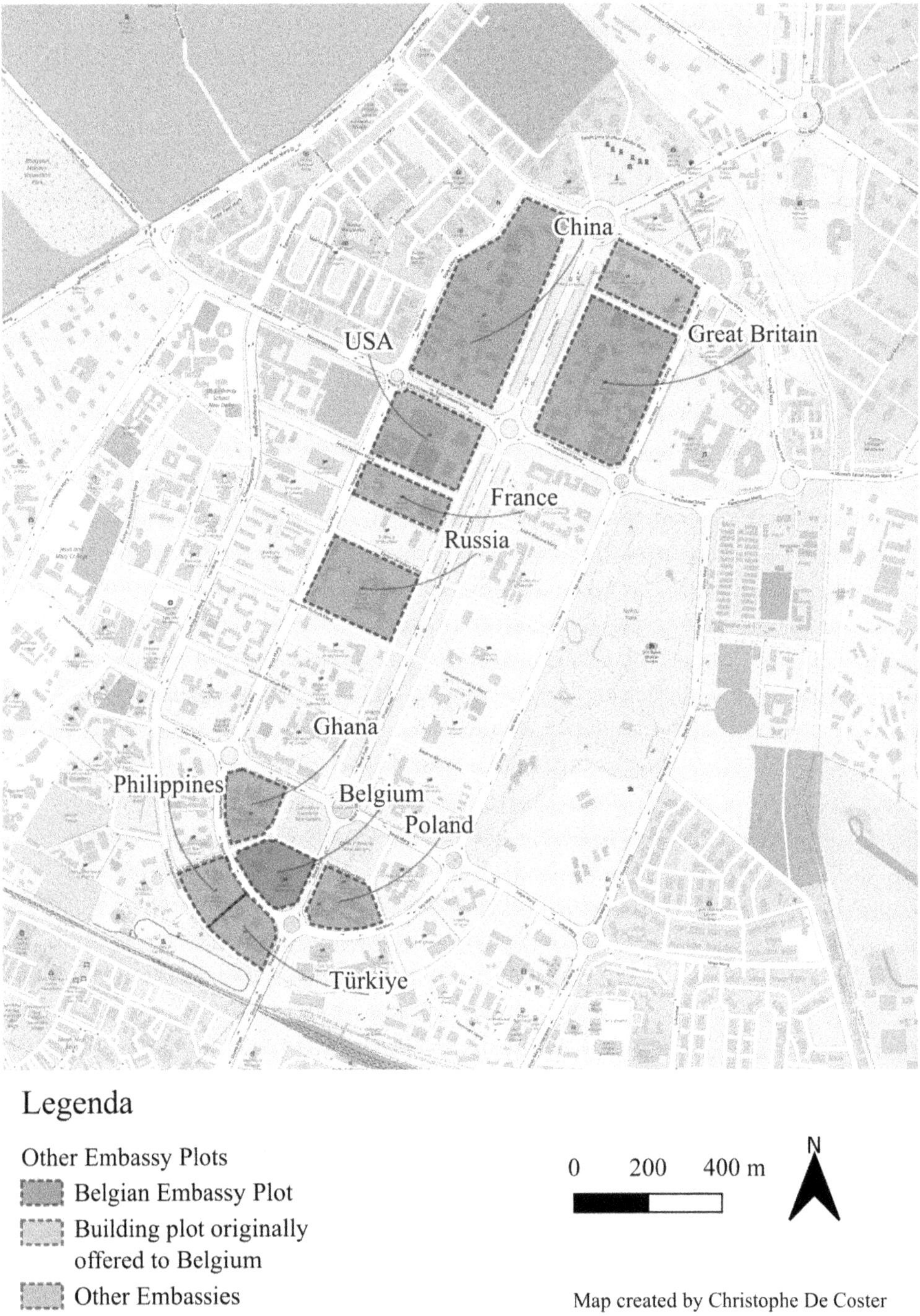

China
USA
Great Britain
France
Russia
Ghana
Philippines
Belgium
Poland
Türkiye
Legenda
Other Embassy Plots
Belgian Embassy Plot
Building plot originally offered to Belgium
Other Embassies
0 200 400 m
N
Map created by Christophe De Coster

Figure 43: Chanakyapuri

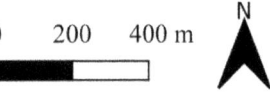

signed the necessary paperwork at a local notary's office. The Belgian state acquired the parcel of land by means of a perpetual lease. The Ministry paid a premium of 4.7 million Belgian francs (1,150,000 euros) and committed itself to paying one symbolic rupee on a yearly basis to the Indian government, serving as a tacit renewal mechanism between both parties. In return, Belgium was allocated the prime building plot on which it could construct its new chancery. The Indian perpetual lease was very similar to the Australian Crown Lease that the Belgian Ministry of Foreign Affairs had signed three years earlier. First and foremost, the perpetual lease made it crystal clear that Belgium could only use the site to construct office and residential buildings with a clear diplomatic purpose. Secondly, the architectural design of diplomatic buildings had to comply with local building codes in New Delhi and the blueprints had to be submitted to the Chief Commissioner of New Delhi for review. Thirdly, Belgium had to abide by the so-called 'drain of wealth' economic theory that made up Nehru's economic agenda. The contract stipulated that:

> The Lessor [Indian government] excepts and reserves unto himself all mines, minerals, coal, gold washing, earth oils and quarries in or under the said land, and full right and power at all times after giving reasonable notice to the Lessee [Belgium] to do all acts and things which may be necessary or expedient for the purpose of searching for, working, obtaining, removing and enjoying the same.[296]

As far as the Nehruvian authorities were concerned, the nation's precious raw materials had to be kept out of foreign hands in the process of allocating sites. The fourth and final similarity between the Australian Crown Lease and the Indian perpetual lease was the stipulation that Belgium landscape, introduce plants to, and thereafter maintain its embassy grounds in Chanakyapuri in an adequate manner. In return, the Indian government committed itself to completing all infrastructural works such as paving the roads, installing street lighting around the site and connecting the site to the municipal electricity network, water supply and sewerage system within two years of the signing of the lease.[297]

It is striking that the Indian authorities did not impose a deadline to sending states to launch construction works. This was a profound difference to the Australian Crown Lease where sending states were contractually bound to kickstart construction works within three years following the start of the lease. The Indian authorities most likely believed that it was not necessary to stipulate such a deadline explicitly in the contract. After all, if a sending state was willing to pay a considerable amount of money to lease a building plot, the Nehruvian state reasoned, then its government would surely be keen on building a new embassy in Chanakyapuri as soon as possible. However, the Indian government would be in for a rude awakening as the Belgian Ministry of Foreign Affairs crowned itself the undisputed champion of procrastination in Chanakyapuri.

The Undeveloped Building Plot: The Symbol of Belgian Disinterest in India

As the Washington and Canberra projects have demonstrated, the fact that the Ministry had a building plot at its disposal did not necessarily mean that it immediately proceeded with construction works. The time between the Ministry's acquisition of the land and the launch of construction works in the United States and Australia were respectively nine and eight years. In the grand scheme of things, however, these time spans were relatively short when compared to the turn of events in New Delhi. In this case, there was a staggering time span of almost three decades between the acquisition of the plot in 1954 and the completion of the purpose-built embassy in 1983 (Table 1). This large timespan not only stands out from the Belgian embassy-building programme as a whole but also from the building activity of other sending states along the main avenue of *Shanti Path*.

The reasons for this procrastination are twofold. The first reason is an all too familiar story by this time. The embassy-building programme continued to be dependent on the goodwill of the Belgian Ministry of Finance for funding. As the allocated funding has historically been modest, the Belgian Ministry of Foreign Affairs opted to invest its limited funding first and foremost in diplomatic postings with economic importance.

This brings us to the second and most important reason for the lack of enthusiasm to build an embassy in New Delhi. As the Nehruvian state did not embrace the free market system that would have enabled Belgian companies to export goods and services easily to India, Belgian policymakers were not committed to going the extra mile to penetrate this foreign market with its high import tariffs and strict regulation culture.[298] Consequently, Brussels did not see the point of making considerable investments in diplomatic personnel and housing in New Delhi. Secretary-General Louis Scheyven may have got his way with the acquisition of land in Chanakyapuri but as far as successive secretary-generals

Sending state	Allocation building plot	Inauguration of the embassy compound	Time span
Afghanistan	1953	1960	7
Australia	1953	1960	7
Belgium	1954	1983	29
Canada	1958	1972	14
France	1978	1985	7
West Germany	1955	1962	7
Norway	1954	1960	6
Poland	1973	1978	5
Soviet Union	1956	1959	3
United Kingdom	1955	1959	4
United States	1953	1959	6

Table 1: Time span between the allocation of embassy plots along the central avenue of Shanti Path in Chanakyapuri and the inauguration of the embassy compound

were concerned, it was out of the question to build in a country that was economically insignificant to Belgium.

The Belgian government drew flak from the opposition in the Chamber of Representatives for its reluctance to build a new chancery in New Delhi. During a parliamentary debate on Belgian exports in 1955, the Christian-democratic MP Emiel Van Hamme (1900-1998) stressed the importance of investing in modern embassy offices where Belgian diplomats could work comfortably and receive guests in style to talk business.[299] As an entrepreneur with business dealings in Asia, Van Hamme had recently made a business trip to India and expressed his dissatisfaction with the apparently deplorable working conditions in New Delhi. He described the leased apartment at Connaught Place as a deficient and cramped work environment that had the appearance of army barracks.[300] Van Hamme considered an embassy building to be a reflection of the importance that the sending state attributes to the receiving one. Framing India as a future economic Valhalla for Belgian entrepreneurs and investors, Van Hamme could not get his head around the fact that the government did not invest in the construction of modern embassy offices in New Delhi.

Emiel Van Hamme went on to call out Minister of Finance Henri Liebaert (1895-1977) of the Liberal Party. Van Hamme criticised him for his allegedly unequal allocation of funding among the different ministry departments. He made the case that Liebaert had his priorities all wrong in terms of government infrastructure. Van Hamme claimed that, while Liebaert had no objections to allocating 500 million Belgian francs (123 million euros) to construct a state-of-the-art ministerial office complex in Brussels for his own administration, the finance minister was too greedy to allocate just ten million Belgian francs (2.4 million euros) to build a chancery in New Delhi.[301] Van Hamme was alluding to the *Cité Administrative d'État*. As one of the largest architectural projects ever launched by the Belgian state, the *Cité Administrative d'État* was designed to physically concentrate the offices of 8,000 civil servants from various ministry departments on one site in Brussels.[302]

Van Hamme concluded that, if the Belgian government truly wanted to improve the working conditions of the diplomatic corps, the 500 million Belgian francs (123 million euros) would be better spent on constructing 50 chanceries worth ten million Belgian francs (2.4 million euros) each all over the world. His pleas to abandon the plans for the *Cité Administrative d'État* and reallocate the funding to the embassy-building programme fell on deaf ears.

Meanwhile, some 6,500 kilometres eastward, the Belgian plot in Chanakyapuri remained untouched. While other sending states kickstarted building projects, the Belgian wasteland was a fitting symbol for the Ministry's disinterest in India. In 1957, just three years after the signing of the perpetual lease, the Ministry considered giving the plot in Chanakyapuri back to the Indian authorities as it had no building plans for the near future.[303] The Inspection of Diplomatic and Consular Missions suggested terminating the perpetual lease in Chanakyapuri at once. Eventually, Spaak discarded the idea because he believed that offering the plot back to the Indian authorities would undoubtedly tarnish Belgian prestige in India. Spaak opted to hold on to the plot of land but allocate future investments in diplomatic housing solely to the purchase of the ambassadorial residence at Hardinge Avenue from the Indian authorities. In the meantime, the embassy offices at Connaught Place were moved to a new location.

With the limited funding at his disposal, Ambassador Count Geoffroy d'Aspremont-Lynden (1904-1979) leased a bungalow in Jor Bagh to house the embassy offices from 1957 onwards. Situated in the southern suburbs of New Delhi, Jor Bagh was a popular neighbourhood for sending states to house their chanceries. Interestingly, MP Emiel Van Hamme also visited the Jor Bagh chancery in late 1957. However, the new location and accommodation did not live up to his expectations. In the Belgian parliament, Van Hamme made a snide comment on the bungalow housing of the chancery. He sarcastically commented that, had it not been for the Belgian flag waving in front of the bungalow, he would have never believed that the Belgian embassy offices were located in such a rundown building.[304]

He yet again urged the government to revive the original building plans of 1952 and construct a chancery in Chanakyapuri at once. However, his pleas were to no avail. Economic relations with India did not justify the launching of an embassy project. In 1957, barely one per cent of the total Belgian export volume was destined for the Indian market.[305]

Even if the Indian subcontinent had been a more lucrative export market for Belgium at the time, it would have been highly unlikely that the Ministry would have commissioned a new embassy in Chanakyapuri. After all, the once excellent diplomatic ties had turned sour. These tensions were intrinsically linked to the turbulent decolonisation of the Belgian Congo during the summer of 1960. As one of the founding fathers of the Non-Aligned Movement and its struggle against Western (neo-)colonialism in Africa and Asia, Prime Minister Nehru criticised the Belgian government for the ill-prepared decolonisation of the Belgian Congo and its involvement in the secession of the resource-rich province of Katanga from the Democratic Republic of the Congo. Belgian diplomats posted to New Delhi reported to Brussels that they were increasingly cold-shouldered by the Nehruvian state because of events in the Democratic Republic of the Congo.[306]

By February 1961, when news broke out that Patrice Lumumba had been executed by the Belgian-supported Katangese regime, diplomatic relations between Brussels and New Delhi reached rock bottom. This became very tangible in the streetscape of New Delhi where several anti-Belgian demonstrations took place. On the afternoon of 14 February 1961, African exchange students raided the Belgian chancery at Jor Bagh, turning the chancery into the focal point of yet another iconoclastic attack against the Belgian diplomatic corps. According to Ambassador Goffart, the Communist Party of India had run a smear campaign against Belgium and incited students to raid the embassy.[307]

Boiling with anger, the students targeted the most tangible symbols representing Belgium. The national coat of arms at the main entrance and the state portrait of King Baudouin in the ambassador's office were both struck down and smashed to smithereens. However, the amount of damage was relatively small when compared to the attacks in Warsaw, Belgrade and especially Cairo where the embassy building was burned to the ground. Ambassador Goffart offered a rather racist explanation for the limited damage. Referring to the ethnic background of the rioters,

190 CHAPTER III

Goffart reasoned that the African students were most likely astounded that a rich Western country such as Belgium housed its embassy offices in a building that looked like an African hut.[308] He claimed that the exchange students had only slightly damaged the embassy interiors because the Jor Bagh chancery reminded them of home. The ambassador therefore not only mocked the living standard of the African students involved but also the apparently parlous state of his chancery building. Goffart's comments serve as a prime example of the biting and sarcastic tone frequently used by Belgian ambassadors to complain about their diplomatic housing.

As the students left the trashed interiors of the Belgian chancery, their fury had not yet calmed down. They marched to Chanakyapuri to also stage an attack against the American chancery. Believing that the American government was also involved in the murder of Patrice Lumumba, the African exchange students meant to teach Washington, D.C. a lesson by attacking its embassy offices. However, the American security personnel put up stiff resistance. Following a scuffle, the exchange students quickly headed for the hills without even coming close to the embassy.[309] Had the students succeeded in storming the US embassy, they would have found themselves in a building that was architecturally a far cry from the rundown Belgian bungalow they had just trashed.

In 1953, just one year before Belgium did so, the US State Department began to lease a spacious plot of land along the central avenue of *Shanti Path*. As part of its policy to hire American architects for major embassy projects, the Foreign Buildings Operations awarded the New Delhi commission to Edward Durell Stone (1902-1978). The Foreign Buildings Operations conceived the future New Delhi chancery as a prestige project to ingratiate itself with the Indian government. Against the backdrop of its rivalry with the USSR for political influence over the Nehruvian state, the New Delhi embassy had to brand the United States a progressive, democratic and above all reliable international partner for India. Following a visit to New Delhi, Edward Durell Stone set about designing the new chancery. His refined design (Fig. 44) comprises a large rectangular architectural structure situated on an elevated platform. This architectural structure consists of a two-storey glass box. Taking Delhi's tropical climate into account, the glass box is protected by a chequered sunscreen made of a white marble-concrete mix. As the flat roof extended well beyond the sunscreen, Stone included a series of sleek columns that were covered in gold leaf to create a colour contrast with the white exteriors.[310] Above the

Figure 44: The American chancery in New Delhi, 1950s

glazed entrance, Stone strategically positioned a large American coat of arms that was also covered in gold leaf. The chancery's scale and horizontal composition gives the chancery the appearance of a temple-like pavilion. This image was further reinforced by the presence of both a waterbody in front of the chancery that reflected the façade and the wide steps. In designing the chancery, Stone added features that were intended to pay tribute to the host country. To this end, he included a Mughal-inspired courtyard in the chancery's interior with endemic plants, a decorative pool for cooling down and small stones from the Ganges as pavement.[311]

Completed in 1959, the American chancery was and still is one of the diplomatic landmarks affirming Chanakyapuri's status as New Delhi's main diplomatic hub. Its refined architectural design showcased to other sending states that commissioning state-of-the-art embassy buildings could not only boost one's self-image through diplomatic architecture but also provide diplomatic personnel with a comfortable work environment in Delhi's tropical climate. Following the completion of the American chancery, a real building frenzy took hold of Chanakyapuri. By the end of the 1960s, more than 20 purpose-built embassy compounds had been erected. All the while, however, the Belgian plot along *Shanti Path* remained a barren landscape, a clear sign that the Ministry lacked the necessary incentives to build.

A Mixed Bag: Deteriorating Diplomatic Housing but an Economic Glimmer of Hope

Whereas the building plot in Chanakyapuri remained undeveloped throughout the 1960s, the Ministry of Foreign Affairs did make some investments in diplomatic housing in New Delhi. In 1960, the Ministry purchased the colonial bungalow at Hardinge Avenue. As the Belgian state henceforth owned the property, successive Belgian ambassadors made considerable efforts to make their ambassadorial residence at Hardinge Avenue a true home. One notable ambassador who turned the residence into a home was Charles Kerremans (1915-1998). Having a green thumb, Ambassador Kerremans loved to garden and took great pride in the residence's well-maintained garden. Kerremans planted greenery endemic to India and even participated in several flora art competitions in New Delhi, often with great success.[312]

Kerremans' green thumb was also picked up by the Inspector of Diplomatic and Consular Missions, Georges Puttevils, who made a site visit to the New Delhi embassy in 1973. In his report, he praised the well-tended garden but noted that the ambassadorial residence had seen better days.[313] Firstly, the walls had become damp as the building had been constructed without proper foundations. Attempts to conceal these damp patches by repainting the walls had all been in vain. Secondly, the sewer system had not been properly constructed. Consequently, it often flooded and spread human faeces across the garden, generating an unbearable smell. Puttevils reported that he had witnessed such an event at first hand following a visit to the toilet. Thirdly and lastly, the neighbourhood in which the ambassadorial residence was situated had witnessed profound changes over the years. As the motorised traffic in New Delhi had significantly increased in the 1960s, the nearby intersection had become an important arterial road. The decibels produced by passing cars and drivers honking their horns, something intrinsically linked to driver behaviour in India, created significant noise pollution. Consequently, it became increasingly difficult for Ambassador Kerremans and his guests to fully enjoy luncheons and cocktail parties in the garden.

In his report, Inspector Puttevils warned his superiors that the bungalow's parlous state and the noise pollution reflected poorly on Belgian prestige. Puttevils also gave his account of the embassy offices. By 1973, the chancery was housed in a leased residential building at Golf Links, a southern suburb of New Delhi. As far as the working conditions in the chancery were concerned, the situation was not exactly better than the living conditions in the ambassadorial residence. In an interview, former embassy staffer Cristina Funes-Noppen recalls that the building was not beautiful to look at and the interior layout was anything but functional.[314] Offices were situated in cramped rooms and it was a logistical nightmare to store archival records safely in the building's cellar. As the property was leased, the Belgian embassy could not make any profound alterations to the building's spatial layout.

Inspector Puttevils put forward suggestions to improve Belgian diplomatic housing. Firstly, he explored the possibility of creating an embassy compound at Hardinge Avenue. Echoing previous ideas, Puttevils suggested constructing new embassy offices in the residence's garden and launching a thorough renovation of the colonial bungalow to restore it to its former glory. The inspector, however, raised a red flag when discussing this possibility. By this time, the Indian government had redeveloped the area into a residential neighbourhood. Only cultural institutions were given permission to build new offices in the district. Puttevils made it crystal clear that the municipal government would never award a building permit to the Belgian embassy.[315]

Secondly, Puttevils suggested reviving an old scheme dating all the way back to the mid-1950s. He reminded his superiors that the Ministry had been leasing a building site in Chanakyapuri since 1954 but had not done anything with it. Puttevils was sold on the idea of building an embassy compound in the diplomatic district. Reading between the lines of his report, he accentuated how the construction of a new embassy had the potential to kill two birds with one stone. Firstly, Puttevils revealed how other countries had already constructed magnificent embassy compounds. They had successfully used diplomatic architecture to boost their self-image and accentuate that Chanakyapuri was the main diplomatic hub of New Delhi. Puttevils argued that if Belgium wanted to boost its self-image, moving into a purpose-built embassy would help tremendously. Secondly, the launch of a building project could help to smooth things over with the Indian authorities. He stressed that the Indian government was growing impatient with Belgian procrastination. The Belgian diplomat Cristina Funes-Noppen even recalls that the lack of Belgian interest annoyed officials at the Indian Ministry of External Affairs who frequently brought up the issue during bilateral meetings.[316] As far as Puttevils was concerned, the Ministry should launch a building project at once. However, in his report he expressed misgivings about the financial feasibility of building abroad given the economic circumstances back home.

Puttevils was referring to the fact that the Belgian economy was going through a rough patch at the time following the oil embargo that the Organisation of the Petroleum Exporting Countries (OPEC) had imposed on the Western world in 1973. The oil embargo crippled the national economy and state finances. Whereas the national budget was still balanced in 1974, the budget deficit had increased to a staggering 279 billion Belgian francs (21.4 billion euros) by 1981.

Confronted with this adverse financial-economic climate, successive Belgian governments drastically reduced national spending in an effort to stay afloat. The Ministry of Foreign Affairs witnessed its fair share of budget cuts. From 1976 onwards, the Ministry faced annual budget cuts of seven per cent that crippled both the material and physical presence of the Belgian diplomatic corps abroad.[317] Several diplomatic and consular missions were closed down while much-needed maintenance and renovation works on embassies were postponed until further notice.[318] Well aware that the Ministry had to work on a shoestring budget, Inspector Georges Puttevils knew all too well that it would be unfeasible to move to Chanakyapuri and commission a new embassy.

Meanwhile, Belgian exports to India had significantly increased by the end of the 1970s. Whereas Belgian companies exported 2.3 billion Belgian francs (328.9 million euros) in terms of goods and services to India in 1973, this figure had risen substantially to 14 billion Belgian francs (1.2 billion euros) by 1978.[319] One of the ways in which India's growing economic importance was reflected was through the status that the Ministry allocated to the New Delhi embassy. In a similar fashion to publication categories in academia, the most prestigious Belgian diplomatic postings were categorised as A1-postings. In the late 1970s, for instance, the Permanent Representation of Belgium to NATO and the Belgian embassies in Paris, London, The Hague, Bonn, Washington, D.C. and Kinshasa were listed among A1-postings. It speaks volumes that New Delhi was added to the list in the late 1970s.

With the New Delhi embassy joining this select group of diplomatic postings, its esteemed status had to be reflected in terms of housing. Therefore, the Ministry's highest echelons had a sudden change of heart at the end of the 1970s regarding the construction of a new embassy in Chanakyapuri. Whereas it had previously been reluctant to launch a building project, the highest echelons now seriously looked into the possibility. In doing so, they wanted to build on the economic momentum of the last couple of years literally and figuratively. As embassy staffer Philippe

Falisse recalls, the Ministry pledged to provide Belgian diplomats with suitable accommodation to receive trade missions in style.[320]

Just a few years earlier, such ambitions would have been unachievable. The parlous state of the Belgian ambassadorial residence at Hardinge Avenue did not ring any alarm bells back in Brussels. However, as India became an ever more important export market by the late 1970s, the Ministry of Foreign Affairs was now determined to build a new embassy in India at once. Judging from the level of funding, the future New Delhi embassy was envisaged to be a key building project. The Ministry of Foreign Affairs spared no expense as it requested 95 million Belgian francs (8.3 million euros) for the project at hand.[321] Taking into account that the Ministry of Foreign Affairs was struggling to make ends meet at the time, this was a considerable amount of money to say the least.

In a similar fashion to previously discussed embassy projects, the building costs were to be partially covered by selling the ambassadorial residence at Hardinge Avenue.[322] The total revenue was therefore entirely reinvested in the nation's diplomatic patrimony. Triggered by the improved trade relations and the horrendous state of Belgian diplomatic housing in New Delhi, the Belgian government allocated the necessary 95 million Belgian francs (8.3 million euros) to the building project at the start of 1979.[323] The Belgian diplomatic corps may have put off its building plans in New Delhi for exactly a quarter of a century but an economic glimmer of hope had finally convinced Brussels that the time had come to build in Chanakyapuri.

Hiring the Artist-Architect Satish Gujral: A Gesture to the Indian National Congress

Having secured the necessary funding by 1979, the Ministry of Foreign Affairs was in need of an architect. By this time, Luc Piot was the Ministry's in-house architect.[324] Like his predecessors, Luc Piot was assigned to the Inspection of Diplomatic and Consular Missions. In his capacity as architect, Piot served as a technical advisor and supervised the maintenance, renovation and refurbishment of the Belgian embassy patrimony.

With regard to the New Delhi project, Luc Piot was not tasked with designing the new embassy. The Ministry continued the practice of calling upon private architectural practices. As luck would have it, the New Delhi project marked a milestone in the way the Ministry awarded commissions to architects. Whereas the highest echelons had previously tended to award commissions to befriended architects or to hire architects suggested by

Belgian ambassadors, the Ministry now opted to organise an architectural competition for the project in 1980.[325] However, it would be too short-sighted to claim that the introduction of an architectural competition was synonymous with a more transparent and impartial award procedure for embassy commissions. After all, an architect had to be invited by the Belgian embassy in New Delhi to enter the contest. As such, an architect had to be already on speaking terms with the Belgian diplomatic corps, underscoring that personal ties remained paramount for an architect. Moreover, the embassy opted to include only Indian architects to its shortlist of invitees.[326]

With Belgian architects excluded from the competition, the Ministry did not envisage the building project as an opportunity to give Belgian architects an international stage to show off their take on diplomatic architecture. In an interview with the Christian-democratic strongman Mark Eyskens, the former Belgian prime minister stressed how the Ministry intentionally opted to hire an Indian architect because of political considerations.[327] Such a move was envisaged as a token of goodwill to the Indian elite. In fact, it was common practice for sending states in Chanakyapuri to collaborate with Indian architects.[328]

One of the Indian architects who made the Belgian shortlist was Satish Gujral (1925-2020), whose presence was striking to say the least. At the time, Satish Gujral was principally known as one of India's leading artists of the second half of the 20th century, making his mark as a sculptor, painter and muralist. Born in 1925 in the province of Punjab in British India, Gujral had a freak accident as a child which resulted in hearing impairment and gradual loss of coherent speech. Nonetheless, Gujral pursued his dream to become an artist. In 1939, Gujral studied art at the Mayo School of Arts in Punjab and then, in 1944, he studied at the Bombay JJ School of Arts. Following the decolonisation of British India in 1947, his home province of Punjab was divided between the newly independent states of India and Pakistan. Gujral witnessed first-hand the devastating effects of this ill-prepared partition as he helped his father with the evacuation of refugees from Pakistan to India during the tumultuous summer of 1947. He was deeply touched by this human tragedy, which became a recurrent element in his artistic work.

In 1952, Gujral was awarded a scholarship to study at the *Palacio Nacional de Bellas Artes* in Mexico City. There he took on work as an apprentice of the renowned Mexican muralist Diego Rivera (1886-1957), who pushed him to explore the art form of muralism. During his stay, Gujral came into contact with influential artists and architects such as Frida Kahlo (1907-1954) and Frank Lloyd Wright (1867-1959). As the renowned American architect had a profound interest in pre-Columbian architecture, Wright frequently visited Mexico and it was most likely in this context that Gujral had the occasion to speak with him.[329] In his memoirs, Gujral remembers bringing up the topic of muralism in a conversation with Wright. He asked Wright why he had never thought of having murals in the interiors of his buildings, to which the American architect allegedly replied, "Well, an architect needs an artist to resurrect a dead wall, but I never design dead walls."[330] As Gujral vividly recalls in his memoirs, these words took root in his mind:

> Murals and sculpture can be used in architecture as ornamental additions, but they cannot help in strengthening a building's spatial or utilitarian aspect. After this realization, I began to look at Mexican murals from another perspective. Whatever their plastic or aesthetic merit, in most cases they made no contribution to the buildings that they adorned. This disillusionment was shattering, but it helped me in making a more objective assessment of Mexican art and the true value and function of murals.[331]

Following his return to India in 1955, Gujral put his newly acquired skill into practice as he designed murals for the Punjab University (1963) in Chandigarh and the Oberoi Sheraton Hotel (1973). However, such high-profile commissions could not take away his growing frustration about the architectural context in which he was asked to work. Gujral recalls:

> The buildings I was asked to paint murals on were essentially not suitable for them. Each time I was working on one it crossed my mind that I would have done a better job designing the building itself.[332]

Putting his money where his mouth is, Gujral set up his own architecture firm, Design Plus, on 25 November 1976 even though he lacked a professional qualification in architecture. Nevertheless, Gujral received commissions from well-reputed Indian entrepreneurs such as Bhupendra Kumar Modi and Ajit Narain Haksar (1925-2005), designing respectively a private residence and a hotel. As Satish Gujral had only recently ventured into architecture and lacked the qualifications, the question remains as to why the Belgian embassy added him to the shortlist.

Yet again, personal ties played a significant role. In the late 1970s, Satish Gujral attended a cocktail party at the Belgian ambassadorial

Figure 45: Inder Kumar Gujral (left), Indira Gandhi (middle), and Satish Gujral (right), 1957

residence.[333] There, he came into contact with the Belgian diplomat Louis-Roland Burny. Both men got on very well and became close friends. In his memoirs, Gujral recalls how Burny informed him of the upcoming project to build a new embassy:

> My Belgian friend Ronald [Roland] Burny [...] told me of the proposal to build the Belgian embassy in Chanakyapuri. He offered to have me included in the shortlist of Indian architects whose plans would be submitted to a committee for selection. My initial response was not enthusiastic. I submitted my plan more to please Burny than in any hope of getting the assignment.[334]

Apparently, a Belgian diplomat faced no difficulties in including a befriended architect to a design competition. On the surface, the introduction of an architectural competition seemed to have paved the way for a more transparent and unbiased selection procedure. However, in reality, there was nothing new when compared to previous award procedures.

At first glance, it seems as though Burny only wanted to include Gujral to the shortlist to do his friend a favour. However, there is more to Gujral's inclusion than meets the eye. Political reasons also came into play. The Gujrals were and still are a well-respected family that belongs to the highest echelons of Indian society (Fig. 45). On a political level, the family has traditionally been affiliated to the Congress Party of Jawaharlal Nehru and his daughter, Indira Gandhi (1917-1984), who served as Indian Prime Minister in the 1960s and 1980s. Moreover, Inder Kumar Gujral (1919-2012), who was the brother of Satish, was a seasoned diplomat and prominent member of the Congress Party.[335] By awarding the prestigious embassy commission to the brother of an influential Indian politician and diplomat, the Belgian diplomatic corps could further cement ties with the almighty Congress Party. Eventually, Satish Gujral accepted the invitation of Burny to enter the architectural competition.

The Embassy's Site Plan: Checkpoints in a Fortress

In order to interpret Gujral's design entry, it is essential to further expand on his personal aversion towards functionalist and modernist approaches to architecture. The urban project of Chandigarh was a particular thorn in his side as Gujral was very critical of Le Corbusier's approach:

> Corbusier based his plans for Chandigarh upon the time-worn cliché of 'form follows function'. His admirers treated it as a sacred mantra. What they called functional architecture turned out to be more of his own concepts rather than the users' or clients' notion of what they wanted. In common parlance, this phrase meant architecture for the sake of architecture. His buildings exhibit a marked indifference towards local cultures around which communities have traditionally created their habitats, in the way birds construct their nests according to the shapes of their bodies. Architecture that ignores this time-tested rule becomes artificial.[336]

Gujral's reading of the Chandigarh project is of course limited. In fact, the local conditions in Punjab had been taken into account by Le Corbusier and his team. For instance, Le Corbusier scaled the Capitol Complex in proportion to the neighbouring Himalayas and extensively employed *brise-soleils* to deal with the climatological conditions of India.[337] However, most buildings in Chandigarh did not feature straightforward references to local building traditions or materials, two aspects Gujral aspired to introduce in his own projects.

Gujral's criticism needs to be seen in the context of fundamental shifts in India's architectural scene during the late 1970s. Indian architects trained overseas witnessed how the modernist project and its universalist claims increasingly drew criticism from the postmodern avant-garde in the West.[338] However, given the technological constraints of India's building industry and crippling housing crisis, renouncing modernist architecture with its functionalist hallmarks was a luxury they initially could not afford. Instead, political developments deeply affected contemporary architectural thinking in India. In 1977, growing criticism of Prime Minister Indira Gandhi's extensive use of the state of emergency and the apparent failure to fight corruption and poverty effectively resulted in a new coalition government, which included Hindu right-wing parties. Believing that Gandhi's socialist agenda had lost touch with local identity, these factions expressed their desire to give Hindu culture a more prominent place in India's society.

This changing ethos was reflected in architecture. Supported by the rising influence of the private sector in commissioning buildings, architectural thinking accentuated the importance of culture, place and identity in designing buildings. For instance, from the 1980s, the Indian architect Charles Correa (1930-2015) opted to incorporate historically charged features such as domes and stupas – a mound-like structure used as a venue for meditation in Buddhism – in several of his designs, such as the Vidhan Bhavan State Assembly in Bhopal (1980-1996). Furthermore, Correa prominently displayed typical local building materials in his projects, including white marble from Makrana, black Kadapa limestone and Agra Red sandstone.[339] Meanwhile, the Indian architect Balkrishna Doshi increasingly opted to include locally embedded symbols and associations in his architectural oeuvre. Initially working as an apprentice for Le Corbusier in the late 1940s, Doshi's oeuvre in the 1980s also featured stupas, as well as references to seventeenth century Mughal architecture.[340] It was in the context of this growing importance of historical and cultural references in Indian architectural thinking that Gujral took on the task of designing the new Belgian embassy. It would, however, be too shortsighted to simply categorise his embassy design as just another example of the changing postmodernist architectural climate in India. In line with the work of Correa and Doshi, Gujral's design tried to strike a balance between traditional and modern references. However, at the same time it showcased a much more crafted and experimental approach to architecture combined with an explicit interest in the overall formal expression of the building. As such, the project is as much an example of contemporary Indian architecture as it is an anomaly within it.[341]

Metaphorical, historical and symbolic associations heavily influenced Gujral's design for the new embassy, as demonstrated in the site plan. In terms of programmatic needs, the Ministry briefed participating architects that the new embassy should include an ambassadorial residence, a chancellor's residence, a chancery and servants' quarters. The triangular plot of land played an instrumental role in the layout of the various buildings. Gujral drew an imaginary axis running from east to west, dividing the parcel of land into two nearly symmetrical parts. The compound's two most important building units, the ambassadorial residence and chancery, were positioned on this axis. To determine the position of the residence and the chancery, Gujral took their respective functions into account. As the front office where people conduct their bureaucratic business with the Belgian administration, the chancery was positioned along Chanakyapuri's main road of *Shanti Path*, making it more convenient for embassy officials and visitors to reach the chancery. To deal with the circulation of cars, a driveway and garages were to be constructed. The ambassadorial residence was situated at the tip of the triangular plot of land along Nyaya Marg, a quieter street. This was to be a welcome change from the busy street of Hardinge Avenue where the ambassadorial residence was situated at the time. A roundabout was to be included in front of the ambassadorial residence, functioning as the main drop-off area for guests attending a dinner party, reception or one-on-one meeting with the ambassador. Parking lots were situated adjacent to where chauffeurs could wait until their passengers came out. The chancellor's residence and the servants' quarters were to be situated on the northern edge of the building plot, opposite to Chanakyapuri's rose garden.

Upon analysing the compound as a whole, it becomes apparent that Gujral positioned all of the building units along the edges of the compound (Fig. 46). In doing so, Gujral wanted to evoke two historical references. Firstly, he envisaged each building unit to be a checkpoint of a fortress for the different approaches to the embassy grounds.[342] Just as checkpoints function as a gateway to a fortress, Gujral designed the physically distant building units as different points of arrival for the diverse groups of people visiting the embassy grounds on a daily basis. Whereas a visa applicant had to enter the chancery through the busy entrance at *Shanti Path*, the chauffeur of an Indian entrepreneur could drive up to the ambassadorial residence at Nyaya Marg away from any prying eyes.

The second reason why Gujral positioned the different building units on the edges was to create a spacious garden between the residence and chancery. Well aware that the old residence at Hardinge Avenue was renowned for its well-tended garden, Gujral wanted to include a large

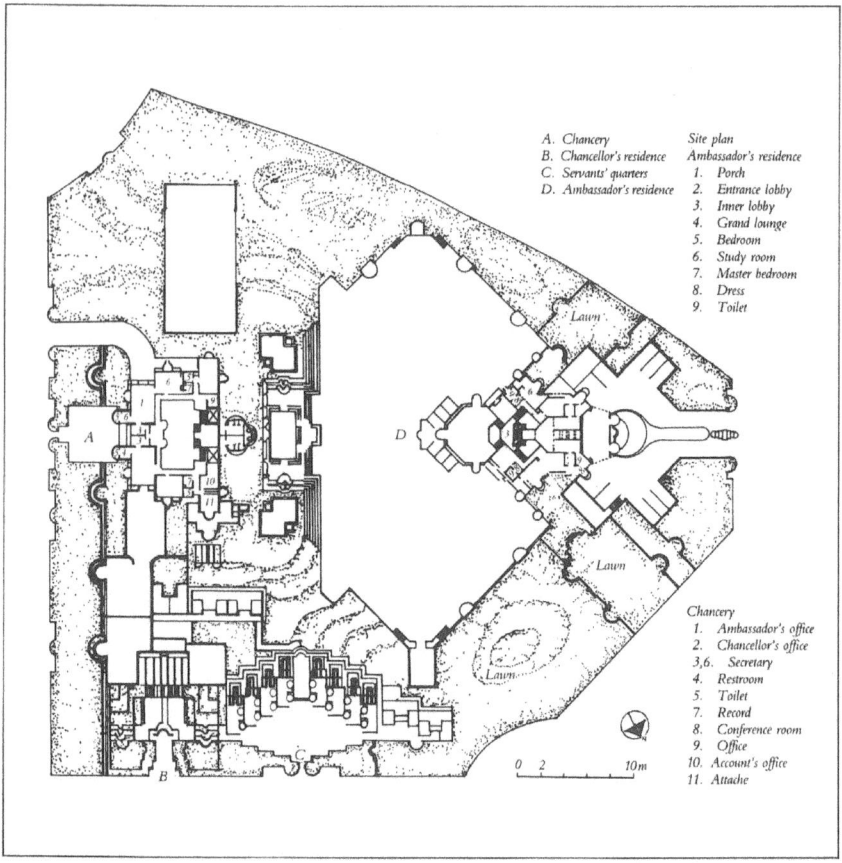

Figure 46: Site plan of the Belgian embassy grounds, made up of the chancery (A), the chancellor's residence (B), the servants' quarters (C) and the ambassadorial residence (D), undated

garden that evoked the image of an enormous inner court similar to an amphitheatre.[343] Gujral framed the garden not only as a place to relax for the Belgian ambassador following a long day of meetings, but also as an area where the head of mission could entertain guests with walks and receptions. To preserve the memory of the old embassy gardens at Hardinge Avenue, Gujral suggested replanting the greenery in the new embassy garden in Chanakyapuri.[344] In order to further evoke this image of an amphitheatre and enhance the sense of privacy in the garden at the same time, the edges of the compound were heightened by an earthen rampart with walls made of local grey stone to further reinforce the fortress-like appearance. The earthen ramparts were to be covered with

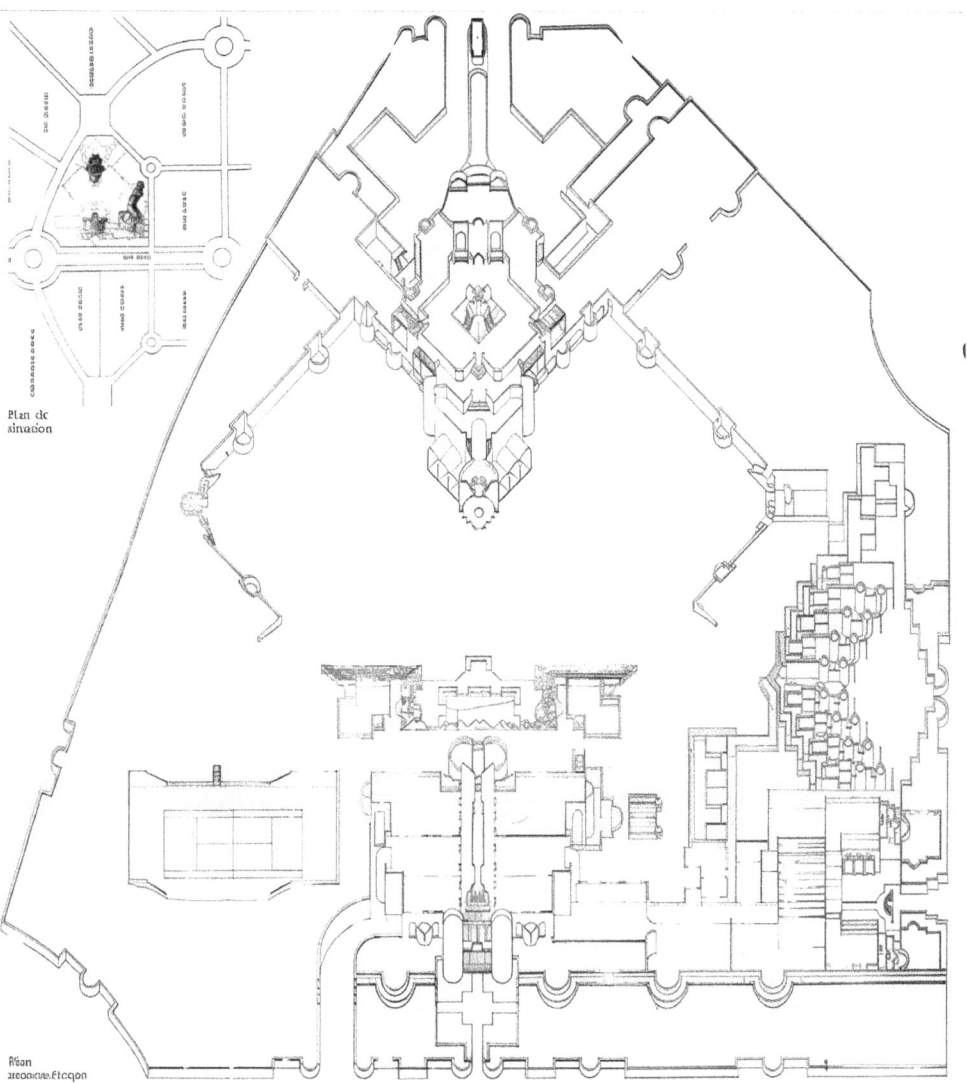

Figure 47: The New Delhi embassy compound, undated

grass and greenery to blend into the garden surroundings in order to further generate a feeling of intimacy and privacy.

Envisaging the embassy garden as more than a meeting place, Gujral invested considerably in adding recreational facilities to refresh the bodies and minds of the ambassador, his/her family and guests. Situated at the back of the chancery, a swimming pool was to be included on a heightened platform. The pool was to be flanked by fountains which added a decorative effect and cooled the garden. Moreover, a tennis court was also included next to the embassy offices. The tennis court proved to be a useful tool for conducting diplomacy in a less formal context. As one of the few sites in Chanakyapuri with a tennis court at the time, the embassy compound turned into one of the district's main sports grounds where Belgian ambassadors could have informal chats with fellow diplomats and Indian politicians between fiercely fought sets.[345]

The man-made earthen rampart (Fig. 47) was also key to integrating the different building units making up the compound. The earth was to be banked against the exterior walls of the embassy buildings, making it unclear where the landscape ended and the building began. Satish Gujral did this for two reasons. Firstly, the earthen rampart would offer cover from Delhi's burning sun, maintaining a steady indoor air temperature in the embassy. Secondly and perhaps most importantly to Gujral, the earthen rampart fitted very well with the organic design he had in store for the embassy buildings.

The Embassy Design: An Architectural Work of Art

In line with the site plan, the aesthetic of the embassy buildings was also shaped by Gujral's profound interest in evoking historical and symbolic associations. According to him, a good architect should take historical knowledge into account when designing a building:

> Historical knowledge is essential for any architect. But if it is true knowledge, it never leads to historicism. An artist is constantly absorbing all that is around him. He then juxtaposes it in his mind to come out with a creation that is his own interpretation, his own style.[346]

Still perceiving himself as an artist who had ventured into architecture, Gujral was not particularly interested in meticulously imitating the design of historically significant buildings to glorify tradition. Instead, he called for a more personal and contemporary reading of historic examples. He was especially interested in showcasing a more crafted and experimental approach to architecture that was firmly embedded in local building traditions.

The compound was made up of a homogenous architectural ensemble. The embassy buildings were characterised by a sculptural appearance, as

Figure 48: The ambassadorial residence, 1981

though they had been carved out of a monolithic block. All buildings were to be covered with exposed red brickwork. In doing so, Gujral aimed to pay tribute to local building traditions, indicating that brick is a material "[...] that in India is still made the way it was made a thousand years ago."[347] Interestingly, Belgian ambassadors gave their own reading of the extensive use of red bricks. To Ambassador Jan Hollants Van Loocke, the first ambassador to reside in the new embassy, the red bricks reminded him of the typical red brick dwellings in Belgium.[348]

The embassy's sculptural aesthetic was further reinforced by moulding the brickwork into historically inspired geometric forms such as arches, domes and lingams. As such, Gujral chose to adopt a similar approach to that which he had adopted at the end of the 1970s for the baronial mansion of the Indian business magnate Bhupendra Kumar Modi, for whom he had designed a stately residence in sandstone with a dome structure and double-arched porches.[349] A noteworthy addition to the Belgian embassy were the lingams. In Hinduism, lingams are small religious objects representing the god Shiva. In the embassy design, Gujral rescaled the formal features of the lingam into massive architectural structures, illustrating his experimental yet locally embedded approach to architecture.

The ambassadorial residence (Fig. 48) was to be the architectural centrepiece. In designing the building, Gujral invested considerably in metaphorical, historical and symbolic associations. The brick exteriors were moulded into a wide range of geometric forms, giving the building its distinctive sculptured aesthetic. The forms – such as the centrally positioned lingam and the Mughal architectural elements, including the double-arched porches and dome structure – were steeped in the rich history of the Indian subcontinent.[350] This architectural approach gives the building the appearance of a fortress-like cave, an appearance that is further reinforced by the earth banked against the exterior walls.

The residence's floorplan (Fig. 49), characterised by a series of spaces clustered around an octagonal lounge area, brings to mind some of the slightly earlier works of the American architect Louis Kahn (1901-1974), such as the spatial layout of the National Assembly Complex in Dhaka.[351] The residence's interior showcases how Gujral employs domes and tower-like structures to create ceremonial spaces. Once guests had been dropped off by car at the roundabout, they would enter the residence through a narrow corridor with a vaulted ceiling. This would lead them to a platform strategically located beneath an octagonal dome with integrated arc-shaped windows to let in natural sunlight. From this platform, one would slowly descend to the octagonal lounge via a double staircase covered with Italian white marble. In addition to its functional purpose, the marble staircase was in Gujral's eyes a key feature that created a more luxurious impression upon entering the residence.

With his typical sense of exaggeration and bombast, Gujral stated that the double staircase was intend to "[...] reinforce the drama of the interior space. As one descends to the lounge, the space explodes on all sides as in a firework."[352] Gujral referred to the fact that, when visitors would descend the stairs, the residence would really open out onto the garden's panoramic view. The lounge is flanked on either side by a private and public wing, accentuating the residence's hybrid character and the fact that the ambassador's professional and personal lives are intertwined with one another. Whereas the residence's southern wing houses the ambassador's living quarters, including the dining room (4), living room (5) and study (6), the northern wing is made up of the grand lounge (1), the reception room (2), and the large VIP dining room (3) where over 25 guests could wine and dine in style with a view on the embassy garden. The VIP dining room was conveniently situated next to the kitchen and storage rooms. In its capacity as a servant space, to use the terms "served" and "servant" spaces as coined by Louis Kahn, the kitchen and storage rooms enabled the VIP dining room to perform its functions.[353]

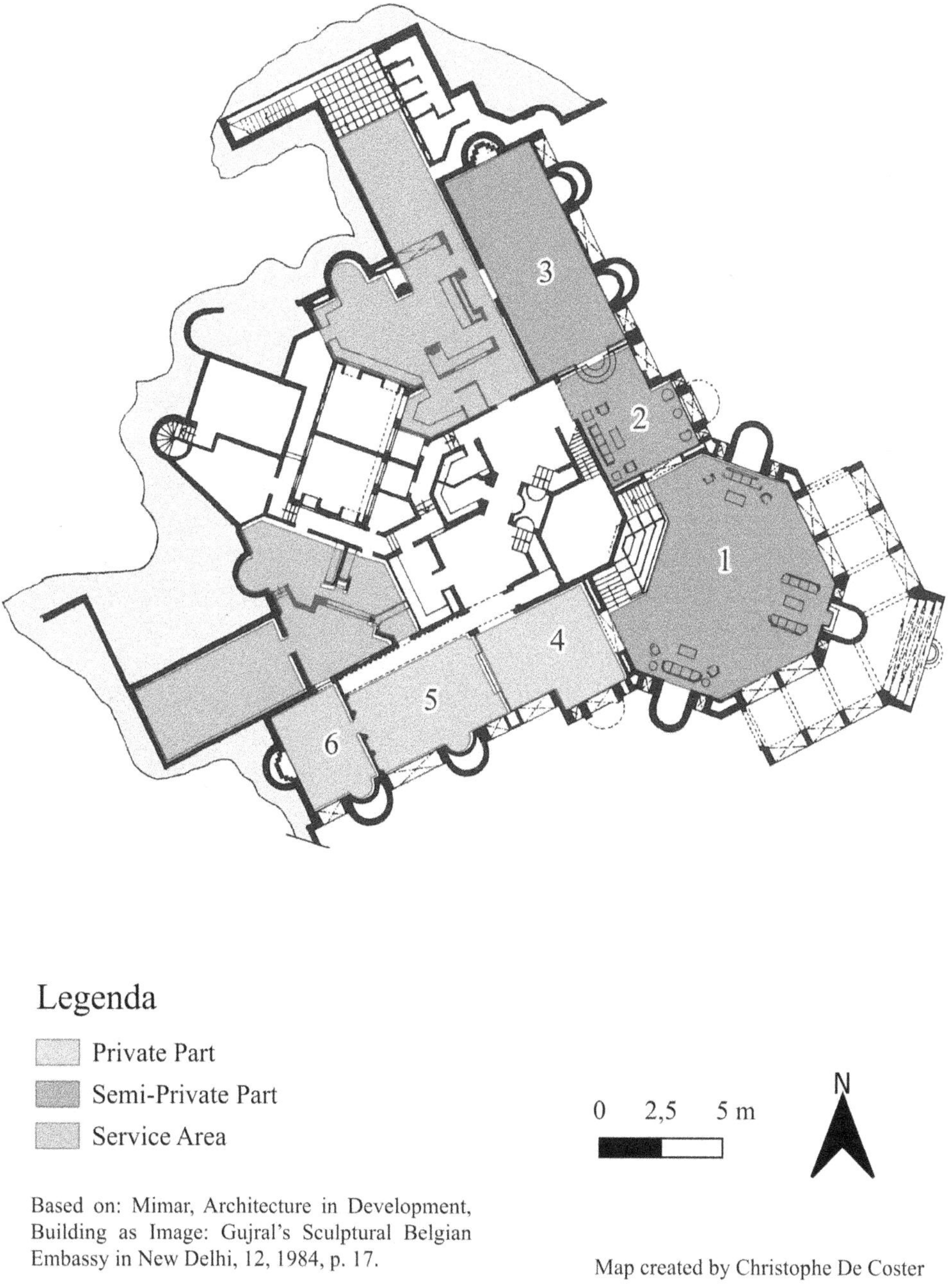

"IT'S THE ECONOMY, STUPID!" 207

Legenda

▢ Private Part
▨ Semi-Private Part
▨ Service Area

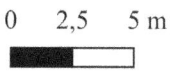 

Based on: Mimar, Architecture in Development, Building as Image: Gujral's Sculptural Belgian Embassy in New Delhi, 12, 1984, p. 17.

Map created by Christophe De Coster

Figure 49: The New Delhi residence

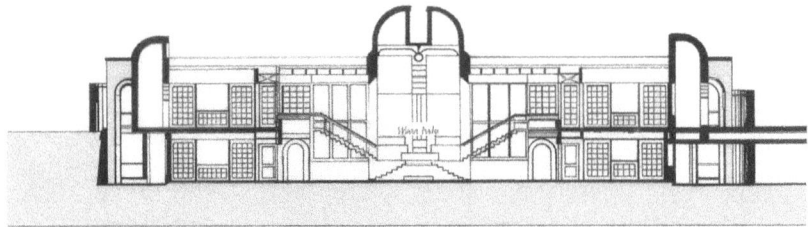

Figure 50: The New Delhi chancery, undated

The spatial layout was Gujral's way of responding to the Ministry's programmatic needs. For the Ministry, it was of the utmost importance that the new residence be well suited to hosting social events. To make its prime function more tangible, the Belgian ambassador had welcomed over 900 guests for dinners and cocktail parties at the colonial bungalow at Hardinge Avenue in 1978 alone.[354] Both wings could be approached by the grand lounge but also had their separate stairs, thus preventing disruption while the lounge was used for a reception. Moreover, both wings could also be closed off by means of wooden sliding doors. As such, the inhabitants could change the atmosphere in the residence by either enhancing the sense of privacy or creating a large open space. Far away from prying eyes, the entire first floor was made up of four bedrooms that were each given a bathroom and small terrace.

From the ambassadorial residence, the Belgian head of mission simply had to cross the garden to make it to the chancery. The chancery (Fig. 50) was a low-rise rectangular structure. In accordance with the residence, the embassy's bureaucratic nerve centre featured a brick façade with a sculptured aesthetic. The roof structure, for instance, was topped off by a horn-shaped brick structure. Moreover, two large lingams flanked the main entrance to the chancery, evoking the image of watchtowers covering the main approach that added to the fortress-like imagery.

The chancery's rear façade, facing the garden, featured a puzzling composition of articulated volumes made of red bricks and grey stones. Gujral described it as a three-dimensional mural that would add a decorative feature to the embassy gardens.[355] Such statements underscore just how much he approached the project as an architectural work of art.

The chancery's spatial layout featured a spacious atrium around which the offices were situated. Gujral envisaged the atrium as a venue for social gatherings such as receptions and exhibitions, even though the ambassadorial residence already offered the Belgian embassy a venue for such occasions. The atrium featured a monumental double staircase, with a base of Indian grey stone and a small fountain, that led to the offices of the senior diplomats. As the atrium already took up a large chunk of space, the available office space was relatively limited. In line with previously commissioned Belgian chanceries, Gujral opted for a cellular office layout. Interestingly, however, the offices of the ambassador, counsellor and secretary were around the same size, standing in stark contrast to other Belgian chanceries. In terms of reconciling functionality with aesthetics, the artist-architect found a creative solution to include toilets, installing them in the lingam-shaped structures.

Architecturally speaking, the design entry of Satish Gujral was like nothing else we have come across in the Belgian embassy-building programme. The locally embedded design, that pays tribute to traditional Indian architecture and religious culture, was in a league of its own. A particularly apt description for Gujral's design is the diplomatic phenomenon of localitis. Localitis refers to diplomats' tendency to gradually lose touch with their home country during their posting and to feel more attached to the receiving state.[356] The New Delhi design would make for an excellent textbook example of architectural localitis as it was first and foremost embedded in the local culture and indigenous building practices instead of being an architectural expression of Belgium on Indian soil. It was a far cry from what Belgium had previously constructed in terms of embassies by this time.

In addition to being an anomaly in the Belgian embassy-building programme, the design also stood out from other European embassies constructed in Chanakyapuri at the time. Situated just opposite to the Belgian plot, the purpose-built Polish embassy (Fig. 51) was erected. In 1972, the Polish government launched an architectural competition for a new embassy. The architectural competition was intrinsically linked to the nation's ambitious modernisation programme, known as 'Second Poland', which aimed to stimulate rapid industrialisation and grand urban projects to both improve the country's standard of living and take on a more contemporary image on the world stage.[357] The design entry of the Polish architects Witold Cęckiewicz and Stanislaw Denko (1943-2021) came out on top. Commissioned in 1978 in collaboration with the Indian architectural firm Kothari & Associates, the new embassy was the architectural expression of the government's agenda of promoting Poland as a modern communist state abroad. The aesthetic is characterised by several architectural features of the International Style, including an articulated

Figure 51: The Polish embassy in Chanakyapuri, 1978

volumetric conception, the extensive use of pilotis and large glass façades. To counter Delhi's harsh climate, *brise-soleils* with a grid-like structure were extensively used and the inner courtyard is equipped with large rectangular bodies of water for cooling. Demonstrating his biting wit, the British architecture critic Roger Connah argued that the design looks more like an oil rig than an embassy.[358]

Meanwhile, the construction of the new Finnish embassy compound was launched in Chanakyapuri in the early 1980s. In a similar fashion to the Polish embassy, the building project was the result of an architectural competition in which the Finnish Ministry of Foreign Affairs called for an embassy that would be the architectural expression of Finland on Indian soil.[359] It selected the entry of the renowned Finnish architects Reima Pietilä and Raili Pietilä, entitled Snow Peaks on the Mountains, which refers to the snow-covered landscapes of Finland and the Indian Himalayas and showcases the architects' organic approach to architecture. Like Satish Gujral, the Pietiläs shared a clear interest in symbolism and metaphors but – in contrast to the Belgian embassy design that only pays tribute to the culture of the host country – they used such elements to establish a visual common ground between Finland and India.[360] The most striking feature is the sculptural rooftop that commemorates Finland's glacial origins (Fig. 52).

Figure 52: The Finnish embassy, 2018

In their own ways, both the Polish and the Finnish embassies reflect the developments within the contemporary architectural scene of their respective homelands. However, this was definitely not the case with the design of the Belgian embassy. One could argue that, from the outside, the national flag and coat of arms would be the only unambiguous indications of the buildings' purpose of representing Belgium on Indian soil. If the Ministry had been poised to follow the example of fellow European countries of radiating nationhood through embassy architecture, then surely ministry officials would have put Gujral's design entry in the recycle bin. However, as luck would have it, things played out very differently.

Satish Gujral: The right man for the job?

In 1980, Gujral submitted his plans to the Belgian embassy. As part of the architectural competition, the Ministry of Foreign Affairs put together a jury. Unfortunately, the memoirs of Satish Gujral are the only source regarding the architectural competition. It remains a mystery what the other design entries looked like and who was part of jury. According to

Gujral, jury members were only presented with the design entries. The identity of the participating architects was kept a secret to ensure an unbiased verdict.³⁶¹ Gujral's design caught the eye of the jury members who ranked it first place. Their call was surprising to say the least. After all, the fortress-like and sculptural design greatly deviated from what the Ministry had constructed up until this moment. So why did the jury opt to make a U-turn for New Delhi?

In retrospect, two possible reasons come to mind. Firstly, former embassy staffer Philippe Falisse argues that the locally embedded design showed to the Indian people that Belgium was a country that paid tribute to the historical building traditions of the host country in commissioning its purpose-built embassies.³⁶² From a diplomatic point of view, the organic design with traditional architectural and religious features was thus the perfect architectural expression of Belgian efforts to ingratiate itself with the Indian political-economic power base.

Secondly and perhaps more significantly, the conspicuous design can be read as a sign of the times. In the early 1980s, the Belgian Ministry of Foreign Affairs was going through an existential crisis. As discussed previously, the day-to-day operation was severely crippled by massive budget cuts. On top of that, the national press openly questioned whether the Ministry of Foreign Affairs was still a relevant government entity.³⁶³ Framing the Ministry as a conservative bastion that was a relic of the past, media outlets deemed the Ministry to have become redundant as successive Belgian prime ministers tended to meet foreign political leaders and mass media such as television already reported what was going on abroad at a faster pace than diplomats ever could.

To top it all off, the Ministry had domestic competition with regard to its core business of representing Belgium abroad. As political tensions rose between the Dutch-speaking and French-speaking parts of Belgium in the late 1960s, the national government set up cultural communities for Flanders and Wallonia that were responsible for all cultural matters. It did not take long before the cultural communities expanded the scope of their activities beyond Belgian territory and sent delegations abroad to sign cultural agreements, much to the Ministry's frustration. In its eyes, the appearance of Flemish and Walloon cultural delegations severely undermined the credibility of the Belgian diplomatic corps in representing the state as a whole.³⁶⁴ Indian state officials, for instance, could not wrap their heads around the fact that they now had to negotiate cultural agreements with two different delegations.³⁶⁵ Confronted with all these challenges, the Ministry of Foreign Affairs was adrift at the time that it unveiled plans to build an embassy in New Delhi. Against the backdrop of this existential crisis that shook the Ministry's very foundations, one cannot help but think that the Belgian diplomatic corps perhaps saw the building project as an opportunity to show that it was still a force to be reckoned with both at home and abroad.

However, as soon as the identity of the winning architect was revealed, support for the design within the Ministry crumbled. This had to do with the fact that the commission would once again be awarded on turnkey basis, making Satish Gujral not only responsible for designing the embassy but also supervising construction works. Given that Gujral lacked a degree in architecture, the Ministry argued that he was unfit to be awarded the commission.[366] His design entry may have been much appreciated in Brussels but his untrained background came back to bite him.

Moreover, the news that Satish Gujral was selected also sparked controversy in New Delhi. The Indian architectural community did not take kindly to the fact that someone without a degree in architecture was awarded such a prestigious commission. In his memoirs, Satish Gujral recalls how Indian architects began to cold-shoulder him.[367] Gujral briefly considered turning down the commission. His friend Louis-Roland Burny had failed to disclose that the commission was going to be awarded on a turnkey basis. Keeping Gujral in the dark about something as crucial as a turnkey commission underscores the questionable manner in which the Belgian diplomatic corps sometimes tackled the administrative aspect of commissioning purpose-built embassies. Like the Ministry, Satish Gujral believed that he lacked the expertise to supervise the construction stage. His older brother Inder Kumar Gujral, who had good contacts in the Indian building industry, reassured him that it would be no problem to accept the commission and subsequently delegate responsibility to subcontractors.[368]

Satish Gujral may have come to terms with what was expected of him, but his involvement was still hanging by a thread as ministry officials in Brussels did not believe that he was really suitable for the job. In his memoirs, Gujral recalls that the Ministry wanted to exclude him from the competition and instead award the commission to the runner-up. Fortunately for Gujral, his close friend Louis-Roland Burny came to his aid. By 1980, the Belgian diplomat had left New Delhi and was reassigned to work at the Ministry of Foreign Affairs in Brussels. From there, he kept a watchful eye on his colleagues at the Inspection of Diplomatic and Consular Missions that dealt with awarding the New Delhi commission.

Upon hearing of the reluctance to work with Gujral, Burny began to pull strings behind the scenes in an effort to convince his colleagues that his Indian friend was the right man for the job at hand.[369] Burny personally vouched that a Gujral-led project would be a success, arguing that his architectural design would put Belgium on the map in New Delhi. Apparently, Burny held a certain sway over his colleagues. He turned the tables in Gujral's favour as the Inspection of Diplomatic and Consular Missions put aside its doubts and awarded him the commission to design and build the New Delhi embassy compound. Finally, construction works could be launched along *Shanti Path*, bringing an end to the Ministry's procrastination that spanned over a quarter of a century.

The Eventful Construction: A Family Affair

In line with Gujral's striking profile and puzzling design, the construction phase added to the project's overall conspicuousness. As he was responsible for supervising the construction works, Gujral strengthened the workforce of his firm Design Plus with an engineer and two assistants. Moreover, he called upon his family to come to his aid during the building phase.

Firstly, he called upon his 18-year-old daughter, Raseel Gujral Ansal. According to ministry records, Design Plus took on the role of contractor but in reality the situation was very different than the documents suggest.[370]

In an interview, the Belgian diplomat Cristina Funes-Noppen – serving at the New Delhi embassy from 1978 until 1982 – reveals that Satish Gujral and his wife Kiran instructed their 18-year-old daughter, Raseel Gujral Ansal, to set up a subsidiary of Design Plus. Allegedly, the subsidiary was not nothing more than a bogus company that only existed on paper. The subsidiary was contracted by Design Plus to construct the embassy. In return, the newly established subsidiary called upon several subcontractors to do the actual work, following the advice of Satish Gujral's brother, Inder Kumar Gujral. It is indeed common practice that contractors call upon multiple subcontractors in order to mitigate project risks, but the scheme set up by the Gujral family was questionable as this system can be susceptible to fraud.

This book does not want to go as far as stating that the system was indeed fraudulent but circumstantial evidence suggests that something shady might have been going on. In his report, Inspector of Diplomatic and

Consular Missions Pierre Anciaux Henry de Faveaux (1920-1995) revealed that there were financial irregularities. The subsidiary sometimes left out the invoices of its subcontractors when it forwarded bills to the Belgian embassy.[371] Consequently, the Belgian embassy frequently made intermediary payments to the subsidiary based on the projected costs mentioned in the building specifications instead of the actual invoices of the subcontractors involved. Such a course of action is especially vulnerable to fraud. Hypothetically, Design Plus could claim to the Ministry that the construction of a specific building unit cost 10 million Belgian francs, but in fact the subcontractors carried out the construction works for 9 million Belgian francs. In this fictional scenario, the main contractor would unjustly enrich itself at the expense of the deceived client by making false statements regarding the building costs.

Invoices provided by the subcontractors could of course clarify the matter but these were often left out. The embassy staffer responsible for making the payments admitted to Inspector Anciaux Henry de Faveaux that she did not always ask the subsidiary to provide supporting invoices. This untransparent payment procedure did not go unnoticed in Brussels. In its capacity as the government's financial watchdog, the Court of Audit gave the Ministry of Foreign Affairs a rap on the knuckles. For a brief moment, the Belgian embassy was instructed to stop payments until the issue of the missing invoices was sorted out.[372]

However, the Belgian course of action was also questionable. As the bulk of the construction materials such as cement and Italian marble were to be purchased abroad, the various Indian subcontractors would have had to pay import duties, costs which they would have directly passed on to the Ministry. However, the Ministry had no intention of paying such duties. It had a trick up its sleeve to avoid paying such duties. Reflecting the privileged position diplomatic missions occupy in society, the *United Nations Vienna Convention on Diplomatic Relations* of 1961 stipulates that sending states are exempt from paying any national, regional or municipal dues and taxes. To put it in other words and to nod towards the political slogan of the American Revolution, there is no taxation for diplomatic representations. As it was exempt from paying such import duties, the Belgian embassy used this legal loophole to its full potential as the embassy staff placed the foreign orders for construction materials instead of the Indian subcontractors.[373]

Moreover, through diplomatic teamwork, the Belgian embassy obtained the necessary soil to landscape the earthen rampart around the compound. The Belgian embassy reached out to other sending states that were constructing embassies in Chanakyapuri. They were invited to drop off their excavated earth on the Belgian plot, an invitation they gladly accepted.[374] Subsequently, bulldozers created man-made slopes on the site.

In September 1980, the construction was launched and took over three years to be completed. The long construction period was the result of Belgium's precarious financial situation. The Ministry of Finance demanded that the construction works be split into phases in order to spread the cost of 95 million Belgian francs (8.3 million euros) over three budgetary years.[375]

Belgian efforts to use the limited financial resources prudently were, however, thwarted by Satish Gujral. Hiring someone who was more of an artist than an architect had its practical downsides as his design was not entirely well thought out. As a painter and sculptor, Gujral framed the construction process as yet another phase in making the final adjustments to his design, as he did with his artistic work. While on the site, he reassessed the dimensions of the buildings that he had designed on paper. For instance, the chancellor's residence was deemed too small, prompting Gujral to enlarge its significantly. Moreover, Gujral increased the number of dwellings in the servants' quarters (Fig. 53) from eight to 16, admitting to Ambassador Jan Hollants Van Loocke that he had underestimated the number of the servants employed at the Belgian embassy.[376] The servants' quarters were designed in a similar way to the rest of the compound and featured brick façades that were moulded into conspicuous cylindrical structures.

The 16 housing units were constructed adjacent to the earthen rampart, shielding off the embassy gardens. Gujral therefore concealed the servants' quarters from people wandering through the gardens. For reasons of prestige, it was out of the question that the humble houses should spoil the view of the Belgian ambassador and high-ranking guests as they walked through the well-tended gardens. To put it metaphorically, the engine room that keeps the cruise ship up and running was concealed from the passengers strolling along the deck. The servants' housing conditions were a far cry from the spacious and lavish ambassadorial residence. Each housing unit was made up of a living room that also functioned as a bedroom, as well as a rudimentary bathroom that only featured a tap, a separate toilet and a courtyard that served as an open-air kitchen. While the dimensions were already small for just one person, the mixed crew of male and female domestic servants lived there together with their partners and children as was customary in Indian society. In total, over 80 people lived in the

Figure 53: The servants' quarters, 1985

servants' quarters by 1984. Inspector Pierre Anciaux Henry de Faveaux was appalled by the cramped living conditions but confided in his report that the Indian servants were actually pleased with their housing given the precarious standard of living of millions of Indians.[377]

Much to the Ministry's frustration, the various alterations had an adverse effect on the budget. The price tag rose to 120 million Belgian francs (7.8 million euros), far more than originally projected in 1980. If Satish Gujral had got his way, he would have also made changes to the design of the residence and chancery. Alarmed by the fact that Gujral pleaded to deviate from the original plans, the Ministry's highest echelons frequently urged Ambassador Jan Hollants Van Loocke to curb the architect's enthusiasm. This once again underscores just how much the Ministry of Foreign Affairs relied on its diplomatic boots on the ground when it commissioned purpose-built embassies. In his published memoirs, Ambassador Hollants Van Loocke recalls the arguments with Satish Gujral, or rather his wife Kiran who used sign language to get the ambassador's message across to her mute husband:

> The many and heated arguments with Satish Gujral, the Indian architect, would on their own fill a novel. Deaf and dumb, he communicated with the aid of his wife while his sparkling eyes, his gestures and expressive face were eloquent

enough. We regrettably often had to temper his creative fits with sordid budgetary considerations, which seemed as mean to him as they were mandatory for us. I fondly remember this artist who was accidentally also an architect.[378]

In addition to his daughter, Raseel Gujral Ansal, his wife Kiran therefore also played an instrumental role in commissioning the embassy. However, this would not be the last family member to support Satish Gujral in his building endeavour.

In November 1980, Satish Gujral had a freak accident on the construction site of a house he had designed for a friend of his. During an on-site visit, he fell into a pit filled with pointed steel bars and had to undergo surgery. Gujral was confined to his bed and ended up with a plaster cast running from his hip to his ankle that prevented him from supervising the works in Chanakyapuri for over half a year.[379] Determined to keep the building project going, Satish Gujral called upon his 21-year-old son Mohit Gujral to take his place. In fact, Mohit Gujral was more qualified than his father to play the role of site manager as he was studying architecture at the School of Architecture at Ahmedabad at the time. In order to devote himself fully to the embassy's construction, Mohit Gujral even temporarily dropped out of school. In his memoirs, Satish Gujral boasted that the embassy's construction was the ideal training ground for his son to follow in his footsteps as architect:

> In six months at the site, he learnt more about architecture and building than he would have in ten years at the school. But for Mohit, I do not know how I would have been able to silence my critics. The international acclaim that the Belgian embassy received was largely due to the help my son gave me in the final stages of the building's construction.[380]

Interestingly, the Ministry once again raised no flags as the function of site manager was given to someone without a degree in architecture. As long as the construction continued unabated, it was willing to turn a blind eye to the fact that an architect without a degree and subsequently an architecture student were responsible for the day-to-day supervision at the building site.

However, this would come back to bite the Ministry. Notwithstanding the design's aesthetic qualities, the involvement of two ill-trained site managers had its repercussions. For instance, the structural features left much to be desired. As the commission was awarded on a turnkey basis, the shortcomings only came to light after the Belgian diplomatic staff had moved into the new embassy. For instance, former embassy staffer Philippe Falisse recalls that the chancery's roof was not adapted to local weather conditions. In June 1984, following the start of the monsoon season with its heavy rainfalls, the roof began to leak. The embassy offices were littered with buckets until adjustments were made to the roof's drainage system.[381] However, more experienced architects working in Chanakyapuri were also caught by surprise by the monsoon rains. When he was designing the American chancery in the early 1950s, Edward Durell Stone miscalculated the impact of wind-driven rain and as a result the inner courtyard was often soaked by monsoon rains.[382] It was a running joke among the American embassy personnel that Stone had visited India outside of the monsoon season.

In addition to a leaking roof, ministry paperwork reveals additional shortcomings in the design of the Belgian embassy. A thorough report highlighted that poor-quality cement or too little cement had been used. Rumour also has it that sand containing salt was used in the mortar.[383] Moreover, several decorative arches showed signs of cracks as these were badly sized during the construction phase. Satish Gujral may have designed an architectural work of art but it did come with a number of teething problems.

Practice in New Delhi What You Preach in Brussels

During the embassy's construction, a new Belgian coalition government consisting of Christian-democrats and liberals took office on 17 December 1981. Headed by the Christian-democratic strongman Wilfried Martens (1936-2013), the newly formed Martens V government saw the country's economic recovery as its political *raison d'être*. Confronted with high unemployment and budget deficits, the centre-right coalition government aspired to revive the economy.

Foreign Minister Leo Tindemans (1922-2014) envisaged an important role for the Ministry of Foreign Affairs in increasing the country's export capacity. During his maiden speech as foreign minister in the Senate, Tindemans publicly committed himself and all the Ministry's resources to boost exports.[384] Tindemans pledged to lead the business community to foreign markets that had been neglected in the past, hoping to introduce Belgian products and technological know-how to untapped markets. Therefore, he especially set his sights on Asia, arguing that this continent was well on its way to becoming the economic centre of the world. However, the growing economic importance of this continent was not reflected in Belgium's exports to Asia, which represented just four per cent of Belgium's total export volume in 1981.[385]

Putting his money where his mouth is, Tindemans unveiled a new foreign trade programme entirely devoted to strengthening economic ties with Asian countries. Entitled 'For a Belgian Asia Policy', the scheme aimed to increase Belgian exports to Asia and attract Asian companies to invest in Belgium. As part of his Asia policy, Tindemans envisaged an important role for Belgian embassies in the region. In a 1983 interview with *Gazet van Antwerpen*, he framed embassies as economic venues where Belgian entrepreneurs could come into contact with foreign state officials and investors. Such encounters would serve as the basis for entering into lucrative contracts that in return would reboot the economy.[386] Therefore, Tindemans argued, it was of the utmost importance that ambassadors should not only see themselves as representatives of the state but also as the spokespeople for Belgian companies.

In order to lead by example, Tindemans played his part in promoting Belgian businesses. In January 1983, he headed an economic mission of Belgian entrepreneurs and state officials to Bangkok, Seoul and New Delhi. The Christian-democratic strongman had particularly high hopes for the visit to New Delhi as, by this time, the Indian government had taken its first steps towards embracing the free market system. The gradual liberalisation of the Indian economy was an opportunity not to be squandered. The Belgian Asia policy framed India's domestic market as an economic Valhalla with 700 million potential consumers ready to buy Belgian products and services.[387] During the economic mission to New Delhi, Tindemans was determined to convince the participating Belgian entrepreneurs that the Martens V government was truly committed to enhancing the visibility of Belgium on Indian soil, even by means of brick and mortar.

To this end, on 18 January 1983, the foreign minister visited the construction site in Chanakyapuri with Belgian businessmen. Tindemans had received a memo with the details of the building project and a site plan, enabling him to guide the businessmen around the site.[388] During the two-hour tour, Tindemans thoroughly briefed the Belgian captains of industry on the buildings' specifics and answered any questions that they

Figure 54: The residence's lounge, 1985

had. Tindemans marketed the new embassy with its conspicuous design as a high-end venue where Belgian entrepreneurs could connect with the financial-economic elite of India in a fitting setting.

Tindemans was not the only member of the Martens V government that showcased the New Delhi embassy as a venue for economic diplomacy. As part of the Belgian Asia policy, State Secretary of Foreign Trade André Kempinaire (1929-2012) of the Liberal Party organised a second economic mission to New Delhi in November 1983. This second economic mission had been intentionally scheduled for November 1983 to coincide with the inauguration of the recently completed embassy. As such, the inauguration ceremony could be attended by the Belgian economic mission, underscoring yet again how the New Delhi embassy was marketed as a venue for economic diplomacy. In addition to 40 Belgian entrepreneurs accompanying Kempinaire to New Delhi, the liberal politician was also accompanied by Crown Prince Albert. At the time, Prince Albert was the Honorary Chairman of the Belgian Office for Foreign Trade. In his capacity as the frontman of the national export agency, Prince Albert would go on to spearhead over 100 economic missions to more than 50 countries between 1962 and 1993, the year he became the new King of the Belgians.[389]

The Prince's presence, which added prestige to the ceremony, was used to its full potential. On 5 November 1983, Ambassador Jan Hollants Van Loocke opened the doors of his newly completed ambassadorial residence and held a reception for the participants of the economic mission, officials of the Indian Ministry of External Affairs, and Satish Gujral and his family. The event took place in the most stunning room, the octagonal lounge area with its monumental stairs covered in Italian marble.

By the time of the inaugural ceremony in November 1983, the residence's interiors had been furnished and decorated. As the Ministry still did not have in-house interior designers, Ambassador Hollants Van Loocke and ministry officials were responsible for furnishing and decorating the embassy (Fig. 54). They opted for an eclectic ensemble that was a far cry from the classic Louis XVI furniture in the old residence at Hardinge Avenue. In front of the red marble fountain, they strategically positioned traditional Indian furniture to pay tribute to the receiving state. Moreover, Indian rugs were included to cover the lounge's marble flooring and evoke a sense of warmth. To match the white walls and marble flooring, a series of white lounge chairs was also included. They contributed to giving the interiors its distinctive all-white look. Belgian designs, such as modern tapestries, also found their place in the lounge. The most striking Belgian feature, however, was two futuristic chandeliers flanking the main entrance. These chandeliers were made up of a multitude of long golden tubes ending in miniature bulbs.

The Ministry used the inaugural ceremony of the New Delhi embassy to its full diplomatic potential. As the opening of a purpose-built embassy is not that uncommon in New Delhi given the urban context of Chanakyapuri, Foreign Minister Tindemans pulled out all the stops to draw attention to the event. As part of the ceremony, Crown Prince Albert awarded Satish Gujral the Order of the Crown, one of Belgium's highest national honorary orders. The diplomatic gesture was widely covered in the Indian press. *The Indian Express*, the leading Indian newspaper, praised Belgium for collaborating with Satish Gujral and handing him the medal.[390] Upon reviewing the Belgian Asia policy, the Ministry of Foreign Affairs labelled 1983 as the watershed moment for Belgian-Indian relations. The two economic missions and the opening of the new embassy had set things in motion and substantially boosted the visibility of Belgium in India.[391] Ever since, the New Delhi embassy has been the scene of numerous networking events and business presentations for Belgian economic missions to India.

"Only Belgium Remains Silent": The Embassy's Critical Reception

Following the embassy's completion, the Inspection of Diplomatic and Consular Missions made a thorough review of the new embassy. It praised the design in terms of aesthetics, calling it an unconventional yet pleasing design that made quite the impression. However, for all its architectural splendour, the Inspection made several critical remarks concerning the embassy's functional qualities. Firstly, the chancery's atrium was deemed too spacious when compared to the overall surface area of the office building. The atrium's surface area was considered to be disproportionate when compared to the medium-sized offices of the embassy staffers. The Inspection warned that if the number of diplomatic staff increased and more office space became necessary, the unusable space of the atrium would come back to haunt the Ministry.

Secondly, the Inspection criticised the lack of security features in the design. Such security concerns were a sign of the times. From the late 1960s onwards, terrorist organisations increasingly targeted diplomats.[392] The Belgian diplomatic corps was not immune to this menacing trend. In 1973, the Belgian diplomat Guy Eid was assassinated by the Palestinian Black September Organisation.[393] Against the backdrop of the surging terrorist threat against diplomats, it is striking that security was anything but a top priority in the design of the new embassy. In fact, Gujral's so-called embassy fortress was nothing more than a house of cards. In its report, the Inspection was alarmed by the low height of the earthen rampart and walls surrounding the compound:

> Where the walls are high, they provide sufficient external protection. But most of the walls are low and climbing them is child's play. This is particularly obvious on one side of the residence, where there are no obstacles in the way of reaching one of the bedrooms.[394]

The Inspection proposed installing high fences around the embassy grounds as other diplomatic missions had previously done in Chanakyapuri. However, given the budgetary situation, the Ministry ruled out this possibility. As Brussels could not make the necessary investments to beef up security, Ambassador Jan Hollants Van Loocke took matters into his own hands. He instructed his gardeners to plant thorny bougainvillea hedges at the vicinity of the residence to serve as a natural barrier. The Inspection applauded the ambassador's resourcefulness but argued that the bougainvillea hedges, even when fully grown, would not be sufficient to shield off the premises from undesired guests.

Of course, it is easy to blame the shortcomings on Satish Gujral who was in overall charge of the project. However, it would have been wise for the Belgian Ministry of Foreign Affairs, in its capacity as awarding authority, to also take a good look at itself. It had failed to stress the importance of office space and security to Gujral, underscoring that its decentralised and guideline-free approach to commissioning embassy buildings came with a price. Paradoxically, it was only upon the completion of a purpose-built embassy that ministry officials clearly articulated their preferences by pointing out what was missing.

The Inspection was right to express concerns regarding the lack of security as several uninvited groups did indeed trespass the Belgian embassy grounds from November 1983 onwards. Fortunately for the embassy staff, these trespassers had no malevolent intentions as they were tourists who wanted to see the new embassy with their own eyes. Triggered by the wide media coverage of the new Belgian embassy, several city tour operators included it as a stop during their sight-seeing bus tours across New Delhi, bringing busloads of tourists to the embassy's doorstep. As Philippe Falisse recalls, the embassy became a victim of its own success:

> No sooner had it been completed, I remember how busloads of tourists would descend on Nyaya Marg. Armed with cameras and with nothing to stop them, they would invade the compound and the private gardens of the ambassador![395]

The traffic nuisance at the old residence at Hardinge Avenue may have been a thing of the past, but the new residence in Chanakyapuri now faced the disruption of mass tourism. Eventually, the Belgian embassy reached out to the Protocol Division of the Indian Ministry of Foreign Affairs to intervene on its behalf which resulted in the removal of the embassy from the list of tourist stops. Apparently, there is also such a thing as too much public diplomacy.

However, the new embassy was not to everyone's taste in India. Following their criticism for hiring an untrained architect as Gujral, Indian architects now spoke out against the design. In an interview with *India Today*, the Indian architect Satish Grover (1940-2005) stated:

> I have absolutely no objection that a painter or sculptor takes to architecture. But the building he produces must not be based only on personal expression.

I think a building is successful if it says what it is. I haven't been inside the Belgian Embassy, but from the outside it doesn't look like an embassy.[396]

Echoing the Beaux-Arts principle of *architecture parlante*, Grover argued that the façade of the building should provide a clear indication of the building's function. Gujral's approach to architecture, however, clearly differed. He was less interested in expressing the purpose or character of the composing parts of a building, and more interested in creating enjoyable environments in which people could live and work. In the same article, Ambassador Jan Hollants Van Loocke countered the criticism by framing the new embassy as an ideal working and living environment that was well suited to its diplomatic function as meeting place:

> If an embassy building is any reflection of a country's presence, then Satish's design helps us in our job: not merely as a prestige symbol but as an instrument for the job we do.[397]

Interestingly, the journalist from *India Today* asked passers-by for their opinions of the new embassy. They wondered what the new embassy was all about. Rather unflatteringly, one person described it as an upturned can of earthworm droppings while another passer-by described it to be a desert casbah that had sprouted lingams. This underscored the embassy's status as one of the more conspicuous embassies in Chanakyapuri.

As can be expected, the creative embassy design caught the attention of well-reputed architectural magazines. Whereas the Indian reactions towards the project were diverse, architectural journalists swamped the new embassy with positive reviews. Most notably, the American architecture and design critic Sylvia Gottwald wrote an article for *Architecture USA* in which she admired how the design combined seemingly opposing qualities. It set an example for contemporary Indian architecture:

> The recently completed Belgian Embassy complex in New Delhi by the Indian artist and architect Satish Gujral is what one feels contemporary Indian architecture should be. One feels it should impress with layers of historical evidence, yet be inventive rather than imitative. It should be full of strong sculptural forms and colours, sensual and mysterious on the outside, yet full of surprises, airy, and light on the inside. It should feel very old, pragmatic and wise, yet very new, vibrant, and creative – all at once.[398]

Mimar, one of the very few journals that solely focused on architecture in the Global South, covered the project as well in a straightforward documentary style by primarily voicing Gujral's own point of view. In the article, the self-made architect tooted his own horn and emphasised the organic qualities of his work, such as the exposed building materials, the relative independence of the building's parts and the harmonious relationship of these parts with one another and with the building location.[399] Finally, the French magazine *L'architecture d'aujourd'hui* discussed the embassy, reading its organic design as Satish Gujral's architectural manifesto in which he showcased his discontent with modernist architecture.[400] Interestingly, the French magazine argued that the design may have been striking but it nevertheless made a fine addition to the diplomatic district of Chanakyapuri which was an architecturally diverse neighbourhood. Continuing along these lines, architecture critic Roger Connah lashed out against the architectural incoherence of the neighbourhood and claimed that Gujral's sculptural and antique-looking building fitted perfectly in the Delhi ghetto of carnival embassy architecture.[401]

The Belgian architectural magazine *A+ Architectuur* also reacted favourably to the sculptural embassy design. In an article with the telling title 'Only Belgium Remains Silent', architectural journalist Eddy Pennewaert joined the international magazines in applauding Gujral's design. In a true moment of chauvinism, the journalist even labelled the Belgian embassy as one of the most significant architectural projects ever constructed on Indian soil.[402] However, there was one matter that bothered Pennewaert. He could not wrap his head around the fact that the newly built embassy had hardly generated any attention in Belgium. In fact, Pennewaert's article is one of the very few contemporary references to it in the Belgian press.

Pennewaert went on to offer an explanation as to why the embassy had flown under the radar of the national press, which leads us to the epicentre of Belgian politics. According to Pennewaert, the socialist opposition blasted the Martens V government for spending so much money on the construction of the embassy while the nation was going through a recession. As the political saying goes, the duty of the opposition is to oppose, but the socialists' criticism was somewhat misplaced. Back in 1979, the socialists had allocated the necessary funding to the embassy project. When the socialists were cast into the opposition in December 1981, they started to speak out against the embassy following its completion. According to Pennewaert, the criticism struck a nerve with

Foreign Minister Leo Tindemans and ministry officials.[403] Consequently, Pennewaert reasoned, the Ministry of Foreign Affairs intentionally gave the embassy as little media exposure as possible in an effort not to draw the general public's attention to the embassy and its price tag. Unfortunately, it is not possible to either verify or debunk such claims as the ministry's archival records do not contain any relevant paperwork on this matter.

However, circumstantial evidence does suggest that Foreign Minister Leo Tindemans was well aware that the embassy's price tag was a source of irritation. During the economic mission to New Delhi in November 1983, participating Belgian entrepreneurs voiced their disapproval to officials of the Belgian Office for Foreign Trade. Upon seeing the ambassadorial residence with their own eyes, the businessmen confided to the trade agency that the diplomatic interiors were too luxurious when compared to the horrendous housing conditions of Belgian ambassadors elsewhere.[404] In their eyes, it was ludicrous to allocate the lion's share of the real estate budget to one prestige project. Instead, the businessmen argued that it would have been far more sensible to distribute the funding over various diplomatic postings to carry out much needed renovations and refurbishments.

The scheme of the Martens V government to brand the New Delhi embassy as the architectural expression of its export-oriented policies therefore backfired. In an ironic turn of events, the Belgian business community – the very group Tindemans wanted to please – spoke out against the embassy and its lavish interior. In an effort to smooth things over, the Ministry's highest echelons reassured the Belgian captains of industry that such prestige projects were from now on a thing of the past and funding would henceforth be allocated in a more balanced way.[405]

The Belgian Embassy in Riyadh: A Diplomatic Fata Morgana in the Saudi Desert

The Ministry's highest echelons may have pledged to stop allocating dazzling sums to prestige projects but their subsequent course of action tells a very different story. In the wake of the New Delhi project, the Ministry was poised to repeat its success in Saudi Arabia, a foreign market that became ever more important to Belgium in the 1980s. Apart from being a major oil supplier to Belgium, Saudi Arabia called upon foreign companies, especially Western ones, to put their expertise to good use by constructing new roads, airports and hospitals to profoundly modernise the country and accelerate the growth rate of the national economy.[406]

Determined to claim its share of the Saudi cake, the Belgian government set up several economic missions to Saudi Arabia in the 1970s and 1980s. The pinnacle of these efforts was the construction of a new Belgian embassy in Saudi Arabia. The embassy was to be the architectural expression of the government's efforts to boost Belgian visibility on the Arabian peninsula. Building on the success of the New Delhi project, the Martens V government envisaged the new embassy as yet another stately economic venue. In terms of funding, the Belgian government spared no expense. One hundred and thirty-five million Belgian francs (8.8 million euros) was allocated to the diplomatic building project in 1983, 15 million Belgian francs (980,000 euros) more than the heavily criticised New Delhi project. This dazzling budget stood in stark contrast to the ongoing budget cuts crippling the Ministry's everyday operations. Just one year earlier, in 1982, the Ministry had been forced to cut spending by 147 million Belgian francs (10.3 million euros).[407] In retrospect, the Martens V government was trying very hard to keep up appearances abroad by investing in embassy projects. To a certain extent, the purpose-built embassy with its hefty price tag can be read as a Fata Morgana. The embassy upheld the erroneous image that Belgium was still in good financial-economic shape and was therefore a viable economic partner to the Saudi government.

The Belgian embassy project was intrinsically linked to the modernisation agenda of the Saudi state. As part of its ambition to brand Saudi Arabia a modern state, the House of Saud expanded the capital city of Riyadh. Situated in the middle of the desert, Riyadh was initially a modest city standing in the shadow of the Red Sea port city of Jeddah. The entire *corps diplomatique*, including the Belgian embassy, was housed in Jeddah because the Saudi Ministry of Foreign Affairs was located there. In its efforts to define Riyadh as the true capital city, the Saudi authorities launched a master plan to further develop Riyadh in the 1970s. Therefore, the Arriyadh Development Authority developed a purpose-built diplomatic quarter of 800 hectares, named *Hay as-Safarat* or District of Embassies, on the western outskirts of the city to speed up the move of diplomatic missions from Jeddah to Riyadh.

In a similar fashion to previously discussed cases, the Arriyadh Development Authority approached sending states with an invitation to lease land on which they could construct embassies. However, the Saudi take on a diplomatic quarter deviated from those in Australia, Brazil and India. Whereas the latter were extensions of the existing urban fabric, *Hay as-Safarat* is isolated from the rest of the city. Moreover, there are few entrances to the district and municipal police monitor them closely. Given that the district itself is partially enwalled and that walls also surround the various embassy premises, the diplomatic district resemblances a gated community alienated from the city of Riyadh. This is further reinforced by the fact that the diplomatic district is a self-sufficient community made up of residential units, public buildings, shops, recreational facilities and parks.[408] As the *corps diplomatique* moved to Riyadh and the Saudi capital became one of the major financial-economic hubs in the Gulf area, the Ministry accepted the offer of the Arriyadh Development Authority to lease a site in *Hay as-Safarat* and build a new embassy. On 1 June 1981 the Ministry started to lease a sizeable plot of 6,750 m² in the northern end of the diplomatic district.

In contrast to its procrastination in Canberra and New Delhi, the Ministry did not waste any time in developing the site, underscoring the necessity to provide economic missions with a stately venue. The commission to design and build the new embassy was awarded to the leading Belgian construction firm BESIX Group. Saudi Arabia was familiar territory for BESIX Group as it was already involved in the construction of new hospitals and port facilities on the Arabian peninsula. One cannot help but think that Brussels awarded the high-profile embassy commission to BESIX Group in order to give the Belgian construction firm additional exposure in Saudi Arabia. After all, Saudi state officials and businessmen would attend social events and wander through the corridors of the future Belgian embassy. Any Belgian ambassador would therefore be able to use BESIX Group as a topic of conversation when showing Saudi guests around the embassy. If the ambassador had a bit of salesmanship running through his veins, the head of mission could promote BESIX Group to Saudi guests if they had any building plans of their own.

In the programme of requirements, the Belgian Ministry of Foreign Affairs outlined its expectations to BESIX Group.[409] The programmatic needs called for the construction of a compound made up of an ambassadorial residence, chancery, servants' quarters, a tennis court and a swimming pool. Going through the requirements, the compound's function as a venue for economic delegations becomes very tangible. The ambassadorial residence had to include spacious reception halls where the Belgian ambassador could invite up to 100 guests. Moreover, the dining room had to be spacious enough to seat 20 guests at a table. Continuing along these lines, the swimming pool was envisaged as far more than a recreational facility. The ambassador had to be able to throw

230 CHAPTER III

Figure 55: The Belgian embassy offices in Riyadh, 2022

receptions around the pool. Architecturally, ministry officials stressed to BESIX Group that the new embassy should radiate national identity on Saudi soil, stating that the embassy's design should express a Belgian way of living and working.[410] However, they failed to mention what kind of architecture they deemed appropriate.

Looking at what was actually constructed, it becomes patently clear that the Belgian Ministry of Foreign Affairs quickly abandoned its nationalist approach. Instead, it greenlit plans that called for a locally embedded design in sync with the traditional way of building in Saudi Arabia. After all, the Riyadh embassy (Fig. 55) was another case of architectural localitis, underscoring that the New Delhi embassy was not a glitch in the Belgian embassy-building programme. Designed by Belgian architects working at BESIX Group, the embassy's design can be read as a clichéd take on Arab architecture. To a certain extent, the design forms a somewhat romanticised version of Arab culture. The compound is made up of a homogenous architectural ensemble of fortress-like buildings, seemingly carved out of a monolithic piece of stone. The two-storied structures feature sand-coloured exteriors which are topped off by flat roofs. In line with the main features of vernacular desert architecture, the embassy

Figure 56: The residence's dining room, 1990s

design was adapted to local climate conditions by means of thick walls and small windows to avoid excessive solar exposure. At the end of the ambassadorial residence, the architects included roofed terraces that function as intimate venues. Moreover, the pool area was tiled so that receptions could also take place near the cooling swimming pool.

The Ministry's ambition to radiate national identity may not have come to fruition in the design of the exteriors but the embassy interiors were a very different story. In the programme of requirements, ministry officials emphasised to BESIX Group that the interiors should be one large exhibition room of Belgian design and craftsmanship:

> Given the representative nature of an Embassy in Riyadh, where the emphasis is on functionality, the interior design is all the more important. Furniture, lighting, upholstery and decoration must reflect the current possibilities in these industries in Belgium.[411]

In other words, Saudi guests had to be introduced to Belgian interior design in the hope that this would generate purchase orders. Ministry officials opted to furnish and decorate the diplomatic interiors in a traditional way.

Staying true to its conservative self-image, the Ministry shipped period furniture such as Louis XVI Cabriolet armchairs and Louis XVI chests of drawers to the ambassadorial residence.[412] Traditional artforms, such as tapestries depicting hunting scenes, also ended up in the residence. However, a notable exception to this traditional furnishing style was the VIP dining room (Fig. 56) where the Ministry opted for a more balanced approach. Whereas the room was decorated with a large tapestry depicting a Roman ruin, a modern dining set with chrome dining chairs was also included. Interestingly, the conspicuous light fixture of golden tubes that was also used in the New Delhi residence found its way to the dining room of the Riyadh residence. It created a sky of artificial stars hovering above the heads of the ambassador and his table guests.

Completed in 1984, the Ministry wasted no time in putting the new embassy to good use. Already in the same year as its completion, the new embassy served as a base for a Belgian economic mission presided by Prime Minister Wilfried Martens.[413] Ever since, the Riyadh embassy has functioned as a high-end venue for dozens of economic missions that enabled Belgian captains of industry to talk business with Saudi state officials and entrepreneurs.

Chapter IV
Plugging the Holes in the Federal Budget
Monetising the Belgian Embassy Patrimony (1999-2020)

In the fall of 1926, the Ministry was in the midst of selling its consulate building in Shanghai. It had received a very generous offer for the property. As this money would come in handy for setting up new diplomatic postings, the Ministry was eager to seal the deal. In the final stretch, however, a significant problem emerged. The title deed was nowhere to be found in the archives. In need of this important piece of paper to finalise the deal, the Ministry was desperately searching for a copy of the title deed. Ministry officials tried their luck at the Court of Audit in Brussels which had received such a copy in 1910. In their letter, ministry officials stressed the urgency of their request, asking the Court of Audit to check its records at once. Ministry officials stated that, if the Court of Audit did not reply immediately, the Belgian state would run the risk of losing the sale and therefore a considerable sum of money. The Court of Audit did respond quickly but its answer was not the one the Ministry was hoping for. As the Court of Audit was not an archival institution, the financial watchdog had destroyed the copy of the title deed.[414]

In addition to showcasing the problematic manner in which records that are paramount for this research have sometimes been archived or rather destroyed, this point of entry demonstrates that the Ministry of Foreign Affairs was poised to capitalise on the property value of its foreign patrimony. By selling properties, the Ministry could quickly generate funds. Such schemes were especially welcome in times when discussions with the Belgian Ministry of Finance were at a deadlock. Putting consulate, legation and embassy buildings on sale turned out to be very lucrative. This was especially the case for embassies accommodating the highest level of Belgium's diplomatic representation abroad. To accentuate their esteemed status, embassies were often housed in high-end real estate. In terms of location, embassies have traditionally been well located within the urban fabric of a foreign capital city. This varies from a site in the central business district or the government district, to the green and peaceful suburbs. In terms of housing, embassies and especially residences have often been located in prime real estate. Conceived as high-end venues where guests should be received in style, ambassadorial residences tend to be situated in majestic and spacious buildings such as mansions, villas, castles and even palaces. Taking both the prominent location and majestic architecture into account, diplomatic properties have been sold by the Ministry for a large sum of money to generate additional funding in times of need.

As previously demonstrated, selling embassy buildings was paramount for financing the Belgian embassy-building programme. After all, the construction of the purpose-built embassies in Washington, D.C., Brasília and New Delhi was partially financed by selling old embassy premises. As such, selling embassies was a well-considered strategy in which the revenues of such sales were fully reinvested in the construction of new diplomatic premises.

Since the turn of the millennium, however, the pendulum has swung significantly further with regard to putting embassy premises on sale. Instead of reinvesting the revenues of such real estate transactions into new embassies, Belgian policymakers have to a significant extent used this source of revenue to plug holes in the national budget. This fourth and final chapter goes to the very heart of this development. It showcases how financial difficulties at home, more specifically high national debt and a derailed budget deficit, incentivised the Belgian state to monetise diplomatic properties. These practices reached their zenith during the Verhofstadt governments (1999-2008), a period during which several government buildings in Belgium were sold as part of controversial sale-and-leaseback real estate deals. In the context of this domestic tendency, the Verhofstadt governments turned their sights on embassy buildings in an effort to balance the budget.

This monetising strategy had a profound impact on the Belgian embassy-building programme, making it the fourth and final steering mechanism affecting the Ministry's foreign building activity. This chapter also demonstrates how the government's quest for money was an incentive to construct new embassies. Adopting the role of project developer and landlord, the Ministry of Foreign Affairs redeveloped embassy sites as part of lucrative public-private partnerships, or built in collaboration with new government entities and befriended European countries that would rent the newly built embassy.

As will become evident, the monetising strategy had a profound impact on the programme and design of purpose-built embassies. In contrast to previous projects, the Ministry of Foreign Affairs now had to commission embassy projects in collaboration with external partners who brought their own wish list to the table. Moreover, designs were heavily influenced by the requirement to house as many staffers as possible in the smallest possible area. As a result, high-rise buildings were introduced to the Ministry's building stock. Architecturally, the design of purpose-built embassies showed a clear deviation from the pre-millennium trend. Belgian embassy architecture became more generic and there was less of an emphasis on expressing nationhood abroad through style, form and materiality.

Chapter four leads us to the two most significant building projects of the new millennium so far: the redevelopment of the Tokyo embassy (2006-2010) and the construction of the Kinshasa chancery (2012-2017). Throughout the chapter, additional real estate projects are discussed to showcase that the Belgian state had money on its mind when it came to commissioning new diplomatic housing.

A. REDEVELOPING THE BELGIAN EMBASSY GROUNDS IN JAPAN: A PUBLIC-PRIVATE PARTNERSHIP

Tokyo's Ground Zero: The Destruction of the Beloved Belgian Embassy

Historically, Tokyo has been one of the most important Belgian diplomatic postings in East Asia. Already in 1921, the Ministry elevated the Tokyo legation to the rank of an embassy. In a similar fashion to previously discussed projects such as Washington, D.C. and Warsaw, the elevation incentivised the Ministry to invest in high-end real estate to house the newly established embassy. In 1928, the Belgian Ambassador Baron Albert de Bassompierre (1873-1956) fixed his gaze on the private estate of former Japanese Prime Minister Count Katō (1860-1926), who had recently passed away. The ambassador saw the Katō estate as the perfect fit for the ambassadorial residence. The estate was well situated in Tokyo's urban fabric. It was located in the high-end Chiyoda neighbourhood, the political centre of Japan. The Chiyoda district was and still is home to political hotspots, such as the National Diet and the official residence of the Prime Minister of Japan, and it is situated adjacent to the Imperial Palace. Moreover, the estate comprised a spacious garden covering an area of almost 8,500 m². Given the urban context of Tokyo with its densely populated neighbourhoods, the vast domain showed off wealth and power. Basically, it was a green oasis in a metropolitan desert.

The design of the Katō residence also corresponded to Ambassador de Bassompierre's taste. In 1911, the English architect Josiah Conder (1852-1920) designed Katō's private residence (Fig. 57). Conder designed a charming residential building that would not have looked out of place in the English countryside. Conder's work demonstrated a high degree of sensitivity to Japanese building traditions. In accordance with the majority of the buildings making up Tokyo at the time, he primarily used natural building materials like wood. The residence's façade was modelled on English country houses that drew inspiration from antiquity. However, Conder included Greco-Roman elements in a very subtle way. The characteristic portico, for instance, only featured pillar-shaped elements incorporated into the exteriors and a soberly decorated cornice.

Seeing the Katō estate as the perfect setting for the new embassy, Ambassador de Bassompierre convinced his superiors in Brussels to purchase the estate. In March 1928, the ambassador personally entered into negotiations with the family of the late Count Katō and reached an agreement. Rumour has it that the family was especially open to the idea of selling the estate to Belgium given the fact that Katō had a good relationship with the Belgian diplomatic corps and Belgium was a neutral country on the international stage. As such, the family would not manoeuvrer itself into a politically thorny situation by selling the estate to one of the contemporary world powers.[415] Being a neutral country had its perks with regard to acquiring prime diplomatic real estate.

Following the purchase, Ambassador de Bassompierre launched additional construction works on the domain. The estate was converted into an embassy compound as a chancery and additional housing units were constructed. The chancery was constructed next to the former residence of Katō in an aesthetic that resembled the latter. In his memoirs, Ambassador de Bassompierre was very satisfied with the embassy compound:

> Thanks to these improvements, Belgium now has a fully-fledged embassy in Tokyo, where the entire service and all the staffers have suitable and comfortable premises in an excellent part of the city.[416]

Following Japan's entry into the Second World War, the Belgian government in exile cut diplomatic ties with the Land of the Rising Sun,

Figure 57: The former Katō residence (left) next to the purpose-built chancery (right), undated

demonstrating to the United States that it was committed to the Allied cause. Consequently, the Belgian diplomatic staff was forced to evacuate the embassy in the Chiyoda district. The Belgian diplomatic corps entrusted the keys of the embassy to the Swedish legation, asking the neutral country to safeguard its premises, furniture and archival records for the duration of the war.[417] The Belgian government may have cut ties with Japan to ingratiate itself with the United States but the latter did not quite return the favour. In the latter stages of the Pacific War, American B-29 bombers reduced Tokyo to rubble in an effort to bomb Japan into submission. The Belgian embassy was hit by American incendiary bombs. Consumed by a firestorm, the compound was levelled to the ground and not a single building was left standing.[418]

Following the Japanese capitulation, Belgium was financially reimbursed for the embassy's destruction. As part of the peace treaty with the Allied powers that was signed on 8 September 1951, the Empire of Japan was forced to compensate the Allied nations financially for the war-time destruction of diplomatic properties. Japan therefore had to reimburse foreign nations even though American bombers had been responsible for levelling their diplomatic premises in Tokyo.

Redeveloping the Tokyo Embassy Grounds: A Familiar Story

The Belgian Ministry of Foreign Affairs received its financial compensation on 30 November 1954. In total, Japan paid some 10 million Belgian francs (2.4 million euros). In order to put the money to good use, Foreign Minister van Zeeland was keen to construct a new embassy on the ruins of the old one. He envisaged the redevelopment plans as a true prestige project that would usher in a new age for post-war relations.

In a similar fashion to the Washington project, van Zeeland reached out to his friend and go-to architect Max Winders. Winders visited Tokyo to see the site and immerse himself in the ins and outs of the local building industry. In April 1953, Winders presented his preliminary design to van Zeeland. His plan called for the construction of an ambassadorial residence and chancery. Deviating from the pre-war layout, Winders opted to house the residence and chancery in separate building units. To accentuate the difference in the functions of both buildings, they were physically distanced from one another by means of water bodies. Moreover, both structures were to be oriented towards different streets surrounding the embassy compound. Reflecting his traditional training and line of work, Winders included a Beaux-Arts inspired garden adjacent to the residence's terrace. The design of the garden relied heavily on formal geometry, a symmetrical composition with a centrally positioned fountain, long vistas and classical sculptures as focal points. At the edge of the garden, recreational facilities were to be included such as a swimming pool and a tennis court.

Architecturally, it remains unclear what kind of design Winders had in store for the new embassy. Unfortunately, only one site plan has stood the test of time. However, judging from his preliminary design of the Washington chancery, one can assume that Winders would have opted for a classically inspired aesthetic. Moreover, in one of his letters to van Zeeland, Winders voiced his preference for limestone façades, claiming that such exteriors would add a sense of grandeur to the embassy buildings.[419]

As part of the Tokyo commission, Winders examined the most suitable building method. Given the danger of earthquakes in Japan, he made the case for erecting reinforced concrete embassy structures to resist seismic waves. Past experiences had already made it abundantly clear to Brussels that such a building method was the way to go. On 1 September 1923, during the Great Kantō Earthquake that wreaked havoc across Tokyo, the Belgian embassy had been significantly damaged.[420] This cautionary tale was, however, soon forgotten within the Ministry's walls. Secretary-General Hervé de Gruben, for instance, openly challenged the idea of using reinforced concrete. In an effort to save money, de Gruben instructed Max Winders to examine whether it would also be feasible to use lighter and more cheap building materials for the Tokyo embassy.[421] Apparently, the construction costs outweighed the safety of the Belgian diplomats who would have to work and live in an earthquake-prone area.

Winders and de Gruben may have been at odds with each other but their part in commissioning the Tokyo embassy was well and truly over before the project could pick up steam. Hervé de Gruben was appointed ambassador to West Germany in 1953. Just one year later, Winders was cast aside because the ministership of his friend van Zeeland ended abruptly following the election defeat of the Christian Social Party in 1954.

What happened next is a familiar story as the history of the Washington chancery repeated itself in Tokyo. With van Zeeland out of the picture, Max Winders was replaced as architect by Hugo Van Kuyck. The Ministry's highest echelons were so pleased with the work Van Kuyck had done in Washington, D.C. that he was also commissioned to design the new Tokyo embassy in the late 1950s. As the Ministry's favourite architect was not accustomed to working in Japan, Van Kuyck joined forces with the Japanese architect Shiro Asabuki (1915-1988). An avowed Anglophile, Shiro Asabuki had studied architecture at Cambridge University in the late 1930s. Asabuki adhered to similar principles as his Belgian partner Van Kuyck. Both architects had a functionalist and rationalist approach towards architecture, opting to design in an exceedingly straightforward aesthetic with a strong emphasis on the building's purpose and function. When discussing the Tokyo project, Asabuki highlighted how such principles had been his guiding light:

> In the old days, an Embassy always reminded us of a solemn and prestigious structure. Nowadays, rather than putting priority on expressing the solemn dignity and authority of a country, the buildings have gradually become functional and even to a certain extent economically efficient. The dignity of the buildings as such is an indispensable factor that does not change, but since the lifestyle of modern humans has changed, Embassies cannot stay behind.[422]

Asabuki called for a mentality shift in designing embassies. Architects had to unshackle themselves from tradition and historicism. Asabuki claimed that, if sending states truly wanted to showcase themselves on foreign soil, it was better to construct modern and innovative buildings than to use historical styles and motifs. In doing so, sending states could showcase themselves as modern and progressive countries that were in sync with the latest developments in architecture.

In the late 1950s, Asabuki and Van Kuyck set about designing the new Tokyo embassy (Fig. 58). By this time, the scope of the project had changed significantly. Ministry officials wanted to use the spacious plot of 8,500 m² to its full potential. In addition to an ambassadorial residence and chancery, the compound had to include housing units for all embassy staffers and domestic personnel. A distinguishing feature of the site plan was its functional efficiency, enabling the diplomatic residents to work and live in comfortable conditions. In accordance with Winders' design, the ambassadorial residence was centrally positioned to accentuate its importance. In front of the residence, an obligatory roundabout was to be paved. However, Asabuki and Van Kuyck did clearly deviate from Winders' site plan. Whereas the latter included a Beaux-Arts inspired garden, the Japanese-Belgian duo opted for a fitting-in strategy. A traditional Japanese garden with a swimming pool was to be included behind the ambassadorial residence, offering the ambassador a green space to unwind and organise receptions. Another notable change was the fact that the chancery was to be attached to the residence. This would facilitate internal circulation between the ambassador's working and living environments, making it more convenient than moving from one building to another as was the case in Winders' design. The additional housing units for the embassy staff and domestic personnel were positioned on the edges of the compound. Ensuring that each staffer had privacy, Asabuki and Van Kuyck opted for detached residential units that were physically distanced from each other. Moreover, each house had its own garden enclosed by high walls and a separate entrance that led straight to the street.

Architecturally, Asabuki and Van Kuyck's design was a far cry from what Max Winders would have designed if he had had the chance. They designed an embassy compound that clearly adhered to modernist architectural principles. They conceived a homogenous architectural ensemble made up of low-rise structures (Fig. 59). Each building unit had a distinctive cube-shaped structure with straight lines, a series of ribbon windows and flat roofs. Each structure had a sober appearance with all-white exteriors and no embellishments. The sober appearance was the common thread running through the overall design but a certain sense of monumentality could be found at the residence's main entrance. A large canopy was

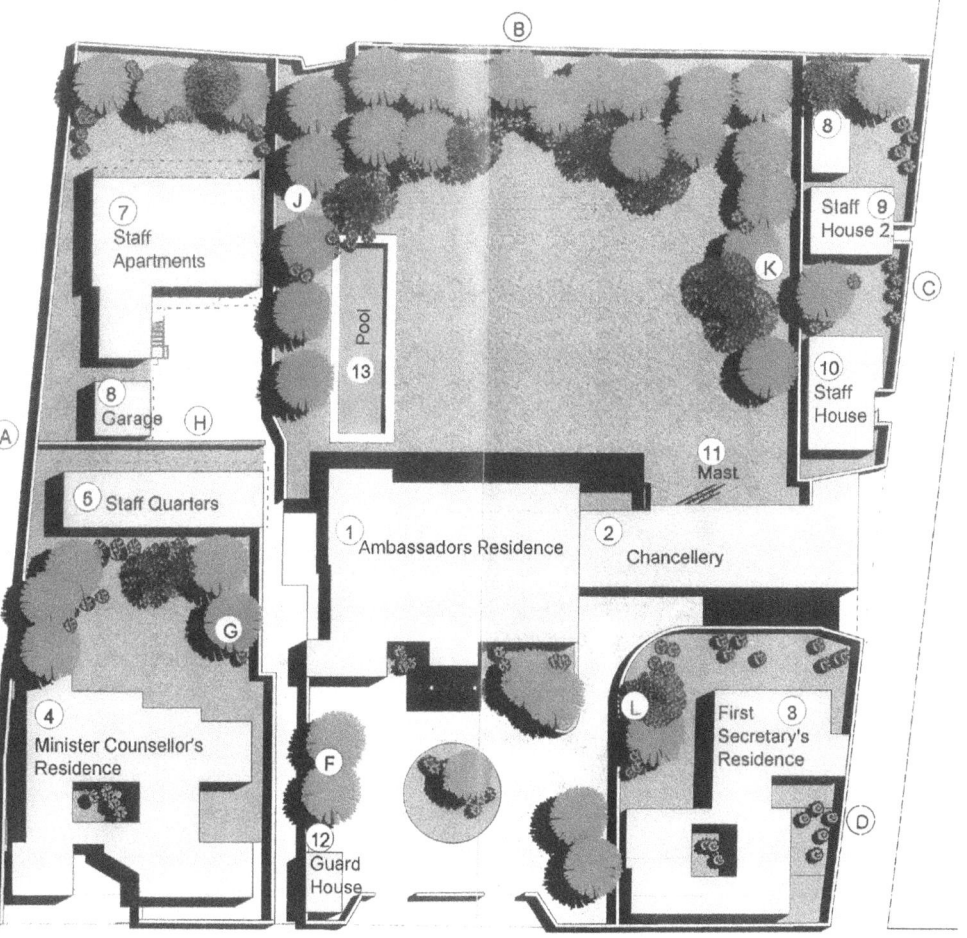

Figure 58: The Tokyo embassy, late 1990s

included that, in an abstract way, gave a pavilion-like vibe to it. In terms of structural details, Asabuki and Van Kuyck built on the preliminary work done by Winders. In line with his suggestion, all building units were made of reinforced concrete to limit the potential risk posed by earthquakes. Building this new compound came with a price tag of approximately 18 million Belgian francs (4 million euros) but a large part of this expenditure could be covered by the Japanese war reparations. Construction works kickstarted in 1959 and were already completed by March 1960.

Shiro Asabuki and Hugo Van Kuyck may have designed a modern embassy compound but they had no say in how the interiors would

Figure 59: The Belgian embassy compound, 1960s

be furnished and decorated. This task was awarded to the Inspection of Diplomatic and Consular Missions. As evidenced in the past, the Inspection had a soft spot for traditional interior designs. The interior of the Tokyo residence, for instance, could have come straight out of the Foxhall Road residence in Washington. The main hall (Fig. 60) featured a classical interior design with Louis XVI armchairs and chests of drawers, several Aubusson rugs and crystal chandeliers. In line with the period furniture, a 16th-century tapestry depicting the mythological figures of Dido and Aeneas was strategically positioned near the spiral staircase. Regarding the discrepancy between the embassy's modernist architecture and classical interior design, the Tokyo embassy was very similar to its counterpart in Brasília. In both cases, the architects involved designed a modern embassy that was in tune with contemporary architectural developments. However, their contemporary approach was not applied to the furniture and decorations within the diplomatic interiors.

Additionally, there was a discrepancy between the embassy compound and its immediate surroundings. The embassy compound with its white concrete structures and flat roofs contrasted greatly with the nearby wooden houses with pitched roofs. Whereas the design of the Warsaw and

Figure 60: The residence's main entrance hall, 1978

Brasília embassies fitted quite well with their respective urban contexts, the Tokyo embassy was the neighbourhood's maverick in terms of architecture and, to a certain extent, it even shielded itself off from its immediate environment. The high walls surrounding the compound further reinforced the notion that the Belgian embassy distanced itself from the neighbourhood. Freddy Cogels, the Inspector of Diplomatic and Consular Missions, jokingly talked about the Belgian embassy ghetto of Tokyo.[423] The Belgian residents very much enjoyed working and living in the embassy compound. In their memoirs, successive Belgian ambassadors had fond memories of the embassy premises and the spacious Japanese garden. By the 1980s, the beloved embassy compound and especially the land on which it stood began to pique the interest of policymakers in Brussels but for reasons that were unrelated to its status as a top-notch diplomatic compound.

Dreams of Monetising the Tokyo Embassy: The Loch Ness Monster of Belgian Politics

The growing political interest stemmed from the fact that real estate prices in Tokyo were going through the roof in the 1980s. Tokyo rose to fame as one of the greatest metropolises and financial-economic hubs of the world.[424] Tokyo witnessed a profound urban transformation that cemented its status as one of the most advanced cities in the world. As a magnet for leading Japanese corporations and multinationals, the city's central business district expanded significantly and absorbed the Chiyoda district where the Belgian embassy grounds were situated.[425] High-rise structures, such as office skyscrapers and luxurious residential towers, became widespread across Tokyo's skyline and reflected Japan's status as an economic superpower. To a certain extent, the growing verticality of the city's urban fabric was a testament to the fact that Japan's economic growth was at an all-time high. The high-rise developments had a profound effect on real estate prices. At the height of the redevelopment frenzy in the mid-1980s, project developers paid 150,000 US dollars (416,000 euros) for just one square metre of land in the central business district.[426]

Dazzled by the astronomical real estate prices in the Chiyoda district, the Ministry entertained the idea of redeveloping the embassy grounds. Determined to use the large and valuable plot of land to its full potential, a part of the newly built embassy was to be leased to commercial tenants. By generating its own revenue, the Ministry wanted to be more self-sufficient and financially independent. After all, the budgetary situation back home was becoming ever more dire. In the mid-1980s, the liberal Budget Minister Guy Verhofstadt, nicknamed Baby Thatcher because of his hardline austerity measures, launched the Sint-Anna Plan. The Sint-Anna Plan entailed a massive programme to cut public spending by 200 billion Belgian francs (11.6 billion euros). As part of the plan, the Ministry of Foreign Affairs had to cut spending. Verhofstadt put pressure on Foreign Minister Tindemans to reduce the Ministry's total budget by ten per cent to meet the requirements set by the Sint-Anna Plan.[427] Consequently, the Ministry's real estate budget was drastically reduced by 400 million Belgian francs (23.2 million euros).

As can be expected, such budget cuts did not go down well with Tindemans. Tindemans developed a deep-seated distaste for Guy Verhofstadt and his budgetary policies, calling him a cold-hearted accountant who has more enemies than allies in the Ministerial Council.[428]

Publicly, however, Tindemans sang a very different tune with regard to the Sint-Anna Plan in the Chamber of Representatives. Whereas his predecessor Wigny had admitted to the opposition that such budget cuts were foolish back in the late 1950s, Tindemans did no such thing as he publicly defended the plan in parliament. The Christian-democratic strongman indicated that it was his moral duty as a loyal member of the national government to do so.[429]

As the Ministry of Foreign Affairs had to make do with less funding, Tindemans examined more creative solutions to fund the real estate budget. He was poised to generate other sources of funding. In this context, he wanted to capitalise on the fact that the Ministry owned a large plot of land in Tokyo, the city with the highest real estate prices at the time.

Marcel Depasse (1933-2006), the Belgian Ambassador to Japan, was instructed to examine various scenarios to monetise the valuable embassy grounds. These scenarios ranged from redeveloping and leasing the site to selling it. Ambassador Depasse considered the construction of a fully state-owned embassy with tenant spaces as the most viable option. He reached out to Takenaka Kōmuten, one of the largest Japanese building contractors at the time.[430] Takenaka Kōmuten was one of the driving forces that transformed Tokyo into a vertical metropolis of high-rise offices and apartments buildings.[431]

On 1 October 1985, the Japanese building contractor presented its redevelopment plans to Ambassador Depasse. The plans offered Belgium a modern embassy complex (Fig. 61) that would be able to generate money at the same time. The preliminary design entitled Belgium in the Heart of Tokyo called for the demolition of the embassy compound that Asabuki and Van Kuyck had designed in the late 1950s. In return, a new embassy was to be constructed that used the land to its full potential. In terms of its layout, the new Tokyo embassy would consist of just one building, a far cry from the existing compound made up of a series of detached building units. Another noteworthy change was the height of the new embassy. Whereas the tallest building within the contemporary embassy compound consisted of just two stories, the new embassy would feature a maximum of six storeys. This modest high-rise embassy was to be more in line with Tokyo's high-rise redevelopment. Takenaka Kōmuten called for the construction of one H-shaped building. The main section, which housed the ambassadorial residence, was characterised by a box-like structure with a glazed façade. In front of the residence, the original roundabout was to be preserved to pay homage to Asabuki and Van Kuyck's original compound. The ambassadorial residence was flanked by two wings, the exteriors of which featured pilotis and ribbon windows that added to the building's modern appearance. Moreover, both wings had conspicuous curved edges. This curved shape was reinforced by the fact that the upper floors were significantly smaller in terms of surface area. This gave a ziggurat-like aesthetic to the ensemble. Both wings added to the dynamic and invigorating vibe of the new embassy complex. Whereas the east wing

Figure 61: The proposed Tokyo embassy, 1985

would house embassy offices, the far longer west wing was to house an absolute novelty in the history of Belgian diplomatic housing, specifically 9,000 m² of prime retail and office space that was to be leased to Japanese businesses.

According to the estimates of Takenaka Kōmuten, the rental revenue could reimburse the construction of the new embassy in just under 15 years. From then on, the Ministry of Foreign Affairs could transfer rental revenues to the diplomatic housing budget. In doing so, the new Tokyo embassy would function as an income-producing property that could help finance investments in Belgian diplomatic housing. For reasons that remain unknown, however, the plan never saw the light of day. Given the dire budgetary situation of Belgium, it is not beyond the realm of possibility that the Ministry did not want to wait over 15 years before it would see a return on its investment. Apparently, it wanted a profit at once. In hindsight, it was good that the Belgian diplomatic corps abandoned such a scheme that depended heavily on rental revenue. After all, in 1992, the Japanese real estate bubble burst and rental prices plummeted.[432] It would therefore have been a financial disaster if Belgium had gone ahead with the proposal of Takenaka Kōmuten.

Nonetheless, the Tokyo embassy grounds and especially its market value became the stuff of legend in Belgian politics throughout the late 1980s and 1990s. Politicians across the political spectrum daydreamed that selling the embassy would generate an astronomical amount of money that would come in handy for balancing the books and reducing the national debt. During budgetary debates in the Chamber of Representatives, it became a running gag to make references to the Tokyo embassy. If members of the opposition could not immediately figure out where non-tax revenues were coming from, they openly wondered whether the government had finally sold the Tokyo embassy.[433] As soon as these claims were debunked, the rumours died down until the next budgetary debate. The Tokyo embassy even got the nickname of the Loch Ness Monster of Belgian politics.[434] Like the legendary creature, the Tokyo embassy had the tendency to show up suddenly in the public debate and disappear just as quickly. At the Ministry of Foreign Affairs, plans to monetise the Tokyo embassy also continued to show up during budgetary discussions.[435] Such plans were, however, abandoned as the Japanese real estate market was still going through a rough patch, making it financially less appealing to sell or redevelop the embassy grounds. It was not until the mid-2000s that the Tokyo grounds once again caught the eye of Belgian policymakers. This had everything to do with the coalition that governed Belgium at the time which took the monetisation of the state patrimony to a whole new level.

The Verhofstadt Governments as Real Estate Tycoon: The Ministry of Foreign Affairs Up For Sale

The national elections of 1999 profoundly shifted the balance of power in Belgian politics. Following the historic election defeat of the Christian-democrats, the liberal strongman Guy Verhofstadt forged an unprecedented coalition of Flemish and Walloon liberals, socialists and greens. For the first time in half a century, the Christian Social Party was cast into the opposition as Verhofstadt became prime minister of the novel purple-green government. Reflecting the ideologically divergent parties making up the coalition, the government's budgetary policy was characterised by a wide variety of left- and right-wing economic policies. These ranged from cutting taxes to increasing social welfare spending so that each political party could leave its mark. Given the enormous optimism at the start of the new millennium, the purple-green government hoped that economic growth would help finance these tax cuts and increase social expenditures.[436]

However, it was not take long before economic growth slowed down because of 9/11 and the dot-com bubble crash in the early 2000s. Consequently, the purple-green government developed a questionable tendency to call upon non-recurring incomes to balance the books. These included privatising state-owned companies, introducing tax amnesties and licencing mobile phone spectrums.

However, an especially lucrative non-recurring income turned out to be the monetisation of the vast real estate portfolio of the Belgian state. As part of the so-called sale-and-leaseback transactions, the government sold state-owned premises to real estate agencies. Subsequently, the government immediately began to lease the very buildings it had just sold. Such sale-and-leaseback operations were especially controversial from a budgetary point of view. In the long run, the Belgian state will pay more in rent than it had originally received from selling the properties. Between 2001 and 2006, 86 state properties were sold for 1.3 billion euros (1.8 billion euros) whereas the total rent for these premises will amount to 1.8 billion euros (2.5 billion euros) by 2035.[437] Moreover, from a representational point of view, the Belgian state was stripped of its patrimony. Basically, the Verhofstadt government sold the family silverware to pay off its credit card debt.

The Ministry of Foreign Affairs also saw its fair share of sale-and-leaseback operations. In 1997, the Ministry moved to a new office complex in the political heart of Brussels. The purpose-built ministry complex was given the name of Egmont I. This name was derived from the Egmont Palace, a majestic neoclassical palace situated just down the street. Designed by Michel Jaspers of the leading architecture firm M. & J-M. Jaspers-J. Eyers & Partners, Egmont I is a massive ministry complex of approximately 36,000 m².

However, just seven years following its completion, the Egmont I complex became the focal point of yet another sale-and-leaseback operation in 2004. By this time, Guy Verhofstadt was leading his second coalition government of liberals and socialists. The Verhofstadt II government sold Egmont I to the Belgian real estate investor Cofinimmo for 170 million euros (274 million euros) which came in handy for balancing the budget from 2004.[438] As part of the deal, Cofinimmo was contractually bound to lease Egmont I to the Ministry for at least 18 years.

Additionally, the Ministry's leadership launched initiatives of its own to generate money from its embassy patrimony. As the Ministry often lacked funding to invest in real estate, the so-called Buildings Fund was introduced. If embassies were sold or generated rental incomes, the money was to be transferred to the Buildings Fund which would cover future real estate investments. Secretary-General Jan De Bock even went to so far as to describe the Buildings Fund as the recycling instrument of foreign patrimony.[439]

In fact, at the end of the 20th century, this tendency was not a specifically Belgian phenomenon. The US State Department also developed a tendency to sell embassy buildings but did so for very different reasons than raising money. The State Department sold high-profile embassies situated in city centres for security reasons. In the wake of the Al-Qaeda bombing attacks on the US embassies in Nairobi and Dar es Salaam in 1998, several landmark embassies were sold and the revenue was used to construct fortress-like embassy compounds in the suburbs.[440]

By the mid-2000s, the Buildings Fund had become indispensable for the Belgian embassy-building programme, covering building costs through two main sources of income. Firstly, considerable efforts were made to find external tenants for Belgian embassies with a high vacancy rate.

One such example leads us back to the Riyadh embassy compound constructed in the mid-1980s. By 2000, the casbah-like compound had become too spacious as the number of embassy staffers had been significantly reduced throughout the 1990s. Consequently, one of the residential units had become vacant. The Ministry asked Ambassador Pierre Colot to find a tenant for the empty house at once. Well, 'asked' is perhaps too mild a word. In fact, the real estate department made it crystal clear to Ambassador Colot that if he did not find a tenant at once, this would reflect poorly on his ambassadorship.[441] Brussels expected its ambassadors to act as rental agents in addition to their already diverse range of duties. Ambassador Colot set to work finding a tenant by sending an email to all foreign diplomats posted in Riyadh. Eventually, a Spanish diplomat came forward to lease the property. In the lease contract, there is a noteworthy condition that indicates what life was like in an embassy compound. During his stay, the Spanish diplomat had to be on his best behaviour as the contract explicitly stipulated that:

> The tenant commits himself to refrain from any act or attitude prejudicial to the character and the functioning of the Belgian diplomatic mission, the quietness of the area and the professional activities or private life of the people living in the compound.[442]

Secondly, the Ministry's leadership increasingly looked into the possibility of selling valuable embassies to balance the books. In the fall of 1999, Foreign Minister Louis Michel of the francophone liberal party *Mouvement Réformateur* (MR) was instructed to cut back spending. Foreign Minister Michel conceived plans to put the Belgian embassy compound in Thailand on sale and use the revenue to meet the budgetary demands. Acquisitioned in 1935, the Bangkok embassy was one of the most majestic Belgian embassy properties. The residence was originally commissioned by a prominent Thai family in the early 1900s who wanted to assimilate itself into a Western lifestyle. This aspiration manifested itself by hiring an Italian architect to design the family residence. He designed a majestic villa characterised by a pitched roof, minimal embellishments and an extensive use of shutters. The villa's all-white exteriors contrasted greatly with the green surroundings.

By the mid-1990s, however, the ambassadorial residence had lost much of its charm. As Bangkok is by its very essence a sinking city, the ambassadorial residence was occasionally flooded. As a result, the flooding had rotted the parquet floors. Moreover, the wooden interiors were being slowly consumed by termites which thrived in the humid conditions. Investments in maintenance works would have prevented this run-down state but budget cuts decided otherwise.

The residence may have been in a deplorable state but the land on which it stood had a significant market value by the early 2000s. As was the case in Tokyo, the Belgian embassy site in Bangkok was situated in a high-end neighbourhood that was being redeveloped by real estate magnates. Capitalising on the fact that developers were looking for sites to construct high-rise commercial and residential buildings, Foreign Minister Louis Michel was keen to sell the Bangkok compound.[443] According to estimates, such a sale could generate the dazzling sum of one billion Belgian francs (43.2 million euros).[444] The Belgian embassy staff did, however, make efforts to change the mind of the liberal strongman. Ambassador Pierre Vaesen, for instance, warned that rumours of a possible sale did not go down well in Bangkok:

> According to the first echoes I have received, a rumour is already circulating in Bangkok about the possible sale of our compound; it is provoking negative reactions from both Thai officials and the Belgian community. We need to remain attentive to the aspect of promoting our image in such operations, which cannot be reduced to purely administrative or financial problems. Under no

circumstances should any change of property be interpreted as a downgrading of our presence in Thailand.⁴⁴⁵

Fortunately for Vaes, external factors thwarted Michel's plans. By the early 2000s, a real estate bust devastated the real estate market in Thailand. Much to his frustration, Louis Michel had to abandon the plans to sell the Bangkok compound. Michel did, however, instruct the embassy to notify him if market conditions started to improve in Bangkok. It is somewhat cynical that just two years later, in the context of writing the preface of the book *Belgium's Most Beautiful Embassies From Around The World*, Louis Michel emphasised that majestic ambassadorial residences such as the one in Bangkok are invaluable to showcasing Belgium abroad and turning ambassadorships into successes. Little did the readers of the book know that Michel was on the verge of selling this embassy because of budgetary reasons.⁴⁴⁶

The third and final strategy to monetise diplomatic patrimony consisted of closing embassies and consulates. By doing so, the Ministry sold or terminated the lease of buildings in places that it considered to be less important from a political or economic point of view. Such a strategy was already implemented throughout the 1970s and 1980s. By 2002, this practice had reached its zenith. Instructed to cut his expenses by 40 million Belgian francs (1.6 million euros), Foreign Minister Michel closed embassies in Sarajevo, Wellington and La Paz while the consulates in Munich, Milan and Lyon met a similar fate.⁴⁴⁷ In the Parliamentary Committee for Foreign Affairs, the Christian-democratic opposition spoke out against the decision, calling it a diplomatic sell-off that would jeopardise the credibility of Belgium at the international level. The liberal strongman went on to publicly defend the decision to close these diplomatic postings, arguing that such operations were the most straightforward and easiest way to cut back spending quickly.⁴⁴⁸ He hammered home the argument that he was actually 'optimising' the country's diplomatic and consular network, a somewhat euphemistically term to say the least.

The three strategies of renting out, selling and closing embassy premises illustrate how policymakers in the early 2000s believed that the nation's embassy patrimony was a cash cow that could raise a significant amount of money in a short time span. It was therefore only a matter of time before the so-called Loch Ness Monster of Belgian politics, the Tokyo compound, caught the eye of policymakers.

Big in Japan: Redeveloping the Embassy Grounds, Part II

The move into Egmont I coincided with a thorough internal reorganisation and computerisation of the Ministry of Foreign Affairs at the end of the 1990s. By this time, Belgium had been transformed from a unitary into a federal state, composed of communities and regions. As part of the Copernicus Reform of the federal government administration, the Belgian Ministry of Foreign Affairs was rebranded into the Federal Public Service Foreign Affairs, Foreign Trade and Development Cooperation (FPS Foreign Affairs) on 8 March 2002.[449] The new name and head offices ushered in a new age for one of the oldest ministries within the Belgian state apparatus.

Meanwhile, the practice of monetising the embassy patrimony continued unabated. By 2004, the FPS Foreign Affairs was headed by Foreign Minister Karel De Gucht of the Flemish Liberals and Democrats (VLD). As a fellow party member of Prime Minister Guy Verhofstadt and one of the VLD heavyweights in the federal government, De Gucht supported the tendency to use non-recurring incomes to balance the books. In his capacity as foreign minister, he chipped in by monetising the embassy patrimony. Consequently, the Loch Ness Monster of the Belgian embassy patrimony reappeared in government circles. Incentivised by budgetary setbacks and the recovery of the Japanese real estate market, De Gucht breathed new life into the scheme of monetising the valuable embassy grounds in Tokyo. Initially, De Gucht examined the possibility of generating money through a long-term lease on the land. The Tokyo grounds were to be leased to a real estate developer for a period of 55 years.[450] The developer was obligated to demolish the embassy compound and construct an office tower housing both the new embassy and commercial spaces that the developer could lease to tenants. At the end of the land lease, the Belgian state would legally recover full ownership of the grounds and the towering edifice. This strategy was to be far more beneficial for the state finances than the sale-and-leaseback operations put in place back in Belgium. In this scenario, the FPS Foreign Affairs would receive a steady income for more than half a century and still remain the full owner of the well-located land in the high-end Chiyoda district.

However, the budgetary situation in Belgium decided otherwise. Following the political summer break of 2006, the Federal Public Service Finance realised that it had made a serious miscalculation in forecasting the federal tax revenues.[451] All of a sudden, the Verhofstadt II government had to find 883 million euros (1.3 billion euros) to balance the budget. Finance Minister Didier Reynders of the MR suggested selling the Tokyo grounds at once instead of setting up a long-term lease. According to him, such a sale would generate at least 115 million euros (177 million euros). With this revenue, the Belgian state could both construct a new embassy in Tokyo and generate funding to balance the budget. Reynders' suggestion effectively ended the original scheme to lease the land, a scheme by which the Belgian state would have remained the sole proprietor of the Tokyo grounds. Eventually, the liberal strongman Reynders got Foreign Minister De Gucht on board. The Ministry launched a public tender for the sale and redevelopment of the Tokyo grounds.

By the mid-2000s, the FPS Foreign Affairs had plenty of experience in organising public tenders. As a result of national and European legislation on government procurements, the Ministry organised a series of seminars for the real estate department on how to organise public tenders in the 1990s.[452] As such, the days in which Belgian diplomats and foreign ministers could singlehandedly award contracts without a notable allocation procedure were well and truly over. Interestingly, however, the leadership of the FPS Foreign Affairs decided to call upon external experts to draft the public tender and assess the various participating bids. The Ministry called upon the services of Deloitte Real Estate, a large strategy consulting business. The decision to join forces with Deloitte Real Estate was by no means incidental. During the early 2000s, Deloitte Real Estate was the go-to real estate expert of the Verhofstadt governments. The company had, for instance, assisted the federal government in the sale-and-leaseback of Egmont I. Deloitte Real Estate was tasked with checking candidates' financial credentials, providing recommendations in the selection of bidders and playing a definite expert role in the negotiation phase in order to maximise the selling price.

Whereas Deloitte Real Estate would deal with the financial aspect of the real estate operation, the FPS Foreign Affairs called upon another external partner to judge the architectural and aesthetic qualities of the participating bids. This partner was none other than Jaspers-Eyers, the very architecture firm that had designed Egmont I. The Tokyo commission further cemented the firm's status as the Ministry's go-to architect, as Max Winders and Hugo Van Kuyck had been in the past. Jean-Michel Jaspers, the son of Michel Jaspers, was tasked with assessing the bids and liaising between the Ministry and the real estate developer that would eventually be assigned the project.

With the help of Deloitte Real Estate and Jean-Michel Jaspers, the FPS Foreign Affairs launched a public tender for the Tokyo redevelopment in 2006. For the sake of convenience, the FPS Foreign Affairs decided that only consortiums could submit a bid. Real estate developers had to submit a joint bid together with an architect and building contractor. As such, the FPS Foreign Affairs only had to conduct negotiations on the concept, planning, construction, finance and management with just one partner.

The scope of the project involved the winning consortium buying part of the embassy grounds and subsequently razing the entire embassy compound to the ground. On its plot of land, the real estate developer could construct a commercial building. On the land that remained in Belgian hands, the consortium had to construct a new embassy. The consortium would be responsible for designing and constructing the embassy but this had to be done in concert with the Belgian architect Jean-Michel Jaspers who would look after the interests of the FPS Foreign Affairs. Bids were evaluated by means of a scoring system. The price that consortiums were willing to pay for partially acquisitioning the embassy grounds was allocated a maximum of 60 points whereas the architectural qualities of the embassy design counted for just 40 points. It goes without saying that the financial aspect trumped the architectural one considerably in redeveloping the embassy grounds.

The Japanese business consortium Mitsubishi-Takenaka was one of the participants. As illustrated previously, Takenaka was no stranger to the Ministry. In the 1980s, the Japanese building contractor had drafted plans to redevelop the embassy grounds but these plans failed to materialise because of the Japanese real estate crash. In the context of the new Belgian public procurement of 2006, Takenaka joined forces with Mitsubishi Corporation, an institution that hardly needs an introduction. Mitsubishi Corporation is the leading business enterprise of Japan, operating across virtually every industry. By 2006, Mitsubishi's Urban Development Division had built up a sound reputation for developing residential properties, office buildings and retail facilities across the Japanese archipelago.

As part of the bid, the consortium Mitsubishi-Takenaka joined forces with the architecture firm Noriaki Okabe Architecture Network that was established by the Japanese architect Noriaki Okabe in 1995. Okabe was and still is one of the best-reputed Japanese architects. He made a name for himself through his collaboration with the Italian architect Renzo Piano. Among others, Okabe supervised the construction of the Centre

Georges Pompidou in Paris. Moreover, in Japan, he designed the Kansai International Airport that is situated on an artificial island. In addition, he worked as an architecture professor at Kobe Design University. By 2006, his architecture firm had cemented its status as an authority and was particularly known for designing corporate headquarters and residential buildings across Japan. The final company making up the consortium was the Bank of Tokyo, one of the nation's leading financial institutions. The Bank of Tokyo provided a bank guarantee to Mitsubishi-Takenaka, showing to the FPS Foreign Affairs that the Japanese consortium would be financially able to deliver on its promises. Given the high-profile entities, the consortium Mitsubishi-Takenaka-Okabe-Bank of Tokyo (MTOB) was a serious contender to redevelop the Tokyo embassy grounds and outdo the bids of the seven other participating Japanese consortiums.

MTOB lived up to the expectations as it did just that. On 14 December 2006, the FPS Foreign Affairs awarded the embassy contract to MTOB. Given the Ministry's scoring system, the odds were definitely in favour of the candidate who was willing to put the greatest amount of money on the table. As luck would have it, MTOB was willing to pay top dollar. The Japanese consortium put the dazzling figure of 419.6 million euros (648 million euros) on the table.[453] This astronomical amount of money reflected the fact that the embassy site was situated in the high-end Chiyoda district, land prices were rising significantly in Tokyo, and the flourishing Japanese business sector was in dire need of rental offices.[454]

The Bank of Tokyo wired the money to the Buildings Fund of the FPS Foreign Affairs. Overall, only a fraction of this figure was immediately reinvested into the diplomatic patrimony. Some 24 million euros (38 million euros) would be used to finance the construction of the new Tokyo embassy that MTOB would erect on the remaining Belgian parcel of land. The remaining 395 million euros (610 million euros) was parked in the account of the Buildings Fund for the remainder of 2006. This was therefore a book-keeping exercise to balance the books of the Verhofstadt II government. Unfortunately for the FPS Foreign Affairs, it was not rewarded for its help to put the derailed federal state budget back on track. Moreover, throughout 2006 and 2007, the Belgian diplomatic corps faced additional budget cuts that severely impacted its presence abroad. At the time when Foreign Minister De Gucht transferred the remaining 395 million euros (610 million euros) of the Tokyo deal to the federal budget, the VLD strongman simultaneously closed down embassies in Gabon, Bolivia and Ecuador for budgetary reasons.[455]

During the meeting of the Parliamentary Committee for Foreign Affairs on 9 January 2007, De Gucht received backlash from the opposition regarding the Tokyo sale. In particular, MPs from the Christian Democratic and Flemish political party (CD&V) spoke out against the redevelopment project. CD&V MP Servais Verherstraeten, for instance, spoke out against selling part of the Tokyo grounds.[456] Verherstraeten framed the sale as yet another book-keeping exercise of the federal government. Yet again, a non-recurring income had to shore up the derailed federal budget. Moreover, Verherstraeten regretted that the embassy patrimony had become the subject of such real estate operations. In his response, Foreign Minister De Gucht boasted about the Tokyo deal that his administration had closed. He hammered home the argument that the embassy compound had seen better days and was in an abysmal state by 2006. De Gucht claimed that, by redeveloping the embassy grounds alongside MTOB, the FPS Foreign Affairs would be able to modernise the Tokyo embassy while simultaneously making a profit of 395 million euros (610 million euros). Given the contemporary mindset, De Gucht went on to say that the profitability of the embassy patrimony would become ever more important in the future and the Tokyo project had set the standard. De Gucht reasoned that, as far as profitability was concerned, the Tokyo redevelopment was a tremendous success that exceeded all expectations.

The Spatial Ramifications of the Public-Private Redevelopment

The real estate transaction may have exceeded the Ministry's financial expectations but what were in fact the real-life effects on the embassy grounds? Basically, the FPS Foreign Affairs received a large amount of money for selling a part of its Tokyo embassy grounds but it paid a hefty price from a representational point of view. After all, the Belgian footprint in Tokyo altered significantly.

Before the deal with MTOB, the FPS Foreign Affairs owned a spacious plot of 8,500 m^2, a true luxury in the densely populated Japanese metropolis. Visually, the embassy compound contrasted greatly with Tokyo's vertical development. Fuelled by a real estate boom, Tokyo had become a city of towers from the late 1970s onward. With booming land prices, real estate developers were paying over the odds for land. Consequently, they maximised the land's value by stacking storey upon storey. High-rise buildings began to dominate Tokyo's skyline as height became the dominant aesthetic for buildings and the main sign of prestige. The high-end Chiyoda district was no exception to the rule of vertical urbanisation. As building upwards became more common in the Chiyoda district, the Belgian embassy grounds turned into an anomaly because of their detached, low-rise embassy buildings immersed in a green environment. This made the Tokyo embassy a highly valuable property for the Belgian state as it was a notable exception in the Chiyoda district. The embassy site was situated in the very city centre but it was not affected by market conditions. All this, however, was about to change because of the partial sale of the embassy grounds to MTOB in December 2006. In fact, the description 'partial sale' is quite an understatement when describing what actually transpired. Of the total area of 8,500 m², some 6,520 m² or three-quarters of the embassy premises were sold to MTOB whereas some 2,000 m² would remain in Belgian hands. Of course, this was still a considerable plot of land by Tokyo standards but a far cry from what the FPS Foreign Affairs used to own.

Situated on a corner block, the site was divided along its full width along an east-west axis (Fig. 62). On the northern end with its surface area of 6,500 m², MTOB could erect the Nibancho Center Building it so eagerly wanted to construct. The Nibancho Center Building was to be a multistorey office building generating rental incomes for MTOB. Interestingly, the FPS Foreign Affairs imposed an important condition to MTOB with regard to developing its parcel. It was agreed that the Nibancho Center Building would not occupy the entire plot. Instead, the FPS Foreign Affairs negotiated a deal by which the north-western corner was to be developed into a square.

It had several reasons to put forward this spatial demand. Firstly, the square had to ensure that the future Belgian embassy would not be overshadowed by the far larger and taller Nibancho Center Building. The square would function as a transition zone between both buildings. Secondly, the square was conceived to be an integral part of the new embassy. In several discussions, ministry officials perceived the square to be the embassy's "antechamber".[457] Orientated towards the embassy's main entrance, the square would create an architectural promenade. Thirdly and lastly, the plaza was included for reasons of national prestige in the Japanese metropolis. To boost national visibility in Tokyo, the plaza was to be named Belgium Square and paved with materials endemic to Belgium.

From a representational point of view, the redevelopment therefore marked a profound shift in Belgian diplomatic housing in Tokyo. The old embassy could only be used by a select group of people such as Belgian

258 CHAPTER IV

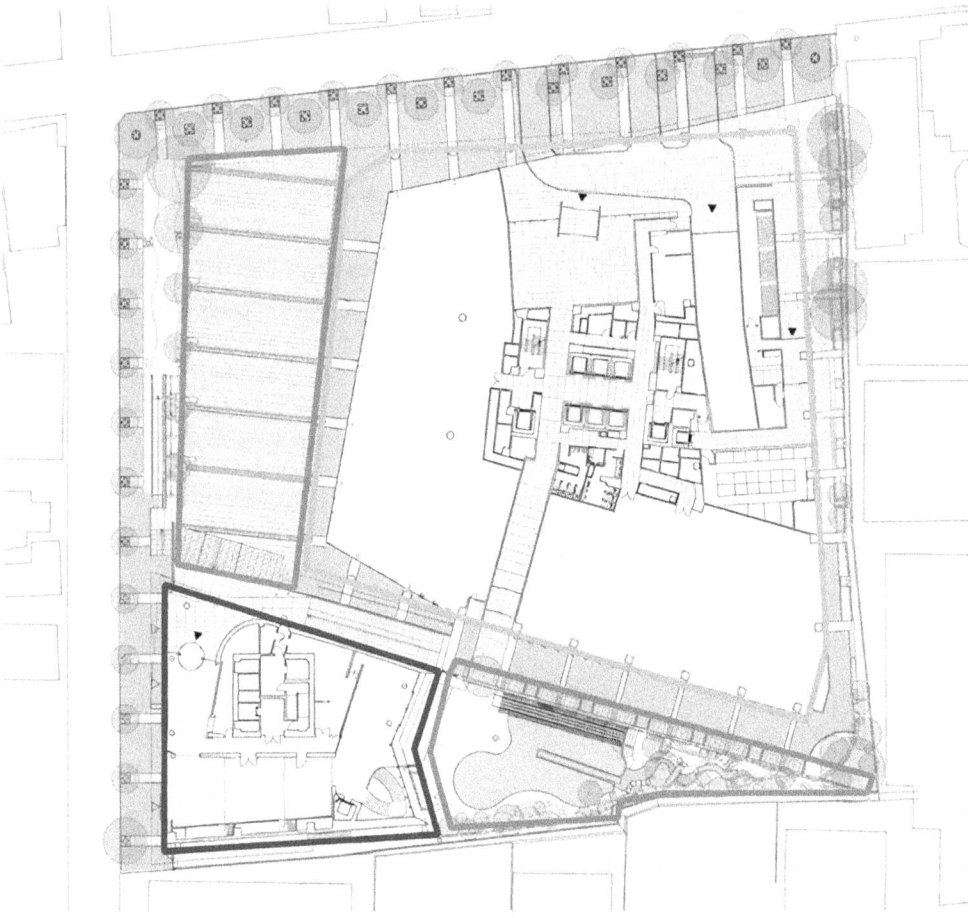

Legenda

☐ The Belgian Embassy
☐ The Belgian Square
☐ The Embassy Garden
☐ The Nibancho Building

Based on: Noriaki Okabe
Architecture Network

Map created by Christophe De Coster

Figure 62: The redevelopment of the Tokyo embassy grounds

diplomats and guests. However, with regard to the new Belgium Square, the average Tokyo resident could enjoy this public space. Belgium Square can be read as an effort to create goodwill among local residents. As an overcrowded metropolis, Tokyo is known for its chronic lack of public space. By forcing MTOB to include a square, the FPS Foreign Affairs created substantial open space which by itself is an expensive commodity given Tokyo's urban fabric. The addition of public space was therefore a significant transformation when compared to the old embassy compound that used to shield itself off from its surroundings.

On the remaining 2,000 m², the new embassy would be erected. The southern triangular parcel of land was significantly smaller than the old embassy compound but it nevertheless had to accommodate similar facilities. This would have a profound effect on the volume and height of the new embassy. The new embassy was to be situated along the street side and prolonged with a garden running parallel to the Nibancho Center Building. In order to visually distinguish the garden from the massive office building, the green space was to be surrounded by a high white wall that marked a clear boundary between both neighbours. The white wall was reminiscent of the wall surrounding the old compound and was a subtle nod to the design of Asabuki and Van Kuyck of the late 1950s.[458]

Form Follows Finance: Designing the Belgian Embassy Tower

In terms of designing the embassy, the Japanese architect Noriaki Okabe had to meet an extensive programme of requirements. The Ministry's wish list consisted of an ambassador's residence, additional housing units for diplomats, embassy offices, a visa section, recreational facilities, a garden and a parking lot. Basically, Okabe was presented with a similar programme as Asabuki and Van Kuyck in the 1950s but he had to work in very different spatial conditions. Given that he had to design an embassy with similar programmatic needs but on a significantly smaller building site, Okabe opted to design a tower building of nine storeys. To a certain extent, the low-rise structures of the old embassy compound were to be stacked upon one another to create a medium-rise development. His approach was a textbook example of what architectural historian Carol Willis has coined as 'form follows finance'. Building on Louis Sullivan's famous axiom of 'form follows function', Willis illustrates how American high-rise developments were more likely to result from speculative development rather than a desire for prestige by building ever higher.[459] Space is a commodity and high-rise buildings are conceived to be nothing more than business endeavours. Accordingly, form follows finance is very fitting description of the redevelopment of the embassy grounds as the financial aspect directly inspired the tower-shaped form of the new embassy.

Given Tokyo's high-rise skyline, Okabe's plan to build a tower structure, especially one of just nine storeys, is hardly worth mentioning. However, the same cannot be said for the Belgian embassy-building programme. The Tokyo project would be the first time that building in a vertical way would be the guiding principle in an embassy project. In so doing, Belgium followed the example of the US State Department which constructed a high-rise apartment building in Tokyo in the mid-1970s.[460]

Given the spatial constraints, the Ministry's leadership was open to the idea of packing a tall building onto the remaining parcel of land. Okabe and his collaborators at the Noriaki Okabe Architecture Network set about designing the new Belgian embassy. In line with Japanese regulations, the new embassy had to be earthquake-proof. Therefore, Okabe equipped the foundations with a state-of-the-art system of seismic dampers.

The tower building was made up of a reinforced concrete frame. The tower itself is a simple rectangular structure. In line with his other work, Okabe added a playful touch to this straightforward building form. Okabe delighted in creating contradictions in his architectural oeuvre. He included such contradictions in his embassy design, giving it a more playful touch. This becomes especially apparent in the exterior cladding. Ministry officials had stressed that the façade had to reflect a certain sense of dignity and should be covered with high-end limestone.[461] Such a statement underscores that the FPS Foreign Affairs considered a building's exterior key in measuring the quality of an embassy design. However, Okabe had no intention of covering the entire building with limestone. He only opted to include limestone exteriors along the entire length of the northern façade whereas the remaining exteriors featured a combination of limestone and glazed façades for the top floors. The abrupt end of the limestone coating (Fig. 63) along the western façade was intended to give a playful and dynamic appearance to the exteriors. It gives the impression that the entire building used to be covered in limestone but parts were peeled off over time. Another dynamic feature was included at the corner of the northern and western façade. Whereas the building has an overall rectangular appearance, this corner is curved which creates a more sensual appearance overall.

Figure 63: The Belgian embassy in Tokyo, 2017

Okabe deemed it imperative to include such conspicuous features in order to distinguish the embassy from the adjacent Nibancho Center Building (Fig. 64) that he had also designed. As this big, boxy office complex would surpass the embassy in terms of height and volume, Okabe wanted to make sure that both structures would sufficiently stand out from one another. Raised on a series of pilotis, the Nibancho Center Building was to be a massive office complex with curtain walls and a ziggurat-like structure on top, which therefore contrasted greatly with the embassy's limestone façade and architectural tweaks. Okabe's diverging architectural approaches had to make it crystal clear to people walking across Belgium Square that both buildings had very different owners and were used for very different activities. From Belgium Square, visitors could make their way to the Belgian embassy by means of a broad flight of stairs leading to the main entrance. Along the street side, Okabe included an entrance to the visa section and a gateway leading to an underground car park. In the past, the roundabout had been the main instrument to guide circulation from and to Belgian embassies but now the various entrances were incorporated into the building itself given the spatial constraints.

Figure 64: The Belgian embassy with the Nibancho Building Center on the left hand side, 2017

In total, the embassy tower had a surface area of approximately 7,500 m² spread over nine storeys. This considerable amount of space had to accommodate the Ministry's bureaucratic, residential and recreational needs. The first storey would feature a large multipurpose hall adjacent to the embassy garden.

The chancery was spread across the second and third storey. Above this bureaucratic nerve centre were additional offices that reflected the changing dynamics in the Belgian state apparatus. These offices were not used by diplomats but rather by a new breed of government officials working in a Belgian embassy, the so-called regional representatives. As part of the constitutional reforms of the Belgian state at the end of the 20th century, the regions were granted the power to represent themselves abroad with regard to attracting foreign investments and stimulating exports. Consequently, the regions were in need of offices abroad for their trade representatives. As had previously been the case with attachés working for various ministry departments, these regional trade representatives were usually allocated office space in a Belgian embassy. Metaphorically, the average Belgian chancery had therefore become a lasagne made up of national and subnational representations, housing the offices of both the diplomats of the federal state and the regional representatives of Flanders, Wallonia and Brussels under one roof. Okabe was instructed to give each of these three regional entities the same amount of office space.[462]

Each regional trade agency was allocated some 200 m² of cellular office space. The FPS Foreign Affairs had learned the hard way that office space was a very delicate matter for the regional trade agencies, as they had the tendency to compare themselves with each other. An interesting case in point, for instance, was the move of the Bangkok chancery to an office complex in 2000. Upon seeing the proposed spatial layout of the chancery, the trade representatives of Wallonia were appalled that the dimensions of their offices were significantly smaller than those allocated to Export Vlaanderen, their Flemish counterpart. The Wallonia trade agency vented its frustration to the FPS Foreign Affairs and insisted that it alter the spatial layout at once.[463]

Additionally, being located within an embassy posed more challenges for the regional attachés. How could they project regional identity within a building that was meant to project the identity of the nation? It is telling that regional representatives tended to make their presence visually known. In order to distinguish themselves from the Belgian diplomatic corps representing the federal state, the regional representatives made efforts to evoke an image of their specific region in their workspace. At the Tunis chancery, for example, the representative of Export Vlaanderen turned his office (Fig. 65) into some sort of Flemish island in a Belgian sea. The flag of Flanders was prominently positioned and a series of images depicting Flemish landmarks such as the Belfry of Bruges were hung on the walls. It was a testament to the growing tendency of the Flemish region to distinguish itself on the international stage.[464]

Against the backdrop of this growing regional awareness, it speaks volumes that the Tokyo design has a generic and neutral architectural setting that makes no significant effort to project nationhood. Moreover, the FPS Foreign Affairs did not instruct Okabe to express Belgian nationhood clearly in the new embassy through its style, form or materiality. It seems as though the generic and neutral architectural design put forward by Okabe was considered fitting to accommodate a multilayered national representation abroad. By commissioning a neutral and generic embassy building, it seems as though the FPS Foreign Affairs wanted to keep away from the thorny issue of projecting national identity in a building that would also house regional agencies.

Figure 65: Office of Export Vlaanderen at the Tunis embassy, undated

In designing the new embassy, Okabe made sure that the staff was able to decompress. Just above the offices, on the fifth storey, the recreational facilities were to be located. These included an indoor swimming pool, a sauna and a fitness area, among others. The upper floors were to accommodate housing units for embassy staffers. The floor arrangement and surface area reflected the power and rank within the embassy's hierarchy. On the fifth storey, apartments of 60 m² were to be included for the supporting Japanese staff who would keep the embassy up and running. On top of these apartments, the diplomatic staff was awarded sizeable apartments of some 250 m². The ambassador, however, got the royal treatment. The ambassadorial residence was spread over the two top floors and also had a roof terrace with a stunning view over the Chiyoda district.

Belgian-Japanese Collaboration: A Clash of Civilisations

Foreign Minister Karel De Gucht was very pleased with the embassy design. In the Parliamentary Committee for Foreign Affairs, De Gucht called it a splendid and modern design that would boost national prestige in Japan.[465] The liberal strongman greenlit the general outlines of the project but several design features still had to be discussed in more depth with MTOB. Therefore, the FPS Foreign Affairs called upon architecture consultant Jean-Michel Jaspers. Jaspers frequently travelled to Tokyo to have face-to-face negotiations with the consortium. Such negotiations were anything but smooth sailing for the Belgian architect. Jaspers indicated that it took him some time to get used to the Japanese style of negotiation.[466] According to Jaspers, there is a fundamental desire in Japanese negotiation culture to avoid discussion. At first, his Japanese interlocutors always seemed to agree with his suggestions. It was only later on, and much to Jaspers' surprise, that MTOB forwarded its objections in writing. This negotiation culture continued to be problematic and turned the negotiations with MTOB into a painstaking endeavour for Jaspers. To make matters even more difficult, there was no lack of disputes regarding the embassy design.

The first issue had to do with the embassy's exteriors. As agreed in the contract, the façade was to be covered with high-quality limestone. In follow-up talks, the FPS Foreign Affairs expressed its desire to use Moca Creme, a beige limestone quarried in Portugal. Under the watchful eye of Jean-Michel Jaspers, a Japanese delegation paid a visit to the Italian city of Carrara with the purpose of selecting slabs of Moca Creme. During the visit, MTOB representatives were impressed by the quality of the slabs and hinted that they would purchase the necessary Moca Creme in Italy. Framing the Carrara visit to be a success, the FPS Foreign Affairs spoke words of praise for MTOB's constructive cooperation. However, it was not long before MTOB backtracked on its previous commitment. The consortium made the case that it would be better to purchase the Moca Creme slabs in Shanghai instead of Carrara, confiding that they knew a local supplier who could deliver similar Moca Creme limestone but at a far more competitive price. Intrigued, Jaspers went to Shanghai in order to inspect the Moca Creme.

In his follow-up report, Jaspers talked the FPS Foreign Affairs out of the idea of purchasing the limestone in Shanghai. The Belgian architect warned that the slabs put on display did not have the same colour as the ones shown in Carrara and were of an inferior quality. He openly questioned whether the slabs shown to him were actually Moca Creme limestone, indicating that the necessary certificates were lacking.[467] Upon receiving Jaspers' remarks, ministry officials were astonished that MTOB was apparently trying to use limestone of an inferior quality. In an internal email between Brussels and the Tokyo embassy, a ministry official resorted to very strong language to describe the state of affairs. According to him, MTOB was deceiving the FPS Foreign Affairs as it was trying to erect the cheapest possible building by using poor quality limestone.[468] Confronted with such allegations, MTOB representatives presented new and seemingly far-fetched arguments in order to defend themselves. They argued that it was raining on the day Jaspers visited Shanghai. The rain had apparently changed the colour of the stones. Moreover, MTOB was unwilling to purchase limestone from an Italian supplier because Italian firms could not be trusted.[469]

Far from convinced by the Japanese arguments, the FPS Foreign Affairs insisted that the limestone had to be purchased in Carrara to ensure that the quality was top-notch. MTOB, however, stuck to its guns. Consequently, discussions on the embassy's exterior cladding were at a deadlock by the summer of 2008. In light of these discussions, the FPS Foreign Affairs and architect Jaspers were also growing increasingly frustrated by the fact that Noriaki Okabe, the very man responsible for designing the embassy, was nowhere to be seen during such pivotal negotiations. Ministry officials expressed their dissatisfaction concerning the architect's absence:

> One of the problems is that the people who have the power to make decisions are not always present around the table. For example, Mr. Okabe was not present either in Shanghai or in Carrara, even though the choice of the façade stone is a crucial element in the aesthetics of the building and every decision or idea must be submitted to him, as he is THE person responsible for the design. This state of affairs meant that we were unable to make any progress whatsoever from an architectural point of view.[470]

The FPS Foreign Affairs had the impression that the renowned Japanese architect lacked interest in the embassy project. Whether this was truly the case remains unclear. In fact, it seems as though something far more fundamental had caused Okabe's absence during these discussions. As the abbreviation MTOB suggests, Okabe was not only in league with the Japanese consortium but he was also one of its prominent members. As he had overall responsibility for the design, Okabe was surely briefed on the discussions concerning the embassy's exteriors. He opted to stay out of any discussions between the Belgian state and MTOB, a professional courtesy by which he signalled to the FPS Foreign Affairs that he fully backed his Japanese associates. As such, the Belgian decision to award the contract to a consortium was therefore a double-edged sword. On the one hand, it tremendously facilitated the redevelopment as the entire project was awarded to just one entity. On the other hand, this made it more difficult for the FPS Foreign Affairs to ask for alterations. It faced one Japanese monolithic block cemented by aligned interests.

Another bone of contention had to do with security measures. The FPS Foreign Affairs wanted to include bullet-resistant glass at the enquiry counters of the visa section. However, MTOB could not wrap its head around the fact that its Belgian client was so adamant that this type of glass had to be included.[471] The Japanese consortium made the case that it would be ludicrous to include bullet-resistant glass given the fact that Tokyo is one of the safest metropolises with a historically low rate of gun violence. The Belgian request was in fact nothing more than standard procedure as bullet-resistant glass was installed in all visa sections. Nevertheless, MTOB felt offended by the Belgian request. The Japanese partners considered it a sign that the FPS Foreign Affairs thought Tokyo was a crime-infested city. Being far from keen to include it, MTOB made the case to Jaspers that bullet-resistant glass could not even be found on the Japanese market.[472] They argued that it had to be shipped from abroad, incurring additional costs.

The final major dispute revolved around Belgium Square (Fig. 66) which was to be included in front of the embassy. Conceived as the embassy's antechamber, the plaza was considered the locus for accentuating Belgium's presence in Tokyo. In order to live up to the name of Belgium Square, the FPS Foreign Affairs wanted to pave the plaza with materials endemic to Belgium. This explicit demand for national references was very striking. After all, the FPS Foreign Affairs did not put forward such requirements with regard to designing the embassy. Apparently, the urge to express nationhood through building materials was confined to the public space in front of the embassy and did not extend to the building itself. Initially, MTOB wholeheartedly supported the idea. However, upon receiving Okabe's blueprints, the FPS Foreign Affairs was astonished to see that MTOB had broken its promise. In the blueprints, Belgium Square was to be paved with black granite from Zimbabwe.[473] MTOB defended itself by stating that it was accustomed to working with Zimbabwean granite, the granite was a high-end material, and that it was available at a bargain price. Antagonised by the Japanese change of heart, ministry officials spoke out against using the African granite. Instead, they reasoned that Belgium Square should be paved with bluestone quarried in the Belgian city of Tournai, a natural limestone with a grey-blue colour. However, MTOB was far from keen to use Belgian limestone and continued to promote Zimbabwean granite. As such, the paving of Belgium Square became yet another point of contention between the FPS Foreign Affairs and MTOB.

Figure 66: Belgium Square, 2017

The various disputes deepened animosity between both parties. Basically, the FPS Foreign Affairs was under the impression that MTOB wanted to cut corners and build a cheap embassy that would be inferior to what was agreed. In a confidential email, a cabinet staffer of Foreign Minister De Gucht claimed that MTOB was scamming the Belgian government by building a third-rate embassy.[474] As MTOB did not show any signs of complying with Belgian demands, the FPS Foreign Affairs significantly raised the stakes to turn things around. None other than Foreign Minister Karel De Gucht sent a letter of complaint to MTOB. De Gucht warned that, if the consortium did not comply with the Belgian demands at once, there would be grave consequences:

> We can no longer approve the way Takenaka Corporation is currently handling the implementation of our agreement. The proposals made by the design team remain far below the level of quality that was agreed upon in the contract. [...] I regret to say that all this is casting a shadow over our cooperation and we are seriously wondering whether we made the right choice when we awarded the sales contract to the MTOB consortium. The project urgently needs to be put on the right track again. [...] Our aim remains to obtain a high quality building with respect for the agreed price and standards. Unless these requirements are met, we will feel compelled to consider more drastic decisions.[475]

Threatening to terminate the contract, De Gucht succeeded in breaking the stalemate. From then on, MTOB took on a more cooperative attitude and complied with the Ministry's wish list. The façade was to be covered with Moca Creme limestone, bullet-resistant glass would be installed, and Belgium Square was to be paved with Tournai bluestone.

Designing the Embassy Interiors: A Belgian-Japanese Museum

The focus now shifted to the embassy's interiors. The FPS Foreign Affairs expressed its desire for sober interiors that still evoked a sense of grandeur. Ministry officials even used telling imagery to get their message across to MTOB. The interiors should evoke the image of a museum and MTOB should use modern exhibition galleries as a point of reference.[476] The interiors should evoke a sense of space and light, a common trademark among contemporary exhibition galleries.[477] Whereas the floors had to be covered with either ceramic tiles or marble, the walls had to be covered with woodwork to evoke a sense of warmth or white plaster to make the room feel bigger.

The most striking example of this museum-like model can be found in the large multipurpose hall situated near the main entrance. Measuring some 500 m², the grand hall was the embassy's largest room and was conceived to be the ceremonial venue for grand social events such as receptions, banquets, business meetings and art exhibitions. The multipurpose hall featured an arrangement of sliding walls that could be hidden from view. Depending on the type of event and the number of attendees, the sliding walls could create the ideal venue for any given activity.

Another noteworthy and especially Japanese feature were the sanitary installations. MTOB opted to install high-tech Japanese toilets. In terms of comfort, this type of toilet surpassed the standard flush toilet. The Japanese toilets in the embassy have lids that open automatically, heated seats, and can even play music to mask unpleasant sounds.

The image of a museum was further reinforced by the abundance of artwork put on display. By the late 2000s, the FPS Foreign Affairs had taken steps to professionalise the manner in which diplomatic interiors were decorated. Firstly, a new position as art curator was added to the Ministry's organigram in November 2002. Ever since, Ilse Dauwe has been the art curator. In her capacity, Dauwe has initiated the development of an internal art depot within the walls of the Ministry and a database listing all the works of art in the Ministry's collection. Such steps were imperative to get an overview of the amount and type of artwork collected throughout the Ministry's long existence. By 2013, the collection already numbered a staggering 4,500 pieces ranging from paintings, tapestries, sculptures, lithographs, photographs, mixed media to video art.[478]

Secondly, the purchase policy witnessed a fundamental change. In the past, ambassadors were often allocated funding to purchase artwork themselves. However, this bottom-up approach made way for a top-down approach. An art commission made up of the art curator, external experts and diplomats now decided what the FPS Foreign Affairs would acquire.[479] Of course, ambassadors could still share their artistic preferences but the days in which a head of mission could solely decide were well and truly over by the 2000s.

Thirdly and lastly, the FPS Foreign Affairs explicitly articulated the role artwork was meant to play in diplomatic interiors. In her mission statement, Dauwe highlighted that artwork should forge an identity for the FPS Foreign Affairs, represent Belgium in a versatile way, initiate an

Figure 67: The embassy's main entrance hall, undated

intercultural dialogue between the sending and receiving states, create a dynamic working environment, sharpen critical minds and offer a reflection on the ever-changing world.[480]

To achieve these lofty ambitions, art curator Dauwe oversaw the purchase of some 40 works of art for the Tokyo embassy. Together with the art commission, she opted for a very different aesthetic. Belgian embassy interiors had traditionally been decorated with tapestries and paintings depicting landscapes and historic battles. However, in line with the modern aesthetic of the Tokyo embassy design, a decision to include more contemporary artwork was made. In the ambassador's office, blueprints of the imaginary vehicles conceived by the renowned Belgian assemblagist Panamarenko (1940-2019) were hung on the walls. Meanwhile, the main entrance hall (Fig. 67) was decorated with a series of conspicuous fluorescent paintings by the Belgian visual artist Anne-Mie Van Kerckhoven that created a strong contrast with the all-white interiors. In fact, the main entrance hall was the space that lived up the most to the Ministry's expectations of evoking a modern museum-like atmosphere. In literature on museum architecture, authors have coined the concept of the 'white cube' to describe the ideal type of gallery space to exhibit contemporary art. They argue that gallery spaces should be an abstract architectural setting or white cube in which everything centres on the artwork on display.[481]

Figure 68: The embassy
garden, 2017

The embassy's main entrance hall with its all-white walls and high ceilings can be read as Okabe's interpretation of the white cube.

The FPS Foreign Affairs also considered the design of the embassy garden (Fig. 68) to be a matter of national prestige. The fact that there was even space for a garden was already a sign of prestige given the densely populated urban context in Tokyo. Designing the new embassy garden was to be a separate commission. Whereas the design of the embassy was a Japanese affair, the FPS Foreign Affairs wanted to call upon Belgian landscapers. In doing so, the FPS Foreign Affairs aimed to strike a balance between the host country and the country that would take up residence in the new embassy. As part of awarding the commission, the FPS Foreign Affairs organised a design competition in 2007. The various design entries would be judged by the FPS Foreign Affairs, MTOB and representatives of the Arboretum Kalmthout, one of the oldest botanical gardens in Belgium. One of the bids was submitted by the Belgian design team Aldrik Heirman,

Wim Oers and Monique Stoop. Making the most of the triangular parcel of land, the trio suggested planting greenery along the edges. From inside the embassy, this created the impression that the garden was considerably larger than it actually was. This effect was further reinforced by including a strip of moving water oriented towards the embassy tower. In their design, Heirman, Oers and Stoop also paid respect to the old embassy garden. Trees, stone slabs and lanterns from the old garden were to be used in the new one, creating a certain continuity with the past. Their design entry was lauded by the jury and Heirman, Oers and Stoop were awarded the commission.

In November 2007, MTOB launched the redevelopment of the embassy grounds. For the second time in its history, the embassy compound was levelled to the ground. Instead of American bombs, Japanese wrecking balls and bulldozers now turned the compound into a lunar landscape. Given the magnitude of the project, it took nearly three years to complete the embassy tower and the Nibancho Center Building.

Finally, on 8 April 2010, the new embassy was officially inaugurated. The brains behind the operation were, however, nowhere to be seen during this event. By this time, the liberal Foreign Minister, Karel De Gucht, had left national politics and was succeeded by Steven Vanackere of the CD&V. Together with CD&V Prime Minister, Yves Leterme, Vanackere travelled to Tokyo to inaugurate the embassy. From a political point of view, both CD&V heavyweights must have felt somewhat uncomfortable. In 2007, MPs from CD&V had criticised De Gucht for partially selling the embassy grounds. Three years later, however, Leterme and Vanackere were now the ones who had to preside over the embassy's inauguration.

However, Leterme and Vanackere were not particularly bothered by this as they did an excellent job in turning the ceremony into a PR success for Belgium (Fig. 69). The inauguration was turned into a momentous occasion with great pomp and ceremony. The event was attended by high-ranking Japanese officials and the *corps diplomatique* that gathered at Belgium Square, just in front of the newly completed embassy. From the steps leading to the embassy, Foreign Minister Vanackere read out a self-composed haiku, a typical Japanese form of short poetry, by which he undoubtedly ingratiated himself with the Japanese attendees. The haiku read as follows: "Cherry trees in spring. Embassy in a garden. Blossoming friendship."[482] In return, Prime Minister Leterme stressed the importance of the new embassy to Belgian-Japanese relations in his speech. He called it the most important investment in Belgian diplomatic housing of the last

Figure 69: From left to right: Japan-Belgium Society President Takao Kusakari, Foreign Minister Steven Vanackere, Japanese State Secretary for Foreign Affairs Tetsuro Fukuyama, Prime Minister Yves Leterme, Chiyoda Mayor Masami Ishikawa, and Belgian Ambassador Johan Maricou cutting the ribbon, 8 April 2010

50 years and went on to say that it reflected the political and especially the economic importance of Japan to Belgium. Subsequently, Leterme and Vanackere cut the ribbon of the new embassy together with Japanese dignitaries while a local orchestra played *La Brabançonne*.

The attending Belgian journalists were impressed by the new embassy. They lauded the design, calling it a modern building that catapulted the Belgian diplomacy into the 21st century.[483] In particular, they found beauty in the building's height and simplified silhouette, and deemed it a perfect fit for the Japanese metropolis. A journalist from *Het Laatste Nieuws* even went so far as to state that the new embassy was an astonishing piece of architecture and the Belgian diplomatic corps would henceforth be housed in a modern and high-end embassy.[484] The financial scheme behind the building project also piqued the interest of Belgian journalists. They were astonished that the partial sale of the embassy grounds had generated a small fortune for the federal government. Amidst all the excitement, *De Standaard* mistakenly reported that the partial sale had generated 4 billion euros (5.6 billion euros) whereas the figure was in fact 'only' some 400 million euros (560 million euros).[485]

B. DIPLOMATIC CO-HOUSING: THE KINSHASA PROJECT

Building an Embassy in the Democratic Republic of the Congo:
A Geopolitical Power Struggle

Following the Congo's independence in 1960, the Belgian Ministry of Foreign Affairs purchased an office building in the centre of Léopoldville to house the chancery. More commonly known as *Le Cinquantenaire* (Fig. 70), the office building was part of a larger apartment and office complex. Completed in 1956, *Le Cinquantenaire* was designed by the Belgian architect Marcel Lambrichs. Inspired by the tropical modernism propagated by Oscar Niemeyer, Lambrichs drew inspiration from the design of the Ministry of Education and Health building in Rio de Janeiro.[486] Architecturally, Lambrichs designed one of the most modern office buildings Léopoldville had to offer in the 1950s.[487] Towering above the ground, the concrete building was supported by a series of pilotis with *brise-soleils* profoundly shaping the building's exteriors. However, from a representational point of view, the office building was not particularly well suited to housing the Belgian chancery. In both a literal and figurative sense, the embassy offices stood in the shadow of the imposing apartment complex making up *Le Cinquantenaire*. The high-rise apartment building eclipsed the chancery both in terms of volume and height. However, the presence of the adjacent apartment complex came in handy as the Ministry leased a dozen apartment units to accommodate diplomatic, military and development aid officials. As such, the Ministry was able to establish a diplomatic hub centred around *Le Cinquantenaire*.

The proximity of living and working space may have been convenient for the embassy staff but political bigwigs in Brussels disdained the chancery. They considered it a dreadful building that did not do justice to the importance that the Democratic Republic of the Congo continued to play in Belgian foreign policy.[488] In the 1980s, there was talk of constructing a new chancery in Kinshasa.[489] Foreign Minister Leo Tindemans believed that the premises had seen better days and he was determined to erect a purpose-built chancery during his time in office. The new embassy was envisaged to be the architectural expression that Belgium was committed to investing in bilateral ties with the Democratic Republic of the Congo and cementing its status as Congo's privileged partner on the international stage.

Figure 70: *Le Cinquantenaire* with the Belgian chancery in the foreground, 1978

Tindemans' aspirations were, however, cut short by the draconic budget cuts of the aforementioned Sint-Anna Plan of Guy Verhofstadt.[490] It was only in 1988, when Verhofstadt and the liberals were cast into the opposition, that Tindemans was able to put the project back on the table. He had his eye on a prime building plot situated on the banks of the Congo River. There were, however, significant rivals in the field for the site. Manda Mobutu (1959-2004), who was the son of the Congolese dictator Joseph-Désiré Mobutu (1930-1997), was toying with the idea of building a luxurious hotel on the site.[491] Worried that thwarting the hotel project of the dictator's son would jeopardise bilateral relations, the Ministry abandoned plans to build along the riverbank. Going against the most powerful political family in the country, especially the Mobutu regime with its kleptocratic ways, was considered diplomatic suicide. Consequently, the Ministry scanned Kinshasa for another site. However, before a new site could be selected, ministry officials pulled the plug on the project all together because of deteriorating diplomatic relations with the Mobutu regime. The fact that the Congolese authorities had violently suppressed student protests in 1990 and had not taken any significant steps in the democratisation process were a thorn in the side of the Belgian government.[492] As bilateral ties hit rock bottom, there was no more Belgian appetite to build a new embassy.

It was only at the end of 2011 that the building plans were revived. By this time, the liberal strongman Didier Reynders had swapped his function as finance minister for that of foreign minister in the new Di Rupo government (2011-14). In his new capacity, Reynders breathed new life into the Kinshasa project. His reasons for doing so were threefold. Firstly, the chancery building near *Le Cinquantenaire* was in an abysmal and run-down state by 2011. Extensive renovations were considered a logistical and financial nightmare. Instead, it was better to start afresh by constructing a new chancery elsewhere. Secondly, the Kinshasa embassy was the most staffed of all Belgian diplomatic postings. At the time, approximately 80 Belgian officials were employed at the embassy. This mixed workforce of diplomats, military advisers and development aid staffers had been steadily growing and it was imperative to move them into modern and spacious offices. Thirdly and perhaps most importantly, Reynders envisaged the building project as a useful tool in the ongoing geopolitical power play for influence in the Democratic Republic of the Congo. By the 2010s, the French and Chinese governments were stepping up their efforts to deepen ties with the Congolese President Joseph Kabila. In return for access to the

Congo's vast resources, both countries launched massive infrastructural works across the country. In this context, the French government made considerable efforts to boost its diplomatic presence in Kinshasa. The French state purchased a majestic mansion that was in a rundown state. From a political point of view, it is somewhat ironic that the mansion was originally constructed by the Belgian colonial administration in the 1930s.[493] As renovation works were completed in 2011, the embellished mansion was an architectural *tour de force* of the French diplomatic corps that symbolised its ambitions to become the privileged speaking partner of the Kabila regime on the European continent.

Worried that the growing French and Chinese influence would jeopardise Belgium's privileged position, Foreign Minister Reynders deemed it imperative to further deepen bilateral ties with the Congolese government. Reynders was impressed by the new French embassy and reasoned that Belgium had to catch up at once.[494] Considering the current chancery a liability that tarnished Belgian prestige, the liberal strongman unveiled plans to construct a new chancery that would put Belgium back on the map. The new embassy building had to reaffirm to President Kabila that the Democratic Republic of the Congo was still an important place for Belgium and that the former colonial power still had a role to play in modern-day Congo. Perceiving his building plans as a matter of diplomatic credibility, Reynders spared no expense. According to estimates, acquiring a prominent building plot and constructing a new chancery would come with a price tag of ten million euros (13.3 million euros). However, as the former finance minister, Reynders was well aware that the budgetary situation of the state finances left little room for such projects.

Consequently, Reynders set up a real estate operation to generate the necessary money through which Belgium said farewell to relics of its tainted colonial past. The FPS Finance put some 20 real estate assets on sale, ranging from villas, office buildings and plots of land across the Democratic Republic of the Congo.[495] These properties used to belong to the Belgian colonial administration and were still the property of the Belgian state by 2011. Even though the majority of the properties were dilapidated because they had been left vacant and had received little or no maintenance, the FPS Finance estimated that these assets could still generate the necessary ten million euros (13.3 million euros).

Co-housing on a Diplomatic Level: Standing Strong Together

While these real estate assets were being sold to the highest bidder, Reynders looked for additional possibilities to make it financially more feasible for the FPS Foreign Affairs to operate the new chancery once it was completed. More specifically, ministry officials entertained the idea of leasing office space in the new chancery to another country, preferably a close international partner. This would generate a sustainable rental income for the FPS Foreign Affairs. The plans to do so were a clear sign of the times. From the late 1990s onwards, there has been a growing tendency among small state actors with close ties to share embassy premises abroad. This diplomatic take on co-housing is more commonly referred to as co-location. Governments can significantly reduce financial burdens by sharing the running and maintenance costs of diplomatic missions. Moreover, co-location is a strong symbolic gesture on the international stage. The countries involved demonstrate that they are close partners that not only share similar ambitions, values and interests abroad but also the same roof.

The Nordic countries were frontrunners in co-location. An example of their diplomatic co-housing (Fig. 71) can be found in Berlin. In the context of moving their embassies to Berlin in the late 1990s, Denmark, Finland, Iceland, Norway and Sweden joined forces by constructing a common diplomatic building complex. The Nordic countries jointly acquisitioned a prominent building plot in Berlin, situated just south of the *Großer Tiergarten*. On the site, five detached chancery buildings were erected. The chanceries were located according to their geographical position in the world and water bodies were included between the buildings to represent the North and Baltic Seas. Each of the five embassy offices were designed by architects from the respective countries.[496] Each architect was instructed to incorporate design features and construction materials that paid tribute to the building tradition of the respective home country. For instance, the glazed exteriors of the Icelandic embassy feature latticework made of red rhyolite, a volcanic rock. Meanwhile, the glazed façade of the Norwegian embassy has been extensively covered with larch wood slats. While each of the five Nordic countries built their own chancery, a common public building was also constructed. Better known as the *Felleshus* or Pan Nordic Building, the Pan Nordic Building serves as the complex's cultural centre and event venue. Members of the general public can visit the Pan Nordic Building to immerse themselves in the culture of the five

Figure 71: The Nordic Embassy Complex in Berlin, undated

countries through exhibitions, lectures and film screenings. In order to further highlight Nordic camaraderie to the outside world, the embassy complex is surrounded by a copper band with a turquoise patina. The band is arranged in wave-like sweeps to symbolise the respective countries status as seafaring nations.

Following the example set by the Nordic countries, the Belgian diplomatic corps also entertained the idea of building a joint embassy in Berlin. In the mid-1990s, the Ministry approached The Hague with an invitation to build a Belgian-Dutch embassy complex in the reunified German capital. The Dutch diplomatic corps, however, kindly declined the offer as it had no interest in sharing a roof with the Belgians.[497]

By the early 2010s, however, The Hague had profoundly changed its mind with regard to co-location. This had to do with the fact that the Dutch Ministry of Foreign Affairs was now also confronted with budget cuts. In 2013 alone, the Dutch Ministry of Foreign Affairs had to cut spending by 100 million euros (132 million euros).[498] To reach his targets, the Dutch Foreign Minister Frans Timmermans took the same steps as the FPS Foreign Affairs. Timmermans closed consulates while several embassies were relocated to smaller and cheaper premises to cut spending. Additionally, Dutch policymakers embraced the notion that sharing embassy buildings with other diplomatic missions could tremendously cut spending. The

Hague perceived Belgium as its preferred partner as both countries have common cultural and linguistic traits as well as, more importantly, aligned foreign policy and security interests.[499]

Applauding the Dutch change of heart, the FPS Foreign Affairs entered into negotiations with its Dutch counterpart. Under the supervision of Reynders and Timmermans, co-location became the buzzword in Brussels and The Hague. By 2013, Belgium and the Netherlands were pooling embassy buildings in Albania, Bosnia and Herzegovina, Kazakhstan and Venezuela. However, not everyone welcomed the tendency to set up joint embassies. In the Belgian Chamber of Representatives, for instance, the Christian-democratic MP Georges Dallemagne warned Reynders that it was unwise to share embassy buildings with Dutch diplomats. Dallemagne confided that his business contacts in the port of Antwerp were anything but happy with the strategy of co-location.[500] With the Dutch port of Rotterdam as their main competitor, the captains of industry in Antwerp deemed it ludicrous to house the Belgian diplomatic corps in the same building as the diplomatic corps of their biggest economic rival. These businessmen feared that Dutch diplomats could eavesdrop on ongoing contract negotiations and other export-related topics, with all the negative consequences that would entail for the port of Antwerp.

Foreign Minister Didier Reynders, however, brushed such concerns aside. Reynders officially invited The Hague to lease offices in the future Belgian chancery in Kinshasa. Much to Reynders' delight, the Dutch Ministry of Foreign Affairs accepted the invitation. The FPS Foreign Affairs had already agreed on a rent fee with The Hague. The prospect of rental income further strengthened Reynders' proposal to build in Kinshasa. He could now showcase to his colleagues in the Di Rupo government that the new Kinshasa chancery would not only be an expenditure but also an investment property thanks to the monthly rent The Hague would pay. Receiving the green light from the Ministerial Council, Reynders could now shift his attention towards commissioning the future Belgian calling card in Kinshasa and therefore the architectural legacy of his ministership.

Land Acquisition in Kinshasa: Resurrecting the Corporate Dead

As discussed previously, Foreign Minister Reynders envisaged the future chancery to be a prestige project. By constructing a new chancery, the liberal strongman wanted to flex Belgium's muscles in Kinshasa. Therefore, it was imperative to turn the purpose-built embassy into a landmark of the Congolese capital. The chancery's landmark status already had to be made evident in its location.

In terms of location, the current chancery at *Le Cinquantenaire* had its pros and cons. The fact that the embassy offices were situated in the bustling city centre was a double-edged sword. On the one hand, it offered Belgian diplomats a front row seat on political life in Kinshasa. More specifically, popular street politics form an integral part of Congolese politics. From their high-rise embassy offices, Belgian diplomats immediately knew if something significant was about to happen in Kinshasa when the streets were either suddenly packed or deserted. On the other hand, the chancery was situated in a crowded environment with street markets and passing traffic. Given the Congo's politically unstable situation, the FPS Foreign Affairs was worried that the embassy offices were vulnerable to an attack. Taking all these elements into consideration, it was decided to look for a more prominent location in a more high-end area of Kinshasa that could also be protected more easily.

In its search for a building plot, the FPS Foreign Affairs did not look too far. Just three kilometres west of *Le Cinquantenaire*, a plot of land caught its eye for a variety of reasons. Firstly, it was a large piece of land measuring almost 6,000 m². This considerable land area was therefore well suited to the construction of the spacious Belgian-Dutch chancery. Secondly, the plot of land had a prominent location as it was situated in the high-end district of Gombe. In 1923, the Belgian colonial authorities launched the development of Gombe.[501] In the context of the racially segregated urban fabric of Léopoldville, Kinshasa's name during the colonial era, Gombe was turned into the European quarter where the administrative buildings and villas of the colonial power base were situated. By the late 2000s, Gombe remained the city's most prestigious and expensive neighbourhood and was made up of the government district, the central business district, luxury apartments and hotels.[502]

Thirdly, the site in Gombe was located along the main boulevard of Kinshasa (Fig. 72) and ran along an east-west axis parallel to the Congo River. The boulevard was well paved, making it especially convenient for embassy staffers and visitors making their way to the chancery by car. Originally, this boulevard was constructed by the Belgian colonial administration and was given the name *Boulevard Albert I*.[503] As part of the decolonisation process, the city's main thoroughfare was given a new name in 1963. Henceforth, *Boulevard Albert I* was better known as

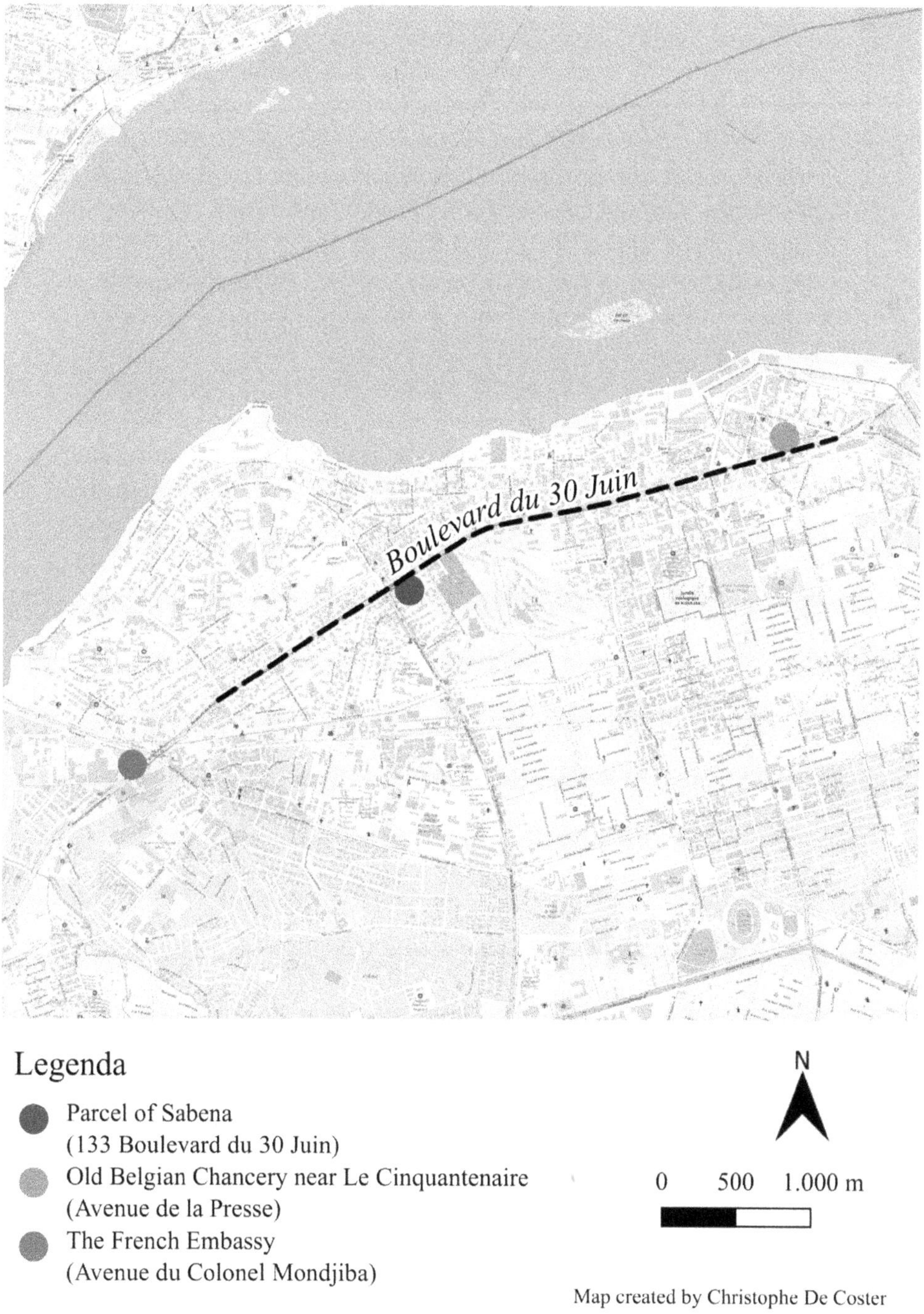

PLUGGING THE HOLES IN THE FEDERAL BUDGET 283

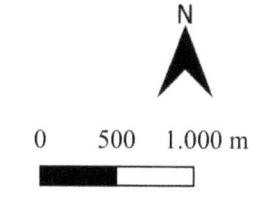

Legenda

● Parcel of Sabena
   (133 Boulevard du 30 Juin)
● Old Belgian Chancery near Le Cinquantenaire
   (Avenue de la Presse)
● The French Embassy
   (Avenue du Colonel Mondjiba)

N

0   500   1.000 m

Map created by Christophe De Coster

Figure 72: Spatial overview of Kinshasa

Boulevard du 30 Juin to commemorate the Congolese independence day. Interestingly, by the 2010s, *Boulevard du 30 Juin* had become a tangible symbol of the geopolitical power struggle of foreign countries for influence in the Democratic Republic of the Congo. In 2008, Chinese mining companies struck a deal with the Congolese President Joseph Kabila. The Kabila regime gave them access to the country's mines and in return the Chinese mining companies allocated three billion US dollars (4.3 billion euros) to infrastructure projects to modernise the Democratic Republic of the Congo.[504] Thanks to Chinese funding, *Boulevard du 30 Juin* was redeveloped into one of the best-paved roads of Kinshasa, a luxury in a city where dirt roads are still omnipresent.[505] Fourthly and lastly, the plot of land was owned by an entity that the FPS Foreign Affairs knew all too well. It was the property of the former Belgian airline Sabena that went bankrupt in 2001.

As Kinshasa was a popular destination of the former Belgian flag carrier, Sabena had built up its own patrimony in the capital city.[506] This comprised a hotel, villas, offices and building plots, among others. Following the airline's bankruptcy in 2001, the keys of the vast patrimony were entrusted to the Belgian lawyer Christian Van Buggenhout. In his capacity as liquidator of the Sabena estate, it was his job to manage and sell this patrimony in order to reimburse the creditors and shareholders of the airline. As a protégé of Reynders, Van Buggenhout suggested to Reynders that he purchase the Sabena grounds along *Boulevard du 30 Juin* for the new embassy.[507] Van Buggenhout hammered home the argument that such a location would tremendously boost national prestige in Kinshasa. Given Belgium's status as a former colonial power, Van Buggenhout reasoned that the Belgian embassy had to be situated in the high-end Gombe district along Kinshasa's equivalent of the Parisian *Champs-Elysées*.[508]

Back in Brussels, Foreign Minister Reynders saw the merits of purchasing the Sabena parcel of land. There was, however, one problem. The plot of 6,000 m² was considered too small for what Reynders had in store. The liberal strongman reasoned that the plot had to be doubled in size to at least 12,000 m². Before he entered into a deal, the neighbouring parcels of land had to be added to the Sabena site. As such, the Belgian state could purchase the entire urban block and use it for the embassy project.

This is where the Kinshasa project allegedly takes a suspicious turn. According to investigative journalist Philippe Engels, Foreign Minister Reynders sent his right-hand man, Jean-Claude Fontinoy, to Kinshasa in 2012 to sort out the issues with the building site.[509] As a long-time cabinet employee and confidant of Reynders, Fontinoy is notorious for being one of the most controversial figures in modern Belgian politics. In recent years, his name has popped up in stories involving bribery in public procurements, lobby regulation violations, money laundering and the intimidation of opponents.[510] It is rumoured that Fontinoy allegedly did things for Reynders that could not stand the light of day.

Reynders sent his right-hand man to Kinshasa where he was involved in a real estate transaction with Sabena. More specifically, Sabena allegedly witnessed an astonishing resurrection overnight even though the company was bankrupt and had gone into liquidation in 2001. Sabena purchased the adjacent plots of land making up the urban block along *Boulevard du 30 Juin*, the very plots that had caught Reynders' eye. According to Engels, the details surrounding these land purchases were anything but transparent as they involved bribery.[511] If this were true, one can only wonder what the creditors and shareholders of Sabena would have made of this brief revival. Of course, it is imperative to stress that one has to be wary of automatically believing such serious allegations. The book of investigative journalist Engels is the only source I have regarding the purchase of the building plot. As the Kinshasa chancery is a fairly recent project, it was impossible to consult the necessary paperwork that would have enabled me to verify or debunk the claims put forward by Engels.

In early 2012, under the supervision of Fontinoy, the Sabena liquidator Christian Van Buggenhout was granted concessions by the Congolese authorities on the adjacent plots making up the urban block.[512] As a result, the Sabena site now had a surface area of approximately 12,000 m². It was only now that the FPS Foreign Affairs stepped in and entered into talks with Sabena on purchasing the entire plot. A deal was struck in which the FPS Foreign Affairs would pay some 3.7 million euros (4.9 million euros) to Sabena for the parcel of land and several villas situated on said land. However, these villas would be demolished immediately after the purchase in order to make room for the new embassy offices.[513] The considerable expenditure was unanimously greenlit by the Ministerial Council of 23 March 2012.

Whatever the case, the land acquisition scheme in Kinshasa demonstrates that the leadership of the FPS Foreign Affairs still had plenty of room for manoeuvre, even as late as the 2010s. Given its status as the maverick within the Belgian state apparatus, the Ministry's real estate transactions continued to be a blind spot for parliamentary oversight and the public eye. As far as Reynders was concerned, he had reached an important milestone and could now devote his attention towards commissioning the new embassy. However, as luck would have it, Reynders allegedly ventured into even more dangerous waters during this stage.

Awarding the Embassy Contract: A Legal Struggle and Allegations of a *Quid Pro Quo*

In March 2013, the FPS Foreign Affairs launched a public tender for the Kinshasa project. Continuing along the lines of the Tokyo project, bids could only be submitted by consortiums made up of building contractors and architecture firms. The FPS Foreign Affairs therefore only had to conduct negotiations with one entity. Participating consortiums had to tick the following boxes when submitting their bid.

Firstly, the programme of requirements stipulated that the chancery should consist of 5,200 m² of office space. These considerable dimensions, especially for a Belgian chancery, demonstrate the importance of the Kinshasa embassy. As discussed previously, this diplomatic mission already had the largest workforce of all Belgian bilateral postings. Moreover, the new chancery had to be especially spacious in order to house the offices of Dutch embassy staffers. Moreover, Reynders had found additional tenants. Together with the trade agencies of Flanders, Brussels and Wallonia, the Belgian development agency Enabel would rent office space as the Congo has historically been its main operations base for development aid projects.[514] Interestingly, representatives of non-state actors would also use the new chancery as a workspace. The Belgian-Congolese-Luxembourg Chamber of Commerce committed itself to leasing 60 m² of office space for a monthly rent of some 1,200 euros (1,570 euros).[515] Together with the rent paid by the other entities, this source of income would turn the Kinshasa chancery into an income-producing property funding the Ministry's Buildings Fund.

Secondly, candidates were instructed to include an extensive visa section with multiple counters. This requirement went against the growing trend among foreign ministries to close down visa sections. With the dominance of the Internet in everyday life, visa and passport applications are increasingly processed online. As the Democratic Republic of the Congo was and still is one of the least Internet-connected countries in the world, the FPS Foreign Affairs opted to include a large visa section in the chancery. This was considered a necessity given the large Congolese community travelling to and living in Belgium.

Thirdly and most significantly, the programme of requirements included an absolute novelty in the Belgian embassy-building programme. The FPS Foreign Affairs stated that the new chancery had to be a passive building. In order to keep outdoor heat out and create comfortable working conditions throughout the year, the embassy's outdoor walls had to be hyper-insulated. Additionally, high-performance glazing and shutters had to be included. By constructing a passive embassy, the FPS Foreign Affairs aimed to kill two birds with one stone. It would both significantly reduce cooling costs and Belgium could showcase itself as a country committed to fighting climate change by building more sustainably.

Fourthly and finally, consortiums had to invest considerably in beefing up the security around the embassy grounds. Given the unpredictable nature of Congolese politics and previous incidents, the embassy had to be shielded off from the streetscape by means of manned checkpoints and high walls. The bid evaluation process used the same scoring system as for the Tokyo project. The construction price counted for a maximum of 60 points whereas the design only counted for 40 points.[516] The financial aspect once again trumped the architectural one considerably.

There were two main competitors for the embassy contract. The first candidate was an old acquaintance of the Ministry, the leading Belgian construction firm BESIX Group. Having previously designed and constructed the Riyadh embassy in the mid-1980s, BESIX was now keen to do the same in Kinshasa. The BESIX bid, which was submitted in collaboration with Brussels-based studio ArtBuild Architects, entailed the construction of a state-of-the-art office building. Immersed in a densely wooded environment, the design (Fig. 73) featured one massive building with an overall rectangular appearance. The main structure was to be four storeys high, housing the visa section and an abundance of offices. A noteworthy feature was that the main building was, to a certain extent, concealed by additional exteriors. For instance, the front façade facing *Boulevard du 30 Juin* had a striking arrangement of wooden slabs. Serving as sun-shading structures, the vertically positioned slabs would run across the façade's length and fitted nicely with the wooded surroundings. On the sides, non-load bearing perimeter walls were to be included that did not reach the roof, creating the illusion that the roof was hovering above the building.

Another noteworthy feature was the three cone-shaped figures on the roof. Breaching the flat roof, these figures gave more texture and a dramatic twist to the structure's overall square appearance. In front of

Figure 73: Design entry of ArtBuild Architects/BESIX for the new Kinshasa chancery, undated

the chancery, a driveway was included so that visitors could be dropped off at the main entrance. Upon making their way to the embassy, visitors would pass a double row of flagpoles that visually illustrated how the embassy was home to various national and subnational entities. The flagpoles would demonstrate that the days of a unitary Belgian representation abroad were well and truly over and had made way for a multilayered foreign representation together with regions, communities and even other countries. Complying with the wishes of the FPS Foreign Affairs, BESIX also added a wall to shield off the embassy grounds. Instead of a dreary concrete wall, however, BESIX opted for a wall with wooden elements that blended in more nicely with the natural surroundings.

The second viable candidate for the Kinshasa commission was Willemen Groep. Willemen Groep is a Belgian construction firm and was the rising star of the national construction industry at the time. In 2013, the Malines-based contractor won the Business of the Year Award as the firm grew three times in terms of personnel and revenue.[517] Willemen Groep had its reasons to compete for the embassy contract. The general manager, Johan Willemen, was keen to penetrate the African market, seeing the continent as an emerging market for building projects.[518] Arguing that the European market had become oversaturated, Willemen saw Africa as the place to do excellent business thanks to increasing prosperity, affordable building materials and growing political stability. In order to gain a foothold on the African continent, Willemen set his sights on the embassy contract. He considered the Kinshasa project to be his ticket in.

Eventually, Willemen Groep was awarded the contract by the FPS Foreign Affairs on 3 May 2013. To justify its decision to turn down the bid from BESIX, the FPS Foreign Affairs stated:

> The references submitted by AMBABEL – BESIX / ART & BUILD were therefore not considered sufficiently relevant to demonstrate its technical capacity to perform the present contract since they do not demonstrate its technical capacity to design a comparable building in sub-Saharan Africa.[519]

Upon reading this justification, BESIX's leadership was flabbergasted and fuming. The FPS Foreign Affairs considered that BESIX lacked the experience to build in sub-Saharan Africa. Such reasoning is remarkable to say the least, given the fact that the contract was awarded to Willemen Groep, a building contractor with no previous building experience in Africa.

BESIX felt that it had been treated unfairly and took legal action. It submitted an application at the Council of State, Belgium's supreme administrative court, to overturn the decision and to start the public procurement all over again. In a press interview, Willemen Groep called BESIX a sore loser that could not come to terms with the fact that it would not build the Kinshasa embassy.[520] The Council of State, however, begged to differ. The Council of State ruled that the arguments to exclude BESIX made no sense.[521] Consequently, the public procurement had to be done again. Relaunching the tender caused considerable delay and reflected poorly on the Belgian state. One can only wonder what the regions and the Dutch diplomatic corps made of the way its future landlord was handling the project. Additionally, the delay was a loss of face for Reynders in the Democratic Republic of the Congo. Unaware that BESIX would take legal steps, Reynders had already made plans for the foundation stone laying ceremony in Kinshasa.

The liberal strongman would preside over the ceremony that was to be attended by the Congolese political and economic elite on 12 August 2013. Given how dear the building project was to him, Reynders had no intention of postponing the event because of the relaunch of the public procurement. Laying the foundation stone may have no longer been a possibility, but Reynders salvaged what he could by altering the event programme. Instead of laying the foundation stone, he brought out his green thumb to the embassy site. In the presence of the highest Congolese echelons, Reynders planted a wenge tree (Fig. 74) that is endemic to Central Africa. It was by no means as symbolic as laying the foundation stone but given the circumstances it was the next best thing in the eyes of Reynders.

Figure 74:
Foreign Minister
Reynders on the
embassy grounds,
12 August 2013

Meanwhile, back in Belgium, the second public procurement for the embassy contract was launched. Yet again, both BESIX and Willemen Groep submitted a tender. Yet again, the outcome was the same as Willemen Groep was awarded the commission for a second time in the fall of 2013.[522]

Rumour has it, however, that the public procurement allegedly fell victim to corruption. In his book on Reynders and his right-hand man, Fontinoy, investigative journalist Philippe Engels argues that the second public procurement was rigged. Based on various testimonies, Engels pushes the narrative that Fontinoy put pressure on BESIX to pay him 50,000 euros (66,000 euros) as a bribe and in return BESIX would get the embassy contract.[523] According to Engels, BESIX did not accept this offer and reached out to its political allies for help but to no avail. Engels argues that, as BESIX was unwilling to pay this bribe, it lost all chances of winning the contract. The Belgian construction firm did not go public with the story as it was worried that its status as whistle-blower would jeopardise its chances of obtaining future public contracts in Belgium.[524] Yet again, one has to be wary of automatically believing such serious allegations. Given the upstanding reputation of investigative journalist Engels, however, it leaves little doubt that the process for awarding the Kinshasa contract was questionable. As such, the practice of monetising the embassy patrimony is twofold: policymakers tended to sell embassies in order to balance state finances but there are also allegations that certain individuals might have tried to enrich themselves by awarding embassy contracts.

Designing the Embassy: State-of-the-art Offices in the Tropics

Having been awarded the contract, Willemen Groep could finally set about constructing the Kinshasa embassy. But what did its calling card on the African continent look like exactly in terms of architecture? Willemen Groep joined forces with the Belgian architecture firm A2M. Founded in 2000 by the Belgian architect Sebastian Moreno-Vacca, A2M has built up an upstanding reputation. The Brussels-based architecture firm is known to be one of the frontrunners in designing passive buildings in Belgium.[525]

A2M approached the design commission in a very different way to BESIX/ArtBuild Architects. Whereas the latter had designed a building with an overall rectangular appearance oriented towards *Boulevard du 30 Juin*, Sebastian Moreno-Vacca and his collaborators opted for a more compact structure with a square footprint. A2M called for the construction of a concrete office building with five storeys. Moreover, A2M clearly deviated from the straight lines dominating the design of BESIX/ArtBuild Architects. Notwithstanding the square footprint, the exteriors had conspicuous sloping surfaces. These were most notable near the main entrance, more specifically in the concrete baseplate and roof structure. The configuration of triangular surfaces (Fig. 75) gave a more dynamic appearance to the façade. This was further reinforced by the extensive use of *brise-soleils* that are tightly packed against each other. Running across all sides of the building, these *brise-soleils* added a sense of rhythm to the exteriors. As part of the passive building design, the rectilinear building volume was to be made airtight by means of hyper-insulated walls and high-performance glazing with aluminium joinery.

In a similar fashion to the Tokyo project, the Kinshasa design has a generic aesthetic that does not seek to project nationhood through style, form and materiality. Instead, the aesthetic is direct and clear, and disassociated from any historical, national or traditional motifs. Although not explicitly stated, a possible explanation for this design may have to do with the multilayered national representation that would work in the new chancery. Instead of embarking on an endeavour to express both Belgian, Dutch and regional elements in the design, it is possible that A2M opted to accommodate the various entities in a more neutral architectural setting.

The chancery's main entrance is oriented towards *Boulevard du 30 Juin*. It was to be fully glazed in order to give the building an inviting appearance. In front of the entrance, an especially wide staircase was included, adding a sense of monumentality. Leading to the second storey

Figure 75: The Kinshasa chancery, 2017

where the offices were to be located, this majestic entrance was to be used by high-profile guests. A2M also included a second entrance along the chancery's eastern façade. In contrast to the main entrance, the eastern entrance was situated on the ground floor and led visitors to the Belgian and Dutch visa section. By physically distancing both entrances and accentuating their respective hierarchy by means of height, A2M opted to separate the circulation of high-profile guests and visa applicants. The separated circulation thus divided the chancery into two sections. The first section was situated on the ground level with the reception desk, waiting room and visa section counters (Fig. 76). The second section was made up of the four upper storeys and accommodated the embassy offices. Both sections were, however, interwoven with each other through a 14-metre-high atrium tying the chancery together. Around the atrium, A2M included an architectural promenade that served as a stage and as a vantage point to gaze from and be gazed at. The atrium and adjoining promenades were to feature all-white walls, ceilings and balustrades that gave a feeling of space and light to the interiors. The dominance of white surfaces in the interiors was to be contrasted by dark tiled flooring. The sense of height and wonder in the atrium was further increased by the natural daylight that would penetrate the central meeting place of the chancery.

In terms of office layout, the Kinshasa chancery marked a true novelty in how the Ministry has historically organised the workspace in

Figure 76: The chancery's visa section, 2019

its purpose-built chanceries. Whereas the Ministry previously had the tendency to go for cellular offices, the Kinshasa chancery was made up of several spacious rooms with an open office layout. In accordance with the *zeitgeist* of corporate culture, the FPS Foreign Affairs chose office spaces made up of shared desks with barriers. The reasons to do so were twofold.

Firstly, it wanted to create a more collaborative and interactive work environment. The open layout, which included coffee corners, was designed to create a sense of togetherness on the work floor. Secondly and perhaps most instrumentally, the open office layout was introduced because of spatial limitations. The Kinshasa chancery may have had the largest amount of office space but it also had to accommodate a small army of Belgian and Dutch diplomats, military attachés, development aid officials, trade representatives from Flanders, Wallonia and Brussels, the Belgian-Congolese-Luxembourg Chamber of Commerce, and administrative staff. In total, some 200 people would work in the new chancery. The amount of office space given to each entity clearly expressed the power balance within the chancery. The Belgian diplomats were allocated 1,790 m², the Belgian development agency Enabel was allocated 480 m², the members of the Dutch embassy staff were allocated 270 m², the regional trade agencies were allocated 90 m², and the Belgian-Congolese-Luxembourg Chamber of Commerce was allocated some 60 m². As it was

Figure 77: The ambassador's office, undated

spatially unfeasible to give each staffer an individual office, the open office layout was the solution. Each entity was allocated its own office space made up of shared desks with barriers. However, as is so often the case with workplace transformations, the introduction of the open office layout did not go down well with Belgian diplomats moving into the Kinshasa chancery. Off the record, a Belgian diplomat confided to me that the idea of sharing desks was ludicrous in a diplomatic workspace that by its very essence handles confidential information. Colleagues could easily overhear each other's sensitive phone calls with Congolese politicians, fellow diplomats, entrepreneurs and journalists. Moreover, the lack of privacy and increased distraction led to frustration and ineffectiveness among Belgian diplomats. My source allegedly recalled how one diplomat was so fed up with the shared desk policy that he moved his desk to the copying room so that he could work separately.

However, some individuals working at the chancery were exempt from working in an open office environment. Senior officials such as the Belgian ambassador were allocated an individual office with a sleek appearance. In accordance with the colour scheme used for the atrium, the ambassador's office (Fig. 77) would feature all-white walls to give the room a sense of brightness and spaciousness. Moreover, this created a colour contrast with the dark parquet floor. A2M also used a colour scheme to distinguish different spheres in the office space. The seating area was to feature all-white furniture, whereas the ambassador's desk had darker surfaces. It is worth noting that clear national references were present but

Figure 78: The embassy terrace, 2019

in a more subtle way. A flagpole with the Belgian tricolour, for instance, was to be included in the corner.

While the general idea behind sharing desks was to strengthen the bonds between staffers working for the same entity, A2M also invested considerably in deepening ties between the various entities throughout the design. The top floor, for instance, accommodated the canteen. During lunchtime, staffers could catch up with colleagues and personnel working for other entities. Next to the canteen, A2M included a roof terrace that was an ideal venue for informal talks. The roof terrace offered staffers a panoramic view over the neighbourhood. In the garden, A2M added another venue where the mixed staff could meet each other. By means of a footbridge, staffers could leave the chancery and make their way to a raised terrace (Fig. 78). Made up of concrete slabs, the terrace was fitted with an arrangement of garden furniture. The terrace was to be a comfortable setting for anything ranging from confidential one-on-one talks to well-attended after-work drinks. The informal and relaxing atmosphere was further reinforced by the palm trees surrounding the terrace.

As the lion's share of the embassy grounds remained undeveloped, considerable attention was given to landscaping the embassy gardens. The barren landscape turned into well-tended lawns that would not have looked out of place at a golf course. Because of its sheer size, the embassy garden could be used as diplomatic décor for social events such as receptions and cocktail parties.

Judging from the glazed main entrance, shared desks and recreational facilities, one can easily get the impression that the chancery presented itself to the outside world as an open and approachable site. However, looks can be deceiving. Given the unpredictability of Belgian-Congolese political relations and a genuine feeling of insecurity, the FPS Foreign Affairs considerably beefed up the level of security. In fact, the Kinshasa chancery is one of, if not the most, well-protected Belgian embassies. As security specifics are classified for obvious reasons, this book only touches upon the general outlines without delving into too much detail. Willemen Groep was instructed to build a wall that turned the embassy into a compound. Visa applicants and visitors have to pass manned checkpoints. Moreover, the FPS Foreign Affairs hired a private security firm to offer around-the-clock surveillance.

Labelling the Kinshasa chancery as an embassy fortress may be somewhat of a stretch but the enhanced security measures nonetheless create a certain tension between the chancery and its surroundings. The building itself has an inviting appearance but the site as a whole shields itself off from the immediate environment. The days in which Satish Gujral could design an embassy in New Delhi shielded off by nothing more than an earthen rampart were well and truly over by the new millennium. The FPS Foreign Affairs may have lagged behind in turning embassies into fortress-like compounds but the Kinshasa project corresponds with the growing international trend to beef up the level of security at diplomatic sites since the turn of the millennium.[526]

The Art of Diplomacy

With the legal issues resolved, the FPS Foreign Affairs could proceed with the construction of the flagship chancery. Its leadership was poised to organise a proper foundation stone laying ceremony this time around. Scheduled to take place on 26 August 2014, the event was envisaged to be a political *tour de force* reaffirming Belgium as a privileged partner of the Democratic Republic of the Congo.

However, the driving force behind the project could not attend the pompous event. During the summer of 2014, Didier Reynders was preoccupied with negotiations to form a new federal government. Reynders entered into coalition talks with the Flemish nationalists of the New Flemish Alliance (N-VA). In the margins of these talks, Reynders unveiled his Kinshasa embassy project to Bart De Wever, the N-VA party leader. According to investigative journalist Philippe Engels, the N-VA party leader spoke out against the impending building project.[527]

In the past, N-VA MPs had frequently criticised Reynders and his predecessors for their close ties with the Kabila regime which was internationally recognised as corrupt with little to no regard for human rights.[528] Aspiring to secede Flanders from Belgium, N-VA politicians also had a deep-seated disdain for the aspirations of the mainstream political parties to continue to play a leading role in the former colony. The Flemish nationalists framed this political interest to be a prime example of what has been coined as *La Belgique à papa*, a strong nostalgia for the time before the state reforms when Belgium was a unitary and politically stable country. For De Wever, it was a bridge too far that his new federal government would construct a new embassy in Kinshasa. According to Engels, however, Reynders was able to defuse the situation. The N-VA strongman allegedly had a sudden change of heart upon hearing that the prestigious commission was awarded to Willemen Groep which is based in Malines. This political U-turn made quite a lot of sense. After all, De Wever had good relations with Johan Willemen whose firm was an important employer in his very own constituency.[529]

Reynders' absence did not put a damper on the festivities. Some 100 guests attended the foundation stone laying ceremony, including high-profile guests such as the Congolese Foreign Minister Raymond Tshibanda, MPs, the *corps diplomatique*, building contractor Johan Willemen and none other than Jean-Claude Fontinoy. From a custom-made stand, the prominent audience witnessed a pompous ceremony that could have come straight out of the time of *La Belgique à papa*. A journalist from *Le Soir* reported to her readers that she was catapulted back in time. The former colony, she wrote, is one of the few places where the illusion of the unitary Belgian state still exists and where Belgium can punch above its weight on the international stage.[530] A Congolese choir sang the Belgian, Dutch, and Congolese anthems. The foundation stone was unveiled by Armand De Decker (1948-2019), a fellow party member of Reynders and former Minister for Development Cooperation. On Reynders' behalf, De Decker gave a solemn speech (Fig. 79) in which he portrayed the new embassy as the architectural testament to Belgium's commitment to the Democratic Republic of the Congo. Moreover, De Decker used the opportunity to send a clear message to the Kabila regime that had a questionable track record when it came to organising fair elections and abiding by the rule of law. In a very subtle way, De Decker alluded to the fact that Belgium would keep a watchful eye on political developments in the Democratic Republic of the Congo:

> This is a moment that will go down in the history of our diplomatic relations. It is a powerful symbol of Belgium's presence in the Democratic Republic of Congo and of the excellent relations between our two countries. It is also Belgium's hope, indeed its conviction, that efforts to democratise and modernise the country will continue for a better future. Beyond the building project, the construction of this new chancery is a political gesture, a gesture of confidence in the future, a demonstration of our desire to deepen our relations even further.[531]

Interestingly, De Decker did not accentuate the Dutch involvement in the project. Apparently, the liberal strongman considered the chancery first and foremost a Belgian calling card. In his eyes, the Dutch presence was nothing more than a minor detail in a construction project that was an architectural *tour de force* of the Belgian diplomatic corps in the Democratic Republic of the Congo. However, during the closing reception, the Dutch presence was made evident by adapted finger food and beverages. Aiming to showcase the Belgian-Dutch cooperation that underpinned the project, specialities of both countries were served to the attendees such as custom-made pralines with the Belgian colours and Heineken beer.

On 1 October 2014, Willemen Groep kickstarted construction works. Erecting a passive office building in Africa turned out to be quite the undertaking. Most building materials and technical installations had to be shipped by container from Europe. Some 60 containers had to make the long journey south.[532] As such, the Kinshasa chancery was somewhat of a paradox from an environmental point of view. On the one hand, the building was going to have a low carbon footprint because of the passive building design. On the other hand, ship and aviation pollution linked to the project nullified the effects of this eco-friendly building method for several years on end. Moreover, engineers from Willemen Groep frequently travelled up and down to Kinshasa to supervise local contractors and monitor construction works.

Given the historical background, it is telling that Belgian actors played the supervising role in building the embassy. It exposes a certain imbalance reminiscent of the time when the Congo was a colony and Belgium

PLUGGING THE HOLES IN THE FEDERAL BUDGET 299

Figure 79: Armand De Decker giving a speech, 26 August 2014

the metropole. Even as late as the 2010s, it was still considered evident that the necessary technical expertise had to come from Belgium in order to get anything done in the Democratic Republic of the Congo. In fact, it speaks volumes that the FPS Foreign Affairs awarded the contract to Belgian firms even though it had been common practice to call upon local architects and contractors to commission embassies. One can argue that Belgium still considered the Democratic Republic of the Congo to be its backyard where Belgian businesses were the preferred partners. Such notions demonstrate the complex relationship between Belgium and the Democratic Republic of the Congo. This line of thought reveals itself in a newspaper interview with the manager of overseas projects at Willemen Groep. The manager noted that he was forced to spread construction works over two years.[533] Willemen Groep allocated twice as much time to the Kinshasa project as it would have needed to erect the same structure in Belgium because the Congolese building industry was less productive and short on construction machines.

The long building phase did, however, offer the FPS Foreign Affairs some much needed time to examine how it was going to integrate and display artwork in the new embassy. In line with the Tokyo project, art curator Ilse Dauwe was tasked with addressing this question. Given the nature of the project, Brussels was determined to go the extra mile in terms of artwork. Therefore, it was decided that artwork would be commissioned. In line with Dauwe's mission statement to foster an intercultural dialogue through art, Belgian and Congolese artists were awarded commissions. However, it is telling that the FPS Foreign Affairs was less interested in expressing the Dutch presence through artwork. The chancery may have housed the Belgian and Dutch embassies but both countries were not equal in expressing their presence, most likely because of their respective capacities as landlord and tenant.

In total, some 20 works of art were commissioned. One such commission was awarded to the Belgian artist Maarten Vanden Eynde. His line of work revolves around studying the ecological impact of humans on the world. During his time in Africa, Vanden Eynde was introduced to a remarkable brick-making technique involving termite hills.[534] Termites bring up high quality earth to the surface that is well suited to making bricks. In the vicinity of termite mounds, one can find ovens where this earth is heated into bricks. Intrigued by this method, Vanden Eynde drew inspiration from this brick-making technique. He designed a total of five brick structures moulded in such a way that they look like termite hills. He

Figure 80: The artwork *Contradictio in Terminarium*, 27 November 2017

accentuated this visual contradiction in the name of his artwork. He named his work *Contradictio in Terminarium* (Fig. 80), a play on words between *contradictio in terminis*, Latin for contradiction in terms, and *terminarium*, Latin for a termite hill. In addition to paying tribute to the African building method, the brick structures were also a nod to Belgium. It was a homage to the saying that Belgians are born with a brick in their stomach, referring to their desire to build their own house. *Contradictio in Terminarium* was given a prominent position near the embassy's main entrance.

Another striking artwork was made by the Brussels-Congolese artist Aimé Mpane. As a well-reputed visual artist in both Belgium and the Democratic Republic of the Congo, Mpane frames art as an instrumental tool to mitigating conflict and redressing power imbalances. He designed a wooden sculpture (Fig. 81) with a Lingala name, *Yambi* which means 'welcome'. Strategically positioned in front of the embassy's glazed entrance, the grid-like sculpture depicts two men, one black and the other white, wearing suits who are about to shake hands. The black man is positioned with his back to the embassy, giving the impression that he is the one coming out of the embassy to greet the white man. This is the ambiguity Mpane aims to include in his work. *Yambi* asks the question who welcomes whom and it is up to people visiting the embassy to decide for themselves.[535]

Figure 81: The wooden sculpture *Yambi*, 2019

On 27 November 2017, high-profile guests gathered on the embassy grounds to inaugurate the embassy (Fig. 82). This time around, Foreign Minister Reynders was present to preside over the event. However, the event took place at a most unfortunate moment in Belgian-Congolese relations. The Kabila regime had just postponed the presidential elections and appointed a new prime minister without parliamentary approval, much to the frustration of the Belgian government. In response, Reynders cut funding for development aid programmes in the Democratic Republic of the Congo. As a result, Belgian-Congolese ties once again lived up to their reputation as a complicated on-again, off-again relationship.

The strained relationship became especially tangible during the inauguration as both President Kabila and his ministers were conspicuous by their absence. Their absence gave a somewhat ironic twist to the event. The embassy itself was envisaged to be a political gesture to the Congolese ruling power base that Belgium attached great importance to Central Africa but the Congolese government chose not to attend its inauguration. Only politicians belonging to the opposition parties accepted the Belgian invitation. Nevertheless, Reynders made the most of the event by giving

Figure 82: Inauguration ceremony of the Kinshasa chancery, 27 November 2017

a high-flown speech. He framed the new chancery as the architectural testament to Belgium's commitment to the Congolese people. Moreover, he expressed his hope that Belgian diplomats working at the chancery could play a role in supporting Congolese politicians' efforts to secure open and transparent elections, a subtle yet clearly pointed remark aimed at President Kabila.

As part of the festivities, a Congolese choir positioned itself on the stairs and sang the Belgian, Dutch and even European anthems, showcasing that the chancery transcended the traditional bilateral context. During the ceremony, the respective flags of the different actors were also hoisted in front of the new chancery. Off the record, a Belgian diplomat told me that the dimensions of these flags had been a bone of contention between Brussels and The Hague. As the awarding authority and landlord, the FPS Foreign Affairs wanted to hoist a Belgian flag that would be significantly larger than the Dutch one. However, The Hague was offended by the idea, deeming it a lack of respect. Eventually, it was decided to give all flags the same size in an effort to diffuse the situation between landlord and tenant.

Commissioning the Kinshasa chancery may have been a long-drawn-out affair for Reynders but he had accomplished his goals by late 2017. Henceforth, Belgian diplomats were accommodated in a state-of-the-art and well-secured workspace. The chancery put Belgium back on the map in the Democratic Republic of the Congo and the property would generate steady rental incomes. However, Reynders' appetite to monetise the diplomatic patrimony was far from satisfied. The liberal strongman stepped up his efforts, even when they came at the expense of the architectural legacy that others within the Ministry of Foreign Affairs had previously built up.

The Washington Sale: A Sign of the Times

During the summer of 2016, Reynders and Fontinoy set their sights on the Washington chancery, the architectural legacy of Silvercruys' ambassadorship. They deemed the time right to sell the property, reasoning that the chancery had become too spacious. In fact, financial incentives were the main impetus for the liberal duo. According to their estimates, a sale could easily generate 25 million euros (32 million euros). Such funds would come in handy both to plug the holes in the federal budget and generate money for the Ministry's Buildings Fund. In return, Reynders and Fontinoy suggested moving the chancery to an apartment building in the city centre.

Their plans, however, drew flak from within the Ministry's walls. The Inspection of Diplomatic and Consular Missions spoke out against the scheme, reasoning that such a sale would be an utter mistake from both a representational and financial point of view. Selling the landmark chancery would undoubtedly tarnish national prestige in the American capital. Moreover, the Inspection indicated that the maintenance costs for the apartment building suggested by Reynders and Fontinoy would be significantly higher than for the chancery at Garfield Street.[536] The sale would only be lucrative in the short run but in the long run it would become a costly undertaking. Instead, the Inspection of Diplomatic and Consular Missions suggested leasing the vacant offices to a befriended diplomatic mission. In doing so, the FPS Foreign Affairs could monetise the spacious chancery without having to sell it. Much to the frustration of the Inspection, Reynders refused to even examine this possibility. Moreover, he brushed the Inspection's concerns aside and pressed on with his plans. Given the strained atmosphere, it speaks volumes that *De Standaard* could not reach the spokesperson of the FPS Foreign Affairs for a comment on the forthcoming sale.[537]

In December 2019, Reynders found a conspicuous buyer for the chancery. The Socialist Republic of Vietnam was willing to pay approximately 20.5 million euros (24.8 million euros) for the property and use it for its

Figure 83: The sculpted Belgian coat of arms in the garden of the Foxhall Road residence, 2025

own embassy offices.[538] As this figure was significantly lower than the estimated 25 million euros (32 million euros), Reynders and Fontinoy had got somewhat ahead of themselves. Nevertheless, the deal with the Vietnamese government was finalised by the end of 2019. It is somewhat ironic that the very embassy building that was intended to showcase Belgium's commitment to the transatlantic alliance was eventually sold to one of the world's last communist countries. Only a fragment of the architectural legacy of Silvercruys' ambassadorship was salvaged. On the initiative of Ambassador Dirk Wouters, the sculpted coat of arms was removed from the façade and placed as a statue in the garden of the Foxhall Road residence (Fig. 83). Ever since, the coat of arms serves as a silent reminder of more glorious times of the Belgian embassy-building programme.

Epilogue

> An embassy is a building that represents a country abroad; through this building a country shows itself to the outside world. Therefore it is important that embassy buildings show a certain style, class without exaggeration, as they are in fact a visit card of the country in question.[539]

Using this statement from the Ministry's real estate department as a starting point, *Building for Belgium* set out to unravel precisely what this statement means, whether the Ministry proclaimed this idea in earlier times, and to what extent it lived up to its own standards. Therefore, this book has reconstructed the historical trajectory of the Belgian embassy-building programme, revealing to what extent the Ministry has purposefully invested in the architectural design and representational role of purpose-built embassies on an everchanging international stage.

The book has illustrated that, throughout the period under investigation, there was no such thing as a well-considered policy that formulated clear guidelines as to how embassy architecture should represent the Belgian state. At no specific moment in time was there an overarching set of ideas, beliefs, values and rules as to how embassy architecture should radiate nationhood and express foreign policy stances abroad. Instead, incidental decisions, private ambitions and personal tastes were the driving forces shaping the embassy-building programme.

This already becomes apparent in how decisions were made to launch a building project. Such decisions were often the focal point of power struggles between the ambassador, foreign minister, the finance minister, MPs and the Ministry's bureaucracy. Each in their own way exerted substantial influence on the embassy-building programme as their actions would decide whether building plans would ever see the light of day. These different players projected their own aspirations on the embassy project which aimed to solve existing accommodation problems, boost national prestige, emphasise the earnestness to cement bilateral ties, facilitate economic missions, and generate revenue for the state finances. Building proposals were complicated by the fact that there was no general consensus on the necessity and added value of investing in purpose-built embassies. Throughout this book, both vocal supporters and ardent opponents have been identified. Therefore, in order to get the green light, the person in office was equally as important, if not more so, as the merits of the building project.

The absence of a leading architectural vision also reveals itself by looking at the way the Ministry awarded commissions to architects. For a long time, there was no such thing as a transparent tendering procedure. Policymakers handpicked architects who were part of their inner circle. Moreover, Belgian diplomats could have a big say in choosing an architect, especially when the Ministry opted to hire a local architect. During their postings, diplomats got to know people of all walks of life, including architects. They often succeeded in convincing their superiors to award the commission to architects they personally knew. It was only in the 1970s that the first traces of an architectural competition can be found. However, these competitions were not immune to personal meddling, as demonstrated in the New Delhi case study. Even in the new millennium with its rigid bidding process for public procurements, there are signs that personal ties and interests have continued to play a pivotal role behind the scenes.

The lack of a well-considered architectural vision becomes especially evident when assessing the diverging architectural designs of the Ministry's building stock. At no point in time did the Ministry develop a guiding template regarding the kind of aesthetic it deemed appropriate to project national, diplomatic and ideological visions abroad. There was no such thing as a series of preconceived ideas or leading principles guiding the embassy-building programme. Instead, the Ministry started each building project with a blank page. In its capacity as awarding authority, the Ministry filled this blank page with programmatic needs but it rarely formulated its architectural preferences on paper. The Ministry never committed itself to a particular aesthetic; instead, it put its faith in the architect hired for the job at hand. Brussels often went along with the architect's preliminary design, calling only for minor alterations to meet the programmatic needs. Claiming that the architects were given complete *carte blanche* may be stretching the truth but in several cases they nevertheless enjoyed plenty of room for manoeuvre.

However, the incidental and ad hoc building programme does not mean that the Ministry was disinterested in embassy architecture all together. During the design phase, individuals within the Ministry shared their preferences through informal talks with the architect. An embassy's design was therefore not so much the result of a closely monitored top-down building programme, but rather the result of personal and shifting tastes and opinions. Moreover, designing an embassy was and still is a collaborative effort in which architects, foreign ministers, ambassadors and ministry officials each have their part to play. However, for a long time, there was no level playing field with regard to this collaborative effort. The Ministry may have been the awarding authority but it had a glaring lack of in-house expertise on how to design and build embassies. In order to fill the void, the Ministry has awarded commissions on a turnkey basis to architects and project developers. This gave the architects involved even more room for manoeuvre, resulting in heterogenous embassy architecture across the globe.

However, the lack of a guiding building policy and procedure should not necessarily be considered a failure. In fact, the decentralised and ad hoc approach has actually been the greatest strength of Belgium's embassy-building programme. It has resulted in a rich and stylistically varied architectural patrimony. As the Ministry did not propagate a particular aesthetic or style, architects and ambassadors had plenty of room for manoeuvre at the design level. They could mould the design to reflect a particular situation, place and timeframe. This constant adaptation runs like a thread through the embassy-building programme. Instead of exporting a generic model abroad that downplayed local conditions, the Ministry's decentralised approach and lenient attitude enabled architects and ambassadors to commission embassy designs that fitted in a given urban context and were often deeply rooted in the receiving state's history and traditions.

This book has coined this tendency as 'architectural localitis' which reached its zenith in the mid-1980s with the building projects in New Delhi and Riyadh. In fact, the tendency to blend into local surroundings trumped efforts to project national identity abroad. Embassy designs responded to specific conditions of site, project-related conditions, and the urban context. As such, adaptability and resourcefulness have been the cornerstones of Belgium's embassy-building programme. This has resulted in a broad palette of architectural projects making up the nation's embassy patrimony. For instance, it is telling that in just three years the Ministry greenlit the construction of a countryside villa in Canberra, a neoclassical palace in Warsaw and a modernist compound in Brasília. This varied approach bore fruit for Belgium's image abroad. Locally embedded embassy designs received much acclaim in the local press and architecture magazines.

In conclusion, Belgium's embassy-building programme has not been marked by the search for a dominant aesthetic to express nationhood abroad but instead by incidental decisions fuelling an already ad hoc building programme.

In the grand scheme of things, the Belgian case has offered us several insights broadening our knowledge of purpose-built embassies. Firstly, the Belgian case reinforces the notion that the tendency to construct purpose-built embassies really boomed since 1945. Before the Second World War, the Ministry of Foreign Affairs showed little to no interest in building abroad. It was only in the post-war period that a building frenzy took hold of the Ministry. This building frenzy was first and foremost launched to solve existing accommodation problems as embassy staff increased and to facilitate the move to new capital cities. Nevertheless, constructing an embassy never became the Ministry's preferred housing strategy.

Secondly, the Belgian case has nuanced the tendency in existing literature to portray foreign ministries as a monolithic block when it comes to commissioning purpose-built embassies. Authors have already demonstrated how embassy-building programmes became the focal point of power struggles between the foreign ministry, the treasury and parliament. However, this book has challenged the notion that a foreign ministry is by default a monolithic block when it comes to launching building projects. The Belgian case has illustrated how suggestions to build were complicated by the fact that there was no general consensus within the Ministry's walls on the necessity and added value of investing in embassy architecture. Building plans often became the focal point of internal power struggles, personality clashes, rivalries and intrigues between the foreign minister, ministry officials and the diplomatic corps.

Thirdly and most significantly, *Building for Belgium* has demonstrated that one should be wary not to succumb to the fiction that an embassy-building programme is by default carefully guided and closely monitored by the state. Belgium provides a telling case in point with its incidental and ad hoc building policy and procedure. Moreover, the building policy and procedure was not marked by a fundamental desire to express nationhood abroad by means of architecture.

Fourthly and finally, this book has illustrated that Belgium lagged behind in terms of moving embassies into fortress-like compounds. For a long time, security was not an important consideration in designing embassies. Even the series of attacks on Belgian embassies in 1961 did not bring about any noteworthy change. It speaks volumes that the New

Delhi embassy, constructed in the early 1980s, was initially only shielded off by an earthen rampart at a time when terrorists increasingly targeted diplomatic premises. It is only in more recent projects that security has become a guiding principle when designing Belgian embassies.

Altogether, it is my sincere hope that this book serves as a stepping stone for further research on diplomatic architecture as a whole and the case of Belgium in particular. *Building for Belgium* has offered a close reading and initial interpretation of the design and construction realisation processes of Belgian embassies. Discussing additional embassy projects might confirm, refine or expand on the dominant dynamics discussed in this book and draw attention to additional dynamics. It is my firm belief that this book is definitely not the final study on the fascinating and insightful subject of (Belgian) diplomatic architecture.

What the future of the Belgian embassy-building programme may hold is anyone's guess. Obviously, the FPS Foreign Affairs will construct future embassies in an ever more challenging context. The deplorable state finances, the possibility of new state reforms dissolving the federal state, the prospect of sharing more embassy premises with European allies, the changing world order, evolutions in the diplomatic profession, and the perpetual quest to define and express national identity in an ever more complex world are just some of the issues the FPS Foreign Affairs will have to deal with in the near future. However, what can be said for sure is that the territories making up current-day Belgium will continue to be represented across capitals far and wide through embassy buildings, the history of which is worth telling.

Notes

1. Special Specifications. Full Design and Build of the new Belgian Chancellery in Washington, D.C., 18 May 2018 (P&O Archives of the FPS Foreign Affairs, files Washington, D.C.).
2. Regie der Gebouwen, *De Regie der Gebouwen*, 87-89.
3. Delcorps, *Dans les coulisses de la diplomatie*, 11.
4. Loeffler, *The Architecture of Diplomacy*, 4; Bertram, *Room for Diplomacy*, 313; Bellat, *Ambassades françaises du XXe Siècle*, 24.
5. Berridge and Lloyd, *The Palgrave Macmillan Dictionary of Diplomacy*, 108.
6. Machiavelli, *Il Principe en andere politieke geschriften*, 368.
7. Bell and Zacka, "Introduction," 1-17.
8. Vale, *Architecture, Power and National Identity*, 14-18.
9. Therborn, *Cities of power*; King, *Writing the global city*; Judin, *Architecture, state modernism and cultural nationalism in the apartheid capital*; Urban, *Postmodern Architecture in Socialist Poland*.
10. Robin, *Enclaves of America*, 63-166; Bertram, *Room for Diplomacy*; Stourton, *British Embassies*; Bellat, *Ambassades françaises du XXe Siècle*; Fülscher, *Deutsche Botschaften*; Kazakova, Архитектура советской дипломатии (The Architecture of Soviet Diplomacy).
11. Hagströmer, "In search of a national vision,"; Gower, "Image Building,"; Damen, "Sober Nederlands Vlagvertoon," 36-49.
12. Chapnick, "The Middle Power," 73-82.
13. Stevens, *Belgium's Most Beautiful Embassies*; Federal Public Service Foreign Affairs, Foreign Trade and Development Cooperation, *Belgian Embassy London*; Similar booklets have also been made for the Belgian embassies in Bangkok, Beijing, and Washington, D.C; Falisse, *Inspirations*.
14. Bekaert and Strauven, *Bouwen in België*, 61-62.
15. Bekaert, "Architectuur + Beleid,".
16. De Standaard, *Belgiës leeghoofdige architectuur*, 13.
17. Luyten, Meynen and Witte, *Politieke Geschiedenis van België*, 360-372.
18. Coolsaet, Dujardin and Roosens, *Buitenlandse Zaken in België*, 396.
19. Bellat, *Ambassades françaises du XXe Siècle*, 21.
20. Loeffler, *The Architecture of Diplomacy*, 3.
21. Loeffler, *The Architecture of Diplomacy*, 3.
22. Le Corbusier, *Vers une architecture*, 73.
23. Berridge and Lloyd, *The Palgrave Macmillan Dictionary of Diplomacy*, 87.
24. Loeffler, "The State Department and the Politics of Preservation," 99.
25. Letter from Arthur Wauters to Paul van Zeeland, Etat des Lieux, 16 April 1952 (DAB, 14.074bis, Notes sur les immeubles de service à l'étranger et à Bruxelles, Moscou).
26. Note pour A/Inspecteur des Postes, 24 April 1952 (DAB, 14.074bis, Notes sur les immeubles de service à l'étranger et à Bruxelles, Moscou). Original citation in French, translated by the author.
27. Note pour A/Inspecteur des Postes, 24 April 1952 (DAB, 14.074bis, Notes sur les immeubles de service à l'étranger et à Bruxelles, dossier Moscou).
28. Hagströmer, "'Swedish Modern' meets international high politics," 171-174.
29. Vanwing, "Ambassadeur Silvercruys en de Belgisch-Amerikaanse relaties (1945-1959)," 282.
30. Highsmith and Landphair, *Embassies of Washington*, 14.
31. Vander Hulst, "De opdracht van Paul Kronacker (1944-1947)," 401-440.
32. Highsmith and Landphair, *Embassies of Washington*, 24.
33. Interview with Mark Eyskens, 8 September 2021.
34. Federal Public Service Foreign Affairs, Foreign Trade and Development Cooperation, *Belgian Embassy Washington*, unnumbered pages.

35 Washington Times Herald, *Belgian Premier Makes Hasty Visit*, 6 October 1947 (DAB, 18.434/4, Papiers Robert Silvercruys).
36 The Washington Post, *Bachelor Embassy Boasts Smooth Efficient Household*, 1 January 1950 (DAB, 18.434/6, Papiers Robert Silvercruys).
37 Note pour Monsieur Le Secrétaire Général, 2 August 1949 (DAB, Notes sur les immeubles de service à l'étranger et à Bruxelles 14.074 bis, dossier Washington).
38 Letter from Silvercruys to Theunis, 18 June 1945 (DAB, 18.434/3, Papiers Robert Silvercruys).
39 Letter from Section A to Silvercruys, undated (DAB, Notes sur les immeubles de service à l'étranger et à Bruxelles 14.074 bis, dossier Washington).
40 Letter from Silvercruys to Theunis, 18 June 1945 (DAB, 18.434/3, Papiers Robert Silvercruys). Original citation in French, translated by the author.
41 Delcorps, *Dans les coulisses de la diplomatie*, 123.
42 This limited diplomatic building activity entailed the construction of a legation building in Beijing (1907), Ankara (1929) and Cairo (1930) and embassy offices in Tokyo (1928).
43 Gutheim and Lee, *Worthy of the Nation*, 162.
44 Cole, *Sir Edwin Lutyens*, 9-27.
45 Stourton, *British Embassies*, 205.
46 Gutheim and Lee, *Worthy of the Nation*, 162.
47 Highsmith and Landphair, *Embassies of Washington*, 103.
48 Highsmith and Landphair, *Embassies of Washington*, 103.
49 Highsmith and Landphair, *Embassies of Washington*, 103.
50 Vanwing, "Ambassadeur Silvercruys en de Belgisch-Amerikaanse relaties (1945-1959)," 248.
51 Letter from Silvercruys to Spaak, 5 April 1947 (Archives of the Belgian Embassy in Washington, D.C.).
52 Letter from Silvercruys to Spaak, 5 April 1947 (Archives of the Belgian Embassy in Washington, D.C.).
53 Letter from Silvercruys to Spaak, 5 April 1947 (Archives of the Belgian Embassy in Washington, D.C.).
54 Letter from Waverly Taylor Inc. to Max Winders, 20 February 1953, (CIVA, Archives Max Winders, Box 6: Washington, New York, Tokyo, Palais Egmont).
55 Letter from Waverly Taylor Inc. to Max Winders, 20 February 1953, (CIVA, Archives Max Winders, Box 6: Washington, New York, Tokyo, Palais Egmont).
56 Letter from Silvercruys to Spaak, 5 April 1947 (Archives of the Belgian Embassy in Washington, D.C.). Original citation in French, translated by the author.
57 Letter from Loridan to Silvercruys, 11 June 1947 (DAB, 18.434/4, Papiers Robert Silvercruys).
58 Report from Hervé de Gruben to Paul Van Zeeland, 30 July 1935 (CegeSoma, Archives Hervé de Gruben, AA699, 15, Rapport d'une mission officieuse à Moscou relative à l'installation matérielle de la Légation de Belgique à Moscou).
59 Interview with Mark Eyskens, Heverlee, 8 September 2021.
60 Silvercruys as cited in: Note pour monsieur le Ministre. Construction d'un bâtiment pour loger la chancellerie de l'ambassade à Washington, 14 January 1948 (DAB 14.074bis, Notes sur les immeubles de service à l'étranger et à Bruxelles 14.074 bis, dossier Washington).
61 Silvercruys as cited in: Note pour monsieur le Ministre. Construction d'un bâtiment pour loger la chancellerie de l'ambassade à Washington, 14 January 1948 (DAB 14.074bis, Notes sur les immeubles de service à l'étranger et à Bruxelles 14.074 bis, dossier Washington).
62 Letter from Gutt to Spaak, 19 August 1948 (DAB, 18.434/4, Papiers Robert Silvercruys). Original citation in French, translated by the author.
63 Letter from de Gruben to Silvercruys, August 1949 (DAB 14.074bis, Notes sur les immeubles de service à l'étranger et à Bruxelles 14.074 bis, dossier Washington).
64 Letter from de Gruben to Silvercruys, 16 April 1949 (DAB 14.074bis, Notes sur les immeubles de service à l'étranger et à Bruxelles 14.074 bis, dossier Washington).

[65] Construction d'un bâtiment pour loger la chancellerie de l'Ambassade à Washington, 3 August 1949 (DAB 14.074bis, Notes sur les immeubles de service à l'étranger et à Bruxelles 14.074 bis, dossier Washington).
[66] Ordre de Service N° 14, Réduction des frais inhérents aux déplacements à l'étranger, 2 December 1947 (DAB, 12.202 Ordres de service).
[67] Ordre de Service N° 14, Réduction des frais inhérents aux déplacements à l'étranger, 2 December 1947 (DAB, 12.202, Ordres de service).
[68] Letter from Eyskens to Silvercruys, 23 March 1949 (DAB, 18.434/5, Papiers Robert Silvercruys). Original citation in French, translated by the author.
[69] Vanwing, "Ambassadeur Silvercruys en de Belgisch-Amerikaanse relaties (1945-1959)," 251.
[70] Letter from Ockrent to Silvercruys, 18 November 1949 (DAB, 18.434/5, Papiers Robert Silvercruys).
[71] Letter from Ockrent to Silvercruys, 18 November 1949 (DAB, 18.434/5, Papiers Robert Silvercruys).
[72] Delcorps, "Le secrétaire général du ministère belge des Affaires étrangères," 201-202.
[73] Dujardin and Dumoulin, *Paul van Zeeland*, 50-65.
[74] Note pour A, 22 January 1948 (DAB, 14.074 bis, Notes sur les immeubles de service à l'étranger et à Bruxelles).
[75] Willies, "Max Winders," 603.
[76] Willies, "Max Winders," 603.
[77] Willies, "Max Winders," 603.
[78] Appraisal of property of the Belgian Government, south-east corner of 34th Street & Garfield Street, N.W., Washington, D.C. Dots 4, 5 and 19 square 2119, 11 September 1952 (CIVA, Archives Max Winders, Box 2: Ambassades Projets).
[79] Letter from Silvercruys to van Zeeland, 10 December 1952 (CIVA, Archives Max Winders, Box 2: Ambassades Projets).
[80] Letter from King to Silvercruys, 29 December 1944 (DAB, 18.434/3, Papiers Robert Silvercruys).
[81] Letter from Silvercruys to van Zeeland, 10 December 1952 (CIVA, Archives Max Winders, Box 2: Ambassades Projets).
[82] Gutheim and Lee, *Worthy of the Nation*, 231.
[83] Vale, *Architecture, Power and National Identity*, 66-67.
[84] Letter from Silvercruys to van Zeeland, Logement des services administratifs à Washington, 13 October 1952 (CIVA, Archives Max Winders, Box 2: Ambassades Projets). Original citation in French, translated by the author.
[85] Minutes of a meeting between Paul van Zeeland and Etienne Ruzette, undated (CIVA, Archives Max Winders, Box 2: Ambassades Projets. Original citation in French, translated by the author.
[86] Report from Winders to van Zeeland, 20 February 1953 (CIVA, Archives Max Winders, Box 6: Washington, New York, Tokyo, Palais Egmont).
[87] Report from Winders to van Zeeland, 20 February 1953 (CIVA, Archives Max Winders, Box 6: Washington, New York, Tokyo, Palais Egmont).
[88] Report from Winders to van Zeeland, 20 February 1953 (CIVA, Archives Max Winders, Box 6: Washington, New York, Tokyo, Palais Egmont).
[89] Questions et réponses, Chambre des Répresentants, Question n° 15 de M. Huysmans du 16 juin 1953, 897 (AMSAB, 625 Archief Camille Huysmans, 625.1313: Stukken betreffende de werkzaamheden in de Commissie voor Buitenlandse Zaken en Buitenlandse Handel, voornamelijk over de bouw van de ambassade in Washington). Original citation in French, translated by the author.
[90] La Libre Belgique, *L'ambassade de Belgique à Washington*, 13 June 1953, 2.
[91] De Standaard, *De bouw van een nieuwe kanselarij te Washington. Camille Huysmans is nieuwsgierig*, 8 August 1953, 2.
[92] Hunin, *Het enfant terrible Camille Huysmans*, 468-470.
[93] Letter from P. Smet to Camille Huysmans, undated (AMSAB, 625 Archief Camille Huysmans, 625.1313: Stukken betreffende de werkzaamheden in de Commissie voor Buitenlandse Zaken en Buitenlandse Handel, voornamelijk over de bouw van de ambassade in Washington). Original citation in French, translated by the author.

94 Letter from Max Winders to Paul van Zeeland, 28 December 1953 (CIVA, Archives Max Winders, Box 6: Washington, New York, Tokyo, Palais Egmont).
95 Letter from Max Winders to the Ministry, 1 March 1954 (CIVA, Archives Max Winders, Box 6: Washington, New York, Tokyo, Palais Egmont).
96 Honoraires de l'architecte, Tribunal Civil de Liège, 18 October 1926 (CIVA, Archives Max Winders, Box 2, Ambassades Projets).
97 Minutes of the Ministerial Council, Session of 9 April 1954 (National Archives of Belgium).
98 Begroting Buitenlandse Zaken, uitgaven voor materiële behoeften en andere werkingsuitgaven (Liberal Archive, Archives of Paul Kronacker, 6.4.3.21. Stukken m.b.t. de begroting Buitenlandse Zaken, 1955, 1956).
99 Schelfhout, *In het kielzog van Hugo Van Kuyck*, 27.
100 De Bremaeker, de Pauw and Janssens, *75 jaar Luchtbal*, 65.
101 Vosbeck, Wrenn and Smith, *A Legacy of Leadership*, 86.
102 Schelfhout, *In het kielzog van Hugo Van Kuyck*, 72-84.
103 Floré, "Technological progress as an obstruction to domestic comfort," 64-79.
104 Basyn, "Van Kuyck, Hugo," 569.
105 Van Kuyck, *Modern Belgian Architecture*, unnumbered pages.
106 De Vos and Geerinckx, "Modernist High-rises in Postwar Antwerp," 113-132.
107 Ryckewaert, *Building the Economic Backbone of the Belgian Welfare State*, 42.
108 Ryckewaert, *Building the Economic Backbone of the Belgian Welfare State*, 42.
109 Basyn, "Van Kuyck, Hugo," 569.
110 Presentation booklet Belgian Chancellery, unnumbered pages (FelixArchief, Architect Hugo Van Kuyck, 28#9562).
111 Stalder, "Turning Architecture Inside Out," 69-77.
112 Pieters, *Bouwen voor de natie*, 87-157.
113 Vanwing, "Ambassadeur Silvercruys en de Belgisch-Amerikaanse relaties (1945-1959)," 83.
114 Calvocoressi, *World Politics since 1945*, 767.
115 Helmreich, "US Foreign Policy and the Belgian Congo in the 1950s," 322.
116 Letter from Silvercruys to Spaak, 10 January 1956 (DAB, 2416 Personnel Extérieur Washington).
117 Presentation booklet Belgian Chancellery, unnumbered pages (FelixArchief, Architect Hugo Van Kuyck, 28#9562).
118 Ripnen, *Office Building and Office Layout Planning*, 26.
119 Van Meel, *The European office*, 38-39.
120 Koolhaas, *Elements of Architecture, Book 8: Balcony*, 74-83.
121 Delcorps, *Dans les coulisses de la diplomatie*, 122.
122 Coolsaet, Dujardin and Roosens, *Buitenlandse Zaken in België*, 294.
123 Unpublished memoirs Pierre Wigny, 32 (National Archives of Belgium, Papiers Pierre Wigny, I 591). Original citation in French, translated by the author.
124 Letter from Gutt to Silvercruys, 17 December 1954 (DAB, 18.434/7, Papiers Robert Silvercruys).
125 Crombois, *Camille Gutt and Postwar International Finance*, 129.
126 Smets, *Lambert: Une Aventure Bancaire et Financière*, 273.
127 Letter from Gutt to Silvercruys, 17 December 1954 (DAB, 18.434/7, Papiers Robert Silvercruys).
128 Letter from Scheyven to Silvercruys, 29 March 1956 (DAB, 18.434/7, Papiers Robert Silvercruys). Original citation in French, translated by the author.
129 Loeffler, *The Architecture of Diplomacy*, 59-78; Bertram, *Room for Diplomacy*, 231-255.
130 Instructions to Bidders, 4 November 1955 (Hagley Museum & Library, John McShain Papers, Box OS 54, Folder 4 Belgian Chancellery).
131 Brauer, *The Man Who Built Washington*, 80-125.
132 Le Soir, *Ambassade de Belgique*, 26 January 1956, 2.
133 The Washington Daily News, *Belgian Chancery to Rise on 34th Street*, 23 January 1956, 23.
134 Floré, "Wood Firm De Coene and the Modern Office," 7.
135 Jaenen, de Bouw, Leus et al., "Congolese Wood in the Antwerp Interwar Interior," 2005-2011.
136 Walter, "Les Bois du Congo dans la Construction et Décoration," 184-186.

[137] Note pour le Ministre, 15 December 1949 (Archives Université Catholique de Louvain, Papiers Paul van Zeeland, file 678, Affaires Etrangères 1949-1950).
[138] Vanwing, "Ambassadeur Silvercruys en de Belgisch-Amerikaanse relaties (1945-1959)," 117-118.
[139] La question des immeubles et du mobilier des postes à l'étranger, 21 January 1948 (DAB, 14.074bis, Notes sur les immeubles de service à l'étranger et à Bruxelles, Nouvelle installation du Ministère des Affaires Etrangères).
[140] Letter from De Coene Frères to Winders, 5 November 1953 (CIVA, Archives Max Winders, Box 6: Washington, New York, Tokyo, Palais Egmont).
[141] Devos and Floré, "Modern met De Coene. De Productie na 1952," 184.
[142] *Stars and Stripes*, 11 May 1955, 12-13 (National Archives of Belgium, Courtrai, Verzameling De Coene NV, BE-A0516/913, folder 328, series of press clippings).
[143] Floré, "Serving a Double Diplomatic Mission," 167-185.
[144] Letter from Silvercruys to Pierre De Coene, 3 May 1957 (Private Collection of Noël Hostens). Original citation in French, translated by the author.
[145] Belgian Commission to the world's fair, *New-York World's Fair 1939-1940*, 21.
[146] Words spoken by Baron Silvercruys. Ambassador of Belgium to the United States of America, Stanford, California, 10 March 1953 (DAB, 18.434/7, Papiers Robert Silvercruys).
[147] Dumont, *Louis Hennepin: Explorateur du Mississippi*, 33.
[148] Words spoken by Baron Silvercruys, Ambassador of Belgium to the United States of America, Stanford, California, 10 March 1953 (DAB, 18.434/7, Papiers Robert Silvercruys).
[149] Excerpts from the *Sunday Star* and *Washington Post and Times Herald*, 10 February 1957 (DAB, 18.434/7, Papiers Robert Silvercruys).
[150] Le Soir, *La nouvelle ambassade de Belgique à Washington*, 10 February 1957, 6.
[151] Le Soir, *La visite de Spaak à Washington*, 12 February 1957, 1.
[152] Damen, "Sober Nederlands vlagvertoon," 38-39.
[153] The Washington Star, *New Belgian Chancery Open*, 10 February 1957.
[154] Le Soir, *La nouvelle ambassade de Belgique à Washington*, 10 February 1957, 6.
[155] Le Drapeau Rouge, *La nouvelle ambassade belge à Washington*, 11 February 1957, 2.
[156] Proceedings of the Belgian Chamber of Representatives, session of 19 May 1959, 16.
[157] Unpublished memoirs Pierre Wigny, 32 (National Archives of Belgium, Papiers Pierre Wigny, I 591).
[158] Publicity folder De Coene, unnumbered pages (National Archives of Belgium, Courtrai, Verzameling De Coene NV BE-A0516/913, file 184).
[159] Cogels, *Souvenirs d'un diplomate*, 197-198.
[160] Letter from E.L.C. Schiff to the Dutch Minister of Foreign Affairs, 29 July 1960 (Nationaal Archief, The Hague, 2.05.118, Dutch Ministry of Foreign Affairs: Code Archive 1955-1964, file 29766).
[161] Letter from Silvercruys to Gutt, 19 February 1957 (DAB, 18.434/7, Papiers Robert Silvercruys).
[162] Comité de Coordination, Session of 17 June 1988 (DAB, 18.913/6: 1985-1988, Ministère des Affaires étrangères, Comité de Coordination – Procès-verbaux).
[163] Création d'une légation en Australie et en Nouvelle-Zélande, 28 June 1947 (CegeSoma, Archives Hervé de Gruben, AA699, Folder 72: Correspondance et notes diverses, 1945-1948).
[164] Brown, *A History of Canberra*, 38.
[165] Brown, *A History of Canberra*, 96-121.
[166] Loeffler, *The Architecture of Diplomacy*, 55.
[167] Boyd, *The Australian Ugliness*, 28.
[168] Letter from Verstraeten to Spaak, Création d'une Légation à Canberra, 22 July 1947 (DAB, Personnel Extérieur 2652 Ambassade Canberra).
[169] Letter from Verstraeten to Spaak, Représentation diplomatique et consulaire belge en Australie, 21 January 1949 (DAB, Personnel Extérieur 2652 Ambassade Canberra).
[170] Crown Lease, Australian Capital Territory. Leases (Special Purposes) Ordinance 1925-1936, 28 May 1951 (P&O Archives of the FPS Foreign Affairs, files Canberra).
[171] Letter from Querton to Spaak, Activité du poste en 1955, 20 February 1956 (DAB, Personnel Extérieur 2652 Ambassade Canberra).

172 Letter from Querton to Spaak, Activité du poste en 1955, 20 February 1956 (DAB, Personnel Extérieur 2652 Ambassade Canberra).
173 Tanner, "Fowell, Mansfield, Jarvis & Maclurcan," 261.
174 The Canberra Times, *Entertaining Tennis at the Embassy*, 12 January 1954, 2.
175 Letter from Stevens to Wigny, Relations diplomatiques entre l'Australie et la Belgique, 12 September 1958 (DAB, Personnel Extérieur 2652, Ambassade Canberra).
176 Décision proposée par le Conseil de Direction, en sa séance du 19 décembre 1958, et approuvée par Monsieur le Ministre, 22 January 1959 (DAB, Personnel Extérieur 2652, Ambassade Canberra).
177 Proceedings of the Belgian Chamber of Representatives, session of 19 May 1959, 16.
178 Letter from Stevens to Fowell, Mansfield & Maclurcan, Proposed Royal Belgian Chancellery Building Canberra, 25 October 1960 (Archives of the Belgian embassy in Canberra).
179 Letter from Stevens to Spaak, 9 January 1962 (Diplomatic Archive of Belgium, Personnel Extérieur 2652 Ambassade Canberra).
180 Letter from Stevens to Fowell, Mansfield & Maclurcan, Proposed Chancellery Building Canberra, 16 March 1960 (Archives of the Belgian embassy in Canberra).
181 Biltekin, "The Performance of Diplomacy," 260.
182 Letter from Stevens to Spaak, Activité du poste en 1961, 9 January 1962 (Diplomatic Archive of Belgium, Personnel Extérieur 2652 Ambassade Canberra).
183 The Sun, *Women's News, Fashion and Gossip*, 28 December 1962; Catholic Weekly, *Many Homes of An Ambassador's Wife*, 21 February 1963 (Diplomatic Archive of Belgium, Personnel Extérieur 2652 Ambassade Canberra).
184 Letter from Stevens to Spaak, 4 January 1963 (Diplomatic Archive of Belgium, Personnel Extérieur 2652, Ambassade Canberra).
185 Goldman, "Warsaw. Reconstruction as Propaganda," 135-155.
186 Goldman, "Warsaw. Reconstruction as Propaganda," 136.
187 Bellat, *Ambassades françaises du XXe Siècle*, 121.
188 Letter from Wauters to van Zeeland, Rapport de fin de mission, 2 June 1950 (DAB, Personnel Extérieur 2549, Ambassade Varsovie).
189 La Pénétration russe en Pologne, undated (DAB, 13.035 Belgique – Pologne, Notes diverses: Expansion russe, église et Etat, politique intérieure, etc. 1944-1955).
190 Kavtaradze and Tarkhanov, *Stalinist Architecture*, 44-79.
191 Kazakova, *Архитектура советской дипломатии*, 126-127.
192 Letter from de Meeûs d'Argenteuil to Spaak, Présentation des Lettres de créance, 24 May 1954 (DAB, Personnel Extérieur 2487, comte-ambassadeur Hadelin de Meeûs d'Argenteuil).
193 Erauw, *Koningin Elisabeth*, 140.
194 Aide-mémoire, 23 March 1955 (DAB, 13.035 Belgique–Pologne, Visite Reine Elisabeth, Varsovie, 1955).
195 Letter from de Meeûs d'Argenteuil to Spaak, Réception Reine Elisabeth, 2 May 1955 (DAB, 13.035 Belgique–Pologne, Visite Reine Elisabeth, Varsovie, 1955).
196 Proceedings of the Belgian Chamber of Representatives, session of 24 November 1955, 18-19.
197 Diary of Pierre Wigny, 13 November 1959, 4 (Archives Université Catholique de Louvain, Papiers Pierre Wigny, Mémoires M2 octobre 1959 à avril 1960, farde 5: Octobre-décembre 1959).
198 Proceedings of the Belgian Chamber of Representatives, session of 19 May 1959, 16.
199 Proceedings of the Belgian Chamber of Representatives, session of 20 May 1959, 14. Original citation in French, translated by the author.
200 Letter from de Meeûs d'Argenteuil to Vaes, 25 May 1962 (DAB, Personnel Extérieur 2487, comte-ambassadeur Hadelin de Meeûs d'Argenteuil).
201 Letter from de Meeûs d'Argenteuil to Spaak, Palais Mniszech. Règlement du Contentieux, 26 July 1963 (DAB, Personnel Extérieur 2549, Ambassade Varsovie).
202 Zaera-Polo, Trüby, Koolhaas et al., *Elements of Architecture, Book 7: Façade*, 46.
203 Olszewski, *An Outline History of Polish 20th Century Art and Architecture*, 90-91.
204 CEKOP, *Ambassade de Belgique à Varsovie*, 1962 (Archives of the Belgian Embassy in Warsaw).
205 Note à la Direction Générale A, 11 October 1962 (DAB, 18.914/1, Notes du Secrétaire général, 1960-1962).
206 De Witte, *De moord op Lumumba*, 205-254.

207 Préliminaires, Varsovie, undated (DAB, 18.678, Lumumba, Décès 1961 Manifestations – Protestations).
208 Calvocoressi, *World Politics since 1945*, 767.
209 *Le Soir*, La nouvelle ambassade des Etats-Unis à Varsovie truffée de micros, 3 November 1964, 5.
210 Cogels, *Souvenirs d'un diplomate*, 220.
211 Letter from de Meeûs d'Argenteuil to Vaes, 25 May 1962; Letter from van den Bosch to de Meeûs d'Argenteuil, 30 November 1962 (DAB, Personnel Extérieur 2487, comte-ambassadeur Hadelin de Meeûs d'Argenteuil).
212 Inventaris van de waardevolle voorwerpen, undated (P&O Archives of the FPS Foreign Affairs, Files Warsaw).
213 L'Éventail, *La Nouvelle Ambassade de Belgique à Varsovie: Le Palais Mniszech*, December 28 1962, 1 (P&O Archives of the FPS Foreign Affairs, Files Warsaw).
214 Letter from de Meeûs d'Argenteuil to Vaes, 25 May 1962 (DAB, Personnel Extérieur 2487, comte-ambassadeur Hadelin de Meeûs d'Argenteuil).
215 Letter from André de Meeûs d'Argenteuil to Hadelin de Meeûs d'Argenteuil, 10 June 1963 (Archives of the Royal Palace, the Secretariat of Queen Elisabeth).
216 Letter from de Meeûs d'Argenteuil to Vaes, 25 May 1962 (DAB, Personnel Extérieur 2487, comte-ambassadeur Hadelin de Meeûs d'Argenteuil). Original citation in French, translated by the author.
217 Frampton, *Building Brasilia*, 76.
218 Mendes, *O Cerrado de Casaca*, 201.
219 Niemeyer, *The Curves of Time*, 170.
220 Bergen, "Oscar Niemeyer," 34.
221 Letter from van Meerbeke to Larock, Nouvelle capitale fédérale. Critiques de M.E. Gudin – Ancien Ministre de Finances, 31 May 1957 (DAB, 13.094, Brésil, Série Générale 1957).
222 Letter from van Meerbeke to Larock, Voyage à Manáos et à Brasilia, 24 October 1957 (DAB, 13.094, Brésil, Série Générale 1957). Original citation in French, translated by the author.
223 Nooteboom and Stierli, *Brasilia-Chandigarh*, 111.
224 Wigny, *Tienjarenplan voor de economische en sociale ontwikkeling van Belgisch Kongo*, XXII-XXIII; De Meulder, "Het Office des Cités Africaines," 99.
225 Floré, "Wood Firm De Coene and the Modern Office," 7.
226 O.C.A. Centre de Léopoldville, Cité Pierre Wigny (Archives Université Catholique de Louvain, Papiers Pierre Wigny, C6: Ministre des Affaires étrangères 1958-1961 (II)).
227 Fiche Kanselarij, Bezitnemingsmodaliteiten (P&O Archives of the FPS Foreign Affairs, Files Brasília).
228 Diary of Pierre Wigny, 10 January 1960, 11 (Archives Université Catholique de Louvain, Papiers Pierre Wigny, Mémoires M2 octobre 1959 à avril 1960, farde 6: 4 janvier-21 février 1960).
229 Diary of Pierre Wigny, 10 January 1960, 10 (Archives Université Catholique de Louvain, Papiers Pierre Wigny, Mémoires M2 octobre 1959 à avril 1960, farde 6: 4 janvier-21 février 1960). Original citation in French, translated by the author.
230 Cogels, *Souvenirs d'un diplomate: du gâteau avec les duchesses?*, 226.
231 Diary of Pierre Wigny, 10 January 1960, 11 (Archives Université Catholique de Louvain, Papiers Pierre Wigny, Mémoires M2 octobre 1959 à avril 1960, farde 6: 4 janvier-21 février 1960).
232 De Robiano, *Le tour du monde insolite d'un diplomate belge*, 125.
233 Bertram, *Room for Diplomacy*, 352.
234 Letter from Lonnoy to Harmel, Ambassade à Brasilia, 14 February 1967 (Archives of the Belgian Embassy in Brasília).
235 De Kooning, "Een theater voor 'het open, onommuurde, handtastelijke leven.' Het paviljoen van Brazilië," 214-229.
236 Van Meel, *The European office*, 33.
237 Diary of Pierre Wigny, 10 January 1960, 11 (Archives Université Catholique de Louvain, Papiers Pierre Wigny, Mémoires M2 octobre 1959 à avril 1960, farde 6: 4 janvier-21 février 1960).
238 Letter from Lonnoy to Harmel, 14 February 1967 (Archives of the Belgian Embassy in Brasília).
239 Mendes, *O Cerrado de Casaca*, 201.
240 Mendes, *O Cerrado de Casaca*, 202-203.
241 De Ridder, *Geen winnaars in de Wetstraat*, 244.

[242] Martens and Vanden Eede, *De Noordwijk: Slopen en Wonen*, 12.
[243] Letter from Bihin to Spaak, Logement à Brasilia, 19 January 1965 (Archives of the Belgian Embassy in Brasília). Original citation in French, translated by the author.
[244] Letter from Lonnoy to Harmel, Brasilia, 8 October 1968 (Archives of the Belgian Embassy in Brasília).
[245] Brazil Herald, *Brasilia: Capital City...One of These Days*, 1 February 1969 (Archives of the Belgian Embassy in Brasília).
[246] Letter from Vanderlinden to Harmel, Transfert du Ministère des Relations Extérieures à Brasilia, 2 January 1970, (Archives of the Belgian Embassy in Brasília).
[247] Letter from Fikoff to Harmel, 11 May 1970 (Archives of the Belgian Embassy in Brasília). Original citation in French, translated by the author.
[248] Letter from Lonnoy to Harmel, Transfert à Brasilia, 16 January 1968 (Archives of the Belgian Embassy in Brasília).
[249] Letter from Lonnoy to the Inspection des Postes, 9 August 1967 (Archives of the Belgian Embassy in Brasília).
[250] Letter from Smolderen to Lonnoy, 14 May 1970 (Archives of the Belgian Embassy in Brasília). Original citation in French, translated by the author.
[251] Mindlin, *Modern Architecture in Brazil*, 74.
[252] Letter from Paternotte de la Vaillée to Harmel, Travaux à Brasilia, 20 December 1971 (Archives of the Belgian Embassy in Brasília).
[253] Letter from Paternotte de la Vaillée to Harmel, Construction à Brasilia 22 January 1971 (Archives of the Belgian Embassy in Brasília).
[254] Letter from Vanderlinden to Harmel, Luchtverkoeling residentie Brasilia, 13 November 1970 (Archives of the Belgian Embassy in Brasília).
[255] Letter from Robinnetterie AVH to Paternotte de La Vaillée, 28 May 1971 (Archives of the Belgian Embassy in Brasília).
[256] Letter from Paternotte de la Vaillée to Hubin, 6 July 1970 (Archives of the Belgian Embassy in Brasília).
[257] Manchete Magazine, *Embaixada da Bélgica*, August 1974, 88-90 (Archives of the Belgian Embassy in Brasília).
[258] Montero, *Burle Marx: The Lyrical Landscape*, 43.
[259] Montero, *Burle Marx: The Lyrical Landscape*, 201.
[260] Letter from Paternotte de la Vaillée to Harmel, Construction à Brasilia, 24 December 1971 (Archives of the Belgian Embassy in Brasília).
[261] Commission du Personnel des Services Extérieures, Séance du 14 juin 1926 (DAB, 14.177, Ministère des Affaires Etrangères, PV: Conseil de Direction, 1926-1963).
[262] Commission du Personnel des Services Extérieures, Séance du 14 juin 1926 (DAB, 14.177, Ministère des Affaires Etrangères, PV: Conseil de Direction, 1926-1963). Original citation in French, translated by the author.
[263] Commission du Personnel des Services Extérieures, Séance du 14 juin 1926 (DAB, 14.177, Ministère des Affaires Etrangères, PV: Conseil de Direction, 1926-1963).
[264] Coolsaet, Dujardin and Roosens, *Buitenlandse Zaken in België*, 282-288.
[265] Curriculum vitae de Son Altesse Eugène de Ligne (DAB, Personnel Extérieur 2353, Ambassadeur Prince Eugène de Ligne).
[266] Letter from Spaak to Holvoet, 27 June 1946 (DAB, Personnel Extérieur 2353, Ambassadeur Prince Eugène de Ligne).
[267] Calvocoressi, *World Politics since 1945*, 427-428.
[268] Abankwa-Meier-Klodt, *Delhi's Diplomatic Domains*, 13.
[269] Metcalf and Metcalf, *A Concise History of Modern India*, 222.
[270] Letter from Hupperts to Spaak, 9 September 1946 (DAB, Personnel Extérieur 2600, New Delhi (Inde) ambassade + Photo).
[271] Letter from Hupperts to Spaak, Ambassade à Delhi, 6 August 1947 (DAB, Personnel Extérieur 2600, New Delhi (Inde) ambassade + Photo). Original citation in French, translated by the author.

272 Murray, *A Handbook for Travellers in India, Burma and Ceylon*, 645.
273 Abankwa-Meier-Klodt, *Delhi's Diplomatic Domains*, 14.
274 Note pour Monsieur le Ministre, Immeuble de l'Ambassade à Delhi, 22 January 1953 (DAB, 14.074bis, Notes sur les immeubles de service à l'étranger et à Bruxelles, New Delhi).
275 De Robiano, *Le tour du monde insolite d'un diplomate belge*, 178.
276 Letter from de Ligne to Scheyven, 22 February 1955 (DAB, Personnel Extérieur 2353, Ambassadeur Prince Eugène de Ligne).
277 Philippe, *Le Val-Saint-Lambert*, 9.
278 Clausset, *Les cristalleries du Val Saint-Lambert*, 26.
279 Abankwa-Meier-Klodt, *Delhi's Diplomatic Domains*, 13.
280 Metcalf and Metcalf, *A Concise History of Modern India*, 235.
281 Prakash, *Chandigarh's Le Corbusier*, 9.
282 Kennedy, *The international ambitions of Mao and Nehru*, 150.
283 Letter from de Ligne to Spaak, 20 September 1947 (DAB, Personnel Extérieur 2353 Ambassadeur Prince Eugène de Ligne).
284 De Messemaeker, "Tussen Kasjmir en Congo. Belgisch-Indiase Politieke Contacten onder Nehru," 204.
285 Guerrieri, *Negotiating cultures*, 164.
286 Note pour Monsieur le Ministre, Construction d'un immeuble pour notre Ambassade à New Delhi, 23 November 1952 (DAB 14.074bis, Notes sur les immeubles de service à l'étranger et à Bruxelles, New Delhi).
287 Note pour Monsieur le Ministre, Construction d'un immeuble pour notre Ambassade à New Delhi, 23 November 1952 (DAB 14.074bis, Notes sur les immeubles de service à l'étranger et à Bruxelles, New Delhi).
288 Note pour Monsieur le Ministre, Construction d'un immeuble pour notre Ambassade à New Delhi, 23 November 1952 (DAB 14.074bis, Notes sur les immeubles de service à l'étranger et à Bruxelles, New Delhi). Original citation in French, translated by the author.
289 De Vylder, "Van Belgische Expansie tot Indiase Heropstanding," 57.
290 Mukherjee, "Drain of Wealth," 70-71.
291 Observations sur la note de A/I.P. du 9-2-1953, 11 February 1953 (DAB 14.074bis, Notes sur les immeubles de service à l'étranger et à Bruxelles, New Delhi). Original citation in French, translated by the author.
292 Observations sur la note de A/I.P. du 9-2-1953, 11 February 1953 (DAB 14.074bis, Notes sur les immeubles de service à l'étranger et à Bruxelles, New Delhi).
293 Abankwa-Meier-Klodt, *Delhi's Diplomatic Domains*, 235-236.
294 Abankwa-Meier-Klodt, *Delhi's Diplomatic Domains*, 82-85.
295 Hagströmer, "'Swedish Modern' meets international high politics," 171-174.
296 Perpetual Lease, 24 May 1954 (P&O Archives of the FPS Foreign Affairs, Files New Delhi, Complexe Résidence-Chancellerie).
297 Perpetual Lease, 24 May 1954 (P&O Archives of the FPS Foreign Affairs, Files New Delhi, Complexe Résidence-Chancellerie).
298 De Vylder, "Van Belgische Expansie tot Indiase Heropstanding," 57-58.
299 Proceedings of the Belgian Chamber of Representatives, session of 16 March 1955, 13.
300 Proceedings of the Belgian Chamber of Representatives, session of 16 March 1955, 13.
301 Proceedings of the Belgian Chamber of Representatives, session of 16 March 1955, 13.
302 Van de Maele, "Architectures of Bureaucracy," 479-480.
303 Letter from d'Aspremont-Lynden to Spaak, Activités du poste en 1956, 20 February 1957 (DAB, 13.125 Inde (New Delhi – Calcutta – Bombay) Série générale 1957).
304 Proceedings of the Belgian Chamber of Representatives, session of 28 January 1958, 18.
305 Note portant sur le développement des échanges commerciaux indo-belges et sur la question de l'envoi d'une mission belge économique en Inde (DAB, 13.125 Inde (New Delhi – Calcutta – Bombay) Série générale 1957).

306 De Messemaeker, "Tussen Kasjmir en Congo. Belgisch-Indiase Politieke Contacten onder Nehru," 208.
307 Letter from Goffart to Wigny, Scènes de violence contre la représentation belge en Inde, 17 February 1961 (DAB, 13.935, Belgique-Inde 1957-61, Mort Lumumba).
308 Telegram of Goffart to the Ministry, Dégâts à la Chancellerie, 4 March 1961 (DAB, 13.935, Belgique-Inde 1957-61, Mort Lumumba).
309 Telegram from Goffart to the Ministry, 16 February 1961 (DAB, 13.935, Belgique-Inde 1957-61, Mort Lumumba).
310 Loeffler, *The Architecture of Diplomacy*, 187.
311 Abankwa-Meier-Klodt, *Delhi's Diplomatic Domains*, 224.
312 De Robiano, *Le tour du monde insolite d'un diplomate belge*, 178.
313 Inspectierapport over de Ambassade van België te New Delhi, Inspectie van het Buitenlands Personeel, 16 November 1973 (DAB, 18.960/24, Rapports d'Inspection des Postes Diplomatiques et Consulaires, New Delhi).
314 Interview with Cristina Funes-Noppen, 11 November 2019, Brussels.
315 Inspectierapport over de Ambassade van België te New Delhi, Inspectie van het Buitenlands Personeel, 16 November 1973 (DAB, 18.960/24, Rapports d'Inspection des Postes Diplomatiques et Consulaires, New Delhi).
316 Interview with Cristina Funes-Noppen, 11 November 2019, Brussels.
317 Coolsaet, Dujardin and Roosens, *Buitenlandse Zaken in België*, 379.
318 Comité de Coordination, Session of 10 March 1978 (DAB, 18.913/4: 1978-1980, Ministère des Affaires étrangères, Comité de Coordination – procès-verbaux); Comité de Coordination, Session of 22 May 1981 (DAB, 18.913/5: 1981-1984, Ministère des Affaires étrangères, Comité de Coordination – procès-verbaux).
319 Office belge du Commerce Extérieur, *Inde*, Bruxelles: Office belge du Commerce Extérieur, 1981, 37.
320 Interview with Philippe Falisse, 9 May 2018, Neupré.
321 Memo titled 'Bouw van nieuwe ambassade in New Delhi', undated (KADOC, BE/942855/1229 Archives of Leo Tindemans, 1394/6, dossier betreffende het officieel bezoek van Tindemans aan Korea, Thailand en Indië van 8 tot 19 januari 1983 en de diplomatieke conferentie in Bangkok op 14 en 15 januari 1983).
322 Comité de Coordination, Session of 13 April 1984 (DAB, 18.913/5: 1981-1984, Ministère des Affaires étrangères, Comité de Coordination – procès-verbaux).
323 Inspectierapport over de Ambassade van België te New Delhi, Inspectie van het Buitenlands Personeel, April 1979 (DAB, 18.960/24 Rapports d'Inspection des Postes Diplomatiques et Consulaires, New Delhi).
324 Nota voor de Inspectie der Diplomatieke en Consulaire Posten, 6 June 1978 (DAB, 3018 Luc Piot).
325 Federal Public Service Foreign Affairs, Foreign Trade and Development Cooperation, *Art in the residence of the Belgian ambassador in New Delhi*, 1.
326 Gujral, *A Brush with Life*, 221.
327 Interview with Mark Eyskens, Heverlee, 8 September 2021.
328 Sending states such as Bhutan (1974), Hungary (1978), Italy (1989), Ghana (1992), Nigeria (1995), Sudan (1996), Bangladesh (1999) and Palestine (2012) hired Indian architects to design their diplomatic premises.
329 Levine, *The Architecture of Frank Lloyd Wright*, 137-140.
330 Gujral, *A Brush with Life*, 135.
331 Gujral, *A Brush with Life*, 135.
332 Gujral, *A Brush with Life*, 216.
333 Interview with Philippe Falisse, 9 May 2018, Neupré.
334 Gujral, *A Brush with Life*, 221.
335 Gujral, *Matters of Discretion*, 51-202.
336 Gujral, *A Brush with Life*, 96.
337 D'Alfonso, *Warm modernity: Indian architecture building democracy*, 130-163.
338 Scriver and Srivastava, *India: Modern Architectures in History*, 242-274.

339 Frampton, *The Work of Charles Correa*, 193-198.
340 Steele, *The Complete Architecture of Balkrishna Doshi*, 133.
341 Khanna, *The Modern Architecture of New Delhi*, 106.
342 Journal of Arts & Ideas, *Architecture to me is about construction of images and associations, interview with Satish Gujral*, 7, April-June 1984, 46.
343 Journal of Arts & Ideas, *Architecture to me is about construction of images and associations, interview with Satish Gujral*, 7, April-June 1984, 46.
344 Letter from Hollants Van Loocke to Tindemans, Onderhouds- en andere kosten en uitgaven nieuw Ambassadecomplex Chanakyapuri, 4 October 1983 (DAB, Personnel Extérieur 3110, Jan Hollants Van Loocke).
345 Falisse, *Inspirations:*, unnumbered pages, chapter devoted to the memories of Christian Fellens.
346 Mimar, *Architecture in Development, Building as Image: Gujral's Sculptural Belgian Embassy in New Delhi*, 12, 1984, 13.
347 Journal of Arts & Ideas, *Architecture to me is about construction of images and associations, interview with Satish Gujral*, 7, April-June 1984, 42.
348 Hollants Van Loocke, *Vogelvrij: Herinneringen van een diplomaat*, 184.
349 "Painter-Muralist Satish Gujral Draws Flak for Turning Architect," India Today, accessed 19 June 2021, https://www.indiatoday.in/magazine/living/story/19831115-painter-muralist-satish-gujral-draws-flak-for-turning-architect-771201-2013-07-15.
350 Asher, *Architecture of Mughal India*, 45.
351 Goldhagen, *Louis Kahn's Situated Modernism*, 192.
352 Journal of Arts & Ideas, *Architecture to me is about construction of images and associations, interview with Satish Gujral*, 7, April-June 1984, 46.
353 Shih and Liou, "Louis Kahn's Tectonic Poetics," 284.
354 Inspectierapport over de Ambassade van België te New Delhi, Inspectie van het Buitenlands Personeel, April 1979 (DAB, 18.960/24 Rapports d'Inspection des Postes Diplomatiques et Consulaires, New Delhi).
355 Gottwald, "A Sculptural and Sensual Embassy for Belgium," 118.
356 G.R. Berridge, *Diplomacy: Theory and Practice*, 107.
357 Lukowski and Zawadzki, *A Concise History of Poland*, 270-280.
358 Connah, *Writing Architecture: Fantômas, Fragments, Fictions*, 306.
359 Connah, *Writing Architecture: Fantômas, Fragments, Fictions*, 302.
360 Khanna, *The Modern Architecture of New Delhi*, 130-131.
361 Gujral, *A Brush with Life*, 221.
362 Interview with Philippe Falisse, 9 May 2018, Neupré.
363 Coolsaet, Dujardin and Roosens, *Buitenlandse Zaken in België*, 365.
364 Delcorps, *Dans les coulisses de la diplomatie*, 540-542.
365 Letter from Hollants Van Loocke to Roelants, 13 April 1983 (KADOC, BE/942855/1229 Archives of Leo Tindemans, 1394, dossier betreffende het officieel bezoek van Tindemans aan Korea, Thailand en Indië van 8 tot 19 januari 1983 en de diplomatieke conferentie in Bangkok op 14 en 15 januari 1983).
366 Gujral, *A Brush with Life*, 221-222.
367 Gujral, *A Brush with Life*, 222.
368 Gujral, *A Brush with Life*, 222.
369 Gujral, *A Brush with Life*, 222.
370 New Delhi – Complexe Résidence et Chancellerie, 29 March 1984 (P&O Archives of the FPS Foreign Affairs, files New Delhi).
371 Rapport d'Inspection, Ambassade de Belgique à New Delhi, April 1984 (DAB, 18.960/24 Rapports d'Inspection des Postes Diplomatiques et Consulaires, New Delhi).
372 Rapport d'Inspection, Ambassade de Belgique à New Delhi, April 1984 (DAB, 18.960/24 Rapports d'Inspection des Postes Diplomatiques et Consulaires, New Delhi).
373 Rapport d'Inspection, Ambassade de Belgique à New Delhi, April 1984 (DAB, 18.960/24 Rapports d'Inspection des Postes Diplomatiques et Consulaires, New Delhi).
374 Interview with Philippe Falisse, 9 May 2018, Neupré.

375 Memo titled 'Bouw van nieuwe ambassade in New Delhi' (KADOC, BE/942855/1229 Archives of Leo Tindemans, 1394/6, dossier betreffende het officieel bezoek van Tindemans aan Korea, Thailand en Indië van 8 tot 19 januari 1983 en de diplomatieke conferentie in Bangkok op 14 en 15 januari 1983)
376 Rapport d'Inspection, Ambassade de Belgique à New Delhi, April 1984 (DAB, 18.960/24 Rapports d'Inspection des Postes Diplomatiques et Consulaires, New Delhi).
377 Rapport d'Inspection, Ambassade de Belgique à New Delhi, April 1984 (DAB, 18.960/24 Rapports d'Inspection des Postes Diplomatiques et Consulaires, New Delhi).
378 Hollants Van Loocke, *Vogelvrij: Herinneringen van een diplomaat*, 184; The English translation has been derived from Falisse, *Inspirations: The architectural marvel of Satish Gujral and memories of seven ambassadors*, unnumbered pages.
379 Gujral, *A Brush with Life*, 223.
380 Gujral, *A Brush with Life*, 224.
381 Interview with Philippe Falisse, 9 May 2018, Neupré.
382 Loeffler, *The Architecture of Diplomacy*, 141.
383 Design and build, renovation and extension of the Belgian Embassy in New Delhi, 18 April 2014 (P&O Archives of the FPS Foreign Affairs, files New Delhi).
384 Tindemans, *Krachtlijnen van de buitenlandse politiek van België: Toespraken*, 50-53.
385 Belgische Ministerie van Buitenlandse Zaken, *Voor een Belgisch Aziëbeleid*, 5.
386 Gazet van Antwerpen, *Minister Leo Tindemans over buitenlandse betrekkingen*, 31 October-1 November 1983, 9.
387 Belgische Ministerie van Buitenlandse Zaken, *Voor een Belgisch Aziëbeleid*, 107.
388 Programme for the official visit of his excellency Mr. Leo Tindemans Minister for External Relations 15th to 19th January 1983 (KADOC, BE/942855/1229 Archives of Leo Tindemans, 1394/6, dossier betreffende het officieel bezoek van Tindemans aan Korea, Thailand en Indië van 8 tot 19 januari 1983 en de diplomatieke conferentie in Bangkok op 14 en 15 januari 1983).
389 Schelfhout, *Albert van België: Gangmaker van de Belgische Export*, 29.
390 The Indian Express, *Belgian Award for Satish Gujral*, 11 November 1983.
391 Belgische Ministerie van Buitenlandse Zaken, *Voor een Belgisch Aziëbeleid*, 107 (DAB, 18.899/26, Belgique-Inde).
392 Frey and Frey, *The History of Diplomatic Immunity*, 479.
393 Delcorps, *Dans les coulisses de la diplomatie*, 493.
394 Rapport d'Inspection, Ambassade de Belgique à New Delhi, April 1984 (DAB, 18.960/24 Rapports d'Inspection des Postes Diplomatiques et Consulaires, New Delhi). Original citation in French, translated by the author.
395 Falisse, *Inspirations*, unnumbered pages, section of Philippe Falisse.
396 "Painter-Muralist Satish Gujral Draws Flak for Turning Architect," India Today, accessed 19 June 2021, https://www.indiatoday.in/magazine/living/story/19831115-painter-muralist-satish-gujral-draws-flak-for-turning-architect-771201-2013-07-15.
397 "Painter-Muralist Satish Gujral Draws Flak for Turning Architect," India Today, accessed 19 June 2021, https://www.indiatoday.in/magazine/living/story/19831115-painter-muralist-satish-gujral-draws-flak-for-turning-architect-771201-2013-07-15.
398 Gottwald, "A Sculptural and Sensual Embassy for Belgium," 117.
399 Mimar, *Architecture in Development, Building as Image: Gujral's Sculptural Belgian Embassy in New Delhi*, 12, 1984, 11.
400 L'architecture d'aujourd'hui, *Trois ambassades à New Delhi*, 247, 1986, 64.
401 Connah, *Writing Architecture: Fantômas, Fragments, Fictions*, 306.
402 Pennewaert, "Belgische Ambassade – New Delhi: Alleen België zwijgt," 18-25.
403 Pennewaert, "Belgische Ambassade-New Delhi: Alleen België zwijgt," 18.
404 Comité de Coordination, Session of 25 November 1983 (DAB, 18.913/5: 1981-1984, Ministère des Affaires étrangères, Comité de Coordination – procès-verbaux).
405 Comité de Coordination, Session of 25 November 1983 (DAB, 18.913/5: 1981-1984, Ministère des Affaires étrangères, Comité de Coordination – procès-verbaux).
406 Yizraeli, *Politics and society in Saudi Arabia*, 142-147.

407 Comité de Coordination, Session of 12 March 1982 (DAB, 18.913/5: 1981-1984, Ministère des Affaires étrangères, Comité de Coordination – procès-verbaux).
408 Cardenas, "The Diplomatic Quarters in Riyadh," 394-395.
409 Programme pour la construction d'un complexe Ambassade à Riyadh, 1983 (P&O Archives of the FPS Foreign Affairs, files Riyadh).
410 Programme pour la construction d'un complexe Ambassade à Riyadh, 1983 (P&O Archives of the FPS Foreign Affairs, files Riyadh).
411 Programme pour la construction d'un complexe Ambassade à Riyadh, 1983 (P&O Archives of the FPS Foreign Affairs, files Riyadh). Original citation in French, translated by the author.
412 Inventaire de la résidence 2007 (P&O Archives of the FPS Foreign Affairs, files Riyadh).
413 Comité de Coordination, Session of 15 June 1984 (DAB, 18.913/5: 1981-1984, Ministère des Affaires étrangères, Comité de Coordination – procès-verbaux).
414 Letter from the Secretary-General to the Court of Audit, 15 November 1926 (National Archives of Belgium, Rekenhof, BE-A0510/ I 572, 1908 dossier inzake de opvraging door het Ministerie van Buitenlandse Zaken van stukken met betrekking tot eigendomstitels van gebouwen in het buitenland, 1926-1927).
415 Belgian Embassy in Japan, *Exhibition 90 Years Belgian Embassy in Kojimachi*, panel 1922-1928 (forwarded to me by the Belgian Embassy in Japan).
416 De Bassompierre, *Dix-huit ans d'ambassade au Japon*, 124. Original citation in French, translated by the author.
417 Telegram of Croy, n° 79, 14 August 1942 (DAB, Personnel Extérieur 2607, Ambassade Tokyo).
418 Letter from Daufresne de la Chevalerie to Spaak, 3 April 1946 (DAB, Personnel Extérieur 2607, Ambassade Tokyo).
419 Letter from Winders to van Zeeland, Reconstruction de l'Ambassade à Tokyo, 21 April 1953 (CIVA, Archives Max Winders, Box 6: Washington, New York, Tokyo, Palais Egmont).
420 Télégramme de Bassompierre, 8 September 1923 (DAB, Personnel Extérieur 1943/I Légation Tokyo).
421 Note pour A/Personnel: Reconstruction de l'Ambassade à Tokyo, 3 March 1953 (DAB, 14.074bis, Notes sur les immeubles de service à l'étranger et à Bruxelles, Tokyo).
422 Belgian Embassy in Japan, *Exhibition 90 Years Belgian Embassy in Kojimachi*, panel 1960-2007 (forwarded to me by the Belgian Embassy in Japan).
423 Cogels, *Souvenirs d'un diplomate*, 265.
424 Flath, *The Japanese Economy*, 110.
425 Sacchi, *Tokyo: City and Architecture*, 28.
426 Meyhöfer, *Contemporary Japanese Architects*, 36.
427 Tindemans, *Een politiek testament*, 320-321.
428 Hoflack, *De premier*, 234.
429 Proceedings of the Belgian Chamber of Representatives, session of 5 June 1987, 25.
430 Takenaka Kōmuten, *Belgian Embassy Development Project Tokyo*, 1 October 1985, 61 (P&O Archives of the FPS Foreign Affairs, files Tokyo).
431 Sacchi, *Tokyo: City and Architecture*, 218.
432 Sacchi, *Tokyo: City and Architecture*, 70-71.
433 Proceedings of the Belgian Chamber of Representatives, session of 6 November 1989, 45.
434 De Standaard, *België breekt ambassade in Tokyo af*, 22 January 2005, 12.
435 Comité de Coordination, Session of 16 June 1989 (DAB, 18.913/7: 1989-1992, Ministère des Affaires étrangères, Comité de Coordination – Procès-verbaux); Ibidem, Session of 17 January 1997 (DAB, 18.913/7: 1989-1992, Ministère des Affaires étrangères, Comité de Coordination – Procès-verbaux).
436 Mouton, 'Het geld is op' *De financiële putten van België*, 55-57.
437 De Morgen, *Sale and lease back gebouwen kost overheid 1,7 miljard euro*, 5 February 2010; Mouton, 'Het geld is op' *De financiële putten van België*, 72.
438 De Standaard, *Cofinimmo koopt Egmont I en terrein voor Egmont II*, 15 May 2004, 26.
439 Jan De Bock, *Belgische Diplomatie: Doelstellingen, Middelen, Methode*, 14 March 2002, 15 (AMSAB, Archives of Rik Coolsaet, yet to be inventoried).
440 Loeffler, *The Architecture of Diplomacy*, 260-280.

441 Mail from DGA to Colot, A41-N-RIH/Derde Woning Ambassadecompound, 3 March 2000 (P&O Archives of the FPS Foreign Affairs, files Riyadh).
442 Lease Contract, 1 July 2000 (P&O Archives of the FPS Foreign Affairs, files Riyadh).
443 Mail from A41 to the Belgian Embassy in Bangkok, 5 October 1999 (P&O Archives of the FPS Foreign Affairs, files Bangkok).
444 Mail from Vanhouche to A41, Waardeschatting complex, 19 May 2000 (P&O Archives of the FPS Foreign Affairs, files Bangkok).
445 Mail from Vaesen to A41, Compound notre ambassade à Bangkok, 23 May 2000 (P&O Archives of the FPS Foreign Affairs, files Bangkok). Original citation in French, translated by the author.
446 Louis Michel as cited in Stevens, *Belgium's Most Beautiful Embassies*, 3.
447 Comité de Coordination, Session of 4 January 2002 (DAB, 18.913/10: 2002-2003, Ministère des Affaires étrangères, Comité de Coordination – Procès-verbaux).
448 Belgian Chamber of Representatives, Committee for Foreign Affairs, Morning Session of 19 February 2002, 22.
449 Coolsaet, Dujardin and Roosens, *Buitenlandse Zaken in België*, 398.
450 Colliers Halifax, Embassy of Belgium – Tokyo, Redevelopment Study, August 2005, 3 (P&O Archives of the FPS Foreign Affairs, files Tokyo).
451 Het Belang van Limburg, *Verkoop ambassade Tokio nog voor dit jaar*, 19 September 2006.
452 Comité de Coordination, Session of 19 April 1996 (DAB, 18.913/8: 1993-1996, Ministère des Affaires étrangères, Comité de Coordination – Procès-verbaux).
453 Project Agreement between the Kingdom of Belgium and Mitsubishi Estate/Takenaka Corporation, 14 December 2006, 58 (P&O Archives of the FPS Foreign Affairs, files Tokyo).
454 Colliers Halifax, *Embassy of Belgium–Tokyo, Redevelopment Study*, August 2005 (P&O Archives of the FPS Foreign Affairs, files Tokyo).
455 Belgian Chamber of Representatives, Committee for Foreign Affairs, 5 July 2006, 3-4; Ibidem, 24 April 2007, 14-15.
456 Belgian Chamber of Representatives, Committee for Foreign Affairs, Afternoon Session 9 January 2007, 34.
457 Meeting Minutes of the Work Session, 26 February 2008 (P&O Archives of the FPS Foreign Affairs, Files Tokyo).
458 Belgian Embassy in Japan, *Exhibition 90 Years Belgian Embassy in Kojimachi*, panel 2009-present (forwarded to me by the Belgian Embassy in Japan).
459 Willis, *Form follows finance*, 182.
460 Loeffler, *The Architecture of Diplomacy*, 234.
461 Meeting Minutes of the Work Session in Brussels, 25 June 2008 (P&O Archives of the FPS Foreign Affairs, files Tokyo).
462 Embassy of Belgium, Nibancho 5, Chiyoda-ku, Tokyo Japan, Architectural practice M. & J-M. Jaspers – J. Eyers & Partners, 8 May 2006, 34 (P&O Archives of the FPS Foreign Affairs, Files Tokyo).
463 Letter from Lorent to AWEX, Déménagement des bureaux de l'Ambassade de Belgique à Bangkok, 24 March 2000 (P&O Archives of the FPS Foreign Affairs, files Bangkok).
464 Gimeno-Martinez, *Design and National Identity*, 121-125.
465 Belgian Chamber of Representatives, Committee for Foreign Affairs, Session of 9 January 2007, 35.
466 De Standaard, *Ambassade van ons land is Japans en Belgisch*, 9 April 2010, 15.
467 Mail from Rogge to Takenaka, Choice of the Moca Creme stone, 17 June 2008 (P&O Archives of the FPS Foreign Affairs, files Tokyo).
468 Mail from Goemans to Bostem, Tokyo – Mission Shanghai, 16 June 2008 (P&O Archives of the FPS Foreign Affairs, files Tokyo).
469 Mail from the Belgian Embassy in Tokyo to Stevens, 16 June 2008 (P&O Archives of the FPS Foreign Affairs, files Tokyo).
470 Mail from Leneau to Rogge, Tokyo – Mission Shanghai, 16 June 2008 (P&O Archives of the FPS Foreign Affairs, files Tokyo). Original citation in French, translated by the author.
471 De Standaard, *Ambassade van ons land is Japans en Belgisch*, 9 April 2010, 15.
472 De Standaard, *Ambassade van ons land is Japans en Belgisch*, 9 April 2010, 15.

473 Meeting Minutes of the Work Session, 26 February 2008 (P&O Archives of the FPS Foreign Affairs, files Tokyo).
474 Mail from Stevens to Buyck, Ontwerp brief aan MTOB, 16 June 2008 (P&O Archives of the FPS Foreign Affairs, files Tokyo).
475 Letter from De Gucht to Danno, Reconstruction of the Belgian Embassy in Tokyo, 24 June 2008 (P&O Archives of the FPS Foreign Affairs, files Tokyo).
476 Mail from Rogge to Chanati, 21 February 2008 (P&O Archives of the FPS Foreign Affairs, files Tokyo).
477 Davidts, *Bouwen voor de kunst?*, 91.
478 Dauwe, De Geest and Janssen, "Kunst in de Belgische ambassades," 1.
479 Dauwe, De Geest and Janssen, "Kunst in de Belgische ambassades," 11.
480 Dauwe, De Geest and Janssen, "Kunst in de Belgische ambassades," 10.
481 Davidts, *Bouwen voor de kunst?*, 94.
482 Het Belang van Limburg, *Premier Leterme opent nieuwe ambassade in Tokio*, 9 April 2010, 5.
483 Gazet van Antwerpen, Ambassade bestand tegen zware aardbeving, 9 April 2010, 6.
484 Het Laatste Nieuws, *Premier opent in Japan ambassade van 25 miljoen euro*, 9 April 2010, 13.
485 De Standaard, *Belgische ambassadeurs moeten meer aan economische belangen denken*, 8 April 2010, 16.
486 Lagae, "Lambrichs, Marcel," 385-386.
487 Cogels, *Souvenirs d'un diplomate*, 208.
488 Interview with Mark Eyskens, Heverlee, 8 September 2021.
489 Comité de Coordination, Session of 19 February 1988 (DAB, 18.913/6: 1985-1988, Ministère des Affaires étrangères, Comité de Coordination – Procès-verbaux).
490 Nota voor de heer Secretaris-Generaal, Kinshasa – terrein Ambassadecomplex, 19 January 1990 (P&O Archives of the FPS Foreign Affairs, files Kinshasa).
491 Telex of the Belgian Embassy in Kinshasa to Tindemans, undated (P&O Archives of the FPS Foreign Affairs, files Kinshasa).
492 Hendrickx, "Belgium and Mobutu's Zaïre: Analysis of an Eventful Era," 86.
493 Toulier, Lagae and Gemoets, *Kinshasa: Architecture et paysage urbains*, 7.
494 Engels, *De Clan Reynders*, 163.
495 Het Nieuwsblad, *België houdt uitverkoop in Congo*, 28 July 2014, 4.
496 Jenssen, *Representativt: Buildings in the Foreign Service*, 77.
497 Comité de Coordination, Session of 19 January 1996 (DAB, 18.913/8: 1993-1996, Ministère des Affaires étrangères, Comité de Coordination – Procès-verbaux).
498 Gazet van Antwerpen, *Nederland sluit consulaat in Antwerpen*, 1 July 2013, 11.
499 Klep and Coolsaet, "Na de Koude Oorlog: Het veiligheidsbeleid, 1989-2010," 262-289.
500 Belgian Chamber of Representatives, Committee for Foreign Affairs, Session of 28 May 2013, 24.
501 Nzuzi, *Kinshasa: Planification et aménagement*, 34-36.
502 Fumunzanza Muketa, *Kinshasa: d'un quartier à l'autre*, 84-101.
503 Toulier, Lagae and Gemoets, *Kinshasa: Architecture et paysage urbains*, 82.
504 Saah, "How has China's economic engagement, as tool of soft power in the Democratic Republic of Congo, evolved?," 50.
505 De Standaard, *Ambassade Cha Cha*, 2 February 2019, 28.
506 Toulier, Lagae and Gemoets, *Kinshasa: Architecture et paysage urbains*, 13.
507 De Standaard, *Jacht op het geld van Sabena*, 27 March 2012, 16.
508 De Morgen, *Congolezen in Brussel betogen tegen Kabila-bezoek Reynders*, 24 March 2012, 3.
509 Engels, *De Clan Reynders*, 164.
510 De Tijd, *Fontinoy voorzitter af bij NMBS*, 13 March 2021, 11; Gazet van Antwerpen, *Voormalige rechterhand Didier Reynders beschuldigd van aanvaarden smeergeld*, 5 February 2021, 11.
511 Engels, *De Clan Reynders*, 164.
512 Engels, *De Clan Reynders*, 166.
513 Letter from Couchard to the Federal Public Service Finance, Achat de terrains et maisons à Kinshasa, 11 June 2012 (P&O Archives of the FPS Foreign Affairs, files Kinshasa).

514 Letter from Achten to Reynders, 24 March 2015 (P&O Archives of the FPS Foreign Affairs, files Kinshasa).
515 Letter from Reynders to Chambre de Commerce Belgo-Congolaise-Luxembourgeoise, 13 April 2015 (P&O Archives of the FPS Foreign Affairs, files Kinshasa).
516 Engels, *De Clan Reynders*, 165.
517 Het Laatste Nieuws/Mechelen-Lier, *Onderneming van het Jaar lonkt naar Afrika*, 10 October 2013, 17.
518 Het Laatste Nieuws/Mechelen-Lier, *Onderneming van het Jaar lonkt naar Afrika*, 10 October 2013, 17.
519 Council of State, Ruling n° 223.822, 11 June 2013, 3. Original citation in French, translated by the author.
520 De Morgen, *Bouw ambassade België in Congo ligt stil*, 21 June 2013, 6.
521 Council of State, Ruling n° 223.822, 11 June 2013, 12.
522 De Tijd, *Bouwopdracht ambassade in Congo is voor Willemen*, 13 November 2013, 16.
523 Engels, *De Clan Reynders*, 168.
524 Engels, *De Clan Reynders*, 170.
525 De Standaard, *Spits of botte bijl*, 20 April 2013, 10; La Libre Belgique, *Quand l'architecture s'approprie le durable*, 14 April 2011, 3.
526 Loeffler, *The Architecture of Diplomacy*, 260-280; Bertram, *Room for Diplomacy*, 447.
527 Engels, *De Clan Reynders*, 170.
528 Monaville, "A Distinctive Ugliness. Colonial Memory in Belgium," 74.
529 Engels, *De Clan Reynders*, 170; "De favoriete bouwpromotor van Bart De Wever (1): Samen aan de feestdis," *Apache*, accessed 4 July 2022, https://www.apache.be/2017/11/16/de-favoriete-bouwpromotor-van-bart-de-wever-1-samen-aan-de-feestdis.
530 Le Soir/Namur Luxembourg, *Une nouvelle ambassade à Kinshasa: La Belgique veut garder son rang*, 27 August 2014, 11.
531 Belga News Agency, *La future ambassade Bénélux à Kinshasa, "symbole fort" des relations belgo-congolaises*, 26 August 2014. Original citation in French, translated by the author.
532 Het Nieuwsblad/Mechelen-Lier, *Willemen Groep bouwt in Congo Belgisch-Nederlandse ambassade*, 17 July 2014, 24.
533 Het Nieuwsblad/Mechelen-Lier, *Willemen Groep bouwt in Congo Belgisch-Nederlandse ambassade*, 17 July 2014, 24.
534 Federale Overheidsdienst Buitenlandse Zaken, Buitenlandse Handel en Ontwikkelingssamenwerking, *Kunst in de Belgische ambassade in Kinshasa*, 7.
535 Federale Overheidsdienst Buitenlandse Zaken, Buitenlandse Handel en Ontwikkelingssamenwerking, *Kunst in de Belgische ambassade in Kinshasa*, 8.
536 De Standaard, *Te koop: Belgische ambassade in Washington*, 10 August 2019, 29.
537 De Standaard, *Te koop: Belgische ambassade in Washington*, 10 August 2019, 29.
538 La Meuse, *L'ambassade belge aux USA vendue!*, 14 December 2019, 20.
539 Special Specifications. Full Design and Build of the new Belgian Chancellery in Washington, D.C., 18 May 2018, 20 (P&O Archives of the FPS Foreign Affairs, files Washington, D.C.).

Bibliography

ARCHIVAL SOURCES

Amsab-ISG, Ghent
- Archives of Camille Huysmans (625)
- Archives of Rik Coolsaet

Archives of Belgian Embassies
- Archival records of the Belgian Embassy in Brasília
- Archival records of the Belgian Embassy in Canberra
- Archival records of the Belgian Embassy in Washington, D.C.
- Archival records of the Belgian Embassy in Warsaw

Archives of the Royal Palace, Brussels
- Archives of the Secretariat of Queen Elisabeth

Archives of the Université Catholique de Louvain, Louvain-la-Neuve
- Archives Paul van Zeeland, BE A4006 FD CEHEC-A19
- Archives Pierre Wigny, BE A4006 FD CEHEC-A20

Belgian Chamber of Representatives
- Minutes of the Committee for Foreign Affairs
  - Session of 19 February 2002
  - Session of 5 July 2006
  - Session of 9 January 2007
  - Session of 24 April 2007
  - Session of 28 May 2013
- Proceedings of the Parliamentary Sessions
  - Session of 16 March 1955
  - Session of 24 November 1955
  - Session of 28 January 1958
  - Session of 19 May 1959
  - Session of 20 May 1959
  - Session of 5 June 1987
  - Session of 6 November 1989

CegeSoma, Brussels
- Archives Hérve de Gruben, AA699

CIVA, Brussels
- Archives Max Winders

Council of State
- Ruling n° 223.822 of 11 June 2013

Diplomatic Archive of Belgium (DAB), Brussels
- 1943: Personnel Extérieur Légation Tokyo
- 2353: Personnel Extérieur Ambassade Prince Eugène de Ligne
- 2416: Personnel Extérieur Ambassade Washington

- 2487: Personnel Extérieur Comte-Ambassadeur Hadelin de Meeûs d'Argenteuil
- 2549: Personnel Extérieur Ambassade Varsovie
- 2600: Personnel Extérieur New Delhi (Inde) ambassade + photo
- 2607: Personnel Extérieur Ambassade Tokyo.
- 2652: Personnel Extérieur Ambassade Canberra
- 3018: Personnel Extérieur Luc Piot
- 3110: Personnel Extérieur Jan Hollants Van Loocke
- 12.202: Ordres de service
- 13.035: Belgique-Pologne, Notes diverses, 1944-1955
- 13.094: Brésil, Série Générale 1957
- 13.125: Indes (New Delhi – Calcutta – Bombay) Série générale, 1957
- 13.935: Belgique–Inde 1957-61, Mort Lumumba
- 14.074bis: Notes sur les immeubles à l'étranger et à Bruxelles
- 14.177: Ministère des Affaires Etrangères, PV: Conseil de Direction, 1926-1963
- 18.434: Papiers Robert Silvercruys
- 18.678: Lumumba – Décès 1961 Manifestations – Protestations
- 18.899/26 Belgique-Inde
- 18.913: Ministère des Affaires étrangères, Comité de Coordination – procès-verbaux
- 18.914: Ministère des Affaires Etrangères – Cabinet du Secrétaire Général. Correspondance
- 18.960/24: Rapports d'Inspection des Postes Diplomatiques et Consulaires, New Delhi

FelixArchief, Antwerp
- Architect Hugo Van Kuyck, BE SA 98026

Hagley Museum & Library
- John McShain papers (2000)

KADOC, Leuven
- Archives of Leo Tindemans, BE/942855/1229

Liberal Archive, Ghent
- Archives Paul Kronacker & Mary Kronacker-Good (8)

National Archives of Belgium
- Rekenhof, BE-A0510/ I 572
- Unpublished memoirs Pierre Wigny, BE-A0510/ I 591
- Verzameling De Coene NV, BE-A0516/913
- Minutes of the Ministerial Council
  - Session of 9 April 1954

Nationaal Archief, The Hague
- 2.05.118, Dutch Ministry of Foreign Affairs: Code Archive 1955-1964, 29766

Personnel & Organisation Archives, Federal Public Service Foreign Affairs, Brussels
- Files Bangkok
- Files Brasília
- Files Canberra
- Files Kinshasa
- Files New Delhi
- Files Riyadh
- Files Tokyo
- Files Warsaw
- Files Washington, D.C.

MEDIA OUTLETS

Belga News Agency, la future ambassade Bénélux à Kinshasa, "symbole fort" des relations belgo-congolaises, 26 August 2014

De Morgen, *Sale and lease back gebouwen kost overheid 1,7 miljard euro*, 5 February 2010

De Morgen, *Congolezen in Brussel betogen tegen Kabila-bezoek Reynders*, 24 March 2012, 3

De Morgen, *Bouw ambassade België in Congo ligt stil*, 21 June 2013, 6

De Standaard, *De bouw van een nieuwe kanselarij te Washington. Camille Huysmans is nieuwsgierig*, 8 August 1953, 2

De Standaard, *Cofinimmo koopt Egmont I en terrein voor Egmont II*, 15 May 2004, 26

De Standaard, *België breekt ambassade in Tokyo af*, 22 January 2005, 12

De Standaard, *Belgische ambassadeurs moeten meer aan economische belangen denken*, 8 April 2010, 16

De Standaard, *Ambassade van ons land is Japans en Belgisch*, 9 April 2010, 15

De Standaard, *Jacht op het geld van Sabena*, 27 March 2012, 16

De Standaard, *Spits of botte bijl*, 20 April 2013, 10

De Standaard, *Ambassade Cha Cha*, 2 February 2019, 28

De Standaard, *Te koop: Belgische ambassade in Washington*, 10 August 2019, 29

De Tijd, *Fontinoy voorzitter af bij NMBS*, 13 March 2021, 11

De Tijd, *Bouwopdracht ambassade in Congo is voor Willemen*, 13 November 2013, 16

Gazet van Antwerpen, *Minister Leo Tindemans over buitenlandse betrekkingen. Diplomatie heeft niet aan belang ingeboet, maar krijgt nieuwe oriëntatie*, 31 October-1 November 1983, 9

Gazet van Antwerpen, voormalige rechterhand Didier Reynders beschuldigd van aanvaarden smeergeld, 5 February 2021, 11

Gazet van Antwerpen, Ambassade bestand tegen zware aardbeving, 9 April 2010, 6

Gazet van Antwerpen, Nederland sluit consulaat in Antwerpen, 1 July 2013, 11

Het Belang van Limburg, *Verkoop ambassade Tokio nog voor dit jaar*, 19 September 2006

Het Belang van Limburg, *Premier Leterme opent nieuwe ambassade in Tokio*, 9 April 2010, 5

Het Laatste Nieuws, Premier opent in Japan ambassade van 25 miljoen euro, 9 April 2010, 13

Het Laatste Nieuws/Mechelen-Lier, *Onderneming van het Jaar lonkt naar Afrika*, 10 October 2013, 17

Het Nieuwsblad/Mechelen-Lier, *Willemen Groep bouwt in Congo Belgisch-Nederlandse ambassade*, 17 July 2014, 24

Het Nieuwsblad, *België houdt uitverkoop in Congo*, 28 July 2014, 4

Journal of Arts & Ideas, *Architecture to me is about construction of images and associations, interview with Satish Gujral*, 7, April-June 1984

L'architecture d'aujourd'hui, *Trois ambassades à New Delhi*, 247, 1986

La Libre Belgique, *L'ambassade de Belgique à Washington*, 13 June 1953, 2

La Libre Belgique, *Quand l'architecture s'approprie le durable*, 14 April 2011, 3

La Meuse, *L'ambassade belge aux USA vendue!*, 14 December 2019, 20

Le Drapeau Rouge, *La nouvelle ambassade belge à Washington*, 11 February 1957, 2

Le Soir, *Ambassade de Belgique*, 26 January 1956, 2

Le Soir, *La nouvelle ambassade de Belgique à Washington*, 10 February 1957, 6

Le Soir, *La visite de Spaak à Washington*, 12 February 1957, 1

Le Soir, *La nouvelle ambassade des Etats-Unis à Varsovie truffée de micros*, 3 November 1964, 5

Le Soir/Namur Luxembourg, *Une nouvelle ambassade à Kinshasa: La Belgique veut garder son rang*, 27 August 2014, 11

The Canberra Times, *Entertaining Tennis at the Embassy*, 12 January 1954, 2

INTERVIEWS

Interview with former Foreign Minister Mark Eyskens, 8 September 2021, Heverlee

Interview with former Ambassador Cristina Funes-Noppen, 11 November 2019, Brussels

Interview with former New Delhi embassy staffer Philippe Falisse, 9 May 2018, Neupré

ELECTRONIC SOURCES

Apache. "De favoriete bouwpromotor van Bart De Wever (1): Samen aan de feestdis." Accessed 4 July 2022. https://www.apache.be/2017/11/16/de-favoriete-bouwpromotor-van-bart-de-wever-1-samen-aan-de-feestdis

India Today. "Painter-Muralist Satish Gujral Draws Flak for Turning Architect, 15 November 1983." Accessed 19 June 2021. https://www.indiatoday.in/magazine/living/story/19831115-painter-muralist-satish-gujral-draws-flak-for-turning-architect-771201-2013-07-15

BOOKS, PERIODICALS AND DISSERTATIONS

Abankwa-Meier-Klodt, Gladys. *Delhi's Diplomatic Domains*. New Delhi: Full Circle Publishing, 2013

Asher, Catherine. *Architecture of Mughal India*. Cambridge: Cambridge University Press, 1992

Basyn, Jean-Marc. "Van Kuyck, Hugo." In *Repertorium van de architectuur in België van 1830 tot heden*, edited by Anne van Loo, 569. Antwerpen: Mercatorfonds, 2003

Bekaert, Geert, and Francis Strauven, *Bouwen in België 1945-1970*, Brussel: Nationale Confederatie van het Bouwbedrijf, 1971

Bekaert, Geert. "Architectuur + Beleid (achter het masker van het architectuurbeleid)." *De Witte Raaf* 79 (May-June 1999)

Belgian Commission to the World's Fair. *New-York World's Fair 1939-1940: The World of Tomorrow: Belgian Section*. New York: Belgian Ministry of Economic Affairs, 1939.

Belgische Ministerie van Buitenlandse Zaken. *Voor een Belgisch Aziëbeleid*. Brussel: Belgische Ministerie van Buitenlandse Zaken, 1984.

Bell, Duncan and Bernardo Zacka. "Introduction." In *Political Theory and Architecture*, edited by Duncan Bell and Bernardo Zacka, 1-17. London: Bloomsbury Academic, 2020

Bellat, Fabien. *Ambassades françaises du XXe Siècle*, Paris: Editions du Patrimoine. Centre des Monuments Nationaux, 2020

Bergen, Emiel. "Oscar Niemeyer." *Bouwen en wonen: Maandblad voor nieuwe vormgeving*, January 1957.

Berridge, G.R., and Lorna Lloyd. *The Palgrave Macmillan Dictionary of Diplomacy*. Basingstoke: Palgrave Macmillan, 2012

Berridge, G.R. *Diplomacy: Theory and Practice*, Basingstoke: Palgrave Macmillan, 2010

Bertram, Mark. *Room for Diplomacy: Britain's Diplomatic Buildings Overseas 1800-2000*. Reading: Spire Books, 2011

Biltekin, Nevra. "The Performance of Diplomacy. The residence, gender and diplomatic wives in late twentieth-century Sweden." In *Women, Diplomacy and International Politics since 1500*, edited by Glanda Sluga and Carolyn James, 254-268. London: Routledge, 2015

Boyd, Robin. *The Australian Ugliness*, edited by Christos Tsiolkas. Melbourne: Text Publishing, 2018.

Brauer, Carl M. *The Man Who Built Washington: A Life of John McShain*. Wilmington: Hagley Museum & Library, 1996

Brown, Nicholas. *A History of Canberra*. Cambridge: Cambridge University Press, 2014

Calvocoressi, Peter. *World Politics since 1945*. Harlow: Pearson, 2009

Cardenas, Maria Margarita Gonzalez. "The Diplomatic Quarters in Riyadh: A western-shaped neighbourhood in an Islamic city?" In *International Planning History Society Proceedings*, 17th IPHS Conference, History-Urbanism-Resilience, edited by Carola Hein, 393-404. Delft: TU Delft Open, 2016

Chapnick, Adam. "The Middle Power." *Canadian Foreign Policy* 7, no. 2 (Winter 1999): 73-82

Clausset, Edouard. *Les cristalleries du Val Saint-Lambert*. Bruxelles: Etablissements Pauwels, 1947.

Cogels, Freddy. *Souvenirs d'un diplomate: Du gâteau avec les duchesses?*. Bruxelles: Hervé Douxchamps, 1983.

Cole, David. *Sir Edwin Lutyens: The Arts and Crafts Houses*. Mulgrave: Images Publishing, 2017

Connah, Roger. *Writing Architecture: Fantômas, Fragments, Fictions. An Architectural Journey Through the 20th Century*. Cambridge Massachusetts: MIT Press, 1989

Coolsaet, Rik, Vincent Dujardin, and Claude Roosens. *Buitenlandse Zaken in België: Geschiedenis van een ministerie, zijn diplomaten en consuls van 1830 tot vandaag*. Tielt: Lannoo, 2014

Crombois, Jean. *Camille Gutt and Postwar International Finance*. London: Pickering & Chatto, 2011

D'Alfonso, Maddalena. *Warm modernity: Indian architecture building democracy*. Milan: Silvana Editoriale, 2016

Damen, Hélène. "Sober Nederlands vlagvertoon. Naoorlogse ambassadegebouwen in Washington en Bonn." *Bulletin KNOB* 118, no. 4 (2019): 36-49

Dauwe, Ilse, Joost De Geest, and Elsje Janssen. "Kunst in de Belgische ambassades." *Openbaar Kunstbezit Vlaanderen*, 2013.

Davidts, Wouter. *Bouwen voor de kunst? Museumarchitectuur van Centre Pompidou tot Tate Modern*. Gent: A&S Books, 2006

De Bassompierre, Albert. *Dix-huit ans d'ambassade au Japon*. Bruxelles: Libris, 1943.

De Bremaeker, Jos, Serge de Pauw, and Filip Janssens. *75 jaar Luchtbal, 1925-2000*. Antwerpen: Stad Antwerpen, 2000

De Kooning, Mil. "Een theater voor 'het open, onommuurde, handtastelijke leven.' Het paviljoen van Brazilië." In *Moderne architectuur op Expo 58. Voor een humaner wereld*, edited by Rika Devos and Mil De Kooning, 214-229. Brussel: Mercatorfonds, 2006

De Messemaeker, Pieter. "Tussen Kasjmir en Congo. Belgisch-Indiase Politieke Contacten onder Nehru." In *Het Wiel van Ashoka. Belgisch-Indiase Contacten in Historisch Perspectief*, edited by Idesbald Goddeeris, 197-212. Leuven: Lipsius, 2013

De Meulder, Bruno. "Het Office des Cités Africaines. Wonen als instrument van instant welvaartskolonialisme in Belgisch Congo [1952-1960]." In *Wonen in welvaart: Woningbouw en wooncultuur in Vlaanderen, 1948-1973*, edited by Tom Avermaete and Karina van Herck, 94-109. Antwerpen: Vlaams Architectuurinstituut, 2006

De Ridder, Hugo. *Geen winnaars in de Wetstraat*, Leuven: Davidsfonds, 1986.

De Robiano, Serge. *Le tour du monde insolite d'un diplomate belge*. Bruxelles: Racine, 2009.

De Vos, Els, and Selin Geerinckx. "Modernist High-Rises in Postwar Antwerp. Two Answers to the Same Question." *Cidades* 33 (2016): 113-132

De Vylder, Gerrit. "Van Belgische expansie tot Indiase heropstanding." In *Het Wiel van Ashoka. Belgisch-Indiase Contacten in Historisch Perspectief*, edited by Idesbald Goddeeris, 51-65. Leuven: Lipsius, 2013

De Witte, Ludo. *De moord op Lumumba: Kroniek van een aangekondigde dood*. Tielt: Kritak, 2020

Delcorps, Vincent. "Le secrétaire général du ministère belge des Affaires étrangères: Fonction, profil et nomination (1944-2002)." In *La biographie individuelle et collective dans le champ des relations internationales*, edited by Michel Dumoulin and Catherine Lanneau, 195-212. Bruxelles: P.I.E. Peter Lang, 2016

Delcorps, Vincent. *Dans les coulisses de la diplomatie. Histoire du ministère belge des Affaires étrangères*. Louvain-la-Neuve: UCL Presses universitaires de Louvain, 2015

Devos, Rika, and Fredie Floré. "Modern met De Coene. De Productie na 1952." In *Kortrijkse Kunstwerkstede Gebroeders De Coene. 80 Jaar Ambacht en Industrie. Meubelen, Interieurs, Architectuur*, edited by Frank Herman and Ruben Mayeur, 183-207. Kortrijk: Groeninghe, 2006

Dujardin, Vincent, and Michel Dumoulin. *Paul van Zeeland, 1893-1973*, Bruxelles: Racine, 1997

Dumont, Georges-H. *Louis Hennepin: Explorateur du Mississippi*. Paris: Dessart, 1942

Engels, Philippe. *De Clan Reynders*. Tielt: Kritak, 2021

Erauw, Willem. *Koningin Elisabeth: Over pacifisme, pantheïsme en de passie voor muziek*. Gent: Stichting Mens en Kultuur, 1995

Falisse, Philippe. *Inspirations: The architectural marvel of Satish Gujral and memories of seven ambassadors*, New Delhi: Bosco Society for printing, 2004

Federal Public Service Foreign Affairs, Foreign Trade and Development Cooperation. *Art in the residence of the Belgian ambassador in New Delhi*. Brussels: Federal Public Service Foreign Affairs, Foreign Trade and Development Cooperation, 2017

Federal Public Service Foreign Affairs, Foreign Trade and Development Cooperation, *Belgian Embassy Washington*, Brussels: Federal Public Service Foreign Affairs, Foreign Trade and Development Cooperation, 2010

Federal Public Service Foreign Affairs, Foreign Trade and Development Cooperation, *Belgian Embassy London*, Brussels: Federal Public Service Foreign Affairs, Foreign Trade and Development Cooperation, 2008

Federale Overheidsdienst Buitenlandse Zaken, Buitenlandse Handel en Ontwikkelingssamenwerking. *Kunst in de Belgische ambassade in Kinshasa*. Brussel: Federale Overheidsdienst Buitenlandse Zaken, Buitenlandse Handel en Ontwikkelingssamenwerking, 2017

Flath, David. *The Japanese Economy*. Oxford: Oxford University Press, 2014

Floré, Fredie. "Serving a Double Diplomatic Mission: Strategic Alliances between Belgian and American Furniture Companies in the Postwar Era." *Design and Culture* 9, no. 2 (2017): 167-185

Floré, Fredie. "Technological progress as an obstruction to domestic comfort: Hugo Van Kuyck and the introduction of the American example in post-war Belgium." In *On Discomfort. Moments in a modern history of architectural culture*, edited by David Ellison and Andrew Leach, 64-79. London: Routledge, 2017

Floré, Fredie. "Wood Firm De Coene and the Modern Office." *Architectural Theory Review* 25, no. 1-2 (August 2021): 99-116. https://doi.org/10.1080/13264826.2021.1957961

Frampton, Kenneth. *Building Brasilia*. London: Thames & Hudson, 2010

Frampton, Kenneth. *The Work of Charles Correa*. London: Thames & Hudson, 1996

Frey, Linda S., and Marsha L. Frey. *The History of Diplomatic Immunity*. Ohio: Ohio State University Press, 1999

Fülscher, Christiane. *Deutsche Botschaften. Zwischen Anpassung und Abgrenzung*. Berlin: Jovis Verlag, 2021

Fumunzanza Muketa, Jacques. *Kinshasa: d'un quartier à l'autre*. Paris: Harmattan, 2008

Gimeno-Martinez, Javier. *Design and National Identity*. London: Bloomsbury Academic, 2016

Goldhagen, Sarah Williams. *Louis Kahn's Situated Modernism*. New Haven: Yale University Press, 2001

Goldman, Jasper. "Warsaw. Reconstruction as Propaganda." In *The Resilient City: How Modern Cities Recover from Disaster*, edited by Lawrence Vale and Thomas Campanella, 135-155. New York: Oxford University Press, 2005

Gottwald, Sylvia. "A Sculptural and Sensual Embassy for Belgium," *Architecture USA*, September 1984.

Gower, Rowan. "Image Building: Examining Australia's Diplomatic Architecture in the Asian Region, 1960-1990." PhD diss., University of New South Wales, 2019

Guerrieri, Pilar Maria. *Negotiating cultures: Delhi's architecture and planning from 1912 to 1962*. New Delhi: Oxford University Press, 2019

Gujral, Inder Kumar. *Matters of Discretion, an Autography*, New Delhi: Hay House India, 2011.

Gujral, Satish. *A Brush with Life*, New Delhi: Penguin Books India, 1997.

Gutheim, Frank, and Antoinette J. Lee. *Worthy of the Nation. Washington, D.C., from L'Enfant to the National Capital Planning Commission*. Baltimore: John Hopkins University, 2006

Hagströmer, Denise. "'Swedish Modern' meets international high politics: The 1959 New Delhi embassy and Ambassador Alva Myrdal." In *Design Frontiers: Territories/Concepts/Technologies, 8th Conference of the International Committee for Design History & Design Studies*, edited by Priscila Lena Farias, Anna Calvera, Marcos da Costa et al., 171-174. São Paulo: Editora Edgard Blucher, 2012

Hagströmer, Denise. "In search of a national vision: Swedish Embassies from the mid-20th century to the present." PhD diss., Royal College of Art, 2011

Helmreich, Jonathan E. "US Foreign Policy and the Belgian Congo in the 1950s." *The Historian* 58, no. 2 (Winter 1996): 315-328

Hendrickx, Colin. "Belgium and Mobutu's Zaïre: Analysis of an Eventful Era." *Journal of Belgian History* 49, no. 1 (2019): 80-112

Highsmith, Carol, and Ted Landphair. *Embassies of Washington*. Washington, D.C.: The Preservation Press, 1992

Hoflack, Kris. *De premier*. Gent: Borgerhoff & Lamberigts, 2021

Hollants Van Loocke, Jan. *Vogelvrij: Herinneringen van een diplomaat*, Leuven: Van Halewyck, 1999.

Hunin, Jan. *Het enfant terrible Camille Huysmans, 1871-1968.* Amsterdam: Meulenhoff, 1999
Jaenen, Marieke, Michael de Bouw, Maria Leus et al. "Congolese Wood in the Antwerp Interwar Interior", *World Academy of Science, Engineering and Technology International Journal of Architectural and Environmental Engineering* 10, no. 9 (2016): 2005-2011. https://doi.org/10.5281/zenodo.1339520
Jenssen, Hugo Lauritz. *Representativt: Buildings in the Foreign Service.* Oslo: Forlaget Press, 2008
Judin, Hilton. *Architecture, state modernism and cultural nationalism in the apartheid capital.* London: Routledge, Taylor & Francis Group, 2021
Kavtaradze, Sergei, and Alexei Tarkhanov. *Stalinist Architecture.* Translated by Robin and Julia Whitby and James Paver. London: Laurence King, 1992
Kazakova, Olga. *Архитектура советской дипломатии.* Ekaterinburg: Tatlin Publishers, 2021.
Kennedy, Andrew Bingham. *The international ambitions of Mao and Nehru: National efficacy beliefs and the making of foreign policy,* Cambridge: Cambridge University Press, 2012
Khanna, Rahul. *The Modern Architecture of New Delhi, 1928-2007.* New Delhi: Random House India, 2008.
King, Anthony. *Writing the global city: Globalisation, postcolonialism and the urban.* Abingdon: Routledge, 2016.
Klep, Christ, and Rik Coolsaet. "Na de Koude Oorlog: Het veiligheidsbeleid, 1989-2010." In *Nederland-België: De Belgisch-Nederlandse betrekkingen vanaf 1940,* edited by Duco Hellema, Rik Coolsaet, and Bart Stol, 262-289. Amsterdam: Boom, 2011
Koolhaas, Rem. *Elements of Architecture, Book 8: Balcony.* Venice: Marsilio, 2014
Lagae, Johan. "Lambrichs, Marcel." In *Repertorium van de architectuur in België van 1830 tot heden,* edited by Anne van Loo, 385-386. Antwerpen: Mercatorfonds
Le Corbusier. *Vers une architecture.* Paris: Flammarion, 1995.
Levine, Neil. *The Architecture of Frank Lloyd Wright.* Princeton: Princeton University Press, 1996
Loeffler, Jane. "The State Department and the Politics of Preservation: Why Few U.S. Embassies Are Landmarks." *Future Anterior* 13, 1 (2016): 99-123
Loeffler, Jane. *The Architecture of Diplomacy: Building America's Embassies.* New York: Princeton Architectural Press, 2011
Lukowski, Jerzy, and Hubert Zawadzki. *A Concise History of Poland.* Cambridge: Cambridge University Press, 2006
Luyten, Dirk, Alain Meynen and Els Witte. *Politieke Geschiedenis van België: Van 1830 tot heden.* Antwerpen: Manteau, 2016
Machiavelli, Niccolò. *Il Principe en andere politieke geschriften.* Translated by Paul van Heck. Amsterdam: Ambo, 2007.
Martens, Albert, and Myriam Vanden Eede. *De Noordwijk: Slopen en Wonen.* Berchem: EPO, 1994
Mendes, Manuel. *O Cerrado de Casaca,* Brasília: Thesaurus, 1995.
Metcalf, Barbara, and Thomas Metcalf. *A Concise History of Modern India.* Cambridge: Cambridge University Press, 2006.
Meyhöfer, Dirk. *Contemporary Japanese Architects.* Köln: Taschen, 1993
Mimar, *Architecture in Development, Building as Image: Gujral's Sculptural Belgian Embassy in New Delhi,* 12, 1984.
Mindlin, Henrique. *Modern Architecture in Brazil.* Rio de Janeiro: Colibris, 1956.
Monaville, Pedro. "A Distinctive Ugliness. Colonial Memory in Belgium." In *Memories of Post-imperial Nations: The Aftermath of Decolonization, 1945-2013,* edited by Dietmar Rothermund, 58-75. Delhi: Cambridge University Press, 2015.
Montero, Marta Iris. *Burle Marx: The Lyrical Landscape.* London: Thames & Hudson, 2001.
Mouton, Alain. *'Het geld is op' De financiële putten van België.* Antwerpen: Vrijdag, 2017.
Mukherjee, Aditya. "Drain of Wealth", In *Key Concepts in Modern Indian Studies,* edited by Gita Dharampal-Frick, Monika Kirloskar-Steinbach, Rachel Dwyer and Jahnavi Phalkey, 70-71. New York: New York University Press, 2015
Murray, John. *A Handbook for Travellers in India, Burma and Ceylon.* London: Murray, 1913.
Niemeyer, Oscar. *The Curves of Time: The Memoirs of Oscar Niemeyer.* London: Phaidon, 2007.

Nooteboom, Cees, and Martino Stierli. *Brasilia-Chandigarh. Living with Modernity*. Baden: Lars Müller Publishers, 2010
Nzuzi, Francis Lelo. *Kinshasa: Planification et aménagement*. Paris: Harmattan, 2011
Office belge du Commerce Extérieur. *Inde*. Bruxelles: Office belge du Commerce Extérieur, 1981.
Olszewski, Andrzej. *An Outline History of Polish 20th Century Art and Architecture*. Translated by Stanisław Tarnowski. Warsaw: Interpress, 1989
Pennewaert, Eddy. "Belgische Ambassade – New Delhi: Alleen België zwijgt." *A+ Architectuur: Belgisch Tijdschrift voor Architectuur* 97, no. 4 (1987): 18-25.
Philippe, Joseph. *Le Val-Saint-Lambert: Ses cristalleries et l'art du verre en Belgique*. Liège: Halbart, 1974
Pieters, Hannes. *Bouwen voor de natie: De Albertina op de Brusselse Kunstberg als monumentaal totaalproject*. Gent: Academia Press, 2021
Prakash, Vikramaditya. *Chandigarh's Le Corbusier. The Struggle for Modernity in Postcolonial India*. Seattle, Washington: University of Washington Press, 2002
Regie der Gebouwen. *De Regie der Gebouwen: Gisteren, vandaag, morgen*. Brussel: Regie der Gebouwen, 1978
Ripnen, Kenneth H. *Office Building and Office Layout Planning*. New York: McGraw-Hill Book, 1960.
Robin, Ron. *Enclaves of America. The Rhetoric of American Political Architecture Abroad, 1900-1965*. Princeton: Princeton University Press, 1992
Rottiers, Charlotte. "Housing the Nation Abroad. The Material Representation of Belgian Diplomacy, 1831-1914." PhD diss., KU Leuven, 2024.
Ryckewaert, Michael. *Building the Economic Backbone of the Belgian Welfare State: Infrastructure, Planning and Architecture, 1945-1973*. Rotterdam: 010, 2011
Saah, Stephani. "How has China's economic engagement, as tool of soft power in the Democratic Republic of Congo, evolved?" Master's diss., University of Antwerp, 2021
Sacchi, Livio. *Tokyo: City and Architecture*. Milano: Skira, 2004
Schelfhout, Charles Emmanuel. *Albert van België: Gangmaker van de Belgische Export, 1960-1993*. Brussel: Dyle, 2004
Schelfhout, Charles Emmanuel. *In het kielzog van Hugo Van Kuyck: Een uitzonderlijke Belg*. Bonheiden: De Dijle, 1988.
Scriver, Peter, and Amit Srivastava. *India. Modern Architectures in History*. London: Reaktion Books, 2016
Shih, Chih-Ming, and Fang-Jar Liou. "Louis Kahn's Tectonic Poetics: The University of Pennsylvania Medical Research Laboratories and the Salk Institute for Biological Studies." *Journal of Asian Architecture and Building Engineering* 9, no. 2 (2010): 283-290
Smets, Paul-F. *Lambert: Une Aventure Bancaire et Financière, 1831-1975*, Bruxelles: Racine, 2012
Stalder, Laurent. "Turning Architecture Inside Out: Revolving Doors and Other Threshold Devices." *Journal of Design History* 22, no.1 (March 2009): 69-77
Steele, James. *The Complete Architecture of Balkrishna Doshi: Rethinking Modernism for the Developing World*. London: Thames and Hudson, 1998
Stevens, Olivier. *Belgium's Most Beautiful Embassies From Around The World*. Tournai: Renaissance du Livre, 2003.
Stourton, James. *British Embassies. Their Diplomatic and Architectural History*. Frances Lincoln: London, 2017.
Tanner, Howard. "Fowell, Mansfield, Jarvis & Maclurcan.", In *The Encyclopedia of Australian Architecture*, edited by Philip Goad and Julie Willis, 261. Cambridge, New York: Cambridge University Press, 2012.
Therborn, Göran. *Cities of power: The urban, the national, the popular, the global*. Verso Books: London, 2017.
Tindemans, Leo. *Een politiek testament: Mijn plaats in de tijd: Dagboek van een minister*. Tielt: Lannoo, 2009.
Tindemans, Leo. *Krachtlijnen van de buitenlandse politiek van België: Toespraken*. Brussel: Ministerie van Buitenlandse Zaken, Buitenlandse Handel en Ontwikkelingssamenwerking, 1982.

Toulier, Bernard, Johan Lagae, and Marc Gemoets. *Kinshasa: Architecture et paysage urbains.* Kinshasa: D'Art, 2010.
Urban, Florian. *Postmodern Architecture in Socialist Poland. Transformation, Symbolic Form and National Identity.* London: Routledge, Taylor & Francis, 2021.
Vale, Lawrence. *Architecture, Power and National Identity.* New Haven Connecticut: Yale University Press, 1992.
Van de Maele, Jens. "Architectures of Bureaucracy. An Architectural and Political History of Ministerial Offices in Belgium, 1915-1940." PhD diss., Ghent University, 2019.
Van Kuyck, Hugo. *Modern Belgian Architecture. A Short Survey of Architectural Developments in Belgium in the Last Half Century.* New York: Belgian Government Information Center, 1946.
Van Meel, Juriaan. *The European office: Office design and national context.* Rotterdam, 010, 2000.
Vander Hulst, Reinout. "De opdracht van Paul Kronacker (1944-1947). De invloed van de handelsmissies op het 'Belgische mirakel." *Belgisch Tijdschrift voor Filologie en Geschiedenis* 95, no. 2, (2017): 401-440.
Vanwing, Thomas. "Ambassadeur Silvercruys en de Belgisch-Amerikaanse relaties (1945-1959): Een diplomatieke rots in de Atlantische Oceaan." Master's Diss., KU Leuven, 2012.
Vosbeck, Randall, Tony Wrenn, and Andrew Smith. *A Legacy of Leadership: The Presidents of the American Institute of Architects.* Washington, D.C.: The American Institute of Architects, 2008.
Walter, Willy. "Les Bois du Congo dans la Construction et Décoration." *Bâtir*, April 1939.
Wigny, Pierre. *Tienjarenplan voor de economische en sociale ontwikkeling van Belgisch Kongo.* Brussel: De Visscher, 1949.
Willies, Alfred. "Max Winders." In *Repertorium van de architectuur in België van 1830 tot heden*, edited by Anne van Loo, 603. Antwerpen: Mercatorfonds, 2003.
Willis, Carol. *Form follows finance: Skyscrapers and skylines in New York and Chicago.* New York: Princeton Architectural Press, 1995.
Yizraeli, Sarah. *Politics and society in Saudi Arabia: The crucial years of development, 1960-1982.* New York: Columbia University Press, 2012.
Zaera-Polo, Alejandro, Stephan Trüby, Rem Koolhaas et al. *Elements of Architecture, Book 7: Façade.* Venice: Rizzoli, 2014.

Illustration Credits

1. Courtesy of Dennis Idnay
2. Courtesy of Dennis Idnay
3. Online via Library of Congress. "Embassies and legations. British Embassy, Chancery from Massachusetts Ave." Accessed 14 October 2019. https://www.loc.gov/item/2019682627/
4. Online via Library of Congress. "The Apostolic Nunciature of the Holy See, or Vatican Embassy, Washington, D.C." Accessed 14 October 2019. https://www.loc.gov/item/2011633768/
5. Diplomatic Archive of Belgium, 18.434/4, Papiers Robert Silvercruys
6. CIVA, Archives Max Winders, Box 3: Brochures, prospectus, souvenirs, booklet *The Pentagon: Hub of National Defence*
7. © Hugo Van Kuyck (FelixArchief, FOTO#42341)
8. © Hugo Van Kuyck (FelixArchief, Architect Hugo Van Kuyck, 28#9562, Presentation booklet Belgian Chancellery)
9. © Hugo Van Kuyck (FelixArchief, Architect Hugo Van Kuyck, 28#9562, Presentation booklet Belgian Chancellery)
10. © Hugo Van Kuyck (FelixArchief, Architect Hugo Van Kuyck, 28#9562, Presentation booklet Belgian Chancellery)
11. Courtesy of Christophe De Coster, University of Antwerp based on © Hugo Van Kuyck (FelixArchief, architect Hugo Van Kuyck, 28#9562, presentation booklet 'the Belgian Chancellery', unnumbered pages)
12. © John McShain (Hagley Museum & Library, John McShain Papers)
13. Courtesy of Noël Hostens, undated
14. © Pierre Wigny (Archives Université Catholique de Louvain, Papiers Pierre Wigny, Divers D2, 1959-1968)
15. © John Horan (The Sunday Star, *New Belgian Chancery Open*, 10 February 1957)
16. © Canberra Federal Capital of Australia preliminary plan 1913, signed by Walter Burley Griffin, National Library of Australia.
17. Courtesy of ACT Heritage Library, image 008788. American Embassy, front view with United States flag flying, March 1957.
18. Courtesy of Elke Van den Broecke and alternated by Christophe De Coster, University of Antwerp
19. Courtesy of the Belgian embassy in Canberra
20. Courtesy of the Belgian embassy in Canberra
21. Courtesy of the Belgian embassy in Canberra
22. Courtesy of Christophe De Coster, University of Antwerp based on Archives of the Belgian embassy in Canberra
23. Courtesy of the Belgian embassy in Canberra
24. Courtesy of the Belgian embassy in Canberra
25. Courtesy of the Belgian embassy in Canberra
26. © *Catholic Weekly*, 21 February 1963
27. Courtesy of the Belgian embassy in Warsaw, Photo album *Ambassade de Belgique à Varsovie*, CEKOP, 1962
28. © Irina Polina/TASS
29. Courtesy of the Belgian embassy in Warsaw
30. Courtesy of Christophe De Coster, University of Antwerp based on Archives of the Belgian embassy in Warsaw

31. Courtesy of the Belgian embassy in Warsaw, Photo album *Ambassade de Belgique à Varsovie*, CEKOP, 1962
32. Courtesy of the Belgian embassy in Warsaw, Photo album *Ambassade de Belgique à Varsovie*, CEKOP, 1962
33. Courtesy of the Belgian embassy in Warsaw, Photo album *Ambassade de Belgique à Varsovie*, CEKOP, 1962
34. Courtesy of Christophe De Coster, University of Antwerp
35. Courtesy of the Belgian embassy in Brasília
36. © Manchete Magazine, *Embaixada da Bélgica*, August 1974
37. © Manchete Magazine, *Embaixada da Bélgica*, August 1974
38. © Manchete Magazine, *Embaixada da Bélgica*, August 1974
39. Courtesy of Peter Serenyi
40. National Archives, London, WORK 10/227, Proposed permanent building in Diplomatic Colony Scheme
41. Courtesy of Wikimapia. "Vatican Embassy (Delhi)." Accessed 22 April 2022. http://wikimapia.org/2831830/Vatican-Embassy
42. Courtesy of the Norwegian embassy in New Delhi
43. Courtesy of Christophe De Coster, University of Antwerp
44. Courtesy of Wikipedia. "US Embassy New Delhi." Accessed 4 March 2022. https://en.wikipedia.org/wiki/Embassy_of_the_United_States,_New_Delhi#/media/File:US_Embassy_New_Delhi.jpg
45. Courtesy of Inder Kumar Gujral, *Matters of Discretion, an Autography*, New Delhi: Hay House India, 2011
46. Courtesy of the Gujral Foundation
47. Courtesy of L'architecture d'aujourd'hui, *Trois ambassades à New Delhi* 247 (1986): 63
48. Courtesy of the Gujral Foundation
49. Courtesy of Christophe De Coster, University of Antwerp based on Mimar, Architecture in Development, Building as Image: Gujral's Sculptural Belgian Embassy in New Delhi, 12, 1984, 17
50. Courtesy of the Gujral Foundation
51. Courtesy of *Stowarzyszenie Architektów Polskich*
52. Courtesy of Randhir Singh, Architectural Photography
53. Courtesy of the Gujral Foundation
54. Courtesy of Peter Serenyi
55. Courtesy of the Belgian Embassy in Saudi Arabia
56. Courtesy of the P&O Archives of the FPS Foreign Affairs, Files Riyadh
57. Courtesy of the Belgian Embassy in Japan, *The old embassy. A photographic tribute to the Belgian embassy in Tokyo*, Japan, Tokyo: Nishikawa Printing, 2007, 10
58. Courtesy of the P&O Archives of the FPS Foreign Affairs, Files Tokyo
59. Courtesy of the P&O Archives of the FPS Foreign Affairs, Files Tokyo
60. Courtesy of the P&O Archives of the FPS Foreign Affairs, Files Tokyo
61. Courtesy of the P&O Archives of the FPS Foreign Affairs, Files Tokyo, Takenaka Kōmuten, *Belgian Embassy Development Project Tokyo*, 1 October 1985, 8
62. Courtesy of Christophe De Coster, University of Antwerp
63. Courtesy of Noriaki Okabe Architecture Network
64. Courtesy of Noriaki Okabe Architecture Network
65. Courtesy of the P&O Archives of the FPS Foreign Affairs, Files Tunis
66. Courtesy of Noriaki Okabe Architecture Network
67. Courtesy of Jean-Michel Byl
68. Courtesy of Noriaki Okabe Architecture Network
69. Courtesy of the Belgian Embassy in Japan. The image has been part of the exhibition: Belgian Embassy in Japan, *Exhibition 90 Years Belgian Embassy in Kojimachi*, panel 2009-present
70. Courtesy of the P&O Archives of the FPS Foreign Affairs, Files Kinshasa
71. Courtesy of Christian Richters. "Nordische Botschaften." Accessed 4 April 2022. https://www.peter-ruge.de/project/nordic-embassies

ILLUSTRATION CREDITS 341

72. Courtesy of Christophe De Coster, University of Antwerp
73. Courtesy of ArtBuild Architects
74. Courtesy of De Standaard. "Beschuldigingen bezwaren Europees examen Reynders." Accessed 20 June 2022. https://www.standaard.be/cnt/dmf20190915_04610128
75. Courtesy of Willemen Groep
76. Online via Facebook. "Embassy of Belgium in Kinshasa." Accessed 21 June 2022. https://www.facebook.com/BEEmbassyKinshasa/photos/pb.100069030985355.-2207520000../2562960953749085/?type=3
77. Courtesy of A2M
78. Online via Facebook. "Embassy of Belgium in Kinshasa." Accessed 21 June 2022. https://www.facebook.com/BEEmbassyKinshasa/photos/pb.100069030985355.-2207520000../2565989170112930/?type=3
79. Online via Facebook. "Willemen Groep." Accessed 22 June 2022. https://www.facebook.com/WillemenGroep/photos/a.497010860402330/497902970313119/
80. Courtesy of Willemen Groep
81. Online via Facebook. "Embassy of Belgium in Kinshasa." Accessed 21 June 2022. https://www.facebook.com/BEEmbassyKinshasa/photos/pb.100069030985355.-2207520000../1718171764894679/?type=3
82. Online via Construction 21 Belgium. "Embassy of Belgium & Netherlands, Kinshasa." Accessed 26 June 2022. https://www.construction21.org/belgique/case-studies/h/embassy-of-belgium-the-netherlands.html
83. Courtesy of Dennis Idnay

Index

Aalto, Alvar, 182
Abele, Julian, 41
Albert II of Belgium, 221, 222
Albert I of Belgium, 128, 282
Alighieri, Dante, 47
Anciaux Henry de Faveaux, Pierre, 215, 217
Asabuki, Shiro, 239–241, 245, 259
Assange, Julian, 23
Baudouin of Belgium, 88, 91, 95, 189
Bekaert, Geert, 26
Bellat, Fabien, 27
Bergstrom, George, 61
Bihin, Paul, 155–157
Boyd, Robin, 103
Breuer, Marcel, 24
Burle Marx, Roberto, 166
Burny, Louis-Roland, 198, 199, 213, 214
Cęckiewicz, Witold, 209
Chanakya, 175
Cicognani, Amleto, 47, 92, 93
Cogels, Freddy, 94, 140, 141, 243
Colot, Pierre, 249
Columbus, Christopher, 47
Conder, Josiah, 236
Connah, Roger, 210, 226
Correa, Charles, 200
Costa, Lúcio, 145, 152
Cromwell, Delphine, 40, 41
Cruls, Louis, 145
Dallemagne, Georges, 281
d'Aspremont-Lynden, Geoffroy, 188
Dauwe, Ilse, 270, 271, 300
Davignon, Étienne, 132
De Bassompierre, Albert, 235, 236
De Bock, Jan, 249
De Coene, Pierre, 88, 89
De Decker, Armand, 297–299
de Gruben, Hervé, 37, 38, 52–58, 99, 100, 104, 178–181, 239
De Gucht, Karel, 252, 253, 255, 256, 264, 269, 273
De Ligne, Eugène, 170–174, 176, 178
De Meeûs d'Argenteuil, André, 128, 143
de Meeûs d'Argenteuil, Hadelin, 127–134, 137, 138, 141–144

Demuyter, Ernest, 129
Denko, Stanislaw, 209
Depasse, Marcel, 245
De Robiano, Serge, 151, 174
De Wever, Bart, 297
Dillman, Anna, 40
Dodge, Horace, 40
Doshi, Balkrishna, 200
Durell Stone, Edward, 190, 219
Eid, Guy, 223
Eisenhower, Mamie, 39
Elisabeth of Bavaria, 127–129, 133, 143
Engels, Philippe, 284, 285, 290, 297
Eyskens, Gaston, 56, 57
Eyskens, Mark, 53, 196
Falisse, Philippe, 195, 212, 219, 224
Fikoff, Nicolaï, 152–154, 158
Fontinoy, Jean-Claude, 284, 285, 290, 297, 304, 305
Fowell, Charles, 107, 108
Fukuyama, Tetsuro, 274
Funes-Noppen, Cristina, 193, 214
Gandhi, Indira, 198–200
Goffart, 189–190
Gottwald, Sylvia, 225
Gouthier, Hugo, 148, 150
Griffin, Marion, 99
Griffin, Walter, 99
Gropius, Walter, 24
Grover, Satish, 224, 225
Guillaume, Jules, 167, 168
Gujral Ansal, Raseel, 214, 218
Gujral, Inder, 198, 199, 213, 214
Gujral, Mohit, 218
Gujral, Satish, 170, 195–206, 208–214, 216–219, 222–226, 296
Gutt, Camille, 41, 42, 48, 54, 55, 81, 95
Haksar, Ajit, 197
Halot, Stéphane, 178, 180, 181, 183
Harmel, Pierre, 159
Heirman, Aldrik, 272, 273
Hennepin, Louis, 90
Herter, Christian, 92
Hitler, Adolf, 123

Hollants Van Loocke, Jan, 205, 216, 217, 222, 223, 225
Hoover, Herbert, 89, 90
Horta, Victor, 68
Hostens, Noël, 87
Hupperts, Albert, 171–173
Huysmans, Camille, 63– 65, 70
Ishikawa, Masami, 274
Jansen, Felix, 104
Jaquet, Paul, 101
Jaspers, Jean-Michel, 253, 254, 264–267
Jaspers, Michel, 248, 253, 254, 264, 265
Jespers, Floris, 89
Kabila, Joseph, 277, 278, 284, 297, 298, 302, 303
Kahlo, Frida, 197
Kahn, Louis, 206
Katō, 235–237
Kempinaire, André, 221
Kerremans, Charles, 192
Kiran, 214, 217, 218
Kronacker, Paul, 40, 69, 70
Kubitschek, Juscelino, 144–147, 151, 154
Kusakari, Takao, 274
Kuzma, Mieczysław, 132, 133, 135–138, 143
Lambert, Léon, 81
Lambrichs, Marcel, 275
Le Corbusier, 31, 145, 159, 160, 175, 199, 200
Le Gallais, Hughes, 92
L'Enfant, Pierre, 61
Leopold III of Belgium, 86
Leterme, Yves, 273, 274
Liebaert, Henri, 187, 188
Loeffler, Jane, 24, 28, 34
Lonnoy, August, 159
Loppe, Jean, 156–158, 162
Loridan, Walter, 52
Lotteringhi della Stufa, Lottieri, 164
Lumumba, Patrice, 139, 189, 190
Lutyens, Edwin, 45, 175
Machiavelli, Niccolò, 21, 22
Maclurcan, Donald, 108
Maes, Markus, 34
Mansfield, John, 107, 108
Maricou, Johan, 274
Martens, Wilfried, 219–221, 226–228, 232
McMahon, Brien, 39
McShain, John, 61, 83, 92
Mendes, Manuel, 155
Menon, Krishna, 171
Menzies, Robert, 121
Michel, Louis, 250, 251
Michiels, Lydia, 141

Mies van der Rohe, Ludwig, 87
Mobutu, Joseph-Désiré, 277
Mobutu, Manda, 277
Modi, Bhupendra, 197, 205
Moir, Malcolm, 102, 107
Moreno-Vacca, Sebastian, 291
Mpane, Aimé, 301
Murphy, Frank, 46
Musin, François, 120
Nehru, Jawaharlal, 171–173, 175, 176, 179, 183, 185, 189, 199
Niemeyer, Oscar, 145, 146, 152, 158, 159, 275
Noguchi, Isamu, 87
Ockrent, Roger, 57
Oers, Wim, 273
Okabe, Noriaki, 254, 255, 259–261, 263, 264, 266, 267, 272
Orsolini-Cencelli, Eliane, 164
Panamarenko, 271
Paternotte de la Vaillée, Alexandre, 162–164, 166
Pellegrino, José, 158, 159, 162, 164
Pennewaert, Eddy, 226, 227
Piano, Renzo, 254
Pietilä, Raili, 210
Pietilä, Reima, 210
Piot, Luc, 195
Pius XII, Pope, 181
Provost, Pol, 86, 87
Puttevils, Georges, 192–194
Querton, Jean, 107, 108
Ramm Østgaard, Rolf, 182
Reynders, Didier, 253, 277–279, 281, 284–286, 289, 290, 296, 297, 302–305
Ribeiro, Paulo, 159–162, 164
Ripnen, Kenneth, 77
Rivera, Diego, 196
Rozhin, Igor, 125
Russel, Robert, 178
Ruzette, Etienne, 62
Ryckewaert, Michael, 71
Saarinen, Eero, 24, 87
Scheyven, Louis, 57, 81, 82, 115, 180, 181, 183, 186
Scheyven, Raymond, 57
Schiff, Emile, 94
Sigismund II Augustus, 141
Silvercruys, Robert, 39–45, 47–61, 63, 67–71, 74, 76–78, 80–90, 92–95, 107, 129, 180, 304, 305
Smet, P., 65
Spaak, Paul-Henri, 48–57, 67, 81, 91, 92, 98–100, 122, 128, 129, 143, 144, 148, 151, 154, 156, 171, 172, 176, 188
Stevens, Lucy, 119–122

Stevens, Willy, 115–119, 121, 122, 132, 138
Stone, Edward, 190, 191, 219
Stoop, Monique, 273
Stynen, Léon, 152
Sullivan, Louis, 259
Taylor, William, 51, 58
Timmermans, Frans, 280, 281
Tindemans, Leo, 219–222, 227, 244, 245, 275, 277
Trumbauer, Horace, 41
Trump, Donald, 53
Tshibanda, Raymond, 297
Turner, Rosemary, 39, 47
Vaesen, Pierre, 250
Vale, Lawrence, 23
Vanackere, Steven, 273, 274
Van Buggenhout, Christian, 284, 285
Vanden Boeynants, Paul, 155
Vanden Eynde, Maarten, 300
Vanderlinden, Ernest, 163
Van de Velde, Henry, 86
Van Glabbeke, Adolphe, 93, 94, 115, 130
Van Hamme, Emiel, 187, 188
Van Houtte, Jean, 130, 132
Van Kerckhoven, Anne-Mie, 271
Van Kuyck, Frans, 70
Van Kuyck, Hugo, 68–72, 74, 76, 77, 82, 87, 94, 152, 239–241, 245, 253, 259

Van Meerbeke, René, 146
Van Roijen, Herman, 92
Vanwing, Thomas, 75
Van Zeeland, Paul, 56–59, 61–68, 72, 74, 80, 81, 178–180, 238, 239
Velikanov, Alexander, 125
Verherstraeten, Servais, 256
Verhofstadt, Guy, 244, 247, 248, 252, 277
Verstraeten, Paul, 103, 104
Von Heinz, Karl, 181
Walker, Ralph, 68, 92
Washington, George, 47
Wauters, Arthur, 37
Wigny, Pierre, 80, 94, 129, 130, 132, 148, 150–152, 154, 155, 244
Wilczek, 128
Wilkinson, Leslie, 108
Willemen, Johan, 288, 297
Willis, Carol, 259
Winders, Jean-Jacques, 58
Winders, Max, 58–68, 72, 86, 238–241, 253
Wouters, Dirk, 305
Wren, Christopher, 46
Wright, Frank, 197
Zawadzki, Aleksandar, 127

www.ingramcontent.com/pod-product-compliance
Lightning Source LLC
Chambersburg PA
CBHW041438300426
44114CB00026B/2933